RELIGION AND PUBLIC LIFE IN CANADA: HISTORICAL AND COMPARATIVE PERSPECTIVES

Academic and popular opinions agree that religion has lost most of its influence in Canadian public life during the last one hundred years. However, as this collection of scholarly case studies reveals, religion once played a major role in all aspects of Canadian society, including politics, education, and culture.

Marguerite Van Die has brought together some of Canada's leading historians of religion, as well as the distinguished U.S. historian Mark Noll, to provide insights into how the relationship between religion and public life has changed in Canada from the mid-nineteenth century to the present. *Religion and Public Life in Canada* examines this relationship in terms of such issues as gender, ethnicity, and regionalism, and considers the recent influence of such previously 'outsider' religions as Judaism and Sikhism.

By challenging the assumption that religion has become a matter of purely private concern, and by showing its historical and continued relevance to public life, this book provides a better understanding of the place of religion in public life today.

MARGUERITE VAN DIE is an associate professor at Queen's University/ Queen's Theological College.

Religion and Public Life in Canada

Historical and Comparative Perspectives

Edited by MARGUERITE VAN DIE

UNIVERSITY OF TORONTO PRESS
Toronto Buffalo London

© University of Toronto Press Incorporated 2001
Toronto Buffalo London
Printed in Canada

ISBN: 0-8020-4461-1 (cloth)
ISBN: 0-8020-8245-9 (paper)

∞

Printed on acid-free paper

National Library of Canada Cataloguing in Publication Data

Main entry under title:

Religion and public life in Canada : historical and comparative
perspectives

Includes bibliographical references and index.
ISBN 0-8020-4461-1 (bound)   ISBN 0-8020-8245-9 (pbk.)

1. Christianity and politics – Canada.   2. Religion and politics –
Canada.   3. Religion and state – Canada.   I. Van Die, Marguerite.

BR115.P7R44 2001   261.7'0971   C00-932928-5

Grateful acknowledgment is made to the Faculty of Arts and Science,
Queen's University, and the Pew Charitable Trusts for providing assistance
in meeting publication costs.

University of Toronto Press acknowledges the financial assistance to its
publishing program of the Canada Council for the Arts and the Ontario
Arts Council.

University of Toronto Press acknowledges the financial support for its publishing activities of the Government of Canada through the Book Publishing
Industry Development Program (BPIDP).

To John Webster Grant,
scholar and ecumenist

Contents

Acknowledgments

In many different ways this book is a collaborative effort. It emerged out of a request by the Pew Charitable Trusts to David Lyon of the Department of Sociology, Queen's University, and myself to carry on in new ways the research into religion and society by our esteemed colleague, the late George Rawlyk. We are very grateful to them for their generous funding of the subsequent project, 'Religion and Politics in Canada and the United States,' of which this book is one outcome. Thanks also to Richard Allen, John Simpson, Brian Clarke, Wil Katerberg, Phyllis Airhart, and Darren Dochuk for taking part in an initial planning meeting to suggest topics and possible contributors.

As editor I found it a pleasure to work with the contributors to this volume, and thank them for their prompt and gracious cooperation throughout the various stages of writing. All the chapters, with two exceptions, were presented for commentary at a conference held at Queen's University, 13–15 May 1999. Ruth Compton Brouwer and Terence Murphy, our official commentators, offered invaluable constructive criticism, for which we are most grateful. Much of the success of that conference was due to the wit and wisdom of its coordinator, Roger Neufeld, and to his assistants, Catherine Gidney, Mike Dawson, Joy Frith, and Gary Miedema, each of whom cheerfully took time out from the rigours of doctoral thesis writing.

At a critical stage in the preparation of the manuscript Susan Goldberg shared her editing skills in cutting the length of a number of chapters, and her efforts, along with the two anonymous reviewers of the University of Toronto Press, have strengthened the volume. Doug Hessler's impressive computer and indexing skills, meticulous attention to detail, and enthusiasm for the project greatly facilitated the final work of manuscript preparation. At the Press, Virgil Duff, Executive Editor, Amanda Foubister, Frances Mundy, and copy editor James Leahy offered unfailingly courteous and efficient assistance.

To all of these, and to David Lyon, fellow project coordinator, I would like to express my sincere gratitude.

The final 'collaborator' who deserves mention is John Webster Grant, who honoured us with his presence at the conference, and whose wise and wide-ranging scholarship over many years has blazed a trail into the field of religion and public life for the contributors of this book to follow. We dedicate the volume to him with respect, gratitude, and affection.

Marguerite Van Die
July 2000

Contributors

MARGUERITE VAN DIE holds a joint appointment in history at Queen's University and Queen's Theological College. With David Lyon she is editor of *Rethinking Church, State and Modernity: Canada between Europe and the USA* (2000). Her publications have centred on evangelicalism, family, and society in nineteenth-century Canada.

Professor WILLIAM WESTFALL teaches humanities and history at York University. He has written widely in the field of Canadian religious and cultural history and is the author of *Two Worlds: The Protestant Culture of Nineteenth-Century Ontario* (1990). He is currently completing a study of the social and theological formation of Anglican clergy.

T.W. ACHESON is a founding member of the board of *Acadiensis*, professor emeritus, and former chair of the history department, the University of New Brunswick. A Maritimer and past president of the Canadian Historical Association, he has a strong interest in the history of societies, economies, and religion and has published widely in Canadian economic and urban history.

BRIAN CLARKE is the author of *Piety and Nationalism: Lay Voluntary Associations and the Creation of an Irish-Catholic Community in Toronto, 1850–1895* (1993) and a contributor to *A Concise History of Christianity in Canada* (1996). His current research interests focus on the symbolic representation of public religion in Victorian Canada.

ROBERTO PERIN is an associate professor in the Department of History at Glendon College, York University. He is the author of *Rome in*

Canada: The Vatican and Canadian Affairs in the Late Victorian Age (1990) and co-editor of *A Concise History of Christianity in Canada* (1996).

J.R. MILLER, a professor of history at the University of Saskatchewan, is a specialist in the history of Native–newcomer relations in Canada. His most recent books are *Shingwauk's Vision: A History of Native Residential Schools* (1996) and (with Arthur J. Ray and Frank Tough) *Bounty and Benevolence: A History of Saskatchewan Treaties* (2000).

ALVYN AUSTIN is the author of *Saving Canada: Canadian Missionaries in the Middle Kingdom, 1888–1959* (1986) and is currently preparing for publication a history of Toronto Bible College as well as a study of British, Canadian, and American evangelicalism and the China Inland Mission.

MARK A. NOLL is the McManis Professor of Christian Thought at Wheaton College, Illinois. He is the author of, among other works, *A History of Christianity in the United States and Canada* (1992).

SHARON ANNE COOK is a professor of education at the University of Ottawa, where she teaches educational history and women's studies. Her latest work is a millennial history of Canadian women, edited with Lorna McLean and Kate O'Rourke, to be published in 2001 by McGill-Queen's University Press.

MARY KINNEAR is a professor of history at the University of Manitoba. Her publications include *In Subordination: Professional Women 1870–1970* (1995) and *A Female Economy: Women's Work in a Prairie Province 1870–1970* (1998), both published by McGill-Queen's University Press.

ELEANOR J. STEBNER is an associate professor of theology and church history, Faculty of Theology, University of Winnipeg. Her publications include *The Women of Hull House: A Study in Spirituality, Vocation, and Friendship* (1997) and *Gem: The Life and Work of Sister Mac*, to be released by Novalis/St Paul University Press in 2001.

DAVID MARSHALL, associate professor, Department of History, University of Calgary, is the author of *Secularizing the Faith* (1992). He is currently working on a biography of C.W. Gordon and a book on the history of religion in Alberta.

DAVID SELJAK is an assistant professor of religious studies, St Jerome's University at the University of Waterloo, Waterloo, Ontario. He has published in the area of religion and nationalism and Roman Catholicism in Quebec.

R.D. GIDNEY and W.P.J. MILLAR often collaborate and their co-authored works include *Professional Gentlemen: The Professions in Nineteenth-Century Ontario* (1994). R.D. Gidney is a professor emeritus, University of Western Ontario, and author of *From Hope to Harris: The Reshaping of Ontario's Schools* (1999).

DON PAGE is currently the dean of graduate studies at Trinity Western University in Langley, BC. Before joining the university as its academic vice president in 1989, he spent sixteen years in the Department of External Affairs and International Trade as deputy director of Historical Research and then as a senior policy analyst and speech writer in the Policy Development Bureau.

GERALD TULCHINSKY, professor emeritus, was a member of the history department and is currently director of Jewish studies, Queen's University. His recent publications include *Taking Root: The Origins of the Canadian Jewish Community* (1992) and *Branching Out: The Transformation of the Canadian Jewish Community* (1998).

For two decades HAROLD JANTZ was senior editor of the *Mennonite Brethren Herald* before becoming the founding editor of *ChristianWeek*, a national evangelical newspaper. He has been involved in a variety of boards within both the Mennonite church community and the evangelical community. He lives in Winnipeg.

HUGH JOHNSTON is a professor and chair of the Department of History at Simon Fraser University. His publications on the Sikh community include *The Voyage of the Komagata Maru: The Sikh Challenge to Canada's Colour Bar* (1989) and, with Tara Singh Bains, *The Four Quarters of the Night: The Life Journey of an Emigrant Sikh* (1995).

RELIGION AND PUBLIC LIFE IN CANADA:
HISTORICAL AND COMPARATIVE PERSPECTIVES

Introduction

Marguerite Van Die

The image of Christian Canada – churchgoing, moral, and devotedly partisan – strikes both believers and unbelievers today as somewhat archaic. Whether we like this image or not, it is unlikely that the church will have sufficient authority in our time to replace it with another.

John Webster Grant, 1967[1]

At the beginning of the twenty-first century, as the state undergoes major restructuring, as market forces undermine national identities, and consumerism nudges faith away from tradition to private 'spiritualities,' this prescient observation by Grant, Canada's foremost historian of Christianity, has been more than fulfilled. Not only has the image of a Christian Canada faded into history, but the very thought that religious institutions and beliefs might have a role to play in public life strikes many today as archaic, if not problematic. Yet, not so long ago, churches, religious societies, and people of faith were prominent in establishing such key social services as hospitals, settlement houses, universities, and credit unions, as well as influencing the nature of public education, the media, legislation, and even the way Canadians spent their leisure time.

Not surprisingly, given this relatively recent shift, the growing separation between the secular and the sacred has become a matter of considerable scholarly debate.[2] As opinion polls continue to register declining religious observance in Europe and North America, religion seems to have become largely a private matter.[3] Informed observers, however, have begun to challenge the conclusion that secularization and the privatization of religion are natural partners. In reality, in the

1980s and 1990s religion has again become a matter of public concern.[4] Without a consideration of religion's galvanizing role in the conflicts of such disparate areas as Northern Ireland, the Middle East, the former Yugoslavia, India, Burma, and East Timor, these situations would be largely unintelligible. Closer to home in North America, peasant uprisings in Chiapas, Mexico; the entry of the 'Religious Right' into U.S. politics; and the 1999 decision of the Duecks, a Saskatchewan evangelical family, to seek alternative medical treatment for their terminally ill son in defiance of the medical services provided by the state, are all reminders that religion continues to be a force to be reckoned with in public life.[5]

As the last example demonstrates, what were once deemed to be private matters have now become matters of public interest. Nor can one overlook the churches' past role as public institutions, a point vividly illustrated by recent court cases related to claims of abuse by Aboriginal youth in the 1960s and 1970s at a number of Canadian residential schools jointly administered by the state and the churches.[6] The accounts of suffering, the laying of criminal charges against several denominations and individuals, and the awarding of large financial settlements have had a devastating impact upon the churches' image in popular perception.[7] As Canadians struggle to understand the nature and ramifications of an education system established in the nineteenth century, it is obvious that the stakes for unravelling the historical relationship between religion and public life in Canada are indeed high.

In the United States, an ever-growing list of publications, mostly with a contemporary focus, examine the complex relationship between religion and public life.[8] In Canada there has been little comparable interest. While the American literature may act as a guide, there are pitfalls in assuming that the Canadian experience faithfully replicates that of the United States. Most obvious are the different constitutional relationships between church and state in the two countries. Whereas the First Amendment to the United States Constitution in 1791 provided that 'Congress shall make no law respecting an establishment of religion, or prohibiting the free exercise thereof,' the British North America Act of 1867 made no mention of a religious establishment or state-supported church, but simply assumed the practical loss of church privilege already in place in the various British colonies at the time of Confederation.[9]

In Canada, the actual implications of the separation of church and state for religious life and national self-understanding remain understudied. Where an older generation of Canadian historians of religion, such as Grant, John Moir, and Jean Hamelin, emphasized the cultural role of the churches in Canada prior to the 1960s, more recently historians have been fascinated by the process of secularization and its presumed corollary, the privatization of religion.[10] It is clear, however, from the contemporary restructuring of the state and decreased spending for social services, and from the re-emergence of religious issues in the courts and the media, that secularization does not necessarily mean that there is no longer a place for religious beliefs and institutions in public life.[11] Given the fact that secularization has not, as was once predicted, turned religion into an exclusively private matter, we need to take a fresh look at the historical relationship between the sacred and the secular in Canadian historical development. The purpose of this book is to provide insight into how this relationship evolved in Canada from the mid-nineteenth century to the present, and to provide a better understanding of the place of religion in public life today.

Through a series of case studies, presented chronologically, the authors of this collection examine how individuals, groups, and institutions have faced the redrawing of boundaries – between church and state and between the public and the private – associated with the process of modernization. None of the authors is primarily interested in examining to what extent at any given time individuals engaged in such practices of piety as prayer, the reading of scripture, or attendance at places of worship, questions that figure prominently in contemporary opinion polls aimed at ascertaining the level of private religiosity among Canadians. Rather, this collection examines the ways in which religious beliefs, traditions, and practices translated into public concerns during a time when Canadian and Western society was restructuring extensively through the formation of the modern state, the impact of science, the growth of the capitalist market economy, and the accompanying increased distinction between the private and the public spheres of life.

This concept of a public sphere or realm separate from the apparatus of the state and the economy, where citizens debate, deliberate, and engage in collective democratic will formation, has become a major interest in political theory. Theorists such as Jürgen Habermas and Seyla Benhabib locate this public sphere within the manifold forms of voluntary associations that constitute civil society in the modern democratic state.[12] Others, notably John Rawls, place it primarily within the more restricted legal sphere and its institutions.[13] The meaning of the term 'public' is, therefore, a matter of cultural definition whose precise perimeters continue to be a matter of lively debate. For the purposes of this book, it is helpful to think of society as divided into three primary sectors: the state, the market, and the voluntary.[14] While churches and religious institutions in medieval and early modern Europe were generally considered part of the apparatus of the state, by the time of the eighteenth-century Enlightenment, there was a growing interest in demarcating them constitutionally from the state and turning them into the voluntary sector. The question remained, however: as a voluntary institution, would religion become a private matter or would it take a public role and continue to interest itself in the common good?

The term 'continue' is important, for the assumed link between secularization and the privatization of religion in much political theory has at times resulted in insufficient recognition of the place of religion as one of the early institutional bases of the public sphere. The relationship between religion and politics, once the exclusive concern of prelates and princes, became a matter of lively debate among the laity during the Protestant reformations of the sixteenth and seventeenth centuries, thereby contributing to the formation of the public sphere of modern society.[15] Central to discussions at that time was the question of church establishment, the state financial support of a single church within a given political territory. The questioning of establishment in Enlightenment thought, the growing challenges to it posed by dissenting or nonconformist churches (such as the Congregationalists in Britain), and the need to reorganize state and church finances ultimately brought this arrangement to an end. Occurring first in the newly formed American republic and in revolutionary France, church disestablishment became a reality in British North America in the mid-nineteenth century. No longer an arm of the state, the church faced the challenge of retaining its role as a public institution under quite new circumstances.

Not only did religion succeed in this endeavour, but also, as a number of the chapters in this collection will elaborate, its influence within public life became hegemonic. Various factors in place in nineteenth-century Canada facilitated this process.[16] As Sidney Mead has argued for the United States, in Canada the main Protestant churches, including the recently disestablished Church of England and Ireland, took on the institutional form of denominations.[17] Calling on the financial and practical support of their members and adherents, and engaged in a wide array of educational, moral, and social concerns that the state was unable to undertake, these denominations assumed many of the attributes of thriving voluntary associations. Denominationalism in Canada did not, however, take on the kaleidoscopic form it assumed in the United States. Whereas the latter saw a 'lively experiment' of denominations competing to exercise their influence upon public life, in Canada religion functioned more like an informal or 'shadow' estab-lishment. The players in Canada were considerably fewer and the ties with Europe remained strong: in francophone Quebec an ultramontane Roman Catholicism dominated, and in the other provinces, the rela-tively small number of 'mainstream' Protestant denominations – Anglican, Presbyterian, Methodist, Baptist, and Congregationalist, all with close ties to their British counterparts – experienced to a greater or lesser degree evangelicalism's emphasis on 'scripture, sin, salvation, service.' These developments and their impact in the nineteenth cen-tury upon Canadian public life provide the focus for the first four case studies in this volume; a number of later chapters examine the more enduring consequences of this informal religious establishment.

Reconstructing the Public: The Impact of Nineteenth-Century Disestablishment

Disestablishment especially affected the United Church of England and Ireland. Not only did the church lose its privileged position as the supported bastion of moral order in Upper Canada, it also found itself on an equal footing with other branches of Christianity in hav-ing to look to the laity for financial support. William Westfall offers insight into the many ways in which this church had seen itself as an indispensable public institution for maintaining peace, stability, and moral order in early-nineteenth-century Upper Canadian society. This self-understanding did not change, he points out, when in 1854 the state removed its financial support. Rather than becoming marginal-ized as a private institution, the Anglican Church – as can be seen in the contrasting architecture, rituals, and symbols of two major Toronto institutions, Trinity College and St Paul's Anglican Church – successfully reconstructed itself as a public religion capable of articu-lating in new ways the church's social responsibility. That this suc-cess was due largely to the active involvement and financial support of an evangelical laity – the same group who benefited most from the economic growth of the late nineteenth century – provides a key to understanding why the separation of the sacred from the secular did not lead to the demise of religious influence in society. Instead, in Ontario, as elsewhere in English-speaking British North America, thanks to enhanced lay involvement in all the mainline denominations, the Protestant churches had achieved sufficient concessions from the state by the time of Confederation that one can speak of an informal establishment.[18]

Among Protestants, as Westfall's chapter intimates, the group who contributed most to ensuring the ongoing public nature of religion was collectively described as evangelical. Emerging during the religious revivals of the eighteenth and nineteenth centuries, evangelicals could be found within the United Church of England and Ireland and the Church of Scotland, but were especially identified with such denominations as the Congregationalists, Methodists, Baptists, and the United and Free Church Presbyterians. Strongly activist, emphasizing individual conversion, spiritual holiness, and biblical authority, evangelicals united in a wide array of organizations directed towards the moral reform of society. In an examination of pre- and post-Confederation New Brunswick, William Acheson notes a marked similarity of that colonial province with the northern United States, where an evangelical denominationalism had become the culturally established religion. Through a host of voluntary associations and in active electoral campaigning for two issues of shared concern – prohibition and public schools – New Brunswick's evangelicals gained control over the public discourse of civil society. There were, however, limits to their political power, as Acheson concludes. Unable to handle the kind of compromise needed for effective government, evangelicals succeeded in achieving control only when they limited their political aims to advancing those few areas of moral concern capable of inspiring consensus within the public realm.

The growing cultural hegemony of Protestantism was visible not only in politics, but also in late-nineteenth-century urban public spaces, as Brian Clarke points out in a chapter exploring religion, holidays, and parades in late-nineteenth-century 'Toronto the Good.' Drawing attention to the differences in involvement by women and Irish Roman Catholics in these public celebrations, he argues that in a society where gender, ethnicity, and religion formed important constituent elements, we need to speak of multiple publics and to keep in mind that the category 'public' is itself elastic. Clarke's point is important in understanding the current rethinking of the public sphere. While some feminists and other spokespersons for politically marginalized groups, he notes, have welcomed the conceptual separation between the public sphere and a state traditionally defined in masculine terms, they have challenged the notion of a single public space. Instead, they have argued that public life can be cultivated in many democratic spaces where obstinate differences in power, material status, and, hence, shared interests can find expression, an observation that will receive further attention in a later chapter by Sharon Cook.[19]

A proliferation of publics within a country can in turn serve as a counterforce to the escalating dominance of the state and of capitalism. Roberto Perin makes a compelling argument to this effect as he analyses the multitude of ways in which the Roman Catholic Church in nineteenth-century Quebec established a rich public culture able to resist the encroachments of a state dominated by an English Protestant elite. Indeed, he concludes, in fashioning a cohesive and self-confident French Canadian identity, the church helped lay the foundations for the Quiet Revolution.

Contested Spaces: The Ambiguities of Religion in the Public Sphere

One of the streams flowing into today's 'identity politics' is the close connection that once existed between state and religious institutions, a relationship that disadvantaged those groups dependent on them for services such as education and social welfare. In Canada, unlike the United States, as J.R. Miller points out, a partnership between 'throne and altar' continued to shape the country's Indian residential school system long after disestablishment and well into the twentieth century. State parsimony, church proselytization, and Aboriginal hopes for education coalesced in a pattern destructive not only to Native identity, but also to Christian integrity. At times the interests of church and state flowed in the same direction; at other times significant crosscurrents provided some space, albeit constricted, for Aboriginals to retain a limited form of self-expression. The federal government and the churches, for example, shared the view that Aboriginal education had to be practical in order to provide graduates with work skills allowing them to adjust to cultural change. Where federal bureaucrats considered the use of English to be mandatory in such instruction, many of the missionaries, concerned with furthering their primary goal of Christian socialization, were open to the use of Native languages. While Miller is unequivocal about the injustices that the residential schools inflicted upon Aboriginal students, he emphasizes that differences, as evident in the policy on language, challenge any facile assumption that residential schools were the result of an 'untroubled and seamless partnership' between church and state against the interests and well-being of the Native population. With the state interested primarily in financial savings, and the churches in effecting religious conversions and helping Aboriginal youth adjust to a world now dominated by non-Aboriginal people and ways, the two partners showed subtle but significant differences. In making such distinctions, Miller's chapter offers a nuanced assessment of a problem whose complexities have been largely misunderstood in current popular discussion of the issue.

The assumptions that brought together missionaries and state bureaucrats to impose a Eurocentric education upon Canada's Native children also found expression in a quite different endeavour, the formation of museum collections. In a wide-ranging chapter that lays the groundwork for several distinct studies of the missionary impact upon Canadian public life, Alvyn Austin describes how, through the idiosyncrasies of clerics, missionaries, and scientists, the Chinese collection of the Royal Ontario Museum took form. As it entered into the realm of contested public spaces, the ROM collection was repeatedly decontextualized and recontextualized according to the changing religious, political, and secular purposes of its curators. The ambiguous influence of the missionary experience receives further attention in a second theme in Austin's paper, the role of 'mish kids,' or children of missionaries to China, in Canadian university life and in the Canadian Department of External Affairs in the decades immediately after the Second World War. Here again, as Canadian public servants whose expertise had been shaped in part by an earlier missionary past, these men and women indirectly assured that the informal establishment of religion continued to cast a long shadow in Canadian public life until well into the second half of the twentieth century.

In *A History of Christianity in the United States and Canada*, American historian Mark Noll also has emphasized the remarkable extent and longevity of Canada's Christianization in the nineteenth century.[20] In his contribution to this volume, he extends his analysis to include Mexico, the third and most recent partner in the integration of North American trade. Focusing on the historical narrative of Mexico's troubled religious and political history, and on the impact of the Civil War upon

American Protestantism, Noll raises the point that memory of civil war can be an important factor in shaping a country's religious self-understanding. Whereas in Mexico religion came to be connected to social violence, Protestantism in the United States was greatly weakened as a spiritual and unifying force within public life.

Claiming 'Their Proper Sphere': Women, Religion, and the State

Searching for the historical antecedents to women's activism, feminist historians have invariably encountered religious belief as a key force in motivating an earlier generation of women to undertake moral reform. Sharon Cook's case study of the war against tobacco in the latter half of the nineteenth century illustrates the parallels between today's social reformers and the concerns of evangelical women at the turn of the century. Analysing female rhetoric and activity, Cook explains how religiously motivated women succeeded in redefining private family matters as public concerns. Ostensibly motivated by a common goal, women could differ in their approach, as Cook shows in her comparison of the rhetoric of working-class Salvation Army officers and the middle-class matrons of the Woman's Christian Temperance Union. Though both groups expressed in evangelical terms their opposition to the use of tobacco, Salvation Army women publicly combated the perceived evil through songs and street revivalism, while their more sedate sisters worked through the educational literature of the WCTU and its youth auxiliary temperance groups.

Despite the fact that historians have devoted considerable thought to religion's role in shaping first-wave feminism, few have asked if religion continued to be a significant force in the life of the 'public woman' of the post-suffrage period. Thoughtfully probing the lives and faith of six prominent Canadian women during the interwar years, Mary Kinnear presents a compelling model of diversity and uniformity, useful for further research into this important question. Although widely different in their political views, each of the women examined by Kinnear was able to draw on a common well of Christianity, permitting each to see commitment to the state as synonymous with service to God. Kinnear's conclusion – that 'participation in public life was for [these women] a manifestation of religious faith' – is an incentive for gender as well as political historians to include religion in any redefinition of the public sphere designed to make it more heterogeneous and inclusive.

Religion's Redefinition of the Role of the State:
The Example of Prairie Populism

Nowhere do the political implications of the enduring links between religion and public life in Canada appear more clearly than in the Prairie populism of the interwar years. In the midst of economic disaster and fuelled by strong regional interests, English-speaking Protestants from the 1930s to the 1950s drew on religious rhetoric and symbols to create social and political movements of both the right and left. Eleanor Stebner and David Marshall explore this theme by focusing respectively on two well-known clerics-turned-politicians: liberal Protestant and CCF and NDP member of Parliament Stanley Knowles, and fundamentalist Ernest Manning, Social Credit premier of Alberta from 1943 to 1968. In many ways opposites, the two men were similar in their conviction that religious faith was not simply a private matter, but by its nature compelled political action. As Stebner and Marshall illustrate by delving into the religious psyches of their subjects, theological reflection, whether in the form of Knowles' liberal Protestantism or Manning's biblical fundamentalism, profoundly influenced each man's response to social and economic conditions. Rather than differentiating between religious and secular spheres, these politicians assumed their unity, though in different ways. Where Knowles exchanged his role of minister of the gospel for member of Parliament in order 'to build the kingdom,' the premier of Alberta in his popular radio broadcast, *Back to the Bible Hour*, freely drew on prophecy and dispensationalist history to encourage his listeners to be 'born again.'

Matters of State: Redefining the Sacred in Public Life, 1960–2000

In Quebec and elsewhere in Canada, growing interventionism on the part of the state in the years after the Second World War would lead to a radical differentiation between the spiritual and the secular, ending the overlap that had characterized the earlier informal establishment of religion. In Quebec, the coincidence of the religious reforms advocated by the Second Vatican Council, the growing influence of the press in public life, and the political Quiet Revolution that dramatically stripped the church of its traditional public functions, brought to a swift and decisive end the public Catholic culture described in Perin's chapter. This did not necessarily mean that religion had become a private matter. In a sequel to Perin, David Seljak describes a new form of public religion, intended to make the church more relevant to the world, as advocated by the influential Dominican journal *Maintenant*, launched in 1962. As Seljak concludes, the fact that this public Catholicism in the end lost its lay participation and became very much a preserve of the church hierarchy reveals an important limitation. Seljak's case makes evident the observation of David Zaret that ever since the religious revolutions of the sixteenth century, religious faith has functioned effectively as a body of public opinion only when it has been defined, defended, and debated in arguments that appeal explicitly to an educated and informed laity rather than primarily to a church hierarchy.[21]

Canada, especially anglophone Canada, has grown increasingly diverse in ethnic background, beliefs, and practices since the 1950s, a fact that has made it more difficult to give religion a unified public voice. The matter of determining the role of religion in the country's public schools is one site of that difficulty. Section 93 of the 1867 British North America Act (later incorporated into the Constitution Act of 1982) gave provincial legislatures the exclusive right to make laws in relation to education. It thereby established a diversity of Canadian educational institutions and ensured that future generations of Canadian children would, in the words of one recent study, continue to experience the 'multiform heritage of mid-nineteenth-century school politics.'[22]

In the multicultural public schools of the post-1960 era, however, 'Canadian' and 'Christian' could no longer be assumed to be synonymous, as they had been for over a century. Provincial ministries of education were left to define a new public policy for religion in schools. Ontario offers an important case study of how institutional inertia, public opinion, and new federal legislation reshaped the policies of an earlier century. Supported by a wealth of research into the governance of public education in the province, R.D. Gidney and W.P.J. Millar underscore the fact that well into the 1960s, far from being religiously neutral, Ontario's public schools by law and practice assumed a non-denominational form of Protestant Christianity. In the wake of the Ministry of Education's efforts to address cultural change by replacing religion with a pervasive 'moral education,' the 'recessional of Christianity' from the curriculum, exercises, and seasonal rhythms of public school life was neither swift nor uncontroversial. Canadians were deeply divided on the issue of religion in schools. The 1982 Canadian Charter of Rights and Freedoms successfully allowed individuals not simply to challenge the privileging of Christianity in the schools, but to banish it permanently. Not only Christianity but also religion per se have in this way become casualties in public education.

For individuals and groups who value the earlier dominance of Christianity, the displacement of religion from the educational system and elsewhere in public life has become a matter of critical concern. In the United States, an explosion of literature in the 1980s and 1990s discusses the need 'to reintroduce religious values into American political life.' Key concepts in this discussion have been those of 'public church' or 'public religion,' concepts intended to bring religious concerns and insights into the public discussion about the nature and future of society.[23] Religious liberals and conservatives in the United States have each in different ways appropriated these concepts. In Canada, where there is no counterpart to the American concept of 'civil religion,' they have had much less resonance. Yet, as Donald Page argues in a study of the Public Service Christian Fellowship, a prayer network within the Canadian civil service in the 1970s and 1980s, conservative Christians in Canada did seek to establish a form of public religion. The author, who played a key role within the movement, draws on the language of narrative to tell a story that until now has remained largely undocumented: the desire of a group of Christian public servants to come together for prayer, their concern to maintain traditional Christian values in a secularizing society, and their expression of faith in public life.

As is clear in different ways from the three chapters in this section, the cultural Christianity – whether Protestant or Roman Catholic – that until recently informed so much of Canadian public life has become part of the past. At the same time, despite the dramatic differentiation between the sacred and the secular in the last forty years, the sacred has not disappeared from public life. To gain some sense of how it may be reconstituting itself, we turn now from the narratives, traditions, and convictions of those faiths that once exercised hegemony and listen to those one might call 'religious outsiders.' The ways in which three of these groups – Jews, Mennonites, and Sikhs – have managed to carve out a role in Canadian public life form the concluding section to this collection.

Bearing Witness: The Voice of Religious Outsiders in Public Life

Gerald Tulchinsky's study examines the social thought of a number of influential Reform rabbis who served Jewish congregations in Toronto and Montreal between 1900 and 1960. He offers important insight into how these rabbis were able to draw on the Jewish prophetic tradition to pursue justice, and at the same time to adapt their faith to new contexts by incorporating universalistic values such as decency, charity, and love. In so doing, he concludes, they were able to step out of the confines of their congregations in order to fulfil a 'larger vision' of a just society, in some ways spiritually akin to that of the Christian 'social gospel' examined earlier by Kinnear and Stebner. A second, though implicit, comparison can be made between the emphasis that these rabbis placed on the choice of prominent synagogue sites and the location of large middle-class Protestant congregations, such as Toronto's St Paul's, examined earlier by Westfall. Not only for the disestablished Church of England, but also for Canadian Jewry, who for so long experienced discrimination and marginalization, buildings signified that religion belongs at the centre of a city's locus of power.

The importance of site and the availability of funds enter also into the experience of a second group of religious 'outsiders,' Mennonites. Like Tulchinsky, Harold Jantz has chosen not to examine the discrimination by state and society that religious minorities endured in the past.[24] Instead, he focuses on two impulses that have moved Mennonites to participate in public life: the Anabaptist tradition of communal action and service, and the more recent evangelical emphasis on witness and conversion. As has been the case with other immigrant groups, Mennonites have moved out of the margins as a result of a growing urban presence and increased investment of funds and human resources, first in the service of the denomination, and later in that of those disadvantaged within wider society. Writing from within the Mennonite tradition, Jantz lists an impressive and ever-expanding range of Mennonite social services, from the Mennonite Disaster Service to the Victim Offender Reconciliation Program to the Food Bank (later reorganized as the Canadian Foodgrains Bank). This case study offers a helpful illustration of how context and tradition join to form a part of that wide network of voluntary associations in civil society that some sociologists designate as a country's 'social capital.'[25] Thus, even when state and church are sharply differentiated, the religious tradition of service continues to be an active force in shaping public life.

Even as marginal groups within the Judaeo-Christian tradition move to the mainstream of public life, peoples of other traditions occupy their old space. As their numbers have grown, the distinctive dress and customs of some non-Western religions have begun more visibly to make a public statement of faith in Canada, thereby challenging the homogenizing impulse of modern Canadian life. At the same time, as Hugh Johnston elaborates in a final case study, which examines the Canadian Sikh community, non-Western religious traditions also challenge that other facet of modernity, the differentiation between the sacred and the secular. Thanks to the Asian Diaspora, factionalism brought about by the Khalistan (the Sikh independence movement in India) has reverberated to distant Canada. In the absence of a well-articulated body of Sikh canon law, Johnston observes, American and Canadian courts have been called upon by rival factions to settle such contested practices as the inclusion of tables and chairs in Sikh temples in North America. As the arm of the state, the police and the courts in North America have managed to forestall civil strife among Sikhs. Such examples illustrate the benefit provided by a clear differentiation between the sacred and the secular when there is a need to settle religious strife within a pluralistic society.

In a variety of ways, each of the chapters in this volume demonstrates that religion continues to be a meaningful factor in Canadian public life. And yet, the scene at the beginning of the twenty-first century is quite different from that of a hundred years earlier. Christianity and culture are no longer interwoven to the same degree; one cannot point any more to a Protestant hegemony or to a Roman Catholic public culture. Religious voices, symbols, and organizations have become only one of many agents in public life. Their role, as these chapters have elaborated, has been defined and redefined during the century and a half that followed the legal separation of church and state. Nevertheless, in the course of that redefinition, religion has not become simply a private concern. Rather, the ongoing differentiation between the sacred and the secular, accelerated by more recent state expansion, has moved religious institutions and voices more decisively out of the centres of power represented by government and economics, and into civil society. No longer a 'shadow establishment,' and clearly differentiated from the powerful forces of the state and economics, religion, one might argue, is now situated clearly within the public realm. Here, having lost most of its earlier privilege and power, and operating through a wide and ever-changing range of voluntary societies and institutions, it has also been extended to include formerly marginal groups and non-Christian religions. When one reflects on some of the more positive and general contributions of religion as examined in the following chapters – the colour of ritual and music, the experience of tradition in negotiating change, the prophetic stance against abuse of power, commitment to a just society, the proliferation of voluntary organizations to address social needs – public life would indeed be impoverished without the presence of the country's religious forces.

Notes

1 John Webster Grant, 'The Church and Canada's Self-Awareness,' *Canadian Journal of Theology* 13, no. 3 (1967): 164.
2 For a succinct analysis of this debate, consult Michael Gauvreau, 'Beyond the Half-Way House: Evangelicalism and the Shaping of English Canadian Culture,' *Acadiensis* 20, no. 2 (Spring 1990): 158–72.
3 Reginald Bibby, *There's Got to Be More! Connecting Churches and Canadians* (Winfield, BC: Wood Lake Books, 1995); George A. Rawlyk, *Is Jesus Your Personal Saviour? In Search of Canadian Evangelicalism in the 1990s* (Montreal and Kingston: McGill-Queen's University Press, 1996). For the United States, see, for example, Robert N. Bellah et al., *Habits of the Heart: Individualism and Commitment in American Life* (New York: Harper and Row, 1985); Robert Wuthnow, *After Heaven: Spirituality in America since the 1950s* (Berkeley: University of California Press, 1998).
4 See José Casanova, *Public Religions and the Modern World* (Chicago: University of Chicago Press, 1994).
5 See, for example, Wilson T. Boots, 'Uprising in Chiapas,' *Christian Century* 111, no. 8 (9 March 1994): 246–7; Joel A. Carpenter, *Revive Us Again: The Reawakening of American Fundamentalism* (Oxford: Oxford University Press, 1997); for the account of Tyrell Dueck of Martensville, Saskatchewan, 'Acts of Faith,' *Saturday Night* 114–15 (June 1999): 42–52.
6 See, for example, 'Hundreds of Cree and Ojibwa Children Violated,' *Globe and Mail*, 19 October 1996.
7 As of November 1999 there are 266 active lawsuits, arising out of alleged abuse at residential schools, naming the United Church of Canada, and 200 naming the Anglican Church. 'Lawsuit Costs Considered,' *United Church Observer* (November 1999): 19.
8 For a comprehensive analysis of recent literature, see the bibliographical essay by Anne Loveland, 'Later Stages of the Recovery of American Religious History,' in *New Directions in American Religious History*, ed. Harry Stout and D.G. Hart (Oxford: Oxford University Press, 1997), 487–502.

9 E.R. Norman, *The Conscience of the State in North America* (Cambridge: Cambridge University Press, 1968).

10 On the cultural role of the Canadian churches, see John Webster Grant, *The Church in the Canadian Era*, 2nd ed. (Burlington: Welch, 1988); John Moir, 'The Canadianization of the Protestant Churches,' *Canadian Historical Association Report* 37 (1956): 46–62; Jean Hamelin et Nicole Gagnon, *Histoire du catholicisme québécois. Le XXe siècle*, vol. 3: 1–2 (Montreal: Boréal Express, 1984); Terrence Murphy and Roberto Perin, eds., *A Concise History of Christianity in Canada* (Toronto: Oxford University Press, 1996). Two recent studies on secularization are Brigitte Caulier, *Religion, sécularisation, modernité: Les expériences francophoniques en Amérique du Nord* (Quebec: Presses de l'Université Laval, 1996): David Lyon and Marguerite Van Die, eds., *Rethinking Church, State and Modernity: Canada between Europe and the USA* (Toronto: University of Toronto Press, 2000).

11 This is Casanova's argument in *Public Religions*, which speaks of the 'deprivatization' of religion.

12 Evan Charney, 'Political Liberalism, Deliberative Democracy, and the Public Square,' *American Political Science Review* 92, no. 1 (March 1998): 97–110; Craig Calhoun, ed., *Habermas and the Public Sphere* (Cambridge: MIT Press, 1992); Seyla Benhabib, 'Toward a Deliberative Model of Democratic Legitimacy,' in *Democracy and Difference*, ed. Seyla Benhabib (Princeton: Princeton University Press, 1996).

13 John Rawls, *Political Liberalism* (New York: Columbia University Press, 1993).

14 Here I follow Robert Wuthnow, *Producing the Sacred: An Essay in Public Religion* (Urbana: University of Illinois Press, 1994).

15 David Zaret, 'Religion, Science, and Printing in the Public Spheres in Seventeenth-Century England,' in Calhoun, ed., *Habermas and the Public Sphere*, 221–3.

16 For an insightful discussion of the nature of hegemony as a process, see Geoff Eley, 'Nations, Publics, and Political Cultures: Placing Habermas in the Nineteenth Century,' in Calhoun, ed., *Habermas and the Public Sphere*, 289–339.

17 Sidney E. Mead, 'Denominationalism: The Shape of Protestantism in America,' *Church History* 23 (December 1954): 291–320.

18 John Webster Grant, *A Profusion of Spires: Religion in Nineteenth-Century Ontario* (Toronto: University of Toronto Press, 1989), 221–37; Jacques Zylberberg and Pauline Côté, 'Les balises étatiques de la religion au Canada,' *Social Compass* 40, no. 4 (1993): 529–53.

19 Nancy Fraser, 'Rethinking the Public Sphere: A Contribution to the Critique

of Actually Existing Democracy,' in Calhoun, ed., *Habermas and the Public Sphere*, 109–42; Mary P. Ryan, *Women in Public: Between Banners and Ballots, 1825–1880* (Johns Hopkins University Press, 1990).

20 Mark A. Noll, *A History of Christianity in the United States and Canada* (Grand Rapids: Eerdman's, 1992), 553–4.

21 Zaret, 'Religion, Science, and Printing,' 212–35.

22 Ronald Manzer, 'Public Philosophy and Public Policy: The Case of Religion in Canadian State Education,' *British Journal of Canadian Studies* 7, no. 2 (1992): 268.

23 For an introduction to these concepts, see Wuthnow, *Producing the Sacred*, which also offers a comprehensive bibliography, 169–78. For the lack of a civil religion in Canada, see Andrew S. Kim, 'The Absence of Pan-Canadian Civil Religion: Plurality, Duality, and Conflict in Symbols of Canadian Culture,' *Sociology of Religion* 54, no. 3 (1993): 257–75.

24 William Janzen, *Limits on Liberty: The Experience of Mennonite, Hutterite, and Doukhobor Communities in Canada* (Toronto: University of Toronto Press, 1990).

25 Robert Putnam, 'Bowling Alone,' *Journal of Democracy* 6 (January 1995): 65–79.

Part One

Reconstructing the Public:
The Impact of Nineteenth-Century Disestablishment

1

Constructing Public Religions at Private Sites: The Anglican Church in the Shadow of Disestablishment

William Westfall

In the last half of the nineteenth century the United Church of England and Ireland in the diocese of Toronto was transformed from an official (if incomplete) colonial establishment into a Victorian denomination. Confronted by a powerful array of political, economic, and social forces, the church surrendered the privileged position it had enjoyed within the state and set about the long and at times painful task of reconstructing itself at a private site. The political and institutional dimensions of this transformation have been examined in some detail. Historians, for example, have charted the tortuous path of church–state relations in Canadian politics and shown how the church, under the leadership of the redoubtable Bishop Strachan, responded very effectively to the crisis of disestablishment by creating new administrative and educational structures, most notably diocesan synods and a new church university.[1] Indeed, as the church moved through this administrative revolution, it found itself coming to share the legal status and institutional character of the other major Protestant churches in Victorian Canada – self-governing, lay-inclusive, and voluntary.

These political and institutional narratives, however, do not do justice to the deeper religious and cultural questions that run through the history of disestablishment. With the demise of King's College in 1849 and the secularization of the clergy reserves in 1854, the old political alliance of church and state was indeed well and truly dead. 'To speak of the Church as in unity with the State in the present state of things,' John Strachan explained to Lord John Russell, 'is as ridiculous as it is untrue.'[2] But the Anglican establishment in Upper Canada was not merely a residue of outdated political and institutional arrangements; it also embodied a distinctive set of religious assumptions about the nature of a church, the duties of the clergy, and the unique ability of religion to perform a vital public role in colonial society. This ecclesiology continued to shape Anglican thought and practice long after the church had lost its privileged position.

Disestablishment created, then, a critical disjunction between the administrative and institutional position of the church and the religious and social role it set out to perform. The Anglican Church was now a private institution, cut off from its former ally, the colonial state. It continued, however, to define itself in public terms, holding on tenaciously to the dogma that its teachings and practices should play a major role in Canadian society. This disjunction between private position and public status raises in turn a series of questions that would be at the very centre of Anglican praxis for the next hundred years: how could the church continue to be a religious establishment when it was no longer part of the official state system? What specific strategies could this new 'private' church adopt in order to carry out its public duty? In the shadow of disestablishment, how do you construct a public religion at a private site?

To understand how the church tried to answer these questions we must first reconstruct the intellectual and cultural context in which they were posed: what were the terms and conditions of being a public religion in the period before disestablishment? How did the social and religious discourse that defined the concept and practice of a religious establishment represent the relationship between religion and public life? By illuminating that largely forgotten religious world of the early nineteenth century we can then focus on two very different ways in which the church, now thrown upon its own resources, tried to reconstruct itself as a public religion at a private site. The first concerns the cultural construction of Trinity College, the church university founded by Bishop Strachan in 1851 in response to the 'secularization' of King's College.[3] Although Trinity was built at a private site and took dead aim at the new secular system of higher education, it also tried to preserve many of the essential features of the old religious establishment, allying itself to a particular class structure and taking on the public roles that religious establishments were supposed to perform. Although its ambition to create a new public religion would fail, the attempt nonetheless offers a fascinating insight into the complex relationship between public and private religions during this period.

The second example focuses upon the cultural construction of another great Anglican monument, the 'new' St Paul's Church on Bloor

Street East in Toronto. This massive neo-Gothic structure, which opened for worship on the eve of the First World War, was built under the superintending providence of the Reverend Henry John Cody, undoubtedly the most renowned Anglican cleric in Canada in the first half of the twentieth century. Under his astute leadership, St Paul's became the very epitome of a successful Anglican parish – wealthy, united, fashionable, and active. This section, however, focuses not so much on Cody himself but the way in which the iconography of 'Cody's Cathedral' can help us appreciate the strategy he developed to integrate so successfully the church and Canadian society – how St Paul's constructed at this private site such a vibrant and powerful public religion.[4]

What, then, is the religious nature of a religious establishment? What assumptions about the character and role of religion lay beneath the very privileged public position the church enjoyed before disestablishment? At the centre of this discourse was a finely tempered balance between the interests of the church and the interests of the state. These two bodies, in the words of Bishop William Warburton, whose text was considered the highest authority on this matter, had entered into 'a politic league and alliance for mutual support and defence.' By the terms of this 'civil' or 'mutual compact,'[5] the church received from the state the protection and financial support it required in order to bring the true happiness of salvation to all the inhabitants of the colony. As it performed its religious duty, however, the church also served the larger interests of the state. The church promoted social order by giving people a higher motive for being good. People became Christians of their own free will – no one was forced by law to go to church – but once they became good Christians they also became loyal subjects of the crown. The two institutions worked together for good; the state played an important role in creating a Christian nation, while the church through its religious ministrations cultivated the public order that was the necessary condition for the very existence of the state itself. The power of this logic to an eighteenth-century mind was truly palpable: 'a Christian nation without a religious establishment,' Bishop Strachan declaimed, 'is a contradiction.'[6]

Running through all these rational and utilitarian tropes was a core assumption about the nature of a church, its place in society, and the type of religion it should propagate. As the heirs of a voluntary evangelical culture, we are encouraged to assume that religion begins in a private place (the heart), that the church is a private institution (supported by the voluntary contributions of its own members), and that worship is something conducted behind closed doors (at a private site) for the benefit of a closed community of like-minded folk. It then follows that churches should be separate from the state and allowed to compete on equal terms in an unregulated religious marketplace for the hearts (if not the minds) of the people. The establishment discourse, however, turned upon a very different set of assumptions. It asserted that above all the church was a *public* institution, that religion was an integral part of society, and that the clergy should play a vital role in the public world.

These assumptions in turn drew the church into the very fabric of political and social life. In the first half of the nineteenth century, religion was not merely an important matter of public policy; religious questions dominated the political life of the colony.[7] Within this political culture the Anglican clergy, as Bob Gidney and Wyn Millar have demonstrated so convincingly, formed an integral part of an official colonial elite. Indeed it was their public position as gentlemen – rather than the possession of some esoteric knowledge – that gave the clergy authority over their congregations.[8] For their part the clergy gloried in this public role. They said prayers for the monarch and all those placed in positions of authority; they assumed a prominent position at public occasions and organized public religious observances. The religious message they preached not only encouraged those less fortunate to accept the existing social order, but also sustained a code of virtuous conduct that was supposed to guard the moral character of public life.[9] The clergy also constituted a primitive civil service, serving as the representatives of the crown and carrying out important religious and social functions on the state's behalf at the local level. These included teaching in the schools, drawing up legal documents, keeping government records, fitting people with spectacles, setting up savings banks, and helping to organize the local militia in times of civil unrest, most notably during the Rebellions of 1837.[10]

This public position was reinforced in turn by the public nature of the church itself. The church building was a public rather than a private site. Indeed, worship was treated as a *public* act – something conducted in a public space, by a public official, according to formularies sanctioned by statute. In truth, baptisms, marriages, the churching of women, and funerals were celebrated in a church in order to transform something that was private into something public, bringing these deeply personal moments into public view, and by so doing conferring upon them official (and often legal) status. For the same reasons, the demarcations of class and social position that characterized the public order were purposefully brought into the church, where they were reproduced and sanctified. In early Anglican churches, for example, the well-to-do owned their own pews (which they proceeded to furnish to their own taste) while the poor sat in free seats in the galleries. Some churches provided special places for the representative of the crown, the members of the legislature, and the military. When the Reverend Henry Scadding, a Victorian cleric with a fine sense of social nuance, recalled the history of St James' Church in the early decades of the nineteenth century, he drew a direct link between the internal appearance of the church and the structure of the society it set out to protect. The little church at York presented a world that was at once hierarchical and integrated:

> Altogether it was a very complete little world, this assemblage within the walls of the old wooden church at York. There were present, so to speak, king, lords, and commons; gentle and simple in due proportion, with their wives and little ones; judges, magistrates, and gentry; representatives of government departments, with their employees; legislators, merchants, tradespeople, handicraftsmen; soldiers and sailors – a great variety of class and character.[11]

Finally, the very character of the religion the church presented was shaped by the public role it was supposed to serve. The religious teachings of an establishment had to be presented in a way that appealed to as wide an audience as possible, for its great goal was to make the church coterminous with the nation, to bring the Anglican message of salvation to every subject of the Crown. For this reason the church needed to reach out to the people; it needed to seek to include dissenters rather than turn them away; it had to be broad and inclusive, never allowing any doctrine or theological posturing to bar a soul from worship. Its creeds and confessions, in William Paley's words 'ought to be as simple and as easy as possible.'[12] John Travers Lewis, the first bishop of Ontario, captured this crucial link between establishments and doctrinal inclusiveness very well. 'A great Church,' he stated, 'cannot have narrow tests. A happy characteristic of our Church is the slight interference with the private opinion of her members, and however varied may be those opinions, it is consolatory to know that men are never so good or so bad as their opinions.'[13]

The current debate over the role of public institutions in Canadian society offers an instructive analogy. In the early nineteenth century the church saw itself as a public institution that provided an essential public service, in much the same way we might look upon hospitals providing public health care or schools providing public education. Like hospitals and schools, the church was linked to the state and supported (although not exclusively) by public revenue. Not everyone, of course, availed themselves of this public service – people were free to worship in a field or swamp just as parents are now free to banish their young to private schools or have themselves cut open by doctors in a foreign land. But this did not make the provision of religion (or the provision of health care or education) any less a public service or any less deserving of public support.

The demise of King's College on 1 January 1850 (the Octave of Christmas) marks a critical moment in the history of the Anglican Church. With consummate surgical skill, Robert Baldwin and his gang of reformers unceremoniously removed the church from the provincial university. Four years later another band of Canadian politicians (including the young John A. Macdonald) attacked with the same devastating effect that other pillar of the colonial establishment, the clergy reserves. The latter group set out 'to remove all semblance of connexion between church and state.'[14] While recognizing 'vested interests' – the claim of clergy who had been drawing their stipends from the reserves – the act stripped the church of its major source of public support, turning the revenue from the reserves to purely secular purposes.

At this point the church faced two critical problems. The first was institutional. With disestablishment the church lost its public position within the state – and as we have noted it responded very creatively to this problem by creating its own administrative and educational institutions. Leaving the state, however, also raised a major religious question. Establishment presupposed a certain type of religion – one that was hierarchical, moral, nondoctrinaire, rational, and inclusive. Now the church was assuming a new institutional form; but it had yet to decide what kind of religion – what culture – it would pour into these new private structures.

The construction of Trinity College offers one very instructive example of the way the church tried to respond to this pivotal problem. Here, however, one must not be misled by the official history of this

institution. Bishop Strachan liked to portray Trinity as the true successor to the old King's College, as the faithful remnant that had held true
to an old and sacred ideal. Trinity is praised without ceasing because it
maintained that unity of church and education that the creation of the
University of Toronto had put asunder. But this myth of creation
obscures the way in which Trinity actually responded to the cultural
crisis that disestablishment presented. King's College was part and
parcel of the old colonial establishment, and its rules and regulations
clearly expressed the inclusive latitudinarian principles that were such
a distinguishing feature of the old establishment discourse. To draw in
dissenters, religious tests at King's had been kept to an absolute minimum; to the same end, the presence of the church was largely unobtrusive and non-Anglicans were not compelled to attend either the
lectures in divinity or the services of worship.[15]

Although born less than a decade after the opening of King's College, Trinity was the child of a very different religious world. The new
college was to be an exclusively Anglican preserve, carefully guarded
from atheists and dissenters by batteries of religious tests, declarations,
and subscriptions. Although students did not have to be Anglican to
gain entry to the college, it was well nigh impossible for any student to
take a degree in any faculty without declaring 'willingly and heartily'
that he was 'truly and sincerely' a member of the church. Within the
walls of the college, students received instruction from professors who
were enjoined by the college statutes to be members of 'the Established
Church of England and Ireland' – the provost and professors in arts
were clerks in holy orders while those who taught law and medicine
had to 'sign and subscribe the Thirty-nine Articles of Religion.' And to
preserve the purity of this Anglican institution from generation to generation, membership on the College Council (and then the Council of
Corporation) was restricted to members of the church, who had to subscribe formally to the articles of religion before they were permitted to
assume their seats.[16] The transformation from Christian inclusiveness
to Anglican exclusiveness was dramatic and complete.

The same enclosed and sectarian attitudes informed all the other
important features of college life. The founders were convinced that a
proper university education had to be conducted within a semimonastic Anglican environment governed by a strict clerical discipline. For
this reason Bishop Strachan selected a site – an old park lot on Queen
Street West – safely removed from the hazards and temptations of the
city. Here amidst an elmy dale arose an imposing Gothic pile that was

Trinity College without additions, 1852–77. Toronto, Menzies and Company, 1914

Entrance gates, Trinity College, Toronto. Toronto, Menzies and Company, 1914

supposed to evoke the spirit of medieval Oxford. The founders then surrounded the college with a fence, placed iron bars across the lower windows, and imposed strict rules upon students entering and leaving the college. All who were confined therein were required to study divinity and attend chapel regularly.[17]

The founders of Trinity College clearly rejected the modern notion that higher education could be separated from the institutional setting of the church. But in order to preserve the relationship between church and college, they were forced to construct the college at a private site. And once they had left the public sphere they no longer felt compelled to maintain the latitudinarian culture of their former life. The education of Anglican youth was to take place within an enclosed, exclusive, and highly regulated monastic environment. And yet Trinity was just as determined to hold on to many aspects of the old establishment culture, continuing to represent itself as a public institution that served an important social role. For example, the college cultivated a close relationship with the traditional social and political elite by establishing courses of instruction for preparing young men for the liberal professions – the law, medicine, and the church. The clergy the college presented to the church were expected to perform the same public role that the clergy had performed within the old establishment. The first provost, the Reverend George Whitaker, who remained in this office for thirty years, returned time and again to this theme when he preached in the college chapel. Using words that may have been taken directly from Bishop Warburton, he asserted that it was the primary duty of the clergy to 'urge the law of God upon the consciences of men.' By so doing the people would not only become 'good Christians,' but also 'good citizens, and honest, sober men.'[18]

The college also tried to replicate within this enclosed private space the public order it felt duty-bound to protect, describing itself in the same language of hierarchy and order that had characterized the old establishment discourse. Trinity College, in Strachan's words, was to constitute a 'great Christian Household' – a social order modelled on an aristocratic establishment of the eighteenth century[19] – in which every member of the college, from the bishop in his palace to the Irish serving girls below stairs, was placed within a carefully ranked social hierarchy. Graduates of the college would then be able to step effortlessly into the highest stratum of society – into a social, political, and religious elite that shared the same social and religious ideology.

Finally, this strategy was sustained by what may seem a curious claim for public status and financial support. Trinity followed with absolute devotion the rules set down by sociologists for the behaviour of religious sects, enclosing itself within a private and absolutely pure religious space, excluding all those who did not conform to this singular standard, and vociferously attacking the inclusive and public University of Toronto. And yet Trinity continued to claim that it should be part of the world of public education and receive public support. To this end the Council of Corporation made provision for grammar schools (which received state grants) to affiliate with the college while pressing the provincial government to extend to the Anglican Church the same educational rights (publicly funded separate schools) it had granted to the Roman Catholics. In effect, it tried to represent itself as a public *and* religious alternative to the public *and* secular state system.[20] In the shadow of disestablishment, the Anglicans asserted that there should be a plurality of public systems, that the Anglican educational institutions could be exclusive and public at the same time.

This grand strategy failed for many reasons. The relationship between this exclusively Anglican college and the learned professions was challenged by the college's own medical faculty, which resigned as a body in 1856 primarily over the policy of imposing religious tests on faculty and students. It was also becoming apparent that the gap between the clergy and the other professions was widening; instead of being identified with an elite group of lawyers and physicians, the Anglican clergy were being increasingly associated with the ministers of the other Protestant denominations – something that Bishop Strachan had fought long and hard to resist. Nor were the clergy able to carry out the public roles they had performed within the old establishment, for once they stepped into the world beyond the college walls they found the terms of their public employment had changed dramatically. The state was supposed to be an ally, but, as Whitaker explained, the task the clergy faced was far 'more arduous than it has been' because they must now 'urge the law of God upon the consciences of men, unsupported by the authority of human law or public opinion.' How can we find solace in the laws of the state, the provost lamented, when those laws often appear 'selfish rather than benevolent, made for others' good rather than our own?'[21]

At the same time, the continuing claim for public status quickly came a cropper in the real world of Ontario educational politics. Only two grammar schools ever deigned to affiliate with Trinity College, and any hope of further additions was dashed when the grammar schools as a whole were subsumed into high schools and collegiate institutes and brought into the secular system as a secondary level of public education. Nor did the state evince any willingness to extend to the Anglican Church the same educational privileges it had given to the Roman Catholic Church. There would be no Anglican separate schools.[22]

As well, the metaphor that Strachan and Whitaker employed so often to represent the College suffered from some very serious problems. The little Anglican society constructed within the semimonastic world of Trinity College bore only a slight resemblance to the type of society that was evolving in Victorian Canada. The language of eighteenth-century aristocratic households may have had a certain resonance when colonial society had been dominated by professional elites and family compacts, but by the mid-Victorian period wealth and power were being drawn increasingly into the hands of a new commercial and industrial class, which was building a bourgeois society very different from the one this metaphor evinced. In truth, during this period Trinity College never learned how to operate successfully in this new world and limped pitifully from one financial crisis to the next.

Finally, many Anglicans rejected the college's exclusively Anglican vision of higher education. It was no surprise that Protestant dissenters and Roman Catholics – those excluded from Trinity's world – supported other programs. Much more unsettling was the fact that a substantial and influential group of evangelical Anglicans (who had no problem mastering the mysteries of commerce and industry) challenged Trinity College at every opportunity. This group strongly supported Trinity's arch rival, the University of Toronto, and in 1877 founded the Protestant Episcopal Divinity School (later Wycliffe College) that provided a way for truly serious young men to prepare for ordination without having to risk being contaminated by the sacerdotal world of Trinity College.

For all these reasons this entire religious and social strategy was quickly abandoned once Provost Whitaker left Trinity and returned to England in 1881. At that time a new provost, the Reverend Charles W.E. Body, set out to take the college in a very different direction, rejecting entirely the exclusivist Anglican vision and transforming the college within a few years into a modern and inclusive University that in almost all important essentials followed the lead of its old rival, the University of Toronto. The similarity of these two institutions would, in turn, provide the context for another provost, the Reverend T.C.S. Macklem, to open negotiations with the government of Ontario that would result in the federation of Trinity College with the University of Toronto in 1904. Now Trinity College would try to define its public religious role as a part of the public system of higher education in Ontario.

St Paul's Church pursued a very different strategy for constructing a public religion at a private site. This parish was created in the early 1840s to serve the village of Yorkville, and grew rapidly as the city of Toronto spread relentlessly to the north. To keep pace the congregation built a new gothic church in 1860, which was twice enlarged, first in 1890 and again 1903.[23] In terms of its religious practice the parish had become thoroughly identified with the extreme evangelical wing of the Anglican Church. Fiercely anti-Catholic and dogmatically committed to the principles of the Protestant Reformation, St Paul's revelled in the plainest forms of prayer book worship, rejecting even such moderate customs as preaching in a surplice and the use of choirs. In sum, St Paul's was a strong Anglican parish in an increasingly prosperous part of the city; it was aggressively evangelical both within its own precincts and within the diocese of which it seemed at times only a reluctant member.

By the start of the new century, however, St Paul's was becoming increasingly identified with a young man who would take the parish in a very different direction. Henry John Cody was born in Embro, Ontario, in 1868. His brilliant academic career took him from Tassie's famous school in Galt to the University of Toronto, where his record of prizes won and honours bestowed may still be without equal. He then enrolled in Wycliffe College, taught briefly at another evangelical bastion, Bishop Ridley College,[24] and in 1892 became student-assistant at St Paul's. Ordered deacon in 1893 and priested a year later, Cody continued to serve at St Paul's, although his position was not officially recognized until 1899, when he was appointed assistant rector. Eight years later upon the resignation of the Reverend T.C. DesBarres, Cody was inducted as rector, a position he would hold until 1932. He died in Toronto on 27 April 1951.

In 1909 Cody was put forward as the evangelical candidate in the hotly contested election for Bishop of Toronto. After several inconclusive ballots, however, both Cody and the high church candidate gave way to a compromise figure, Archdeacon J.F. Sweeney. Unable to attain the one episcopal office he truly desired, Cody proceeded to transform

The church front. Courtesy St Paul's Anglican Church, Toronto

St Paul's into a cathedral in all but name. In the aftermath of his election defeat, the parish of St Paul's, at Cody's urging, undertook the enormous task of constructing a new church. Begun in 1910 and opened for worship in 1913, the new St Paul's was the largest – and one of the most imposing – Anglican churches in the Dominion of Canada. Cody filled the church Sunday after Sunday, and the parish prospered; indeed St Paul's became the very epitome of a successful Anglican parish, and Canon Cody became one of the most famous Canadian clerics within the world-wide Anglican communion, his status confirmed by the offers he received to become bishop in dioceses in Canada, England, and Australia.

What were the keys to St Paul's undoubted success? As one might expect, those at the time and historians who have followed have focused almost exclusively upon the life and work of the rector. Cody's role was undoubtedly very important. He had strong administrative abilities and was a popular preacher (although neither theatrically extravagant nor emotionally intense). But there were other great preachers and fine administrators who did not enjoy the same success. Nor does the privileged location this church enjoyed, juxtaposed so nicely between the old wealth of Jarvis Street and the new wealth of Rosedale, adequately explain the church's good fortune, for other Protestant churches (including another Anglican Church) shared this general location, and their histories followed a very different course.[25]

Understanding St Paul's success returns us to the central focus of this chapter, for its rise to fame and fortune can be best analysed in terms of the broad strategy it followed for constructing a new kind of public religion at a private site. Three aspects of this strategy are especially significant: the high position accorded to the laity within the church; the ability of the parish to cultivate close relationships with other social and religious groups; and the way the parish integrated into its worship popular public ideologies, most notably the powerful currents of romantic nationalism. The first addresses the internal character of the parish; the second the relationship between the parish and the public world; and the third the ideology that drew the church and society together.

Both the external appearance and internal composition of this church proclaim in unmistakable terms the prominent role of the laity within this parish. Indeed, the cost and splendour of this neo-Gothic edifice[26] is such an obvious marker of the wealth of this congregation that one is tempted to read the material fabric of the building as a sign of the apparently insatiable appetite of the upper-middling classes for social respectability.[27] The church, however, acknowledged the role of the laity in a very particular way, celebrating the laity not for their social position but for the important roles they played within the religious life of the church. The memorials that line the walls of the church, for example, commemorate those who were active in Sunday school and mission work, those who served as church wardens or on the many committees that oversaw the day-by-day life of the parish. They celebrate especially those members of the parish who made the ultimate contribution to the spiritual life of the church and society by laying down their lives for others in war.

The actual composition of these memorials reinforces the fact that they were meant to be read as a religious text. Inscribed upon marble and brass, often with the addition of religious figures (such as angels) and a passage from the Bible, the memorials link the specific contribution of individuals and families to both the life of the church and an overarching sacred goal or divine purpose. Grouped together on the walls of the church, they reinforced the collective role of the laity within this sacred order. At the same time, they proclaimed visually a religious doctrine that stood at the very centre of Anglican evangelical culture. Alan Hayes has drawn our attention to the way the laity in the diocese of Toronto expounded the doctrine of the priesthood of all believers in order to assert its power and position in relation to the bishop and the clergy. Cody accepted this doctrine without question, and the new St Paul's proclaimed the supremacy of the laity at every opportunity.[28] In fact, one could argue that the laity supported this church so strongly not to acquire power and position, but because the church already acknowledged so fully the critical role of the laity within the life of the church.

Second, St Paul's set out to expand the boundaries of the parish by drawing in groups not directly identified with the Anglican Church. Historians who have examined Ontario culture at the turn of the century have commented upon the process of social and cultural interchange among members of different denominations.[29] St Paul's offers an instructive example of how this Protestant interchange worked in practice. Having the most impressive church building in the city, of course, helped to draw in 'new' people, especially for the Sunday evening service when it was the custom to visit other churches. At the same time, St Paul's actively linked the parish to a wide range of organizations and institutions that elevated the public presence of the church. Canon Cody played a crucial role in this process; indeed not since the days of Bishop Strachan had a cleric in Canada brought together so dramatically the public and the private, the civil and the religious. Cody was a canon of St Alban's Cathedral, the rector of St Paul's Church, and the Archdeacon of York. He was also very well connected with the Tory government of the day; he served on royal commissions, sat in the provincial parliament for North Toronto, and entered the cabinet as Minister of Education. He identified strongly with the University of Toronto, serving inter alia as a professor at Wycliffe College, a member (including the chair) of the board of governors, as well as the president (and later the chancellor) of the university.

The parish of St Paul's also cultivated a close relationship with elite private schools. Havergal College, an evangelical school for girls on Jarvis Street, was directly linked to St Paul's, and the church served as a place of worship and a venue for special events for both Branksome Hall and its sibling school, St Andrew's College. The church also formally welcomed the corps of the St John's Ambulance, the members of the Toronto police force, the St George's Society, the Royal Commonwealth Institute, and the Queen's Own Rifles. The association with these groups was not merely nominal; they literally marched into the church (often in uniform), and special services, plaques, memorials, and flags celebrated their connections to the parish.

Third, worship at St Paul's was constructed very self-consciously to appeal to a broad public audience. Here the great battles over ritualism in the Anglican Church may have obscured the important changes that were taking place in the conduct of religious services under Cody's leadership. Cody was an evangelical but he carefully led his congregation away from its customary puritan practices towards a more ceremonial and visually impressive form of worship.[30] While avoiding the markers of ritualism – not even a simple cross was allowed to desecrate the Lord's table – the rector introduced a number of major innovations. He preached in a surplice, and with the opening of the new church he encouraged the development of what was known as a cathedral style of worship. A gowned choir now processed up the central aisle and sat in carved stalls in the chancel. Healey Willan was hired in 1913 to improve the place and quality of church music, and although his relationship with Cody was often strained he remained at St Paul's for eight years. These fine pageants of worship also helped to draw an ever-widening audience into the church.

What precisely St Paul's was worshipping, however, raises a more complex question. Religious services at St Paul's may have been conducted according to the Book of Common Prayer, but in this church prayer book worship was placed within a setting that drew a direct link between the spiritual mission of the church, the British Empire, and the Canadian nation-state. All around the church were clear expressions of these imperial and national associations – flags, coats of arms, and carved figures of medieval knights. Indeed, at the most sacred site within the church these religious and imperial associations were brought together in one of the most elaborate and fascinating pieces of ecclesiastical art in Canada. Between 1922 and 1926 the parish planned, supervised, and installed a reredos behind the communion table as its major memorial to the members of the parish who had given their lives in the Great War. Customarily filled with the images of saints, a reredos generally marks a high church parish, but as in the case of choirs and processions the parish seems to have had little difficulty in turning such a Catholic artifice to its own purposes. The famous English firm of ecclesiastical art workers, J. Whippell and Company, composed the original design, which Cody and the congregation then revised before it was transported to the site (in 436 pieces) and installed in the church in 1922.[31]

Carved almost entirely from alabaster and marble, the central part of the reredos consists of three gables with crockets in which appear plants with direct national associations – the maple leaf, rose, thistle, shamrock, lily, and daffodil. These soar above the three canopies that overhang the central scene in the composition – a detailed relief of the Last Supper. Above the central canopy is the figure of St Stephen (the first Christian martyr and an obvious reference to the life of St Paul), and in the four niches surrounding Christ and the apostles, where Whippell's had proposed to place the four evangelists, are figures of David, Jonathan, Joshua, and Moses (three warriors and a lawgiver). The congregation also revised the plan in order to remove a cross from the central part of the reredos. Leaving aside one's own sensibilities, the quality of the carving and the scene presented – the first celebration of Christ's own sacrifice for the world – were absolutely in keeping with the events the reredos was intended to memorialize.

The reredos, however, takes on a more remarkable character as one turns to the side panels that flank the Last Supper. Here on a solid block of white alabaster in the centre of each panel are carved the names of the war dead with kneeling angels on each side holding a laurel wreath and torch. Once again there are biblical inscriptions – as well as a quotation from John Bunyan. At the borders of each side panel are six niches where the Whippell's design had placed on the left facing the reredos (the liturgical north) six saints associated with Great Britain and on the right (liturgical south) six saints associated with the Allied powers. At considerable cost, however, the parish insisted that these saints be replaced by lay figures – saints, as it were, of a different order: Drake, Nelson, Beatty, King Richard of the Lion-Heart, Edward the Black Prince, and Henry V of Agincourt grace the left panel; King George V, Kitchener, Florence Nightingale, Marshal Foch, Earl Haig, and Lord Byng grace the right.[32]

Two cultural discourses clearly inform this part of the reredos. As we have already noted, St Paul's celebrated a very lay-centred religion,

Alabaster reredos and screens. Photography by Pringle and Booth Ltd. In
William C. White, *Canon Cody of St Paul's Church* (Toronto: Ryerson Press, 1953)

and these changes to the original design yet again privileged the role of
the laity not only within the religious life of the church, but within the
grand religious passion of the war itself. At the same time, the composition of the reredos inserts into this religious lay discourse a popular
and public ideology. All these carved figures were imperial warriors
and their presence clearly commemorated their role in the formation,
defence, and expansion of the British Empire. In this way the reredos
sanctified the history of the British Empire and drew together the
worship of God and the powerful and popular currents of imperial
nationalism.

Once again these associations served a number of purposes. At a
very practical level they appealed strongly to the thousands of British
immigrants who had settled in Toronto in the two decades before the
Great War and swelled the ranks of the Anglican Church. At the same
time, as historians such as Jonathan F. Vance have shown, linking God
and empire helped to explain and justify a massive and devastating

Detail of screen, Henry V. Photography by William Westfall

war that other thoughtful Canadians found deeply unsettling if not beyond comprehension.[33] More important for our concerns, the celebration of empire linked the church to a prominent public ideology that, as Carl Berger has shown, explained to many English Canadians the true character of the Canadian nation-state.[34] Celebrating this imperial nationalism within St Paul's not only associated the church with this popular public ideology but also imbued imperial nationalism with a powerful spiritual quality: Canada was not only a rising nation in political and economic terms, it also took a leading role in the noble mission to build the Empire of Christ upon the earth.

Canon Cody was himself the archetypical imperial Canadian – a young lad from the colonies who had risen to international celebrity as one of the leading figures in the Imperial Anglican Church. His sermons, whether delivered to a congregation of worshippers or a group of businessmen at the Board of Trade, provide a fitting panegyric to this new public religion. In 1934 the city of Toronto asked Cody to deliver the principal address at the city's centennial celebrations. He took as his text the second verse of the fifty-fourth chapter of Isaiah: 'Enlarge the place of thy tent ... Lengthen thy cords, and strengthen thy stakes.' At one level this public sermon was pure boosterism, a benediction to Toronto's accomplishments over the last century. At the same time, however, Cody engaged the language of Christian idealism to draw the new trinity of God, Empire, and Nation together in a grand spiritual quest. Here, he drew together the commercial, industrial, social, educational, political, and moral ideals in one grand spiritual movement:

> Shall we not realize a *religious* ideal that will create goodness of character, that will vindicate the inherent worth of every man and strengthen him against the tyranny of the many; that will deepen his sense of responsibility to God and man in the exercise of his various rights and the discharge of his various duties, and that will emphasize his obligations to serve and to give, more than his claim to domineer and to get?[35]

What, then, had St Paul's achieved? Looking back, one is immediately struck by the way this parish revitalized so effectively the basic religious strategy upon which the old Anglican establishment had tried to construct a public religion. A public religion celebrated a particular form of social organization; it eschewed restrictive notions of orthodoxy in favour of an inclusive religious message; and it set out to perform an important public role, securing the social order essential to the very existence of society. St Paul's, like Scadding's church in the old town of York, celebrated the close relationship between the church and the state, although these were now lay-centred institutions drawn together through the romance of imperial nationalism. At the same time, the religious and social world of middle-class Toronto had replaced the carefully structured social hierarchies of the early nineteenth century. Through its strategy of institutional outreach, St Paul's renewed those older latitudinarian assumptions that had formed such an important part of establishment thinking, drawing into the church new institutions and social groups.

St Paul's set out to perform the same public role that the church had performed within the old establishment. 'Christianity and the State,' Canon Cody explained to the good people of St Paul's, 'is a subject of great practical importance. If religion be divorced from secular life both suffer; one becomes worldly, the other loses strength and fibre. Though the will of God is chiefly concerned with spiritual things and spiritual ends, yet the will of God concerns itself with all that touches human life. Therefore a good man will be a good citizen.' Here Cody once again returns to one of the defining characteristics of a public religion. In phrases that recall the very words of Bishop Warburton, he asserts that a certain kind of relationship between Christianity and the state serves the interests of both institutions, although this community of interest is now expressed through the language of Christian idealism – a good Christian will be a good subject, 'a good man will be a good citizen.'[36]

These attempts to construct a public religion at a private site suggest, in the first instance, a new way of looking at the history of the Anglican Church in Canada. Here the traditional categories of Anglican historical analysis – evangelical versus Tractarian – are subsumed within a more substantial nexus of religious and social issues. In a period of profound social and religious change, the church set out to address important questions while redefining its relationship with Canadian society. What is the proper relationship between Christ and culture? How should the church as a religious body respond to the new world created by disestablishment?[37] Indeed, one might suggest that Canon Cody, that noted evangelical, appears far more Catholic and universal in his answers to these questions than the supposedly high church founders of Trinity College, who adopted a position of religious exclusiveness worthy of the most extreme Protestant sect.

The Anglican story also offers an important commentary on the religious and social assumptions historians have brought to their studies of the changing place of religion in public life. José Casanova, for example, in his fine study of public religions in the modern world, uses the term 'deprivatization' to describe the process whereby a wide range of religious movements throughout the world have reasserted themselves in public life.[38] At the same time, a group of historians in Canada have adopted the term 'secularization' to describe the process whereby religious institutions, in their view, surrendered the fundamentals of their faith in order to reach an accommodation with the modern world.[39] Although these studies differ markedly in their interpretation of religious and social change, both deprivatization and secularization represent change as a movement from private to public and take as their starting point a time when religious institutions are separated from public life. For the Anglican Church, however, the trajectory of public and private was very different. The church entered British North America as a public religion – a church thoroughly integrated, both institutionally and doctrinally, with the colonial and imperial state – and it sought to maintain its public position throughout this period.

The ongoing commitment of the Anglican Church to a public religion raises in turn important questions about the very conception of public and private religions. Here we have noted the importance of distinguishing between the site a church occupies and the character of the religion it presents. While the Anglican Church had lost its traditional position within the public world, it did not give up the belief that religion should play a major public role in Canadian society. In effect, disestablishment not only redefined the relationship between organized religion and the Canadian state, but also altered the very concepts of public and private. In the shadow of disestablishment the terms themselves became problematic as the former symmetry of public religions and public space was broken apart, leaving the church to try to redefine over time a new relationship between religion and public life. As other contributions to this collection make clear, the Anglicans were by no means alone in trying to make sense of this new world.

Finally, the story of the Anglican Church suggests the need to reconceptualize the character of Ontario Protestantism itself. Here historians have tended to focus upon the critical role played by a broad alliance of evangelical churches – those denominations that traced their origins to the great waves of evangelical revivalism and opposed the very idea of a public state-supported religion. Within this alliance the Anglican

Church appears to have played at best only a marginal role. And yet the type of religion that came to dominate Ontario life was in many respects a reconstruction of the religious world the discourse of Anglican establishmentarianism had clearly envisioned – a religion that was irenic, nondoctrinal, practical, morally focused, and fully cognizant of the critical social role it should play in public life. To understand the formation of such a formidable public religion in Canada, should we not explore in a new light the history of the church that at one time laid claim to being a public religion and absolutely delighted in the close relation it enjoyed with the state? We might well find in the strategies the church developed to maintain its distinctive public role an important formative influence upon that Christian world in Canada that some have argued is one of the nation's most distinguishing features.[40]

Notes

1 John S. Moir, *Church and State in Canada West: Three Studies in the Relation of Denominationalism and Nationalism, 1841–1867* (Toronto: University of Toronto Press, 1959); T.R. Millman, 'Beginnings of the Synodical Movement in Colonial Anglican Churches with Special Reference to Canada,' *Journal of the Canadian Church Historical Society,* 21 (1979): 3–19; R.V. Harris, *An Historical Introduction to the Study of the Canon Law of the Anglican Church of Canada* (Toronto: General Synod, 1965); and Curtis Fahey, *In His Name: The Anglican Experience in Upper Canada, 1791–1854* (Ottawa: Carleton University Press, 1991).

2 Society for the Propagation of the Gospel Archives, D Series, D.14, 'A Letter to the Right Honourable Lord John Russell, etc. On the Present State of the Church in Canada by the Bishop of Toronto,' 20 February 1851.

3 T.A. Reed, ed., *A History of the University of Trinity College, 1852–1952* (Toronto: University of Toronto Press, 1952).

4 For material on Cody and St Paul's see: D.C. Masters, *Henry John Cody: An Outstanding Life* (Toronto: Dundurn, 1995); William C. White, *Canon Cody of St Paul's Church* (Toronto: Ryerson, 1953). I also wish to thank Mr Alex Camp, the archivist of the parish, who pointed me to a number of important sources and was especially helpful with visual materials.

5 The main texts in this discourse were William Warburton, *The Alliance between Church and State, or the Necessity and Equity of Established Religion and a Test-Law, Demonstrated* (1736), William Paley, *The Principles of Moral and Political Philosophy* (1785), and Edmund Burke, *Reflections on the Revo-*

lution in France (1790). '[The church] is yet a blessing to the land over-shadowed by her wide-spread branches; and rightly had she adhered to her obligations in the civil compact. But has a like fidelity been evinced by the state in discharging its share of the mutual compact?' *The Church,* 5 September 1845.

6 John Strachan, *A Sermon Preached at York, Upper Canada, Third of July 1825, on the Death of the Late Lord Bishop of Quebec* (Kingston: Macfarlane, 1826). See also William Westfall, *Two Worlds: The Protestant Culture of Nineteenth Century Ontario* (Montreal and Kingston: McGill-Queen's University Press, 1989), chap. 4.

7 This fact has unfortunately been overlooked in the recent work on state formation. See Allan Greer and Ian Radforth, eds., *Colonial Leviathan: State Formation in Mid-Nineteenth-Century Canada* (Toronto: University of Toronto Press, 1992).

8 R.D. Gidney and W.P.J. Millar, *Professional Gentlemen: The Professions in Nineteenth-Century Ontario* (Toronto: University of Toronto Press, 1994), esp. part 1.

9 Cecilia Morgan, *Public Men and Virtuous Women: The Gendered Languages of Religion and Politics in Upper Canada, 1791–1850* (Toronto: University of Toronto Press, 1996); and Katherine M.J. McKenna, *A Life of Propriety: Anne Murray Powell and Her Family* (Montreal and Kingston: McGill-Queen's University Press, 1994).

10 For a popular account of the wide range of clerical work, see Anne Wilkinson, *Lions in the Way: A Discursive History of the Oslers, 1862–1902* (Toronto: Macmillan, 1956).

11 Henry Scadding, *Toronto of Old*, abridged and edited by F.H. Armstrong (Toronto: Oxford University Press, 1966), 85. See also Shirley Morriss and Carl Benn, 'Architecture,' in *The Parish and Cathedral of St James Toronto, 1797–1997*, ed. William Cooke (Toronto: University of Toronto Press, 1998), 179–215.

12 Paley, *The Principles of Moral and Political Philosophy*, book 6, chap. 10.

13 Donald Shurman, *A Bishop and His People: John Travers Lewis and the Anglican Diocese of Ontario, 1862–1902* (Kingston: Ontario Diocesan Synod, 1991), 64.

14 Michael S. Cross and Robert Lochiel Fraser, 'Robert Baldwin,' *Dictionary of Canadian Biography*, vol. 8, 45–59; and Moir, *Church and State in Canada West.*

15 Ontario Archives, Strachan Papers, Strachan to the Earl of Elgin and Kincardine, 9 November 1849.

16 Trinity College Archives, The Calendar of the University of Trinity College (1853), 15. In addition, all the professors had to subscribe to the three articles of the Thirty-Sixth Canon.

17 Trinity College Archives, Statutes of Trinity College, Minutes of the Council of Corporation.

18 'St John the Baptist, an Exemplar to Christian Ministers,' *A Sermon Preached in the Chapel of Trinity College, Sunday June 14, 1860 by George Whitaker, MA, Provost of Trinity College*, published at the request of the professors and students of the College (Toronto: Henry Rowsell, 1860), 11; and 'The Holy Spirit's Sealing,' *Sermons Preached in Toronto for the Most Part in the Chapel of Trinity College by George Whitaker, MA* (London: Rivingtons, Toronto: Willing and Williamson, 1882).

19 Strachan, Opening address at the laying of the cornerstone of Trinity College, 30 April 1851, as quoted in *The Rise and Progress of Trinity College, Toronto; with a Sketch of the Life of the Lord Bishop of Toronto as Connected with Church Education in Canada* by Henry Melville, M.D. (Toronto: Henry Rowsell, 1852), 120–1. See Alison Prentice, 'Education and the Metaphor of the Family: The Upper Canadian Example,' in *Education and Social Change*, ed. Michael B. Katz and Paul Mattingly (New York: New York University Press, 1975), 110–32.

20 Robert Gidney and Wyn Millar point out that the modern equation of state and public had not been fully articulated and that the ambiguity of the word 'public' left space for a variety of educational institutions to claim public status. See R.D. Gidney and W.P.J. Millar, *Inventing Secondary Education: The Rise of the High School in Nineteenth-Century Ontario* (Montreal and Kingston: McGill-Queen's University Press, 1990).

21 'St John the Baptist,' 11, 'The Holy Spirit's Sealing,' 152.

22 See Gidney and Millar, *Inventing Secondary Education*. Partly for this reason, Trinity was forced to cultivate such close relations with private schools, especially Trinity College School and Bishop Strachan School.

23 The 1860 church was designed by George K. and Edward Radford, the additions in 1890 by Gordon and Helliwell, and those in 1903 by E.J. Lennox. Eric Arthur, *Toronto, No Mean City*, revised by Stephen A. Otto (Toronto: University of Toronto Press, 1986), esp. chap. 4.

24 Stephen Leacock had applied for the same position; Leacock would go on to teach classics at Upper Canada College, although there is no clear evidence at this point that UCC should be regarded as (at least) second-best.

25 The Church of St Simon the Apostle – just a few blocks to the east – remained a well-to-do but comparatively small Anglican parish church while Jarvis Street Baptist Church, a few blocks to the south, actually lost its position as the largest and wealthiest Baptist church in the city. It too had a famous preacher, but in this case a large group of moderate evangelicals,

unable to abide the leadership of the Reverend T.T. Shields, left Jarvis Street to found Park Road Baptist Church. See Paul R. Wilson, 'Baptists and Business: Central Canadian Baptists and the Secularization of the Businessman at Toronto's Jarvis Street Baptist Church, 1848–1921' (Ph.D. diss., University of Western Ontario, 1996).

26 The architect E.J. Lennox, who was also a member of the congregation, described the internal decoration of the church as taking its inspiration from 'the decorative Gothic period.' Archives of the Diocese of Toronto, St Paul's Archive Material Stored with Diocesan Archivist, Memorials and Stained Glass Windows, Letter to J. Whippell and Company, 8 September 1924.

27 See Lynne Marks' equation of new churches and the drive for social respectability. Lynne Marks, *Revivals and Roller Rinks: Religion, Leisure, and Identity in Late-Nineteenth-Century Small-Town Ontario* (Toronto: University of Toronto Press, 1992).

28 Alan L. Hayes, 'Managing the Household of Faith: Administration and Finance 1867–1939,' in *By Grace Co-Workers: Building the Anglican Diocese of Toronto 1780–1989*, ed. Alan L. Hayes (Toronto: Anglican Book Centre, 1989), 235–57; and William H. Katerberg, 'Redefining Evangelicalism in the Canadian Anglican Church: Wycliffe College and the Evangelical Party, 1867–1995,' in *Aspects of the Canadian Evangelical Experience*, ed. G.A. Rawlyk (Montreal and Kingston: McGill-Queen's University Press, 1997), 171–88.

29 Most notably John Webster Grant, *A Profusion of Spires: Religion in Nineteenth-Century Ontario* (Toronto: University of Toronto Press, 1988).

30 Similar changes were also taking place in other evangelical parishes, such as Grace Church and St James. See Cooke, *The Parish and Cathedral of St James.*

31 Archives of the Diocese of Toronto, St Paul's Archive Material Stored with Diocesan Archivist, Memorials and Stained Glass Windows, 'War Memorial Screens in St Paul's.' Correspondence between J. Whippell and Company and St Paul's Church. The reredos was unveiled on 28 March 1926. The stained glass windows in the chancel are also part of the war memorial.

32 Memorials and Stained Glass Windows, J. Whippell and Company to Canon Cody, 27 November 1924. An additional sum of 135 pounds per figure was needed in order to portray accurately the portrait, decorations, and uniforms 'as compared with a medieval figure in a robe, when no exact likeness has to be copied.'

33 Jonathan F. Vance, *Death So Noble: Memory, Meaning, and the First World War*

(Vancouver: UBC Press, 1997). Compare Vance's treatment of the impact of the war with David B. Marshall, *Secularizing the Faith: Canadian Protestant Clergy and the Crisis of Belief, 1850–1940* (Toronto: University of Toronto Press, 1992).

34 Carl Berger, *The Sense of Power: Studies in the Ideas of Canadian Imperialism, 1867–1914* (Toronto: University of Toronto Press, 1970).

35 White, *Canon Cody*, 164. On the intellectual origins of idealism in Canada, see A.B. McKillop, *A Disciplined Intelligence: Critical Inquiry and Canadian Thought in the Victorian Era* (Montreal and Kingston: McGill-Queen's University Press, 1979).

36 White, *Canon Cody*, 36.

37 Marguerite Van Die, *An Evangelical Mind: Nathanael Burwash and the Methodist Tradition in Canada* (Montreal and Kingston: McGill-Queen's University Press, 1989), 178–96.

38 José Casanova, *Public Religions in the Modern World* (Chicago: University of Chicago Press, 1994), esp. chap. 8.

39 Most notably Ramsay Cook, *The Regenerators: Social Criticism in Late Victorian Canada* (Toronto: University of Toronto Press, 1985); and Marshall, *Secularizing the Faith*. See also Nancy Christie and Michael Gauvreau, *A Full-Orbed Christianity: The Protestant Churches and Social Welfare in Canada, 1900–1940* (Montreal and Kingston: McGill-Queen's University Press, 1996).

40 Mark A. Noll, *A History of Christianity in the United States and Canada* (Grand Rapids: Eerdmans, 1992); Mark Noll, 'Christianity in Canada: Good Books at Last,' *Fides et Historia* 23 (Summer 1991).

2

Evangelicals and Public Life in Southern New Brunswick, 1830–1880

T.W. Acheson

Between the American Revolution and the Civil War, the United States witnessed the disestablishment of all religious traditions and the development, especially in the northern part of the country, of an evangelical Protestant denominationalism that, in the words of José Casanova, became the culturally established American religion and 'gained hegemonic control over the public discourse of American civil society.'[1] That transition saw the rejection of early attempts to privatize religion and create a public order free from an overt religious influence. Evangelicals had as an agenda the creation of a Christian society through the reformation of life and habits. Their interdenominational efforts created a 'benevolent empire' of organizations ranging from Bible and tract societies to societies for the preservation of the sabbath, the abolition of slavery, the control of alcoholic beverages, the education of the poor, and the reclamation of prisoners and 'fallen' women.

The British crown colony of New Brunswick was also a creation of the American Revolution. Designed as a refuge for those who rejected the revolution and its values, it became a place where early leaders attempted to create a British social order, including an established Church of England. Despite the nature of its foundation, howeyer, the religious institutions and assumptions of New Brunswickers after 1830 increasingly resembled American rather than British society. The dominant thread in this transition was the growing influence of evangelicalism, a transdenominational Protestantism characterized by biblicism, conversionism, crucicentrism, and social activism.[2] These shared characteristics propelled evangelicals into public life as they sought to reform society in their own image.

By 1860, a generation later than in the United States, evangelicals, organized denominationally, had become the culturally dominant civil religion in New Brunswick; ritualists (mainly Roman Catholics and the wing within the Church of England influenced by the Oxford or Tractarian movement of the 1830s), as well as remnants of the traditional religious establishment, increasingly found themselves on the political periphery. The pattern of development was very similar to that in neighbouring New England, and included a rapid expansion of evangelical numbers and influence largely through conversion; propaganda; the development of aggressive denominations; the emergence of interdenominational evangelical agencies; the great moral and social crusades; and the move from the private, the local, and clergy leadership to the public, the province, and lay leadership. The transition from the paradigm of religious establishment to a public evangelicalism produced one significant difference in New Brunswick: the political instrument through which evangelicals came to influence public policy in the province was by cooperation with the party of liberal reform.[3] This transition occurred largely between 1830 and 1880 and corresponded with the political careers of three prominent evangelical Liberals: Lemuel Allen Wilmot, Samuel Leonard Tilley, and George Edwin King. This chapter focuses on the three dominant issues that brought evangelicals into the forefront of New Brunswick public life: church disestablishment; moral reform through temperance, total abstinence, and prohibition; and the creation of a nonsectarian (but broadly Christian) public school system.

By 1830 demography and history assured evangelicals a place as an emergent ascending social force within the civil society of New Brunswick. Building on the late-eighteenth-century arrival of Massachusetts Congregationalists and Yorkshire Methodists, evangelical strength grew quickly as a result of large-scale British immigration after 1815, especially of Protestant Irish. Among the immigrants were not only members of dissenting or nonconformist churches such as the Wesleyan Methodists and the Baptists – both free will and Calvinist – but also significant numbers of evangelicals within the Church of England and Ireland, and, after the 'Disruption' of the Church of Scotland in 1843, those who left to enter the new Free Church of Scotland.

The half-century after 1830 witnessed a dramatic expansion of the Baptist, Disciples, and Methodist denominations, largely the result of aggressive programs of revival that produced conversions among children of members, the unchurched, and supporters of other denominations. By 1871, southern New Brunswick had become an almost continuous evangelical stronghold, with the exceptions of the Acadian settlements and the urban centres of Saint John, St Andrews, and Fredericton. At that time, the nine southern counties of the province contained nearly 70,000 Baptists – divided in a 3 to 2 ratio between Calvinist and free will – along with 27,000 Wesleyan Methodists, 18,000 Free Church and Reformed Presbyterians, 40,000 adherents of the Church of England, 6,000 Church of Scotland Presbyterians, and 47,000 Roman Catholics.[4]

Despite their sometimes fierce competition for souls through revivals, evangelicals were ecumenical in attitude towards their counterparts in other denominations. They recognized the legitimacy of each others' faith and order, and usually worked cooperatively in matters of social and moral improvement, and in such distinctly evangelical institutions as the Sunday School movement and the Bible Society. This shared understanding of faith and morals led to the creation of broadly based evangelical alliances, the goals of which were the proclamation of God's Kingdom and the creation of a Christian environment. The earliest efforts to fulfil these goals took place in the private arena. In Saint John, the largest urban centre in the Atlantic coastal colonies, they began with the formation of the New Brunswick Auxiliary of the British and Foreign Bible Society in 1819, the Union Sunday School Society in 1823, and the Religious Tract Society in 1832. Sunday School rallies, picnics, teachers' meetings, and teas became common features of evangelical life within the city.

The growing strength and prestige of the evangelical movement became apparent after 1825 when it turned to issues of public morality. Evangelical efforts initially focused on the enforcement of sabbath regulations. In the late 1820s evangelicals turned their attention to theatres and grog shops. In 1828 the city's evangelical clergy persuaded the mayor to close the principal theatre on the grounds that it posed a threat to public morals.[5] The alliance was instrumental in creating the Saint John Temperance Society, dedicated to restricting the consumption of 'ardent spirits.' Evangelical cooperation sometimes extended to the creation and support of charitable institutions, such as the Female House of Industry for destitute women and their children, established in 1832, and later for the school for black children at the Baptist Chapel and the Ragged schools in South Saint John.[6] From 1830 onward the Bible Society, the Temperance Society, and the Sunday School Union remained causes around which evangelicals rallied. These issues would later form the basis of their political agenda.

The Attack on Church Establishment

While all evangelicals rejoiced in a common 'Great Mission' of proclamation and reclamation, they were deeply divided over the issue of the
religious establishment. Evangelicals within the Church of England
accepted the establishment, seeing in it a means of securing and pre-
serving a Protestant community. Wesleyan Methodists and free will
Baptists traditionally acquiesced to it; Calvinist groups, whether Baptist, Presbyterian, or Congregationalist, always demanded disestablishment.[7] The pietism of some of the early evangelical groups –
notably the Wesleyans, who in the eighteenth century had been part of
the Anglican Church – along with the arrangements of colonial government, permitted the religious establishment in New Brunswick to
survive well into the nineteenth century, as will be discussed below.

Economic difficulties were the catalyst that provoked the shift
towards disestablishment. The early 1840s witnessed the beginning of
the disintegration of the imperial trading arrangements under which
colonial timber had entered the British market under substantial tariff
protection.[8] The result was a severe depression, which gripped the
commercial life of the colony through much of the decade. Coupled
with this was the potato famine that devastated Ireland through much
of the decade and brought to New Brunswick a flood of impoverished
Irish immigrants – mostly Roman Catholic – that threatened to remake
the denominational structure of the colony. The personal and commercial distress occasioned by the depression coupled with the threat of
displacement by ancient enemies created great tensions within the
urban areas of the colony, tensions that frequently resulted in violence.[9]
The sense that a loyal people had been betrayed and abandoned by a
thankless homeland produced a spirit of New Brunswick nationalism,
one sometimes manifest in attacks upon the institutions that had been
privileged by the colonial order, including the established church.

Between 1842 and 1846 four British evangelical ministers, representing the Free Church of Scotland, the Presbyterian Synod of Ulster, and
the Congregational Union of Great Britain arrived in Saint John, bringing with them the concerns of English, Scottish, and Irish nonconfor-
mity and providing a catalyst for the growing discontent within the
colonial community. All were supporters of the Anti-State Church
Association of Great Britain, a lobby group supported by most Protestant dissenters as well as most British liberals. They quickly assumed
the leadership of a radical evangelical movement. Of the four, the Con-

gregationalist J.C. Gallaway was particularly active. In 1846 he took the decisive step of inviting the ministers and office holders of the evangelical churches of Saint John – but not of the Church of England and the Church of Scotland – to come together to form the Evangelical Alliance of New Brunswick. This organization was based on the English Evangelical Alliance formed in 1845 in reaction to a perceived expansion of papal influence in the British Isles, a perception fuelled by the shift to ritualism within a sector of the Church of England as a result of the Tractarian movement.[10] The New Brunswick Alliance adopted the program of its English parent, including the declaration that all Protestant denominations, saving the Unitarian, possessed a valid ministry, a true teaching, and spiritual equality. Significantly, however, it added a resolution decrying the claims of one church to primacy over the others. Within a few months a number of Evangelical Alliance members formed the New Brunswick Election Society, a party designed to contest the 1846 elections for the Legislative Assembly in the interest of the Alliance. The party platform reflected the Alliance's liberal biases and the long-standing grievances of dissenting or nonestablished denominations. It contained demands for religious equality, the sharing of public offices among the several denominations, a universal system of education available to all, efficient and cheap government, and the abolition of pensions to government functionaries. In preparation for the election, branches of the Election Society formed in Kings and Westmorland counties, and candidates were nominated in the multimember riding of Kings, Westmorland, Saint John City, and Saint John City and County.

Liberals and more moderate evangelicals greeted this entry into the public arena by the radical evangelicals with anger and consternation. The leadership of the Orange Order, that bastion of the Irish Protestant ascendancy and often a place of evangelical sentiment, saw the formation of a new party as a 'horrid depravity' that would hopelessly shatter Protestant strength.[11] Anglican liberals of evangelical leanings, like George Fenety, editor of the influential *News*, urged the Society to put its faith in the liberal churchmen, who would attempt to rectify the grievances of the dissenters.[12] In the end the reformers failed to elect any candidate running under their banner. A few days after the election, the principal evangelical clergy of the city published a public letter repudiating the activities of the Election Society but declaring their support for the principle of the equality of all denominations.[13]

So ended the first attempt to create a political organization structured around explicitly religious goals. In New Brunswick, as in the United States, a party perceived as the agent of a particular religious interest had little appeal. Moreover, it flew in the face of a long-standing provincial tradition in which legislators ran as individuals rather than representatives of organized partisan groups. Most significantly, it divided the evangelical movement and privileged the liberal political issue of disestablishment over the evangelical goal of spiritual and moral reform. Although the Evangelical Alliance remained a significant forum for interdenominational cooperation among the traditional Protestant dissenters, radical evangelical leaders increasingly abandoned divisive state–church concerns for issues that contributed to the creation of a Christian moral order. Through the next decade temperance and education consumed most of their energies.

Temperance, Total Abstinence, and Prohibition

Temperance permitted a symbolic societal purging of the potential demonic forces unleashed by the consumption of alcohol. It appealed particularly to the perfectionist tendencies of many evangelicals, and in its advanced form of total abstinence became an act of self-giving in which followers of Christ, in response to the injunction of the apostle Paul, denied themselves for the sake of the weak. The temperance societies of the 1820s, supported by all evangelicals, had been led by much of the social élite of the province, and by the clergy of the churches of England and Scotland.[14] They discouraged the use of liquor (but not of wine or ale), importuned local magistrates to limit the number of tavern licences issued in their communities, and had tried, by example, to improve the quality of life in these communities. In Saint John they had succeeded in reducing the number of taverns from 206 to 104; by 1834 more than 1,400 adults in the city had signed the short oath to abstain from liquor.[15] However, these societies had limited their programs to public meetings and processions. They provided little active support for total abstinence, and did little to rescue those who had fallen into alcoholism.

After 1832 total abstinence societies increasingly supplemented and supplanted the efforts of the temperance societies. The Saint John Total Abstinence Society was composed of those prepared to sign the long oath not to consume or serve any alcoholic beverage, including wine or beer, nor permit it in their homes or workplaces.[16] The more activist approach of the abstainers appealed to evangelicals: those who had fallen into alcoholism were sought and saved; those recovered were kept secure in an environment where alcohol was never present. By 1840 the Saint John Society had 758 members, of whom nearly a third were women and nearly half were freemen of the city, two-thirds of whom were artisans or tradesmen.[17] The 1840 recruits included two young Anglican Sunday School teachers, Samuel Leonard Tilley and his friend Joseph W. Lawrence. By 1843 one in four adults in the city were members of the Total Abstinence Society.[18] The local societies maintained an active program of recruitment, creating groups in virtually every hamlet in southern New Brunswick. The evangelical roots of the organization were reflected in regular meetings, public lectures, publication and distribution of tracts, and provision of books and speakers to schools and public institutions. By 1845, with the strong support of Lemuel Allen Wilmot, the legislature provided a grant for the production of a weekly newspaper, *The Temperance Telegraph*. Virtually all evangelicals were found in one of the manifestations of the temperance movement. The Total Abstinence Society, with its emphasis on personal asceticism, saving the fallen, and social concern for those retrieved from addiction, attracted the most committed evangelicals. They in turn provided the bedrock on which the prohibitionist movement built.

Prohibitionist organization in New Brunswick took place through fraternal groups linked to groups in New England and England. By far the most significant was the Sons of Temperance, founded in New York City in 1843. By 1849, the Sons of Temperance had 4,500 adult male members in southern New Brunswick. The order was supplemented by special organizations for women and children, and its life was distinguished by a full round of social activities, the sacred symbols and regalia of a secret society, public torchlight parades, and the security offered by sickness and burial funds. Like total abstinence supporters, prohibitionists were strongest among the Wesleyans and Baptists, strong among the Free Church Presbyterians and members of the Church of England, and weakest within the Church of Scotland. Their members were found particularly among young men twenty to thirty years of age. The Saint John officers, reflecting the evangelical leadership of the city, were drawn mainly from minor merchants and functionaries, small master craftsmen, and shipwrights, while membership generally was drawn from the traditional crafts headed by a petite bourgeoisie of evangelical origins. The traditional leaders of the city – patricians, great merchants, major functionaries, and lawyers – were largely absent from this group.[19]

The arrival of the prohibitionists changed forever the traditional role of religion as either subordinate servant to the state or as dissenting denominations functioning in the private sphere. Unlike the abstainers, who appealed to individual willpower, prohibitionists had a broader and more unitary vision, one that could be fulfilled only through state control. Ultimately this meant entering the political arena with a clear public purpose and a willingness to participate in the exercise of power to enforce that purpose.

The opportunity to enter the political arena came in 1849 with the formation of the New Brunswick Colonial Association, a broad-based political alliance of mildly reformist interests formed in reaction to Britain's abandonment of its mercantilist policies. The association represented a movement of rudimentary New Brunswick nationalism emphasizing the protection of producers, industrial development, liberal political reform, and reciprocity with the United States. Charles Simonds, the venerable long-time speaker of the Assembly, presided over this mid-century effort to create a new community consensus. Other leaders included prominent prohibitionist evangelicals such as Samuel Leonard Tilley and W.R.M. Burtis. In the election of 1850 the association produced a seven-point manifesto of political and administrative reforms that included efficiency in government, the abolition of privilege and political favour, the secret ballot, and reciprocity with the United States. It also endorsed slates of candidates in most constituencies.[20] This move represented one of the first attempts at colonial party organization. Traditionally, candidates for election ran as individuals or as part of local coalitions, and votes in the Assembly were largely the result of personal relationships or sensibilities. In the 1840s a few assemblymen, notably Lemuel Allen Wilmot, had begun to describe themselves as 'Liberal' or 'Reformer,' and to talk in terms of 'responsible government,' but there was never a consistent party.

The Colonial Association offered the possibility of creating an organization with a comprehensive agenda that might capture control of the state. While the presence of Tilley and other prohibitionists linked the association with the temperance movement, the association platform contained no reference to temperance, and many of its leaders were unsympathetic to its aims. Despite this, in the eyes of many, temperance became part of the mythology of political reform. In many constituencies prohibitionists were the backbone of the movement, and the *Temperance Telegraph* threw its support behind the association in the election of 1850.[21] By 1852 prohibitionists had so identified with liberal and moral reform that the Grand Patriarch for New Brunswick, James Johnston, declared the interests of the Sons and the Association to be identical.[22]

Despite great hopes for the Association, it failed to gain control of the Assembly in the election of 1850, and government continued very much in its traditional form for the next four years. That failure was perhaps fortunate for the prohibitionists: in the interim they were able to establish a moral influence in the public sphere quite independent of that of the liberal reformers. Reacting to the passage of the prohibitory acts in Maine and Massachusetts in 1851, the New Brunswick prohibitionists prepared the Great Petition for the 1852 sitting of the legislature.[23] This single scroll, signed by more than 9,000 men and women from the southern counties, asked for the prohibition of imports of all alcoholic beverages into New Brunswick. A majority of surprised assemblymen gave the petitioners half the loaf they desired: they passed an act to prevent the manufacture and sale of liquor, but specifically exempted beer, ale, and porter. This legislation proved impossible to enforce and was quietly repealed in 1853. Nonetheless, the prohibitionists had decisively demonstrated their potential electoral strength.

The prohibitionists' principal leader in the Assembly was Samuel Leonard Tilley, soon to become Grand Patriarch of the Sons of Temperance throughout the United States and British North America. Tilley's reputation as a man of great integrity, and his command of the temperance battalions, gave him a standing in the reform movement rivalling that of the party leader, Charles Fisher. After a nonconfidence vote following the 1854 general elections, Tilley entered the first Liberal government in the history of the province as provincial secretary (treasurer) – effectively deputy leader. At the 1855 sitting Tilley moved to introduce a prohibitory bill that would prevent the import, manufacture, or sale of all alcoholic beverages including ale and beer. The bill passed on a 21 to 17 division in the House, and the act, which came into force on 1 January 1856, produced a situation akin to civil war.[24] The traditional élites of the province, including much of the legal community, openly defied the law. The lieutenant-governor, who had opposed the legislation, now exceeded his authority and dissolved the Assembly.

The 1856 election was fought on the issues of prohibition and of the governor's arbitrary use of power. Those supporting the governor, including John Medley, the Tractarian bishop of Fredericton, were dubbed 'Rummies.' Those opposing him became 'Smashers.' Tilley, who as champion of the Evangelical party within the Church of England had sometimes opposed the bishop on theological issues, now found himself confronting him in the political arena. The evangelical press of the province stood firmly with the Smashers.[25] While the Rummies won the election, it was a short-lived victory. A significant core of Smashers were returned to the Assembly in 1856 and within a year had succeeded in defeating the Rummies' government in the Assembly. They won another general election in 1857 and remained in power until 1865.

The Prohibitionists were the first broadly based populist movement in the history of New Brunswick. They provided the basis of support and the discipline that permitted the creation of the first genuine party in the province.[26] While the political party was essentially an alliance of various groups of reformers, the temperance forces provided the troops and the organization without which the party could not survive.[27]

The formation of an evangelically based social movement with a mildly reformist political ideology is revealed in Gail Campbell's study of voting behaviour in Charlotte County between 1846 and 1857.[28] The second most populous county in the province, Charlotte was a constituency that returned four members to the Legislative Assembly. In 1846 there was little evidence of 'slate' voting, in which a significant part of the electorate voted for the same four candidates. Less than 3 per cent of electors in 1846 voted a slate. By 1857, however, more than 60 per cent did so, and more than two out of every three of these voted the Smashers ticket. By 1857 religious affiliation was the best predictor of party preference. Baptists, Methodists, and smaller groups of dissenters such as Universalists, Disciples, and Congregationalists, supported the Smashers by margins of two or three or four to one, although Baptists – reflecting their strong radical evangelical origins – and native Methodists were at the high end of Smashers support, while British-born Methodists were at the lower end of the spectrum. Roman Catholics divided rather evenly between Smashers and Rummies. The response of the traditional state churches was more ambiguous. While a clear majority of Anglicans and Presbyterians supported the Rummies, nearly a third of the former and 40 per cent of the latter voted for Smashers candidates, a reflection of the strength of the evangelical and temperance movements within these traditions.

The evangelicals represented by the temperance groups within the

Smashers movement fit easily into its mild liberalism, a transition assisted by the process of religious disestablishment. The process was aided when, in 1856, the Bishop of Fredericton resigned his seat on the Legislative Council in the face of an expected Smashers' victory. The major remaining element of the establishment was the publicly supported King's College at Fredericton, with its Anglican chair of theology. In 1858 the Smashers' government created a university out of the Wesleyan seminary of Mount Allison at Sackville. The following year, after an acrimonious debate, Lemuel Allen Wilmot prepared legislation secularizing King's College and transforming it into the University of New Brunswick,[29] an act that effectively completed disestablishment in the colony.

The Education Debate

The other central concern of evangelicals, one they shared with their liberal partners, was public education. Liberals aimed at creating a trained and educated citizenry through an education system available to all children. Evangelicals supported the concept of equal access and vocational preparation, but also insisted the system should reinforce a common Christian culture through access to biblical literacy and moral understandings unmediated by institutions. With the election of the Smashers there was a general assumption that the educational systems of the province would be reformed and improved.

In the city of Saint John about 60 per cent of all children attended some school in 1851.[30] Perhaps a quarter of these attended parish schools, which were established by statute and received about half of their revenues from the province under the authority of the Schools Act. The remainder were in the Roman Catholic and Anglican Charity schools (including the Monitorial Madras schools), and in the Methodist, Presbyterian, Baptist, and interdenominational Commercial schools, all funded in part by annual grants from the governor-in-council.

The debate over educational reform centred on three questions: Should the parish schools be sectarian, religious, or nonreligious? Should nonparish schools continue to be supported by the state, integrated into the parish schools, or left as private schools? Should the parish schools become a common compulsory school system maintained by a general assessment on the community, as the liberal utilitarians within the government wished? Evangelicals, on the other hand, convinced of the necessity of scripture reading and moral training based on Christian ideals, coalesced around the position that Bible reading without commentary was essential in any public school system. The Free Christian (free will) Baptists preferred separate denominational schools, but would accept a common school provided that Bible reading was required. Led by their bishop, the Roman Catholic community petitioned for common schools and Catholic schools in any districts where educational assessments were levied.[31] City evangelicals responded with two petitions containing identical signatures: the first requested that any school law require scripture reading in any tax-supported school; the second that the law be preserved from any provisions of a sectarian nature.[32] These petitions were headed by almost all of the Protestant clergy in the city and its suburbs. The great mass of the signatures were those of artisans, mechanics, grocers, and labourers. As with the prohibition petitions, few great merchants, functionaries, or barristers supported evangelical schools.

It finally rested with the Executive Council to take the decision. While the government preferred a compulsory educational system of common schools maintained by general assessment, such a radical position was both financially and politically unfeasible. Instead, the government permitted private and charity schools to retain their annual grants and provided more resources to the parish schools in an effort to achieve voluntarily what it was unwilling to do through coercion. The real debate centred on the common schools. Some executive councillors favoured their secularization, but Tilley, speaking for the evangelicals, was prepared to destroy the government on the issue of Bible reading.[33] In the end the Schools Act of 1858 required every teacher to read a chapter of the King James Bible every day without comment, and to offer appropriate moral lessons to their students. In Roman Catholic districts the Douay Bible could be read. Despite the latter concessions, the effect was to model the public school system in an image acceptable to the province's evangelicals.

By 1860, then, the Smashers' alliance had permitted the evangelicals to experiment with prohibition and to begin to develop a public school system designed in accordance with their values. They had also participated in the broader Smashers program, transferred the initiation of money bills and the great offices of the crown to the executive council, created the Wesleyan Mount Allison University at Sackville, and destroyed both the Church of England establishment at King's College, Fredericton, and the political role of the bishop. Moreover, in keeping with their agenda for middle-class reform, they reduced the influence of the Legislative Council and introduced the spoils system to the political culture of the province, restricted the influence of the lieutenant-governor and of the Colonial Office, produced the largest publicly owned railway in British North America, subsidized a program of railway construction, provided a system of relatively high tariffs for the protection of provincial producers, promoted reciprocity with the United States, and suspended the Militia Act. Evangelical influence in public life continued to expand over the next decade. When the premier, Charles Fisher, was involved in corruption in 1861 and forced to resign in disgrace, he was succeeded by Tilley, who held the reins of power until shortly before Confederation.

Confederation in 1867 shattered the provincial Smashers alliance through which most evangelicals had participated in the public life of the province. Tilley and most of the provincial leadership chose to enter the federal arena, leaving evangelicals without an effective leader in the Assembly. The new provincial Assembly was divided between supporters and opponents of Confederation, and the government contained both Smashers and Rummies from the previous decade who supported Confederation. As well, the province lost most of its traditional revenues to the federal government in the new constitutional arrangement and became dependent on Ottawa for compensation for those losses.

Public education was again the central issue for most evangelicals in the late 1860s, a cause made more pressing by the loss of provincial revenues on the one hand, and by the perception of a growing Roman Catholic and Tractarian aggressiveness. In its acrimony and divisiveness, the campaign for New Brunswick public schools echoed the struggle for prohibition two decades earlier. In this case, however, the social implications were far wider and the instruments of power, notably the Executive Council and the office of lieutenant-governor, were more firmly in the hands of the evangelicals and their allies.

Lemuel Allen Wilmot led the movement for a single compulsory public school system. At Tilley's urging, Wilmot was named lieutenant-governor of New Brunswick. As early as the 1840s Wilmot had argued for a public school system supported by property tax. The champion of public education in the Legislative Assembly was George King, a young Methodist Smasher lawyer from Saint John, and a close friend of Tilley's. In 1870, at the age of thirty, King became premier and attorney-general, leading an unstable coalition of Liberals and Conservatives joined only by their common support of Confederation.[34]

The outcome of the general election of 1870 had been uncertain. King had prepared a Schools Bill for the sitting. At the meeting of the House, Wilmot read the speech from the throne in which the government committed itself to the bill's passage. On the third day of the sitting, realizing he could not survive a nonconfidence motion, King offered the government's resignation to Lieutenant-Governor Wilmot. In an effort to save the Schools Bill, Wilmot offered the premiership to one of the opposition leaders, George Hatheway. The new government was a coalition of Hatheway and King supporters in which King served as attorney-general. An anti-confederate, Hatheway was a committed public schools supporter, and thus King's public school policy had some chance of success.[35]

In April 1871 King reintroduced the Schools Bill to the House. It provided for a common compulsory school system supported by general assessment. On amendment it was declared that all schools under the act must be nonsectarian.[36] Religious instruction was required as set out in the 1858 Schools Act. The debate was long and sometimes bitter, uniting most Roman Catholics, some Anglicans, and those opposed to compulsory assessment against the largely evangelical majority. The act finally passed by a vote of 25 to 10, with two Roman Catholic Acadian members voting with the majority.[37] Passage of the act was followed by the abolition of all grants to Madras, Roman Catholic, Wesleyan, and Baptist schools in the province.[38] The new educational system provided for local trustees and for a central administration consisting of the Board of Education and its superintendent. The prominent Nova Scotia Baptist educator, Theodore Harding Rand, became the first superintendent. During the autumn the executive council prepared the regulations to the act, which the editor of the *Freeman*, underscoring its evangelical leanings, characterized as the work of Pope Wilmot and his Methodist cardinals.[39]

Hatheway died in 1871 and King reassumed the premiership just in time to meet the mounting assaults on the new Schools Act. New Brunswick Roman Catholics appealed to Ottawa to disallow the legislation on the grounds that the reading of the Douay Bible permitted by the pre-Confederation 1858 legislation constituted the creation of distinctive Roman Catholic schools. Their attempts to secure federal disallowance of the legislation were thwarted in part by the influence of Tilley and Maritime Protestant members of the federal Liberal-Conservative caucus.[40] In scenes redolent of the prohibition crises of 1851 and 1855, Roman Catholic leaders in the province defied the Assessment Acts and refused to pay school taxes; many ordinary Catholics refused to send their children to public schools. By late 1872, 731 school districts had complied with the law, and 571 had not. The federal government, while not disallowing the Schools and Assessment Acts, pressured the province to retreat by withholding increases in federal subsidies to the province, funding judicial appeals of the Roman Catholic minority, and removing Wilmot, rightly seen as a central figure in the debate, from the post of lieutenant-governor and replacing him with Tilley, now the federal customs minister, who was seen as a more conciliatory figure. But this did not achieve the anticipated end. Tilley might have been more conciliatory, but he was as much an evangelical and just as committed to the Schools Act as was Wilmot. Even the defeat of the federal Liberal-Conservative government and its replacement by the Liberal administration of Alexander Mackenzie in 1873 did not weaken the evangelical position. Tilley was replaced in the new federal cabinet by Isaac Burpee, a Saint John merchant and president of the New Brunswick Evangelical Alliance.

Unlike its predecessor in the 1855 prohibition crisis, the King government proceeded into the eye of the controversy. Having created the system, the government left the administration of the assessment laws in the hands of the local trustees, who used court orders to seize the property of recalcitrants. Federal opposition simply confirmed to the majority the rightness of their convictions. The debate reached its peak at the 1874 sitting of the Legislative Assembly when a motion to repeal the Schools Act was defeated on a vote of 24 to 12, and a motion protesting federal and imperial interference in the affairs of the province was carried by the same margin. On this note Tilley dissolved the House and King took the issue to the people.

The 1874 election was the most partisan ever fought in the province. King set the tone with the refrain, 'The ticket, the whole ticket, and nothing but the ticket.' The themes of 'no surrender' and 'no compromise' ran through what became known as the 'Protestant Election.' Most of the press and virtually the entire evangelical community supported King. His language was that of the evangelical dissenters of the previous generation. The enemy was not only the Roman autocracy, it was also the privileges accorded to state churches: 'If we once abandon the strong line of defense that is along the heights of equality ... the end will be the overthrow of our rights and independence of action.'[41] King's government won 36 of the 41 seats in the Assembly in support of the Schools Act. The five opposition members were Roman Catholics. While the government supporters continued to include a small number of Conservatives, 28 of 36 government supporters identified themselves as Liberals, including King.[42] The party had returned to its Smashers roots. The Schools Act was clearly saved and untouchable – so untouchable that when the government later made minor concessions to the bishops in an effort to restore civil order, they had to do so through regulations, and even those regulations were not published.[43]

By 1876 the political coalition in which evangelicals played a decisive role had secured uncontested control of the political institutions of the province. The 1871 Schools Act was the most significant piece of social legislation in nineteenth-century New Brunswick. Its place in the culture and public discourse of the province was so profound that it absolutely eclipsed the other elements in the agenda of the King government.[44]

Late in the decade the evangelicals managed to secure prohibition, the remaining element in their public agenda. Since the successive failures of prohibition in the 1850s, Smasher administrations had avoided another prohibitory act, preferring instead to limit access to alcoholic beverages by restricting vendors' licences to areas where consumption would be tolerated. In the 1870s, Reform clubs and the Woman's Christian Temperance Union strengthened the strong fraternal temperance movements. In 1878 Alexander Mackenzie's federal Liberal government passed the Canada Temperance Act, permitting any municipality to impose prohibition following a plebiscite. The first municipality in Canada to vote for prohibition under the act was the city of Fredericton. The results of these plebiscites clearly demarcated the areas of evangelical influence. While in Saint John City the prohibition referendum failed by two votes (1,076 to 1,074),[45] within the counties the prohibitionists carried every parish in which Baptists, Methodists, and Free Presbyterians constituted a majority of the population.

By the 1870s New Brunswick evangelicals, like their counterparts in the United States, had come to dominate the arena of public discourse. They shared control of the state with the utilitarian liberals, whose views on moral reform, equality of opportunity, and the centrality of the individual they found most congenial. Together they had shaped a broad liberal program, which between 1854 and 1880 facilitated significant constitutional, economic, and social change. Divided on such issues as disestablishment, their specific political goals as evangelicals had been limited to those few areas of broad consensus that were part of their tradition: the authority of Scripture and the need to redeem society from the obvious moral destruction caused by intemperance. Their Christian culture was reflected in the public order they sought to impose on the larger society through prohibition and public schools. As their influence over public policy expanded, they prevented the creation of purely secular schools, eliminated sectarian schools – some of them evangelical – that offered divergent paths and values, and established a common Christian public literacy centred in the rhetoric and precepts of the King James Bible.

Notes

1 José Casanova, *Public Religions in the Modern World* (Chicago: University of Chicago Press, 1994), 53, 137.
2 These characteristics are defined by David W. Bebbington in *Evangelicalism in Modern Britain: A History from the 1730s to the 1980s* (London: Unwin Hyman, 1989).
3 This interpretation modifies that of Robert Kelley, who argues that evangelicals within the British Empire were part of the cultural periphery and were aligned with the Liberals, who were the defenders of pluralism. See Robert Kelley, *Transatlantic Persuasion: The Liberal-Democratic Mind in the Age of Gladstone* (New York: Knopf, 1969), chaps. 9, 10.
4 The nine counties include Charlotte, St John, Albert, Westmorland, Kings, Queens, Sunbury, York, and Carleton. There were dramatically different rates of denominational growth between 1861 and 1881: Baptist numbers increased nearly 40 per cent, while the Church of England, thanks to a new emphasis on ritualism resulting from the Oxford or 'Tractarian' movement supported by Bishop John Medley, grew by just 5 per cent.
5 *City Gazette*, 26 March, 22 and 29 April, and 18 June 1828.
6 *Observer*, 20 January and 23 August 1835.
7 See T.W. Acheson, 'Hugh Johnston' and 'Duncan M'Coll,' *Dictionary of Canadian Biography*, vol. 6, 354–6, 429–32. George Marsden and Richard Carwardine have drawn the distinction between Arminian pietists and Calvinist activists in the United States in the same period. See George M. Marsden, *Fundamentalism and American Culture: The Shaping of Twentieth-Century Evangelicalism, 1870–1925* (New York: Oxford University Press, 1980), 85–93; and Richard Carwardine, 'Evangelicals, Politics, and the Coming of the American Civil War: A Transatlantic Perspective,' in *Evangelicalism: Comparative Studies of Popular Protestantism in North America, the British Isles and Beyond, 1700–1990*, ed. Mark A. Noll, David W. Bebbing-

ton, and George A. Rawlyk (New York: Oxford University Press, 1994), 199.

8 See T.W. Acheson, 'The 1840s: Decade of Tribulation,' in *The Atlantic Region to Confederation: A History*, ed. Phillip A. Buckner and John G. Reid (Toronto: University of Toronto Press, 1994), 307–33, esp. 307–14 and 326–7.

9 Scott W. See, *Riots in New Brunswick: Orange Nativism and Social Violence in the 1840s* (Toronto: University of Toronto Press, 1993), chaps. 5–8.

10 *The News*, 12 January, 28 March, 9 May 1846.

11 *Loyalist and Conservative*, 25 September and 8 October 1846.

12 *The News*, 5 October 1846.

13 *New Brunswick Courier*, 11 October 1846.

14 Useful studies of the movement are James K. Chapman, 'The Mid-Nineteenth-Century Temperance Movement in New Brunswick and Maine,' *Canadian Historical Review* 35 (March 1954): 43–60; and Jan Noel, *Canada Dry: Temperance Crusades before Confederation* (Toronto: University of Toronto Press, 1995), chaps. 1–3.

15 *New Brunswick Courier*, 3 May 1834.

16 *New Brunswick Courier*, 20 June 1832.

17 The Saint John Total Abstinence Society membership rolls 1832–1840, New Brunswick Museum Archives, Saint John.

18 *New Brunswick Courier*, 23 December 1843.

19 These generalizations are drawn from analysis of the 1850 officers of four city divisions.

20 *New Brunswick Courier*, 28 June and 4 August 1849, 8 June and 15 September 1850; *Journal of the Quarterly Session of the Grand Division, New Brunswick Sons of Temperance* (28 July 1852), 293.

21 *Temperance Telegraph*, 6 June 1850.

22 *Journal of the Quarterly Session of the Grand Division, New Brunswick Sons of Temperance* (28 July 1852), 293.

23 RLE/52, pe. 406, Provincial Archives of New Brunswick (PANB).

24 This discussion is informed by William Stewart MacNutt, *New Brunswick: A History, 1784–1867* (Toronto: Macmillan, 1963), 350–60.

25 Ibid., 361.

26 Ibid., 362–3.

27 Ibid., 362–3.

28 Gail Campbell, '"Smashers" and "Rummies": Voters and the Rise of Parties in Charlotte County, New Brunswick, 1846–1857,' *Historical Papers* (1986): 86–116, esp. tables on pp. 93 and 114.

29 *Dictionary of Canadian Biography*, vol. 10, 711.

30 T.W. Acheson, *Saint John: The Making of a Colonial Urban Community* (Toronto: University of Toronto Press, 1985), 258.

31 RLE/858, pe. 212, 122, PANB.

32 RLE/858, pe. 155, 156, PANB.

33 MacNutt, *New Brunswick*, 366.

34 T.W. Acheson, 'George Edwin King,' *Dictionary of Canadian Biography*, vol. 13, 544–8.

35 RS9, Minutes of the Executive Council, 22 February 1871, PANB.

36 W.M. Baker, *Timothy Warren Anglin, 1822–96: Irish Catholic Canadian* (Toronto: University of Toronto Press, 1977), 150.

37 Peter Toner, 'The New Brunswick Separate Schools Issue' (master's thesis, University of New Brunswick, 1967), 36.

38 James Hannay, *History of New Brunswick*, vol. 2 (Saint John: Bowes, 1909), 296–7.

39 Toner, 'The New Brunswick Separate Schools Issue,' 40.

40 Baker, *Timothy Warren Anglin*, 154–6; C.M. Wallace, 'Sir Leonard Tilley, A Political Biography' (Ph.D. diss., University of Alberta, 1972), 129–31.

41 New Brunswick, *Debates of the House of Assembly* (1874), 126–8.

42 See Hannay, *History of New Brunswick*, vol. 2, 329–30.

43 The compromise permitted local public boards to rent schools from the Catholic Church in which members of religious orders could wear their habits and religious instruction could be carried out after regular school hours. Members of religious orders were required to write teachers' licensing examinations with other students, but were permitted to take instruction in their own institutions. Offending passages would be removed from the prescribed English history text. The effect of these regulations was to severely limit the presence of Catholic schools outside of Saint John.

44 See *Dictionary of Canadian Biography*, vol. 13, 544, 547.

45 The votes are summarized in Ruth E. Spence, *Prohibition in Canada* (Toronto: Ontario Branch of the Dominion Alliance, 1919), 577.

3

Religion and Public Space in Protestant Toronto, 1880–1900

Brian Clarke

'The most conspicuous role of religion in nineteenth-century Ontario,' John Webster Grant has argued, 'was to provide ... a set of discrete landmarks' that performed a variety of functions, not the least of which was to claim 'space and time for the spiritual' in society and to enable 'people to give symbolic expression to their religious attitudes.' These landmarks were many and varied but, as Grant has noted, religious parades and processions were a prominent feature of the cultural landscape.[1] Funeral processions, Orangemen's parades, the marches of fraternal societies to hear a sermon, the militia unit's parading to a church service, all were familiar occurrences in Victorian Ontario and a recognized part of civic life. As this list suggests, the association that these parades had with religion took two forms. Some parades were directly associated with organized religion. A militia unit's church parade would fall into this category. This association can, however, take another form, that is in terms of the social identity that a parade expresses or affirms, as in the case of parading Orangemen. The reader needs to be reminded that although religion was a pervasive cultural presence in such parades and holidays, this did not turn these into 'religious' events narrowly understood.

Religious parades were very popular and highly public events. At the same time, they were also part and parcel of a much larger cycle of public holidays and other civic ceremonies, and so they bring us to the interstices of religion, popular culture, and public life. As a result, historians have looked at parades and other civic ceremonies in terms of their social function or as windows to a culture.[2] Both approaches can yield valuable insights but, as Grant's comments also suggest, civic celebrations such as parades and holidays were important in their own right. Not only did they have their own cultural conventions and forms of sociability, they also constituted a significant part of the public culture of the time. As Mary Ryan has pointed out, it was through such celebrations that people gained access to various urban spaces and transformed these spaces into what were generally recognized public spaces.[3] This chapter will look at how people, both men and women, used the cityscape and, in doing so, came to define and map public space. Various identities were at play here, not surprising given the Victorians' preoccupation with religion, class, ethnicity, and gender. Sometimes these identities overlapped with one another; sometimes they contended with one another. Whatever was the case, the result was a variegated and plural public.

By their very nature, parades and other civic ceremonies are local events, and no city in the province of Ontario had a more vibrant street life and a more vociferously Protestant civic ceremonial than did Toronto. While Montreal was the country's largest city, and Ottawa the nation's capital, Torontonians saw their city as their province's and their nation's preeminent British city. In 1880, Toronto had a population of some 86,000 people, and over the next two decades the city's population would more than double in size to include 208,000 people, making it by far the largest city in the province. Toronto was an expanding city, but it remained an overwhelmingly British and Protestant city. More than nine in ten of the city's residents traced their ancestry to the United Kingdom, and four-fifths of them identified themselves as Protestant.[4] This identification was far from passive. Protestantism was very much a part of the city's public ethos and civic identity, as the city's myriad of blue laws proudly proclaimed. Moreover, the city was home to many expressions of Protestant militancy such as sabbatarianism, prohibition, and the Orange Order.[5] For good reason the city claimed for itself the title as the Queen City of English-speaking Canada. Thanks to the prosperity brought by industrial and commercial expansion, Toronto could boast of a cityscape that bolstered that claim and, in addition, offered its inhabitants plenty of spaces where they could gather, parade, and celebrate.

Impressive buildings lined Toronto's downtown streets, such as Timothy Eaton's shopping emporium at Queen and Yonge, the Grand Opera House on Adelaide Street built in the distinguished style of the Second Empire, and the new city hall on Queen Street with its soaring clock tower.[6] Moreover, the city could boast some of the largest churches in the Dominion – in the case of the Methodists' Metropolitan

Church, the largest in the British Empire. There was no shortage of public and semipublic places where people could gather, and in addition to these enclosed spaces, Toronto's inhabitants also gathered outdoors in Queen's Park, at the Exhibition grounds, and in the city streets.

To be sure, these outdoor spaces had a variety of uses in day-to-day life. There were occasions, however, that set these spaces apart from daily life and transformed them. Parades and civic ceremonies were such occasions, and both were tied into the public calendar of holidays. The annual cycle of holidays started with New Year's Day, followed by Saint Patrick's Day, Good Friday, the Queen's Birthday, Dominion Day, the Twelfth of July, the Civic Holiday (typically held sometime during the first part of August), Labour Day (an official holiday beginning in 1894), Thanksgiving (officially 6 November but not consistently observed on that date, or any other day for that matter), and Christmas Day. In addition to these annual holidays, Sunday was a weekly holiday, one that in Toronto the Good was enforced with increasing rigour during this era.

The first thing, then, to be noted about this holiday calendar is its connection to religion. Indeed, only a few holidays were purely civic in origin. Second, the legal and social status of these holidays also varied. Some of these holidays were official public holidays with the full sanction and imprimatur of the Canadian Parliament. Other holidays were semiofficial, but nonetheless generally observed. The Twelfth of July was such a holiday in Toronto, and most businesses closed for that day. And finally, there were holidays observed by a minority of the city's inhabitants, as was the case with Saint Patrick's Day.

Holidays were celebrated in a variety of ways and in a variety of places. Irish Catholic celebrations on Saint Patrick's Day give an indication of one range of possibilities. Beginning in the early 1860s, Saint Patrick's Day had been marked by an annual parade organized by the city's Irish Catholic nationalist organizations. During the 1880s, however, indoor celebrations gradually replaced this mass public demonstration on the streets in importance. Parades were held only sporadically, and after 1895 Irish Catholics ceased to parade at all on that day. Mass, especially the High Mass at St Michael's Cathedral, became the main event of the day, and the evening would feature a sitdown dinner at a hotel, and perhaps an entertainment in one of the city's larger theatres.[7] Even though Irish Catholics no longer massed on the streets to celebrate Saint Patrick's Day, that day still retained its historic symbolic role of signifying the opening of the parade season.

After that date, fife and drum bands associated with the Orange Order and brass bands associated with the militia braved the city streets' muck (which was both plentiful and deep during the spring wet season that stretched from March through to May) to prepare for the big parades of the season.

The major civic holidays of summer – the Queen's Birthday, Dominion Day, and the August Civic Holiday – point to another range of observations as well as places where people could gather and celebrate, and like those places where people congregated on Saint Patrick's Day, these too spanned the spectrum between the semipublic and public. These summer holidays were usually celebrated in a low-key fashion and were not normally marked by parades or by officially sponsored civic rituals. Instead, citizens went to a variety of pleasure spots, some taking out-of-town excursions, others ranging closer to home, visiting the city parks or the many places of commercial amusements such as theatres, hotels, dance halls and the like. Taken together, these holidays indicate the range of places, both indoors and outdoors, where people could gather together to celebrate. Then as now, the Queen's Birthday or Victoria Day represented the beginning of summer, and it set the pattern for the annual summer holidays that followed. Newspapers celebrated the Queen's Birthday as a family holiday. Those who could afford it would stream out of the city to enjoy the cool breezes of the lake and visit Hamilton, Buffalo, Queenston Heights, and Niagara Falls. Others would take the railway and take a day trip to Orillia or Barrie.[8]

Most people would stay closer to home, but even here commercial entertainments also beckoned: Hanlan's Point, Lorne Park, and Victoria Park all featured music and dancing till the late hours. For those who could ill afford these pleasure spots, the streetcars did a booming business taking picnickers to Queen's Park and Riverside Park, where admission was free. In the evening, crowds made their way to the Horticultural Gardens, where they promenaded to the strains of music provided by a militia band.

Not everyone wished to celebrate the day touring, promenading, and picnicking. Sporting events were also popular. Certainly there was no shortage of choices: baseball, boat races, and lacrosse – by far the most popular sport of the time, especially when Montreal's Shamrocks visited the city – all vied for the sports fan's attention and wallet. And for those who after a winter's hiatus ached for the horse races, the Woodbine track opened on the Queen's Birthday, as always.

Fraternal organizations such as the Oddfellows and Foresters frequently timed their annual excursions and picnics to be held on one of the summer's civic holidays. By contrast, church picnics, socials, and excursions rarely coincided with these holidays and were typically held at other times. There was one exception to this pattern, and that was the city's Roman Catholic parishes. Parishes frequently hosted picnics on Dominion Day and the Civic Holiday, and on the Queen's Birthday a citywide picnic was always held for the benefit of the House of Providence.

The House of Providence picnic had many of the components of an official civic ceremony: speeches, games, military marching bands playing music, and, to cap off the day, a display of fireworks. At these festivities Toronto's Roman Catholics honoured Canada's principal institutions and so demonstrated their community's loyalty to their country and to the British Empire. At the same time they used these civic holidays to gather their community together and to support and celebrate their own institutions. In doing so, they signalled how important their religious distinctiveness was to them and how much it set them apart socially and culturally from their Protestant neighbours.[9] Through their holiday celebrations, as in many of their other practices and observances, Irish Catholics created a parallel social universe, to use Mark McGowan's evocative phrase.

The Roman Catholic celebrations on civic holidays were clearly community events complete with a full round of church-sponsored ceremonies. In the rest of the city, however, these holidays were not usually marked with the trappings associated with official civic ritual. There were no parades, no speeches by dignitaries, and, more frequently than one would suspect, no fireworks – no doubt much to the disappointment of many. Observers did note that on these holidays there were more flags flying than was usual, and occasionally the streetcars were decorated with small flags and evergreens. But on the whole, the city lacked a festive appearance. Nevertheless, Protestant Torontonians insisted that their activities and pastimes on these holidays were likewise national celebrations and expressions of patriotism.

At first glance it may seem that there is little patriotic about taking an excursion, attending a sporting event, going on a promenade, or spreading out a blanket on the grass and sitting down to have a picnic. Yet the symbolic value of these holidays as a time set apart seemed obvious to Torontonians, especially on the Queen's Birthday. On that day, they joined with their fellow citizens in communities across

Canada and with British subjects around the globe to observe a common holiday to demonstrate their loyalty to their monarch and those British institutions that bound them together.[10] In observing the holiday the way they did, Torontonians were in effect performing a set of rituals that they shared with others across the British Empire. Through these rituals people gained entry into what Benedict Anderson has termed 'imagined communities.' Such communities, Anderson explains, are imagined by its members who 'will never know most of their fellow members, meet them, or even hear of them, yet in the minds of each lives the image of their communion.'[11] In taking to the open spaces of the city, and observing the customs of the day, Torontonians created a sense of belonging to a wider community and so forged a relationship with those imagined others, who were presumably doing the same thing. Ritual was not only a way people entered into this community, it was also a means by which this broader community came into being and was sustained.

Newspaper coverage also yields clues as to the cultural significance of the day's pastimes. Newspaper editorials commenting on the Queen's Birthday recited largely the same themes: the ongoing growth of the empire, Canada's continuing prosperity, and finally what is most salient here, the Queen's moral character and family life, all of which editorialists held up for the readers' edification.[12] In these renditions, Queen Victoria was the very personification of British Protestant womanhood. As the embodiment of domestic virtue and Protestant piety, the Queen cast a 'holy light' upon her empire, just as she had done among her own family.[13] The news columns reporting how the holidays were spent, with but a few exceptions, noted with pride the good order that prevailed and the peaceful conduct of the city's inhabitants.[14] The connection between the themes celebrated in the daily papers' editorial columns and those lifted up in their news columns was usually not made explicit. It did not need to be.

Torontonians in the late Victorian era were very much aware of leisure's symbolic potential, and they appreciated its expressive value. 'The whole city,' an editorial writer in the Toronto *Mail* observed, 'seemed bent on enjoyment.'[15] Nor were these comments intended to be critical. A few years later another editorial writer from the same paper commented that 'Dominion day in Toronto was a holiday in the true sense of the term.' 'It was a quiet, restful day, and as a result the people will return to their duties refreshed and invigorated.'[16] Far from being seen as a wasteful extravagance, commercialized forms of leisure

came to be valued for their restorative properties and their respectability. Respectability had many connotations and was associated with a
wide range of identities, but however it was understood, it signalled
moral worth. And at the time in the eyes of many, moral worth was
inseparable from religion (though, as we shall see in the case of men,
religion could be appropriated in ways that the clergy far from
approved). Having good, clean fun was thus almost as Protestant as
the work ethic itself. Consumerism and consumption went hand in
hand with being God-fearing, hard-working, and loyal subjects of the
Queen.[17] On this issue, newspapers captured the prevailing popular
sentiment that on such occasions Torontonians spent their day in pursuits and pastimes that did credit to themselves, their country, their
sovereign, and their religion.

One of the chief ways many Torontonians – especially middle-class
Torontonians – thought they did credit to their sovereign was to emu-
late her by celebrating the day as a family holiday. In this regard, the
Queen's Birthday and Dominion Day were far from unique. During
the Victorian era, a variety of holidays became increasingly family centred, the most notable example being Christmas.[18] What distinguished
these summer holidays, however, was that holidaying on these days
was one of the many attempts to transform urban public places into
spaces for the enactment and display of heterosociality.[19] On these holidays, women were present in the city's public and semipublic spaces,
but their presence there was vested with a particular symbolic significance in which they represented those values associated with women's
domestic sphere. Public holidays, then, became occasions for domesticity to be publicly enacted and displayed. The way men and women
comported themselves and related to others signified their membership in a common moral community, a moral community which their
Queen epitomized. Because of this association holiday pastimes were
as much expressions of patriotism and Protestant respectability as they
were means for instilling patriotic sentiments as well as the morals and
virtues associated with religion. Not only was the choreography of the
holiday celebrations gendered, so too were the meanings that were
attached to the various pastimes and social activities that set the holiday apart from quotidian life and made it a day for the public demonstration of fealty to God, crown, empire, and country.

The Queen's Birthday and Dominion Day were usually celebrated in
a quiet way, often without the fanfare of civic-sponsored events and
celebrations. There were those, however, who believed that these civic

holidays did not do nearly enough to cultivate patriotism. They preferred a much more overtly didactic approach to celebrating the holiday, one that would inculcate appropriate sentiments through civic ritual. One such person was George Ross, who as minister of education was in a unique position to create a new set of school celebrations and exercises that would do exactly that. Schools, Ross remarked, 'are public institutions, maintained for the purpose of developing the highest type of citizenship.' What could be more effective to realize this purpose, he thought, than devoting the school day just before the Queen's Birthday (usually 23 May) to patriotic exercises, a day he decided to name Empire Day. Like many Ontarians of his day, Ross saw no conflict between Canadian patriotism and British imperialism.[20] 'The one,' he explained, 'is but the expansion of the other.'[21]

The first Empire Day, celebrated on 23 May 1899, was primarily a school-oriented occasion. The following year, the Toronto Board of Education introduced a crucial change in the program that would soon be emulated across the province. Following school exercises in the morning, the student cadets paraded from the armouries to the provincial Parliament Buildings in Queen's Park. The school cadets' parade and review immediately became a fixed feature and the high point of the day's celebrations. The parade transformed the day into a community event and, in the eyes of many, an event that set an appropriate tone for the civil holiday to follow.[22]

As we have seen, religion held an important place in the holiday calendar. What, then, was its connection to civic fêtes such as Empire Day? As it happens, many of the themes that orators lifted up on Empire Day were very similar to those central to the speeches offered on the Orange Order's day of celebration, Twelfth of July, the city's vociferous annual celebration of the British Empire and of the Protestant religion. Although the Twelfth of July was not a legal holiday, it was, as orators and reporters frequently remarked, a red letter day in the Toronto holiday calendar. With all the trappings associated with officially sponsored civic celebrations, the Twelfth easily outshone all the other summer public holidays. One measure of the Twelfth's importance was that the parade held by the Orange Order to celebrate the day was by far the largest of the year. With nearly five thousand men mustering, the line of march could stretch along as many as ten city blocks. Newspaper men with pocket watches in hand reported that the parade would take between thirty-five or forty minutes to pass by any given point. The Orangemen's parade was so large that it easily rivalled those parades that mustered for special celebrations, such as the Queen's Golden Jubilee held in 1887.

Size, however, was not the only thing that signalled the parade's importance. The route taken by the parade was also fraught with meaning. The usual staging area and point of departure was in Queen's Park, by the Parliament Buildings, which were then in the northern part of the city. Marching out of Queen's Park, the Orange parade would head east to Yonge Street, then proceed south on Yonge to Queen Street. Once downtown, the parade would wind its way through the business district, and after some three hours of parading would end up in the Exhibition grounds at the western end of the city. At other times, the parade would depart from City Hall, in the eastern part of the central business district, or another site close by. On such occasions, the parade would pass along both Queen and King and so circumambulate the downtown core. Whatever the exact route, the marchers filed past many of the city's principal commercial establishments and public buildings, and they did so quite deliberately. By marching past the city's premier buildings, many of which were decorated in orange and white bunting for the occasion, the members of the Orange Order affirmed their importance and displayed it for all to see.

Crowds filled the sidewalks along the parade route, and in the centre of town were so plentiful that male spectators spilled into the streets. Women, too, thronged on the sidewalks to cheer the parade on, even more gathered at windows high off the street, and when the marchers passed by, a sea of white handkerchiefs filled the cityscape. And when the parade ended, another three to five thousand people – spouses, girlfriends, and others – joined the marchers at the Exhibition grounds to indulge in refreshments, listen to speeches, and witness athletic games.

Parades can have numerous components, mark numerous kinds of occasions, convey a wide range meanings, and serve many different purposes. In this sense, parades are ceremonies that can be adapted and transformed to create new forms, what Eric Hobsbawm has called invented traditions – traditions that are actually innovations but gain acceptance as being traditional. Labour Day and Labour Day parades, first officially celebrated in 1894, were one such invented tradition. So too were the parades held on the Twelfth. Though malleable and adaptable, parades are characterized by order, and so through a series of generally recognized rituals and symbols can communicate the messages that the marchers wish to convey and are readily understood by those witnessing the parade.[23] Parades can do this because, as Peter Goheen has pointed out, not only do they have their own codes but the very act of parading changes the meaning and role of space. Marching on the streets requires stopping traffic, creating a distinction between participants and audience. It transforms the street from its daily use as a means of transit into a stage for performance and communication.[24]

In Mary Ryan's memorable words, parades followed a well-established 'gender choreography of celebration,' whose conventions and meanings were well known to marchers and onlookers alike.[25] Parades were typically male-only events. In a departure from the usual and exclusive custom of parading, women occupied a significant place in the Orange Order's annual parade. Some two hundred women from the True Blues, an Orange auxiliary organization that had separate branches for boys and women, usually rode in carriages at the head of the procession. In order to explain the significance of their presence in the parade one must first look at the values that the Orange Order wished to convey to the general public when marching, as well as the protocols that governed marches.

The presence of the women True Blues in the line of march was a recent innovation, and it coincided with a general change in the tone and tenor of the Orange Order's parade. Before the 1880s these parades were fairly raucous affairs, one index of which was the use of alcohol. Individual lodges would often pay a carter to haul a beer keg so that their members could quench their thirst at will while marching. The results of this custom were predictable, and not a few marchers finished the parade rather much the worse for wear, that is, if they managed to finish the parade at all. In this regard, the parade was of a piece with much male sociability of street and tavern, whose pastimes ran counter to middle-class ideals of sobriety, self-discipline, and domesticity.[26]

By the 1880s, however, the Orange Order banned alcohol from all its official functions. At the same time it transformed its post-parade celebrations from a homosocial pastime, when Orangemen visited their favourite tavern with their lodge mates, to a heterosocial event at the Exhibition grounds, where women were welcome to take part in the by now time-honoured pastimes of a civic holiday: picnicking, promenading, and the like. Women's presence was especially welcomed for its symbolic value, something that is most evident in the case of the women True Blues riding in their carriages. They occupied the most prestigious position in the parade, an honour usually accorded only to elected officials and other civic dignitaries. This honour, however, was intended to convey Orangemen's gallantry. Women were present in the great parade on the Twelfth, but their role was primarily an allegorical one that functioned as cyphers for conveying male concerns.[27] In their carriages, the women True Blues were a mute, but nonetheless highly symbolic, presence that testified to the Orange Order's commitment to the ideals of domesticity and respect for feminine virtue. On the Twelfth, the Orangemen displayed themselves as sober citizens, hard-working breadwinners, devoted husbands, and loving fathers. Like other civic ceremonies, parades offered a forum for the expression of a variety of social identities as well as a crucible for their formation.[28] And nowhere was this most evident than when the members of the Orange Order proclaimed themselves to be Her Majesty's most loyal, Protestant subjects.

Parades monopolize space and so make claims to privilege and are expressions of power.[29] On the Twelfth, the Orange Order claimed the privilege of representing the city's moral order to their fellow citizens, showing that theirs was indeed a Protestant and British city. As will be seen, this was repeatedly affirmed in the orations to mark the occasion, but it was also a message that the parade itself conveyed. Marching down the main streets of the city, the marchers wore regalia that marked them as the descendants of Ulster's great heroes who, in the seventeenth century, rose up to defend that colony's British institutions. Gender was central to Orangemen's identity as true Protestant Britons. Like their reputed forbears, they were men of pluck, ever ready to come to the defence of the realm and the religious principles upon which it was established. The Orangemen not only claimed to act on behalf of their community, they also claimed authority to act as arbiters of its values, a point that was often made in Twelfth of July speeches. And as we shall see, there was an unmistakably hard edge to that claim.

Once the parade made its way to the Exhibition grounds, members of the Orange Order and their friends were regaled with speeches by prominent public figures who were also ardent Orangemen. School inspector J.L. Hughes, and mayors William Howland and E.F. Clarke among others were regular favourites. The speeches delivered at the celebration of the Twelfth in 1897 were fairly typical. Wilfrid Laurier and the Liberals had taken power a year before, and the Laurier-Greenway agreement that would put the Manitoba School Controversy to rest was still some four months away. The event celebrated – William III's victory over James II at the Battle of Boyne in 1689 – set the tone for these speeches. As every right-thinking Protestant at the time knew, that battle clinched the victory of constitutional rule over despotism and secured for Protestantism the succession to the British throne. That victory, Howland reminded his listeners, represented the triumph of civil and religious liberty. Howland did not remind his listeners, but they would have known from speeches from previous years that both the British constitution and Protestantism were essential to preserve these freedoms – the first, because it ensured the rule of law; the second, because it, of all religions, was based upon freedom of conscience, or so it was believed. As loyal Britons and devoted Protestants, Howland affirmed, Orangemen 'love liberty in speech, freedom of conscience, right of action for every man and woman in the land.' 'We demand for ourselves,' he explained, 'no more than we are willing to grant to others.' What that meant in practice was spelled out with characteristic bluntness by John Hewitt, the deputy county master: 'as I have said before, and I must repeat it, that separate schools in this province must go.'[30]

E.F. Clarke could not have agreed more. 'This demonstration,' he affirmed, 'is not a menace against the minority, against their creed, or rights as British subjects.' This celebration, he continued was 'a declaration of our principles and fealty to that constitution which was won for us 200 years ago by gallant sires from those who would destroy our race and nation.' In dedicating themselves to defend this liberty as a matter of principle, Clarke continued, Orangemen 'stood for what a British subject ought to be.' 'But,' Clarke concluded with evident pride in his voice, 'Orangeism is a menace to certain classes in our Dominion ... against those classes that are not satisfied with fair play, those classes that are not satisfied with equal rights.'[31]

During times of religious controversy – in the aftermath of the Northwest Rebellion, the Jesuits' Estates Controversy, and the Manitoba Schools Question – the celebrations held to mark the Twelfth easily became demonstrations of political protest and fuelled the flames of anti-Catholic sentiment. But these celebrations also served another purpose. In honouring William III, members of the Orange Order exhibited their loyalty to the British monarchy, revelled in Canada's constitutional connection to Britain, and affirmed the fundamentally Protestant character of their nation. These were among the touchstones of English-speaking Canadians' patriotism. When Orange orators invoked these themes they appealed to beliefs that were deeply held by the vast majority of the city's inhabitants. E.F. Clarke boasted that 'it was quite evident from the vast crowds of ladies as well as gentlemen who lined the streets that the hearts of the people beat in unison with Orange and Protestant principles, and that Toronto is Protestant and Orange to the core.'[32] And that, as Clarke well knew, was no idle boast.

The parade held on the Twelfth was the city's most important parade of the season, but throughout the summer smaller parades occurred regularly. Marching bands, for example, took to the streets in the humid evenings of summer so often that their presence was rarely noted in the press. For the men who participated in these parades the attraction was obvious enough. Certainly part of the attraction was the opportunity to indulge in male camaraderie. In addition to allowing men to hang out with their friends, parades also offered an opportunity for grabbing attention. In parading through the streets they demonstrated their musical prowess, and showed off their fancy uniforms – always a hit with the opposite sex. In addition to the chance of being at the centre of attention, parades also offered an opportunity for marchers to affirm and to proclaim their identity, sometimes as workers (in the case of the bricklayers' Harmony Band), sometimes as Irish Catholics (in the case of the Irish Catholic Benevolent Union), and sometimes as Protestant youths (in the case of the Orange Young Britons).

Rivalry between the Orange and the Green sometimes resulted in violence, but such violence was comparatively restrained and had a ritual quality to it. Over the course of the 1880s this kind of religiously motivated violence became increasingly rare, and by the 1890s it had disappeared. One reason why this violence declined was a growing police force that would not turn a blind eye to such incidents as it formerly had. Here the police were responding to growing public pressure to suppress unruly behaviour in public places.[33] Fraternal organizations also reflected this sentiment. This was especially the case in organizations such as the Orange Young Britons that catered to young men, where the overall trend was to more structured, better-supervised pastimes. And in general, fraternal organizations encouraged their members to indulge in more subdued pastimes and forms of conviviality. Only temperance drinks – pink lemonade being the foremost – were allowed at formal Orange functions for example. Certainly, in the case of the Orange Young Britons, the diminished intake of alcohol contributed to the peace and quiet of Toronto's streets.[34] But there were other considerations at work. Religious riot was not merely suppressed, it was also replaced by other pastimes, and these pastimes reflected different sensibilities on the part of the young men who belonged to the Orange Young Britons and other similar organizations.

Other types of parades also expressed social identity but had an explicit association with organized religion. One such type of parade was the church parade. Militia units, fraternal organizations, and the like would gather at their meeting halls and then parade, often to music set by their marching band, to a church where they would attend a regular Sunday service or, more commonly, attend a special service of their own which featured a sermon commissioned for the occasion.[35] Church parades were a regular event. Militia units would parade to church several times a summer, fraternal lodges at least once, often on their official founding date. When one considers – to take just one example – that there were thirty to forty Orange lodges in Toronto during this period, the number of such church services mounts up considerably. One other form of parade connected with religion was the funeral procession.[36] Funerals for prominent people entailed long processions of several hundred mourners during which shops and businesses would be closed in respect for the deceased.[37] But the funeral processions of ordinary people who were members of a fraternal organization could be quite sizeable, ranging anywhere from fifty to two hundred or so processionists. And in some cases the funeral procession would be headed by a marching band.

In the eyes of Toronto's Protestant clergy there was one thing that was clearly wrong about church parades and funeral processions: their propensity to be held on Sundays. The case against funerals on the sabbath was that they required cemetery workers to work on that day of rest. With regard to church parades, the ministers had two objections. First, these parades disturbed the sabbath's peace and quiet. Second, since they were often held in the early afternoon, they attracted crowds of youngsters who instead should have been in Sunday school class. One can readily understand, however, why many people preferred to hold funerals on a Sunday if they possibly could. It was the one day people were sure of having off and so could pay their respects. Then, too, a large turnout was a sign of the esteem with which the deceased was held and was a source of consolation to the surviving family members. But on this issue the ministers largely prevailed, and both St James and Mount Pleasant cemeteries were generally closed for burials on Sundays.[38]

By contrast, when it came to the militia units' and fraternal organizations' parades to attend Protestant church services, the city's ministers broke ranks. Church parades continued to be held on Sunday afternoons, and it is worth pointing out that the practice continued only because ministers were all too willing to preach the requisite sermon. When it came to the dead, dispensing with a funeral would be unthinkable, and so in the end the clergy could dictate the terms upon which they would conduct funeral services. Such was not the case, however, with church parades. Militia units and fraternal organizations did after all have the option to cancel their parades to church. And they were a constituency that the clergy were determined to cultivate. In general, men had a much more ambivalent relationship to institutionalized Christianity than did women, and church parades were one way for the clergy to demonstrate that manliness and Protestantism were compatible.[39] Not surprisingly, in this instance the clergy chose the path of accommodation, and the city's militia and fraternal organizations continued their church parades much as they had before.

Parades and civic ceremonies were an important part of Toronto's social life. As we have seen, they conveyed a variety of religious meanings, of which concepts of gender and ethnicity were constituent elements. Moreover, they occupied different kinds of social locations, something that brings into question the usefulness of binary understandings of the public and the private. All of these considerations reinforce a point that feminist historians and political theorists have been making for several years: that instead of speaking of the public sphere we should be speaking of publics, in the plural.[40] At the same time that we can speak of multiple publics, then, it is also the case that the category 'public' is itself elastic. In late Victorian Toronto, this category included a fairly broad spectrum of rituals and ceremonies associated with religion that were highly valued by Torontonians as occasions for the expression of social identities as well as arenas for their formation. As a consequence, religion had an unmistakable, if at times diffuse, public presence in the city.

Notes

1 John Webster Grant, *A Profusion of Spires: Religion in Nineteenth-Century Ontario* (Toronto: University of Toronto Press, 1988), 235.
2 For two fairly representative approaches, see Elizabeth Hammerton and David Cannadine, 'Conflict and Consensus on a Ceremonial Occasion: The

Diamond Jubilee in Cambridge in 1897,' *Historical Journal* 24 (1981): 111–46; and Tori Smith, '"Almost Pathetic ... but Also Very Glorious": The Consumer Spectacle of the Diamond Jubilee,' *Histoire sociale/Social History* 29 (1996): 333–56. See also Keith Walden's comments in *Becoming Modern in Toronto: The Industrial Exhibition and the Shaping of a Late Victorian Culture* (Toronto: University of Toronto Press, 1997), xii–xiii, xvi, and 25–6; and those of Mary Ryan, 'The American Parade: Representations of the Nineteenth-Century Social Order,' in *The New Cultural History*, ed. Lynn Hunt (Berkeley: University of California Press, 1989), 132–3.

3 Mary P. Ryan, *Women in Public: Between Banners and Ballots, 1825–1880* (Baltimore: Johns Hopkins University Press, 1990), 3–4, 7, 55, and 59; idem, *Civic Wars: Democracy and Public Life in the American City during the Nineteenth Century* (Berkeley: University of California Press, 1997), 15, 31, 37, 60, and 74. On this issue see also Walden, *Becoming Modern*, 20–1, 24–5, 171, 188, and 299–304.

4 J.M.S. Careless, *Toronto to 1918: An Illustrated History* (Toronto: James Lorimer, 1984), 202–3.

5 Christopher Armstrong and H.V. Nelles, *The Revenge of the Methodist Bicycle Company: Sunday Street Cars and Municipal Reform in Toronto, 1888–1897* (Toronto: Peter Martin, 1977), 6.

6 Careless, *Toronto*, 133 and 135–6.

7 Mark G. McGowan, *The Waning of the Green: Catholics, the Irish, and Identity in Toronto, 1887–1922* (Montreal and Kingston: McGill-Queen's University Press, 1999), 95; *Mail and Empire*, 18 March 1895.

8 This and following paragraphs draw on sources from the *Telegram*, 25 May 1881, 25 May 1882, 25 May 1883, 23 and 26 May 1884, 26 May 1885, 25 May 1888; and the *Mail and Empire*, 25 May 1895, 25 May 1898, 25 May 1899, and 25 May 1901.

9 *Mail and Empire*, 25 May 1899, 25 May 1900.

10 *Mail*, 24 May 1895.

11 Benedict Anderson, *Imagined Communities: Reflections on the Origin and Spread of Nationalism* (London: Verso, 1983), 15.

12 *Telegram*, 25 May 1880; *Mail*, 25 May 1891, 24 May 1895, 24 May 1897, 24 May 1898, and 24 May 1899.

13 *Mail*, 1 July 1887; and *Globe*, 1 July 1887.

14 *Telegram*, 25 May 1881, 25 May 1883, and 25 May 1888.

15 *Mail*, 2 July 1892.

16 *Mail and Empire*, 3 July 1899.

17 I owe this point to Walden, *Becoming Modern*, 24.

18 Leigh Eric Schmidt's *Consumer Rites: The Buying and Selling of American*

Holidays (Princeton: Princeton University Press, 1995) plots this process for the United States. See also, Ryan, *Women in Public*, 37–40 and 50–1.

19 David Scobey, 'Anatomy of the Promenade: The Politics of Bourgeois Sociability in Nineteenth-Century New York,' *Social History* 17 (1992): 204 and 214; Ryan, *Women in Public*, 79.

20 On this issue see Carl Berger, *The Sense of Power: Studies in the Ideas of Canadian Imperialism, 1867–1914* (Toronto: University of Toronto Press, 1970).

21 Robert M. Stamp, 'Empire Day in the Schools of Ontario: The Training of Young Imperialists,' *Journal of Canadian Studies* 8 (1973): 34.

22 Stamp, 'Empire Day,' 34–7; *Mail and Empire*, 24 May 1900.

23 Ryan, 'The American Parade,' 133–4 and 138–9.

24 Peter G. Goheen, 'Symbols in the Streets: Parades in Victorian Urban Canada,' *Urban History Review* 18 (1990), 237 and 239; idem, 'Parading: A Lively Tradition in Early Victorian Toronto,' in *Ideology and Landscape in Historical Perspective: Essays on the Meanings of Some Places in the Past*, ed. Alan R.H. Baker and Gideon Biger (Cambridge: Cambridge University Press, 1992), 332, 338, and 348; idem, 'Ritual of the Streets in Mid-19th-Century Toronto,' *Environment and Planning D: Society and Space* 11 (1993), 128–9; Craig Heron and Steve Penfold, 'The Craftsmen's Spectacle: Labour Day Parades in Canada, the Early Years,' *Histoire sociale/Social History* 29 (1996): 361 and 363–4; and Eric Hobsbawm, 'Introduction: Inventing Traditions,' 1–3, and 'Mass Producing Traditions: Europe, 1870–1914,' 269–71, 286–7, 303–7, in *The Invention of Tradition*, ed. Eric Hobsbawm and Terence Ranger (Cambridge: Cambridge University Press, 1983).

25 Ryan, *Women in Public*, 30.

26 Walden, *Becoming Modern*, 249–50; Lynne Marks, *Revivals and Roller Rinks: Religion, Leisure, and Identity in Late-Nineteenth-Century Small-Town Ontario* (Toronto: University of Toronto Press, 1996), 85–6, 88–90, and 120–1.

27 E.A. Heaman, *The Inglorious Arts of Peace: Exhibitions in Canadian Society during the Nineteenth Century* (Toronto: University of Toronto Press, 1999), 283; and Ryan, *Women in Public*, 35 and 53–4.

28 Ryan, 'The American Parade,' 153.

29 Goheen, 'Parading: A Lively Tradition,' 342.

30 *Mail*, 13 July 1897; *Orange Sentinel*, 15 July 1897.

31 *Orange Sentinel*, 15 July 1897.

32 Ibid.

33 Nicholas Rogers, 'Serving Toronto the Good: The Development of the City Police Force 1832–1884,' in *Forging a Consensus: Historical Essays on Toronto*, ed. Victor L. Russell (Toronto: University of Toronto Press, 1984), 133.

34 Gregory S. Kealey, 'The Orange Order in Toronto: Religious Riot and the

Working Class,' in *Essays in Canadian Working Class History*, ed. Gregory S. Kealey and Peter Warrian (Toronto: McClelland and Stewart, 1976), 26–31; and idem, *Toronto Workers Respond to Industrial Capitalism 1867–1892* (Toronto: University of Toronto Press, 1980), 115–23.

35 *Telegram*, 6 November 1880; 2 May, 30 May, and 15 August 1881; 29 April and 6 November 1882; 5 July 1884; 13 July and 10 October 1885; 22 May and 10 July 1886; 23 April, 25 April, 25 June, 29 October, and 31 October 1887; 23 April, 21 May, 29 October, 10 November, and 17 November 1888; 6 April, 29 April, 11 May, 15 May, and 24 August 1889.

36 *Telegram*, 5 July 1880, 29 July 1882, 5 November 1883, 2 June 1884, 3 October 1884, 19 August 1885, 6 November 1888, and 21 September 1889.

37 Grant, *A Profusion of Spires*, 235.

38 *Telegram*, 17 May, 22 May, and 1 June 1886; 3 June and 28 March 1887.

39 On men and religious involvement, see Marks, *Revivals and Roller Rinks*, esp. chap. 2.

40 Nancy Fraser, 'Rethinking the Public Sphere: A Contribution to the Critique of Actually Existing Democracy,' in *Habermas and the Public Sphere*, ed. Craig Calhoun (Cambridge: MIT Press, 1997), 123–5; Mary P. Ryan, 'Gender and Public Access: Women's Politics in Nineteenth-Century America,' in ibid., 264 and 272–3.

4

Elaborating a Public Culture: The Catholic Church in Nineteenth-Century Quebec

Roberto Perin

At the end of the Second World War French-speaking Quebeckers entered a new phase of their history. For a century, Catholicism as a cultural force and the church as a social institution had occupied a central place in their reality. Now this preeminence was being challenged on all sides. The first salvo came in 1948, when together with other artists Paul-Émile Borduas published the highly provocative manifesto, *Refus global* (Total Rejection). Soon mainstream analysts such as the editorial writer André Laurendeau and the youthful contributors to the magazine *Cité libre* took up Borduas' call, although in more muted tones. Even members of the clergy, Archbishop Joseph Charbonneau of Montreal being the most prominent, were questioning the traditional role of both the church and religion in society. In this period of social and intellectual change, amateur and professional historians began the process of reinterpreting the past, proposing a generally negative assessment of Catholicism. In doing so, they anticipated (and their followers later reflected) the values of the Quiet Revolution – secularism, pluralism, and transparency in public affairs.

In the mid-fifties, the liberal thinker Pierre Elliott Trudeau and the nationalist historian Michel Brunet offered a scathing critique of what they regarded as the dominant thought of French Canada, which, according to them, had been formulated and propagated by the clergy. Although differing with each other on the causes of this dominance, they agreed that it had contributed to the intellectual, social, and even political backwardness of their compatriots.[1] Some years later, historians of various ideological persuasions went further, arguing that the church, a fierce opponent of liberalism and inordinately attached to the ideas of the ancien régime, sought to set up a theocracy in Quebec.[2]

Control was apparently exercised either directly from the pulpit, the confessional, or clerically run social institutions – as when priests told their flock how to vote – or indirectly through elaborately stage-managed spectacles drawing French Canadians closer to the reactionary causes of the papacy under Pius IX.[3] To the charge of perpetuating intellectual and political backwardness was added that of contributing to either the economic lag of Quebec or the exploitation of French Canadians.[4] While these criticisms did not go unchallenged,[5] a wide consensus still exists among liberal, nationalist, and Marxian historians, who hold the church responsible for the deficiencies of French Canadians as a North American people.

More recently, such views have been convincingly disputed in the collectively written two-volume history of Quebec, which marked a historiographical milestone.[6] Among other things, this work clearly established that the church was neither omnipresent nor omnipotent. Its authors emphasized the integration of Quebec into the North American capitalist market and the dominance of its secular élites in the economic, social, and political spheres. Subsequent studies also correctly challenged the notion advanced by Trudeau and Brunet concerning the hegemony of clerically inspired nationalism. Instead Quebec was represented as having a variegated ideological landscape where a liberalism of moderate hue was well-rooted, if not dominant in the nineteenth and twentieth centuries, through its hold on Quebec's social élites and their supporters.[7] Such studies have certainly sharpened our perception of Quebec's past, but what still remains to be clarified is the place occupied by the church and religion in the century following the Union of the Canadas in 1840, Catholicism's period of grandeur. An overview of this question is therefore in order.[8]

Nor has English-Canadian writing provided much insight into the question. In the secularizing 1960s, when the issue of the constitution and language seemed almost to dominate public discourse, the story of la survivance was cast in constitutional and linguistic rather than religious terms.[9] At the same time, religion was being abandoned as an area of study by most professional historians, who increasingly identified it with a sectarian and bigoted past. Forsaking ancestral totems bestowed an aura of objectivity on those who would later become privileged commentators in the national unity debate. While acknowledging the church as the agent of survivance, they identified the object of its solicitude as a linguistic community that received constitutional protection through provincial autonomy.

The primacy of language in defining identity found convenient confirmation in the slogan 'La langue gardienne de la foi.' This maxim, however, did not so much describe the French Canadians of Quebec as their compatriots living in other parts of North America in the late nineteenth century, who were fighting against the efforts of English-speaking coreligionists to impose the language of the majority upon them. Using the Irish as prime evidence, advocates of the French-Canadian diaspora argued that a common language with the Protestant majority actually caused defections from the ancestral faith. In Quebec, however, the issue of cultural survival had been faced some fifty years earlier by a majority that exercised complete control over its church. The difference between these two situations faced by French Canadians inside and outside Quebec has not been stressed enough in the literature. Nor have commentators clearly explained how autonomy, which relates to the scope of provincial power, actually ensured la survivance in Quebec, one of the least interventionist states on the continent. It is necessary for us to look beyond legislative and constitutional considerations, seeing language in its proper social context as a lived reality.

After all, a distinct language and legal system, as well as constitutional autonomy, did not prevent the loss of Louisiana's cultural character. Demographic and sociological factors intervened to turn the tide in this other French outpost in North America. Although facing similar challenges, Quebec was more successful than Louisiana because of its ability to forge a new identity based on more than just language and to give that identity a public character in a period of rapid social and cultural change.

The Church and a French-Canadian Public Space

The Union years witnessed the dramatic takeoff of the church as an institution and religion as a phenomenon of popular culture. Although intimately related, these developments are considered separately here. The first can best be understood within the political context of the period. The failure of the Insurrections of 1837–8 had underlined the futility of patriot aspirations to a lay, sovereign state under Canadian control. Not only did Britain reject such ambitions outright, but in order to reinforce its own interests on the continent, it transformed the majority into a minority within an expanded colony, thus depriving Canadians of what they regarded as their state. The Union of the Canadas also consolidated the economic, social, and political power of Montreal's British élite, previously the target of patriot obstructionism. This class was now free to become a truly metropolitan bourgeoisie whose economic power would span an entire continent. It was under its aegis that Quebec would become industrialized and urbanized. The Union therefore perpetuated the political and social inferiority of French Canadians, as they now called themselves and were called by others.

Confederation did not alter this basic reality. Despite French-Canadian perceptions of the event as more of a separation than the birth of a new nation, the Quebec government's ability to act on behalf of the collective well-being of French Canadians was severely limited by two factors: the federal government's preeminence over the provinces and the formal and informal guarantees wrested by the Anglo-Protestant minority of Quebec.[10] As long as Montreal continued to be the seat of the English-Canadian bourgeoisie's power, French Canadians would be effectively deprived of a state apparatus. In this regard, it is telling that until the Quiet Revolution, the position of provincial treasurer (minister of finance) was occupied almost entirely by English speakers. Anti-statism may therefore have been less an infantile aberration, as Brunet suggested, than a strategy to recover a public space lost with the dissolution of the Lower-Canadian assembly, a space that would be free from the now pervasive influence of the English-speaking élite and their French-Canadian allies in politics, business, and the press.

By taking away the instrument of their self-promotion as a people, Britain anticipated the Canadians' assimilation. Durham's report suggested that this would occur naturally. Canadians were destined to come into closer contact with their British superiors, and without an assembly to encourage vain hopes of nationality, their 'character and institutions' could be assimilated with those of the empire. Louisiana was given as an example of how this could be achieved without unseemly coercion.[11] Already the principal cities of Lower Canada had British majorities, and the skill and enterprise of British capitalists were attracting Canadian labourers in ever-larger numbers. Ethnic barriers could be further broken down and the intermingling of peoples fostered by the creation of nondenominational schools where English would be the language of instruction. This was clearly the intent of the first education bill of the legislature of the United Canadas.

The goal of assimilation, however, miscarried largely because the Quebec church, a body entirely under French-Canadian control, succeeded in creating an alternate public space in those crucial years. The church's efforts were concentrated in the cities, especially Montreal, where Durham correctly believed the future of British dominance lay. In the early 1840s the Canadian metropolis had about 45,000 inhabitants, roughly half of whom were Catholic. There was only one parish to care for them, and the provision of educational, health, and welfare services was barely adequate in the context of a rapidly industrializing city.[12] Ignace Bourget, bishop of Montreal from 1840 to 1876, wasted no time organizing an institutional network that would give French Canadians cohesion and act as a powerful obstacle to their assimilation.

In order for this network to function, however, a large infusion of religious personnel was needed. New orders were founded and others were brought mostly from France within a short time. The results of this recruitment drive were truly astonishing. From 1830 to 1880, the ratio of priests to faithful rose from 1/1800 to 1/500. The overall number of women and men in religion in the second half the century increased tenfold, from 900 to 8600. Isolating the female component in these figures makes clear that 77 per cent of the group were women.[13] As Marta Danylewycz reminded us, religious life offered them the opportunity to escape the narrow confines of their gender and pursue careers in Quebec, North America, or overseas normally reserved for men. Quebec would eventually have the distinction in the Catholic world of possessing the highest proportion of women in religion relative to its female population.[14]

During his episcopate, Bourget fought hard and long to break the monopoly of parish life in Montreal which the Séminaire de Saint-Sulpice had held since French colonial times, making it the uncontested religious authority in the area. After the Conquest, the Séminaire developed an almost obsessive fear of offending the British and therefore encouraged the practice of a discreet form of Catholicism. By 1865, however, the bishop had broken Sulpician obstruction to the division of their parish, and this would have a direct impact on the expression of popular piety in the city. At the end of the century the Catholic population of Montreal, which stood at 160,000, had twenty-four parishes to serve them. These played a crucial role in fostering the integration of French-Canadian settlers from the countryside and providing them with a structure for dealing with the challenges of industrialization and urbanization.[15] The parish stood at the centre of the French-Canadian institutional network. The end of Sulpician hegemony also meant that religious communities could create more schools, convents, colleges, hospitals, chronic-care and welfare facilities of all kinds. In the process these orders helped institutionalize a culture that until then had a weak institutional expression. Montreal set a pattern that would be followed by women and men in religion in other Quebec cities.

Later, the church would encourage the creation of indigenous economic institutions, such as cooperatives, as well as trade and credit unions, that would play such a crucial role in French Canadians' economic strategy during the Quiet Revolution. In the 1960s, for example, the prominence of the Confederation of National Trade Unions, a secular outgrowth of the syndicats catholiques, ensured that, in marked contrast with the past, the Quebec union movement as a whole would be sensitive to nationalist aspirations. In the same period, the Mouvement Desjardins, a federation of French-Canadian credit unions, became an active participant in the program of French-Canadian economic emancipation.

Throughout this period ultramontanism was used to advance the church's claim of autonomy from the provincial state. Instead of reading this discourse literally as a bid for theocratic control, historians should see it as an argument in favour of a French-Canadian public space free from the influence of political parties dominated, as we have seen, by outside elements.[16] Beginning in 1840 the church came to dominate health care, welfare, and education from primary school to university – areas that would later be given to the provinces under the British North America (BNA) Act. Provincial autonomy, therefore, sanctioned a preexisting arrangement in which the church largely delimited a French-Canadian public space. The Quebec government would later exercise its autonomy indirectly and by proxy, relegating public powers to a private institution for the benefit of the majority of its population. This made Quebec clearly distinct not only in Canada, but in the rest of North America.

Religion as Public Culture

After the Conquest, popular culture had become increasingly politicized as a result of the ideological ferment generated by the American and French Revolutions, as well as the extraordinarily broad franchise granted by the Constitutional Act of 1791, which made a voter out of every censitaire – that is, every habitant holding land under the seigneurial system. This process was intensified by successive crises that shook Lower Canada, pitting the legislature against the colonial executive in the first, third, and fourth decades of the nineteenth century. Allan Greer has masterfully described the elements of a popular culture – charivaris, maypole celebrations, popular assemblies, and the election of military and judicial officials – which, although rooted in the peasant past, now took on an unmistakable political coloration.[17] Historians have depicted Canadians of this period as being far from devout, even if, on the whole, they fulfilled their religious duties.[18] In the climate of growing political confrontation, the church was popularly regarded as the handmaiden of the British. At the same time, it was fashionable for patriote leaders to describe themselves as fervent advocates of secular liberalism in politics and deists in religion. Politics, not religion, was the badge of identity.

During the Union years, the opposite became true. The defeat of the Insurrections initially ushered in an atmosphere of spiritual and emotional despondency. But soon these dark clouds dissipated under the pressure of a massive religious revival initiated by the indefatigable Charles de Forbin-Janson, bishop of Nancy in France. An eloquent and dramatic speaker, the prelate was the principal speaker at retreats all over North America. He spent fourteen months in Quebec and Acadia, where he drew people in the tens of thousands anxious to heed his fire-and-brimstone message of repentance and salvation.

Conversion was not simply a private matter, but a social event involving masses of people. The thirst for religious renewal was so great that the local clergy often could not keep pace with it. The church's resources were severely strained as the faithful flocked to the sacraments in numbers never before seen. Crosses were erected in the countryside as a tangible sign of the public commitment to spiritual rebirth. The largest of these, measuring 100 feet, was placed atop Mont Saint-Hilaire on the south shore of Montreal. Described by Montreal's Catholic newspaper *Mélanges religieux* as 'a gigantic flag protecting Catholic Canada,' it was inaugurated in an imposing six-hour ceremony presided over by four bishops and attended by 15,000 people.

Forbin-Janson also fostered the founding of temperance societies in a population that had plumbed the depths of alcoholism in the 1830s. After his departure, clerical orators such as the rivetting Charles Chiniquy kept up this fervour by preaching temperance crusades all over the province.[19] Family heads were given a black cross as a tangible sign of their solemn public pledge to drink in moderation. It is estimated that a total of 400,000 people made such a commitment. The work of religious renewal was later sustained by male orders newly established in Quebec, especially the Oblates, Redemptorists, and Franciscans, who conducted periodic missions in parishes throughout French Canada. No one can doubt that the revival of the 1840s was a mass movement.

The results of these efforts can be gauged by levels of religious practice. In the Montreal area, the proportion of those performing their Easter duty rose from 60 to 95 per cent between the years 1840 and 1880.[20] Indeed, those who failed to observe this precept – the minimum required to be considered a Catholic – were virtual outcasts. The expression 'community of faith' therefore had real meaning, even in the cities. On its own, however, doing one's Easter duty is an insufficient indicator of religiosity and must be combined with evidence suggesting intensity of practice.

French-Canadian religiosity in the period after the Union was rooted in ultramontane piety. Fervid and extroverted both in expression and focus, such piety was especially popular among women, a fact that would later be derided by the postwar generation of intellectuals. Tridentine devotions, involving frequent public recitation of the rosary and relating to Christ's passion, his presence in the blessed sacrament, or Mary's travails, were rediscovered and ardently espoused. Such practices were reinforced by widely read, if somewhat saccharine, devotional literature, as well as by vast quantities of relics of presumed Christian martyrs unearthed during recent digs in Roman catacombs and transformed into instant objects of veneration. Pierre Savard documented the spread of the cult to St Philomena as a result of this archeological work. Devotional societies such as confraternities suddenly flourished after floundering for more than a century. Pilgrimage sites dating back to New France were revitalized and new ones inaugurated, attracting throngs of people in search of extraordinary favours. Special events such as novenas and retreats involving the whole parish or select groups in a closed setting became common. But what set Quebec apart from English-speaking North America was not ultramontane piety per se. Others in fact have documented how widespread it was across the continent. It is rather its public character.

The chief architect of this transformation was the irrepressible Bishop Bourget. His model was Rome, which he described as 'the most perfect image of heavenly Jerusalem that we can possess here below,'[21] and more specifically the Rome of the Counter-Reformation. In the late sixteenth and early seventeenth centuries, the Catholic Church attempted to make religion more accessible to the common people in order to check the attraction and rapid expansion of Protestantism in Europe.

Art both expressed this ambition and played a key role in the process. In contrast to the works of the Renaissance, which tended to be rational, erudite, idealist, and thus remote, the production of the Counter-Reformation was immanent both in theme and technique. The popular appeal of this art came in part from its theatricality, embodied in some of Rome's public squares that resemble stage sets (Piazzas Navona, San Pietro, and del Popolo, all by Gian Lorenzo Bernini); in sculptures such as Bernini's *Ecstasy of St Theresa*, which is actually set in an imaginary theatrical space with marble spectators in their box seats absorbed in the saint's mystical rapture; and in paintings depicting life's dramatic moments, such as Caravaggio's *The Calling of St Matthew* and his *Conversion of St Paul*. The extensive use of putti (angels in the form of babies) who, like the marble spectators just mentioned, seduce the viewer into engaging with the work of art, as well as techniques such as trompe l'oeil, delighted the dilettante then as now. Caravaggio, for his part, eschewed Bernini's use of idealized figures, consciously depicting major personages of Christianity as ordinary people performing everyday tasks. This sense of realism, immediacy, and intimacy heightened the broad appeal of his painting. Was Counter-Reformation art a refined form of manipulation or a means of communicating complex notions in a straightforward and accessible way – the word made flesh? I believe that the idea of social control inherent in the term 'manipulation' cannot account for the public's response, the awe and delight evoked by its warmth, drama, and accessibility.

Like the figure in the painting that invites the viewer to enter the imagined space, Bourget made Rome immanent for French Canadians. In a pastoral letter following the first of seven trips to the eternal city, the bishop associated his diocesans with his visit: 'You were there when we attended the magnificent ceremonies that succeed one another without interruption in this happy city, and when we visited these sacred monuments which by their number seem to make of this great city a single magnificent temple.' He established a link for his diocesans not only to the stones, but to the men of Rome. Bourget depicted the pope not as a remote ruler, much less the reactionary despot of rouge lore, but a wise and kindly father, a Christ-like figure who bore betrayal and suffering with patient forbearance and thus shared the human condition: 'The tears that often fall from his eyes indicate well enough the tender emotions of his naturally sensitive soul.' Characterizing as 'tender and paternal' the relationship between the pope and his bishops, Bourget then went on to establish a direct and personal bond between the faithful and their spiritual head: 'You are the object of the solicitude of the first of these pastors, who in fact could not forget any of his sheep, no matter where in the world it finds itself.'[22] Rejecting Gallican practices that still characterized aspects of local worship, Bourget ensured a total harmony between the liturgical calendar and ceremonies of Rome and Montreal. The two churches would beat with one heartbeat. The non-rouge press of the period celebrated the lavishness, sensuality, and theatricality of the new liturgy, which contrasted markedly with the starker worship favoured by the predominantly Irish hierarchy of English-speaking North America.

The bishop of Montreal felt that by emphasizing the intensely sensual nature of ritual, religion could be made immediate for the laity. Fully a year after the event, he vividly evoked for them a thirteen-hour ceremony that he had presided over in France:

> The hymns that were so touching, the indescribable sighs that I heard there, still resound in my ears. The pleasant odour of this incense of prayer that rose heavenward from that sacred precinct still delights my sense of smell; that sweet fragrance by ascending toward heaven undoubtedly extended to you because of the union that so intensely bound us together during my trip.[23]

Religious ritual, however, could not be confined only to such 'sacred precincts.' It had to be a part of the daily life of both individuals and society. Contrary to predominant nineteenth-century Protestant notions of worship as an indoor or at least spatially contained phenomenon, Bourget stressed the ultramontane view that it should spill out into outdoor public spaces, including city streets. His position was in sharp contrast to that of the Séminaire de Saint-Sulpice. Fearful of offending the English-language majority of Montreal, the Sulpicians discouraged public displays of religion.

In the early years of his episcopate, Bishop Bourget insisted on holding the Corpus Christi procession outdoors 'with all the possible pomp [so as] better to rouse the faithful with this outward splendour.'[24] The priest and his attendants would process outdoors in the rich vestments reserved for worship. The instruments of ritual – candles, incense, monstrance, canopy – would be taken into the streets for everyone to see. Organized by age, gender, and devotional society, participants in the procession wearing costumes or insignia would follow leaders carrying banners aloft. All would proclaim their faith by reciting prayers aloud and singing hymns. Catholic spectators, for their part, were expected publicly to exhibit their reverence for the sacrament by kneeling and crossing themselves as it passed by them. Such public demonstrations of religion in Montreal were a living manifestation of the theatricality that had found expression in the architecture of Counter-Reformation Rome.

Bourget's efforts to romanize the local church included his imposition of the soutane and Roman hat, new forms of clerical garb prescribed by Pius IX following the abortive Roman Revolution of 1848 to highlight the clergy's separation from the world. In religious education at both the primary and advanced levels, the bishop fought tenaciously – sometimes against his fellow bishops – for the adoption of catechisms, textbooks, and authors favoured by Rome. He also promoted an ultramontane press whose task it was to comment on the events of the day, in light not of currently fashionable ideas, but of eternal truths emanating from the eternal city.

Nothing better illustrates the bishop's passion for things Roman than his plan for the cathedral that was to replace the old one destroyed in the great fire of 1852. Against the advice of his architect, Victor Bourgeau, who claimed that it was unfeasible, Bourget wanted to reproduce St Peter's basilica on a reduced scale. If, as Brian Clarke so clearly illustrates, Toronto was the Belfast of North America, Montreal would be its Rome. But just as important as the symbolism of the building's style was its location, a dimension that sheds light on the significance of the movement in favour of romanization. Against the prominent Catholic citizenry, who favoured the former site in the heart of the French-speaking quarter, Bourget chose the rapidly expanding west end, where the Grand Trunk Railway station was situated. Quite apart from the advantages of this location, among which were its centrality and proximity to modern transportation, the fact is that the bishop had opted for the district where the Anglo-Protestant bourgeoisie resided.

It was as if Bourget would not leave unchallenged ethnic claims to money, might, and progress that this area symbolized. He would erect a monument there to French-Canadian strength, endurance, and fidelity, a beachhead in a foreign space that would rival and ultimately overwhelm British claims to superiority. The bishop triumphed over the misgivings of his architect, who went on to erect neobaroque churches throughout the Montreal area. In fact, the neobaroque was made to exemplify the values of Pius' papacy in the same way that the neogothic, favoured in the rest of English-speaking North America, epitomized the ideals of nineteenth-century Protestantism.

Bourget's, however, was only one man's vision. The astonishing growth of the numbers of men and women in religious life during these years certainly helped to transform it into reality. Still, a culture cannot be created by one man's will alone. It requires the active collaboration of a population, and French Canadians wholeheartedly incorporated Roman symbols, doctrines, teachings, liturgies, and practices into their lives. The cult of Pius IX, for example, was widespread in French Canada and reached its peak in two critical periods: during the Roman Revolution and in the decade culminating in 1870 in the fall of Rome to troops fighting for Italian unification. Conservative politicians, such as George-Étienne Cartier, and writers, such as the poet Octave Crémazie, did not hesitate to exploit the pope's popularity in French Canada in order to promote themselves.

Defending the pontiff's right to exercise authority over a sovereign territory, five hundred French-Canadian young men enlisted as volunteers in the papal army in the 1860s. Perceived as selfless, their gesture inspired 15,000 Montrealers to gather together for a church service to honour the first contingent departing for the Italian peninsula. Also attended by two hundred priests, the event included a musical concert performed free of charge by three hundred artists, a sermon given by the most celebrated ecclesiastical orator of the day, Bishop Laflèche, the blessing of the zouave flag, also the object of a solemn oath pronounced by the would-be soldiers, as well as the benediction of the blessed sacrament. Significantly, the spectacle was not confined to Notre Dame church.

The zouaves were paraded there by a musical band and officers of fraternal and patriotic associations. After the ceremony, a smaller group escorted the young men to cries of 'Long Live the Pope-King.' The following day to the ringing of church bells, 20,000 people lined the streets to the train station in order to bid the contingent a final and by all accounts tumultuous farewell. Parishes throughout French Canada rivalled one another by holding similar, though smaller-scale, festivities. The zouaves' return from Italy again prompted public ceremonies of celebration, including parades, official banquets, and religious services. In 1870 a crowd estimated at 50,000 – as many people as protested the hanging of Louis Riel at the famous rally in the Champ de Mars – greeted the returned soldiers in Montreal.[25]

Processions not only marked festivities related to the liturgical calendar, but other forms of religious celebration as well. When in 1856 Bishop Bourget returned from his third trip to Rome, which had lasted two years, the Catholic newspaper *True Witness* gave the following account of his reception: 'It was in fact a general 'turn out' of the entire population ... all intent in one object. So dense was the crowd ... that it was impossible to carry out the program of the procession originally agreed upon. When His Lordship set foot on shore, one deafening shout arose from the assembled thousands.'[26] Some twenty years later the arrival of the apostolic delegate, Bishop George Conroy, at the port of Quebec attracted a throng of 20,000 people, providing the occasion for yet another procession of archbishops, bishops, priests, university professors and students, as well as members of Catholic associations.

But the climax of such events was undoubtedly the Eucharistic Congress of 1910, which brought together an estimated half-million participants. A huge throne was erected outside of Montreal's St James Cathedral, from which the guest of honour, the papal legate Vincenzo Cardinal Vannutelli, blessed 30,000 school children who paraded before him. The open-air mass held in Mount Royal park at the foot of the mountain attracted a huge crowd, as well as sixty bishops, two thousand priests, and a choir of three hundred voices. The procession from Notre Dame basilica to the park was so long that three and a half hours after its inception the sacrament finally left the church. Along the route, residents decorated their houses with flags, banners, and draperies. The streets were strewn with flower petals. At strategic points makeshift triumphal arches were erected, some by French-speaking communities outside Quebec. Perhaps the most exotic of all was the one by the French Canadians of Manitoba and Alberta covered in Prairie wheat.[27]

Such events were simply unimaginable in other parts of North America. In most regions of English-speaking Canada the minority status of Catholicism discouraged outdoor manifestations of religious diversity. The disturbances in Toronto surrounding the processions that marked the jubilee year decreed by the pope in 1875 are a convenient reminder of the limits of Catholic worship within a Protestant society. Similarly, when they tried to bring religion into the street, Toronto's Anglo-Catholics encountered angry threats and incidents of violence by Protestant enthusiasts, who viewed these Anglicans as the 'enemy within' and therefore dangerous subversives. English-speaking Catholic priests outside Quebec often refused to wear soutanes in public for fear of being physically molested. Not even episcopal office was a shield against violent expressions of anti-Catholic sentiment. Soutanes, in fact, became a hotly contested issue among the clergy throughout Canada: French speakers accused their English-speaking counterparts of being afraid or embarrassed to manifest their faith in public, while the latter just as vehemently accused their colleagues of separatism, that is, of frustrating thé effort to convert North America by failing to fit into the dominant culture.[28]

Conclusion

The church and religion filled a large vacuum in French-Canadian public life following the dissolution of the Lower-Canadian assembly and the elimination of both the patriot party and the political culture that it had generated. In order to consolidate the power of conservative forces that emerged triumphant from the Insurrections and instil a spirit of subservience in the people, Britain lifted the tight controls imposed on the Catholic Church at the time of the Conquest. Little did it realize that in the process it was unleashing a powerful force for the regeneration of French-Canadian public life.

In the era of dramatic change ushered in by the Union of the Canadas, the question was whether French Canadians could maintain the social cohesion that they had known in the countryside for almost two centuries. Clearly, Britain did not think this was possible: the demographic and economic dominance of the British in the cities would inexorably lead an urbanizing population into the orbit of British culture. However, with the help of the leading French-Canadian political party, the church created an institutional space in this 'foreign' territory, providing services by French Canadians for French Canadians from the cradle to the grave. This space had a necessarily physical dimension that gave Quebec cities their 'French' character within a North American environment.

This arrangement was tacitly recognized in the BNA Act, which gave the provinces jurisdiction over health, education, and social services, in this way formally removing these sectors from the control of the English-Canadian majority in Parliament. But because the Quebec government was itself subject to pressures from Montreal's powerful English-Canadian élite, the church had to ensure an arms-length relationship vis-à-vis the provincial state. Ultramontane ideology was accordingly invoked in order to maintain the autonomy of this public space.

The classic statement of this position is found in Siméon Pagnuelo's *Études historiques et légales sur la liberté religieuse en Canada* (1872), commissioned by Bishop Bourget in order to refute claims to state supremacy in the question over the division of the parish of Montreal. So strong is the parallel in this treatise between ultramontane discourse and the idea of French-Canadian autonomy that if one were to replace the terms 'Catholic Church' with 'Quebec state' one would almost find the statement of Quebec's current, minimal constitutional demands. But were church men and women conscious of fulfilling a national mission? Bishop Bourget, for one, unquestionably placed religion above all things. But his concept of religion, without being totalitarian (he did respect the rights of Quebec's Protestant minority), was very broad. In fact he made it the defining element of nationality. As a result, there could be no contradiction between ultramontanism and upholding French Canada's national interests. His vigorous defence of both Louis Riel following the Insurrection of 1869 and Catholic rights in the New Brunswick Schools Question of 1870, discussed by William Acheson elsewhere in this volume, clearly indicate this. Ultimately, what matters more, however, is what these women and men in religion did, not whether they were conscious of the implications of their actions.

It is well to remind ourselves, however, that the church was not the state. As Linteau and others have shown, there was another public life – involving the economic and political sectors – that was outside the church's control. Speaking as some historians do of theocracy, a term implying clerical mastery of *state* structures, is therefore both misconceived and misleading.

Viewed from today's individualistic perspective, the century that saw the dominance of religion in Quebec marked the triumph of social and moral conformity. Already expressed by some rouge intellectuals in the nineteenth century, this criticism became widespread in the 1950s. Pius IX's church was undeniably opposed to liberalism in both its political and intellectual dimensions. While this position made it difficult for Catholics worldwide to expose themselves to currents of modern thought, it did not impede their integration into the industrial and urban world. As Lucia Ferretti showed, French Canadians did so on their own terms, successfully adapting a traditional culture to modern-day exigencies. Theirs was not the anachronism of a folk society, a preindustrial remnant surviving intact in a modern milieu; it was a fully industrial and urban Catholic culture, one that both gave its people a sense of belonging and filled them with pride in the face of English-Canadian pretensions to superiority. Was this a false consciousness or rather a culture taking root at a time when the signposts of a preceding culture had been knocked down?

It has almost become a truism to say that the Union condemned French Canadians to a mediocre existence. Certainly the church could not resolve the issue of French Canadians' systematic underrepresentation at all the higher levels of economic life. Only the state could accomplish that. I suspect, however, that commentators had precise models in mind when they made such statements. They were judging the culture born of the Union against the standards of the United States and France in the twentieth century. In doing so they too easily forgot that Quebec under both the French and British was a colony and, by definition, a backwater, demographically insignificant when compared with the emerging American Republic. What intellectual and artistic heights do they imagine an autonomous Quebec under Louis-Joseph Papineau would have scaled? They should instead marvel at the church's ability to institutionalize French-Canadian culture in such a short period of time, as well as religion's role in fashioning a cohesive and self-confident identity. These were the foundations upon which the Quiet Revolution was built.

Notes

1 P.E. Trudeau, 'Quebec on the Eve of the Asbestos Strike,' in *French Canadian Nationalism: An Anthology,* ed. Ramsay Cook (Toronto: Macmillan, 1969), 32–48; M. Brunet, 'Trois dominantes de la pensée canadienne-française: L'agriculturalisme, l'anti-étatisme et le messianisme,' in *La présence anglaise et les Canadiens* (Montreal: Beauchemin, 1958), published in an English version in *Society and Conquest: The Debate on the Bourgeoisie and Social Change in French Canada, 1700–1850,* ed. Dale Miquelon (Toronto: Copp Clark, 1977), 162–71.

2 This view is shared by the liberal Philippe Sylvain in 'Quelques aspects de l'antagonisme libéral-ultramontain au Canada français,' *Recherches sociographiques* 8 (September-December 1967): 275–97; and by the Marxian Nadia Fahmy-Eid in *Le clergé et le pouvoir politique au Québec: Une analyse de l'idéologie ultramontaine au milieu du XIXe siècle* (Montreal: Hurtubise HMH, 1978). This charge was recently renewed in Yvan Lamonde, *Louis-Antoine Dessaulles, 1818–1895: Un seigneur libéral et anticlérical* (Montreal: Fides, 1994).

3 For electoral control, see the study by Marcel Bellavance, *Le Québec et la Confédération: Un choix libre? Le clergé et la constitution de 1867* (Quebec: Septentrion, 1992). For stage-managed spectacles, see René Hardy, *Les zouaves: Une stratégie du clergé québécois au XIXe siècle* (Montreal: Boréal, 1980).

4 Conrad Langlois, 'Cultural Reasons Given for the French Canadian Lag in Economic Progress,' *Culture* (June 1960); Louis Maheu, 'Problème social et naissance du syndicalisme catholique,' in *Aspects historiques du mouvement ouvrier au Québec*, ed. Fernand Harvey (Montreal: Boréal, 1973), emphasized the limitations of Catholic trade unionism in promoting workers' interests; Yolande Pinard, 'Les débuts du mouvement des femmes,' in *Les femmes dans la société québécoise*, ed. Marie Lavigne and Yolande Pinard (Montreal: Boréal Express, 1977), 63–87, argues that the church in general and women's religious orders in particular presented an obstacle to the emancipation of women. For the church's role in class exploitation, see Brian Young, *In Its Corporate Capacity: The Seminary of Montreal as a Business Institution, 1816–1876* (Montreal and Kingston: McGill-Queen's University Press, 1986); Normand Séguin, *La Conquête du sol au 19e siècle agriculture et colonisation au Québec* (Montreal: Boréal Express, 1977), chap. 9; Gérard Bouchard, 'Les prêtres, les capitalistes et les ouvriers à Chicoutimi (1986–1930),' *Mouvement social* 112 (July-September 1980), which all insist on the church's collusion with capital to better keep the lower orders in a state of economic and social subjugation.

5 William Ryan, *The Clergy and Economic Growth in Quebec* (Quebec: Presses de l'Université Laval, 1966), contested the idea that the church was an obstacle to Quebec's economic development. Joseph Levitt, *Henri Bourassa and the Golden Calf: The Social Program of the Nationalists of Quebec (1900–1914)* (Ottawa: Éditions de l'Université d'Ottawa, 1969), showed that the dominant ideology described by Brunet, with its emphasis on anti-statism, the agricultural way of life, and the providential mission of French Canadians in North America, did not apply to Henri Bourassa and his disciples; Jacques Rouillard, *Histoire du syndicalisme québécois* (Montreal: Boréal, 1989), documents the evolving militancy of Catholic trade unions. Marta Danylewycz, *Taking the Veil: An Alternative to Marriage, Motherhood, and Spinsterhood in Quebec, 1840–1920* (Toronto: McClelland and Stewart, 1987), presents religious life as a tool in women's emancipation.

6 P.A. Linteau, René Durocher, and Jean-Claude Robert, *Quebec: A History 1867–1929*, trans. Robert Chodos (Toronto: Lorimer, 1983); P.A. Linteau, R. Durocher, J. C. Robert, and François Ricard, *Quebec since 1930*, trans. Robert Chodos and Ellen Garmaise (Toronto: Lorimer, 1991).

7 Fernande Roy, *Progrès, Harmonie, Liberté: Le libéralisme des milieux d'affaires*

104   Roberto Perin

francophones à Montréal au tournant du siècle (Montreal: Boréal, 1988); *Histoire des idéologies au Québec aux XIXe et XXe siècles* (Montreal: Boréal Express, 1993). These studies confirm the findings of an earlier work which concluded that clerico-nationalism rarely found expression among Quebec politicians and was entirely absent from legislative debates. See Marcel Hamelin, *Les premières années du parlementarisme québécois (1867–78)* (Quebec: Presses de l'Université Laval, 1974).

8 This seems to be the view expressed in Ronald Rudin's latest work, *Making History in Twentieth-Century Quebec* (Toronto: University of Toronto Press, 1997).

9 See, among others, Donald Creighton, 'Confederation: The Use and Abuse of History,' *Journal of Canadian Studies* 1 (May 1966); and in the same issue, W.L. Morton, 'Confederation, 1870–1896: The End of the Macdonaldian Constitution and the Return to Duality'; Ralph Heintzman, 'The Spirit of Confederation: Professor Creighton, Biculturalism, and the Use of History,' *Canadian Historical Review* 52 (September 1971): 245–75; Ramsay Cook, *Canada and the French Canadian Question* (Toronto: Macmillan, 1967); Arthur Silver, *The French Canadian Idea of Confederation* (Toronto: University of Toronto Press, 1982).

10 These are described in my 'Answering the Quebec Question: Two Centuries of Equivocation,' in *Negotiating with a Sovereign Quebec*, ed. Daniel Drache and R. Perin (Toronto: Lorimer, 1992), 30–46.

11 Gerald Craig, ed., *Lord Durham's Report* (Toronto: McClelland and Stewart, 1964), 47. Louisiana is discussed on pages 154–7.

12 Huguette Lapointe-Roy, 'Le renouveau religieux à Montréal au XIXe siècle et le rôle des Sulpiciens dans le domaine de l'éducation,' Société canadienne d'histoire de l'Église catholique (SCHEC), *Sessions d'étude* 53 (1986): 51–62; *Charité bien ordonnée: Le premier réseau de la lutte contre la pauvreté à Montréal au 19e siècle* (Montreal: Boréal, 1987).

13 Louis-Edmond Hamelin, 'Évolution numérique séculaire du clergé catholique dans le Québec,' *Recherches sociographiques* 2, no. 2 (April-June 1961): 237; Bernard Denault and Benoît Lévesque, *Éléments pour une sociologie des communautés religieuses au Québec* (Montreal: Les Presses de l'Université de Montréal, 1975), 50.

14 Danylewycz, *Taking the Veil*; Nicole Laurin, Danielle Juteau, and Lorraine Duchesne, *À la recherche d'un monde oublié: Les communautés religieuses de femmes au Québec de 1900 à 1970* (Montreal: Le Jour, éditeur, 1991), 171.

15 Lucia Ferretti, *Entre voisins: La société paroissiale en milieu urbain Saint-Pierre-Apôtre de Montréal 1848–1930* (Montreal: Boréal, 1992).

16 In *Le Curé Labelle: Messianisme, utopie et colonisation au Québec 1850–1900*

(Montreal: Hurtubise HMH, 1983), Gabriel Dussault made a similar plea not to interpret the discourse of agriculturalism literally, but rather as a call for French Canadians to take possession of their homeland.

17 Allan Greer, *The Patriots and the People: The Rebellion of 1837 in Rural Lower Canada* (Toronto: University of Toronto Press, 1993).

18 Jean-Pierre Wallot, 'Religion and French Canadian Mores in the Early Nineteenth Century,' *Canadian Historical Review* 52, no. 1 (March 1971): 51–94; Brigitte Caulier, 'Les confréries de dévotion traditionnelles et le réveil religieux à Montréal au XIXe siècle,' SCHEC, *Sessions d'études* 53 (1986): 23–40.

19 See Jan Noel, *Canada Dry: Temperance Crusades before Confederation* (Toronto: University of Toronto Press, 1995).

20 Louis Rousseau, 'Les missions populaires de 1840–42,' SCHEC, *Sessions d'études* 53 (1986): 7–21. See as well Louis Rousseau and Frank Remiggi, eds., *Atlas historique des pratiques religieuses: Le sud-ouest du Québec au XIXe siècle* (Ottawa: Presses de l'Université d'Ottawa, 1998).

21 From his 1858 pastoral letter 'Sur l'allocution prononcée par Sa Sainteté, Pie IX, contre les erreurs du temps, le 9 décembre 1854,' cited in *Ignace Bourget, écrivain*, ed. Adrien Thério (Montreal: Éditions Jumonville, 1975), 131.

22 Ibid., 136.

23 Cited in Léon Pouliot, *La réaction catholique de Montréal, 1840–1841* (Montreal: Imprimerie du Messager, 1942), 118 n. 59.

24 Philippe Sylvain and Nive Voisine, *Réveil et consolidation (1840–1898)*, vol. 2 of *Histoire du catholicisme québécois*, ed. Nive Voisine (Montreal: Boréal, 1984), 356.

25 Hardy, *Les zouaves*, 192–200.

26 Léon Pouliot, *Monseigneur Bourget et son temps*, vol. 3. (Montreal: Éditions Bellarmin, 1972), 139 n. 45.

27 *XXIe congrès eucharistique international, Montreal* (Montréal: Beauchemin, 1911), 61, 95–100.

28 Matteo Sanfilippo, '"Une occasion d'humiliations": L'abito talare, il clero cattolico e l'ovest canadese agli inizi del XX secolo,' in *Le stelle e le strisce. Studi americani e militari in onore di Raimondo Luraghi*, 1, ed. Valeria Gennaro Lerda (Milan: Bompiani, 1998), 61–73.

Part Two

Contested Spaces: The Ambiguities of
Religion in the Public Sphere

5

The State, the Church, and Indian Residential Schools in Canada

J.R. Miller

It was a big day for Grace Lavallé. She was selected to meet and be photographed with Louis St Laurent, Canada's prime minister, when he visited her residential school at Lebret, Saskatchewan.[1] Such ceremonial visits were common at the Oblate residential school in the Qu'Appelle Valley, which was easily accessible by rail and road from Regina. On numerous occasions when officials visited residential schools, an elaborate display of amity and cooperation between church and government occurred, for such visits were as much about public relations and promotion of the interests of the Department of Indian Affairs as they were about highlighting the accomplishments of students such as Grace.[2] These carefully orchestrated visits also reinforced the impression that Native residential schools were a harmonious and productive combination of throne and altar for the benefit of both Aboriginal peoples and Canadian society.

While the state-created residential schools that existed in Canada from the 1880s to the 1970s are fairly described in most historical literature as a partnership between the state and the church, within the relationship of throne and altar there were both tensions and differences of emphasis that produced some interesting side-effects. Such crosscurrents in church–state relations were a feature that Canadian mission schools and their American counterparts shared, although in the United States cooperation of government and churches had been much more short-lived than it was north of the border. And even in Canada the apparent partnership of missionary and bureaucrat that formed the implicit background to the photograph of a grinning Grace Lavallé and a benignly smiling prime minister masked important differences in objectives, and sometimes also in outcomes.

Although these residential schools existed as a state creation from 1883 to Ottawa's decision to terminate them in 1969, there was also a 'pre-history' to the story of residential schooling that stretched back to seventeenth-century New France, with important developments in late-eighteenth-century New Brunswick and mid-nineteenth-century Ontario.[3] In this earlier period, leadership was almost invariably provided by Christian missionaries, whether Jesuits and Ursulines in New France or New England Company and Methodists in British North America. In the prehistorical period of residential schooling, Christianity often looked in vain for encouragement and support from the state. Consequently, when the Dominion of Canada turned in the 1870s to the development of a schooling policy for the 'Indians' for whom it had constitutional responsibility, there were missionary precedents and ongoing missionary-run boarding schools in Ontario, the Prairies, and British Columbia.[4]

The immediate inspiration of the Aboriginal educational policy that emerged in the 1880s were the seven treaties that Canada signed between 1871 and 1877 with the First Nations of northwestern Ontario and the Prairies. Since each of these pacts contained a clause obligating the Dominion to provide schooling for the Aboriginal groups, Ottawa was induced to begin a leisurely search for a means of implementing its commitment. Following investigation of American schooling experiments, in particular the famous institution conducted by Captain Richard Pratt in Carlisle, Pennsylvania, the Department of Indian Affairs in 1883 created the first three of what it styled industrial schools in what are now Alberta and Saskatchewan. These initiatives joined and coexisted with a number of small boarding schools that operated under Roman Catholic, Anglican, New England Company, Methodist, and Presbyterian auspices, and in the 1890s the burgeoning system spread to British Columbia. Between 1883 and 1923 the Department of Indian Affairs sponsored both industrial and boarding schools, but in the latter year they were amalgamated into a single category, residential schools, in recognition of the reality that meaningful distinctions between the ambitious industrial and the modest boarding schools had withered to insignificance. At its height in the 1920s the Canadian residential school system totalled eighty institutions, but persistent shortcomings and growing Indian opposition led as early as the 1940s to government efforts to wind the system down, and ultimately in 1969 to a decision to eliminate the remainder of the schools.

Although American practice had definitely had an influence on the creation of industrial schools in 1883, there was an important difference between residential educational facilities north and south of the international border. In Canada, all the residential schools were operated on the government's behalf by Christian church bodies, leading to their usually being described, as noted, as a partnership between throne and altar. In part this arrangement was motivated by racist ideology and in part by parsimony. As Prime Minister Sir John A. Macdonald explained, 'secular education is a good thing among white men but among Indians the first object is to make them better men, and, if possible, good Christian men by applying proper moral restraints.'[5] Besides, as the man commissioned by the government to recommend a school policy after treaty-making had argued, it would be cruel to deprive Indians of 'their simple Indian mythology' without putting Christianity in its place. To him it was obvious that 'Missionary teachers were essential. The advantage of calling in the aid of religion is, that there is a chance of getting an enthusiastic person, with, therefore, a motive power beyond anything pecuniary remuneration could supply.'[6] Cheaper, too, of course.

In the United States, in contrast, although the churches had a role in the operation of Indian boarding schools in the latter decades of the nineteenth century, they were largely eliminated from the field by the twentieth. From the 1870s until 1900 the Bureau of Indian Affairs supported what were termed 'contract schools,' church-run Indian schools that existed along with its own day and boarding institutions, by granting land and funds for construction of the school, and by paying the missionary body an annual per capita grant for operating expenses. However, the contract schools became unpopular among American Protestants, especially as Roman Catholic missionaries availed themselves of the program enthusiastically, and Congress decided to end contracting in 1897.[7] Although American missionaries continued to participate in schooling for Native Americans well into the twentieth century, they never enjoyed the government approval or reliance that marked the Canadian experience. State dominance and greater distance between government and church were features of the American approach that were alien to Canada.

In other respects, though, there were important similarities between the American and Canadian systems of residential schooling for Native children. In terms of their day-to-day operation, none was more important than the 'half-day system' that Captain Pratt had pioneered at Carlisle and that Canadian schools followed until the 1950s. In fact, the Upper Canadian pre-Confederation experience with residential schooling had also included this system. As the term suggests, the half-day system meant that most residential school students spent half the day in the classroom receiving academic instruction and the other half working in kitchens, barns, fields, or workshops at tasks whose theoretical purpose was vocational instruction, but whose real raison d'être was the subsidization of the operation of the schools. One of the early champions of residential schools, Methodist public school pioneer Egerton Ryerson, had even allowed himself to hope before Confederation that 'with judicious management, these establishments will be able in the course of a few years very nearly to support themselves' thanks to student labour.[8] The half-day system, which was eliminated in the more prosperous mid- and late-1950s in Canada, was the source of many ills: overwork, insufficient classroom instruction, and physical mistreatment at the hands of impatient supervisors.

The other negative feature that Canadian and American schools shared was their denigration of Aboriginal culture and their persistent attempts to assimilate the Native child. Products of the nineteenth century, an era notorious for Euro-American intolerance towards non-white peoples and for virulent theories of Caucasian racial superiority, residential schools were thoroughly imbued with a desire to replace Aboriginal identity, belief, and practice with attitudes and behaviour associated with non-Native communities. In Canada, this was merely the pedagogical manifestation of the thoroughly racist assumptions and objectives that framed all of the state's policy towards the indigenous peoples.[9] The heart of Canadian Indian policy, codified in the Indian Act in 1876 and maintained through innumerable amendments for over a century, was a program, chillingly and accurately described by an American Bureau of Indian Affairs official: 'the extinction of the Indians *as Indians* is the ultimate end' of Canadian Indian policy.[10]

Canadian policy, ironically, began by defining some Aboriginal people as separate and distinct. In Canadian law 'Indian' was a legal category administered by the Department of Indian Affairs, admission to which was determined by the government of Canada. The irony arises from the fact that the definition was made solely for the purpose of identifying who was to be encouraged, tutored, and, if necessary, coerced to exchange the status of 'Indian' for the title of citizen. At the heart of Canadian policy was a procedure known as enfranchisement, by which educated and acculturated 'Indians' would apply and qualify for citizenship, necessitating their loss of 'Indian' status and the removal of a share of reserve land in a freehold grant to the new citizen. And, of course, it was to tutor and encourage young Native people to aspire to and qualify for enfranchisement that Indian schooling in general, and residential schools in particular, existed. Although U.S. policy lacked the concept and practice of enfranchisement, principally because American judicial treatment of Native Americans had been different, residential schools in both countries discountenanced Native ways and promoted Euro-American belief and practice.[11] Schools in both countries, unfortunately, were institutions that denigrated things Aboriginal and exalted everything deemed to be Christian and European.

Although in Canada church and state both appeared to subscribe to a thoroughly assimilative program in the residential schools, a project that was only a portion of the larger campaign for the 'extinction of the Indians *as Indians*,' below the surface there was less than unanimity in the aims and practices of the two non-Native partners in the residential schooling story. To summarize crudely, Canadian state policy sought the assimilation of First Nations society through its young in residential schools primarily to limit, reduce, and ultimately eliminate the federal government's financial obligations to Native society. On the other hand, missionary bodies, who were not unanimous about the desirability and necessity of coercive assimilation through the schools, viewed residential schooling as a component of a broader approach that sought first to convert Indians religiously and second to assist Native communities to make the difficult adjustment to coexisting with and thriving alongside a newly dominant Euro-Canadian majority. If Ottawa was motivated by the balance sheet, seeing assimilation as an aid to reducing expenditure, the churches were focused upon the afterlife, while simultaneously working to help their Aboriginal charges survive in this world.

For the government of Canada, in dealing with Aboriginal peoples in general, and with status Indians in residential schools in particular, the bottom line was the bottom line. This governmental fixation on financial considerations was true of schooling policy in two distinct, but related, senses. First, so far as government was concerned, the dominant objective in all its policies was to bring or drive Aboriginal peoples to economic self-sufficiency so as to reduce and end Ottawa's financial obligations. So long as status Indians in particular were financially vulnerable, the federal government, which had constitutional responsibility for this group, was potentially liable for the wherewithal to maintain them. During the immediate post-treaty years in the Prairie region, the time and place that gave rise to an industrial schools policy in 1883, this was more than a potentiality, because the total collapse of the bison-based economy by 1879 had devastated the Plains nations. The Department of Indian Affairs (DIA), which was established in 1880, constantly worked to reduce expenditure on the 'wards' for whom it had responsibility, in part because non-Native society did not value Aboriginal peoples very highly and in part because their advancing weakness militarily and politically meant they were no longer regarded as a threat. Residential schools, and DIA schools in general, were expected swiftly to bring Aboriginal communities to a sufficiently acculturated level that 'Indians' would apply for enfranchisement under the Indian Act. Schooling would lead to enfranchisement, which would reduce the number of 'Indians' and the extent of reserve land, eventually rubbing out Ottawa's constitutionally based financial liability for 'Indians and lands reserved for the Indians.'[12]

The second way in which a bottom-line mentality shaped Indian Affairs' approach to residential schools was that the same thinking caused the department constantly to look for ways to hold down governmental spending on the operation of the institutions. That thinking was the major underpinning of the half-day system by which residential schools operated from the 1880s to the 1950s, much to the detriment of the health and learning of the students, for the system both reduced the students' time in class and shifted some of the burden of maintaining the schools onto their backs. Similarly, the federal government frequently looked for ways to hold down its contribution to the schools' operation. As early as 1892, for example, it cajoled and strong-armed reluctant missionaries to shift the financing of both industrial and boarding schools from a line-budget basis to a per capita system. The change meant that henceforth school administrators would have to manage on the revenue they derived from approved enrolment, rather than being able to call on the government to make good their expenditures on an authorized set of services and goods. Ottawa's rationale for shifting from the latter to the former basis of financing residential schooling was brutally clear:

> When the whole cost of the Institutions is borne by the Government it follows that the same economy is not used as would be employed under other conditions; demands are made for articles of outfit, and for supplies which, if the outlay was covered by a grant, would be found unnecessary; and employees are engaged who would be dispensed with if the payment of their wages formed a direct charge against the per capita grant.[13]

The consequences of this shift in funding were enormous: more work for students, poorer facilities and supplies, and the admission of unhealthy recruits for the revenue they would bring no matter the danger they posed to other students in the schools.

The same governmental attitudes that brought the per capita system into effect in 1892–3 led to periodic reductions in funding at moments of financial stringency. Behind the reductions in the per capita grant during the Great War, Great Depression, and Second World War was the simple fact that Indian Affairs and Indians were not very important politically in Ottawa. When cuts had to be made, the weakest and most vulnerable in Canadian society – Indian children – were forced to bear the worst of them. Although these cuts were restored – often after ferocious, united lobbying by the normally competitive churches – while they were in operation they caused enormous problems for missionary bodies as well as residential school students. It is fair to say that financial matters were the single greatest and most frequent irritant between missionaries and government throughout the existence of the schools. Government regularly attempted to offload more of the cost of the schools on students and missionaries. The latter absorbed some of the cost through increased contributions by their non-Native adherents, but there were very definite limits to how deep congregations, especially in the non-Catholic churches, were willing to dig to support Native missions and residential schools. As the twentieth century wore on, enthusiasm for these missions and schools ebbed, particularly in the United Church, to a lesser extent in the Anglican communion, and least of all among Roman Catholics. When the government began moving from segregated, largely residential, schooling to an emphasis on 'integrated' schooling – significantly, for financial as well as ideological reasons – after 1945, it was only the Catholics who resisted the move strongly.[14]

Government utilized and appreciated the missionaries' work in the residential schools, but largely for instrumental reasons that were not congruent with the aims that motivated the evangelists. Christian missionaries were desirable as teachers and child-care workers from the government's point of view because ethical instruction was as important as secular learning for Native children and because missionaries could be induced to work more cheaply than non-evangelists. Both these ideas, as noted earlier, had been articulated by founders of the industrial schools in the nineteenth century. Prime Minister Macdonald had said that Indians required instruction by missionaries because 'moral restraints' were what they needed to become 'good Christian men.'[15] Edgar Dewdney, an Indian Affairs official and later cabinet minister, in 1884 argued that the Indian child 'must receive one spiritual training unhampered by any other influence' because otherwise instruction would lower, rather than elevate, the youth.[16] The assumption behind these beliefs, an assumption shared by missionaries and politicians, was that moral weakness, rather than intellectual deficiency, was the principal obstacle to success in Native schooling. 'The Indian problem,' the department's annual report contended, 'exists owing to the fact that the Indian is untrained to take his place in the world. Once teach him to do this, and the solution is had.'[17] A Presbyterian inquiry early in the twentieth century pinpointed what type of teaching was required: 'His failure in life is not because he is intellectually dull but because of moral weakness.'[18] Another Prairie evangelist agreed that 'moral strength is the element in their natures that is so lacking.'[19]

Besides striving to inculcate this moral strength, missionaries worked cheaply. There were several reasons for this welcome phenomenon. Among the Roman Catholics, clerical celibacy and large numbers of female religious who had taken vows of poverty and chastity ensured that school workers did not have families who had to be housed and fed, and that the workers themselves would accept minimal remuneration. Among Christian missionaries in general, the evangelistic motivation that had brought them into 'the work,' as it was usually termed, ensured that they would not expect the same rates of pay that workers in similar lines elsewhere were getting. As the report that Macdonald's government had commissioned in the late 1870s expressed the point: 'The advantage of calling in the aid of religion is, that there is a chance of getting an enthusiastic person, with, therefore, a motive power beyond anything pecuniary remuneration could supply. The work requires not only the energy but the patience of an enthusiast.'[20] From Ottawa's perspective religion was important in the residential schools for both pedagogical and financial reasons.

From the missionary's viewpoint, such thinking was short-sighted: evangelists saw the primary purpose of the schools as Christian conversion. Indeed, on the missionaries' part, the primacy of evangelization was a consistent and long-standing feature of their multi-denominational labours in Canada. From the days of New France, through the broadening campaign that developed in the nineteenth century, until the 1960s at least, persuading Aboriginal peoples to abandon their animistic world-view and practices in favour of Christianity, whether Catholic or Protestant, had always been the primary motivating aspiration of the thousands who volunteered for 'the work,' whether in schools, missions, or hospitals. The inner proselytizing pulse that made Christianity such a revolutionary force in the world was captured in the biblical Great Commission: 'Go ye into all the world, and preach the gospel to every creature.'[21] Whether the clerical revolutionaries were Jesuits, Church Missionary Society laymen, Sisters of Saint Ann, or Methodist saddlebag preachers, all were animated at some level by this injunction. And it was pursuit of that goal – conversion of Aboriginal society through the Christian schooling of their young – that was the first objective of those who served in residential schools in Canada.

Where Christian missionaries varied was in the details of their methods. Did religious conversion require cultural assimilation? This had been a matter of debate since seventeenth-century New France, although in nineteenth-century Canada evangelists moved towards a consensus in their answer. In New France the first male missionary order, the Récollets, had believed francization was an essential precondition to conversion, but their successors, the more experienced Society of Jesus, eventually came round to the viewpoint 'that the best mode of Christianizing them was to avoid Frenchifying them.'[22] Early-nineteenth-century missionaries, both Roman Catholic and Protestant, were much more ambivalent about the notion that conversion required a cultural transformation.

This ambivalence came through most clearly in the language practices and policies that the missionaries of this era followed in their work with Native communities. In the first half of the nineteenth century, at least, all the major denominations utilized Native languages in their missions, including the schools. The Church Missionary Society (CMS), evangelical standard-bearer for the Church of England, followed a 'native church policy' that aimed at the indigenization of Christianity by adapting the new religion to the culture of the foreign field, rather than the reverse. In keeping with this approach, male missionaries were expected by the CMS to learn the Native language that prevailed in the mission field. The CMS missionary who learned Swahili or Ojibwa as part of his early duties was under instructions to promote Native advancement to ordination and control of the mission.[23] The Methodists, too, most notably in Upper Canada before 1850 but also in their labours in the Prairie west, had missionaries who learned and used the Native languages in their work. Names like James Evans and McDougall, both George and John, were and are synonymous with facility in Aboriginal languages and customs. As John McDougall once put it in the columns of the *Christian Guardian*, he had 'held service in the schoolhouse, and had the privilege of preaching the glorious Gospel to an earnest people in the "language wherein they were born," which, after all, is the only way to reach the hearts and thoughts of any congregation.'[24] The Jesuits, who returned to British North America in the early 1840s, and the Oblates, who came a bit later to share the labours in the Catholic mission field, similarly regarded mastery of the language of the Aboriginal group to whom they ministered as their first assignment. Like the Methodists, Church Missionary Society workers, and Jesuits, the Oblates became famous for the facility in Aboriginal languages of some of their missionaries.[25]

Although this missionary proclivity for Native languages did not represent a culturally relativist stance towards Aboriginal communities, it was noticeably different from the post-Confederation governmental attitude. Instructions to indigenize the missionary congregation did not obliterate the assumptions of cultural and racial superiority with which many Englishmen and Canadians came to the evangelistic work, and willingness to adopt and employ Aboriginal languages did not imply acceptance of Native peoples' religious beliefs and social customs. Moreover, as will be noted later, missionary openness to Aboriginal languages declined during the late nineteenth and early twentieth centuries. However, the existence, however temporarily and however attenuated, of a willingness to make use of Native languages the better to convert was evidence that missionaries placed much greater emphasis on religious motives – evangelization for its own sake – than did the state.

The second most important missionary motive, assisting Native people with economic adjustment, was one on which there was congruence, not just between state and church, but also between those Native groups that desired schooling and the non-Native partners in residential schooling. Among Aboriginal leaders from Peter Jones and Shingwaukonce in Upper Canada to the pro-treaty Plains chiefs like Ahtakakoop and Mistawasis in 1876 to leaders who appeared before the Special Joint Committee on the Indian Act in the 1940s and told the parliamentarians 'Our greatest need to-day is proper education,' there was a consistent theme.[26] Those First Nations leaders who favoured Euro-Canadian schooling did so primarily for its practical vocational potential. Missionaries strongly supported this objective and saw schooling as the most effective means of achieving it expeditiously. Where the evangelists differed from the bureaucrats and politicians in Ottawa was that the missionaries wanted to promote economic adjustment because it was beneficial for Aboriginal communities, while the Ottawans favoured it as much because it would benefit government by reducing financial obligations to Indians. The differing motives that the three parties in residential schooling had for supporting vocational training help to explain the varying levels of attachment to the goal. The federal government always subordinated the training goal to its fixation on economy, most notoriously in the 1930s and 1940s when its policy was to promote manual training in the schools but its Indian Affairs administration never provided funds adequate to enable schools to carry the policy out effectively. Churches were more supportive of practical training than government, but by the interwar period of the twentieth century they were no longer willing or able to provide the funds to make up the shortfall in government financing.

For First Nations communities, the vocational training aspect of Euro-Canadian schooling was probably its most attractive feature. While their leaders often were ambivalent about the religious or moral component of instruction, they usually recognized that literacy and training in agriculture and trades held the potential to advance their people economically. Such thinking had underlain the views of nineteenth-century Native missionaries such as Peter Jones and Plains treaty negotiators in the 1870s.[27] What all of these leaders, missionary and non-Christian alike, shared was an assumption that vocational and rudimentary academic learning could be acquired in the newcomers' schools without loss of Aboriginal culture and identity. This assumption, of course, proved tragically ill-founded.

In sum, the three parties to residential schooling – Indians, missionaries, and government – had multiple motives for supporting, at times equivocally, residential schools. Sometimes their motives overlapped to a greater or lesser degree; other times there were divergences between them. State and church agreed on the importance of Christian instruction, though for subtly different reasons. All were in favour of using the schools to provide practical instruction that would equip graduates with work skills that would enable them to thrive in the changing world around them; however, Native communities were regularly frustrated by the failure of their non-Native partners to provide adequate funding to enable the schools to accomplish this goal. The frictions, tensions, and open criticisms that became audible over this aspect of the pedagogical program in the post-1945 period constitute but one of many indicators that the supposed partnership of crown and altar in residential schooling was an uneasy one. Another, similar area that taught the same point was the provision of secondary schooling in the twentieth century. As the need for education beyond the elementary level became ever more obvious by the period of the Second World War, the federal government frustrated its partners by dragging its feet in funding more advanced instruction.[28] The reason was straightforward: the governmental parsimony that had marred residential schooling since at least 1892. The logjam was broken only when the Jesuits and the Daughters of the Heart of Mary went ahead on their own and provided limited secondary facilities at their schools at Spanish, Ontario, in 1946.[29]

Another topic that revealed the crosscurrents in the apparently smooth relations between church and government in residential schooling was the matter of languages, more particularly Aboriginal languages in the schools. This is a topic that is, invariably and rightly, mentioned in any account of residential schooling. What is much less often remarked is the fact that until well into the twentieth century most missionary bodies did not agree with the government's desire for a complete ban on the use of Native languages. This issue actually arose in the prehistory of the story of residential schools, because the government of the Province of Canada in the 1850s had insisted that the Jesuits stop permitting the use of Ojibwa at its mission and schools on Manitoulin Island.[30] During the period of federally supported residential schooling after 1883, government officials applied heavy pressure on school administrators to force uniform use of English (or French in parts of Quebec after the Second World War). As a note to the 'Programme of Studies' in the 1894 Annual Report of the Department of Indian Affairs put it, 'Every effort must be made to induce pupils to speak English, and to teach them to understand it; unless they do the whole work of the teacher is likely to be wasted.'[31] Researchers into the history of residential schools are treated to the spectacle of missionaries born and educated in France having to correspond from the field in British Columbia or the Prairies in English with bureaucrats in distant Ottawa. Little wonder that one French Oblate was reported to have complained to an Oblate conference 'that French was spoken in Heaven and that we should therefore learn that language.'[32]

Over time missionary and bureaucratic attitudes on language

became more similar, as Native missions became ideologically closer to Canadian society in general. So far as the Anglicans were concerned, a major stimulus to this process was the switch of administration of the missions, including schools, from the England-based Church Missionary Society to the Missionary Society of the Church in Canada in the early decades of the twentieth century. So far as Methodists and Presbyterians were concerned, after the pioneering generation of evangelists who went west from Ontario in the middle decades of the nineteenth century, their missionary workers had little interest in languages other than English, including Native languages. Part of the nationalizing process that has been observed at work in the Protestant churches was acquisition of the growing intolerance, including impatience with linguistic diversity, that typified Ontario in particular from the late decades of the nineteenth century onward. And even the Oblates found themselves gravitating away from the use of Native languages, as the priests increasingly paid more attention, particularly in western Canada, to immigrants from Europe and eastern Canada than to the nearby Native missions and schools in the region. (The Oblates attempted after 1936 to restore an emphasis on Native languages in their Prairie missions.)[33]

Whatever the outlook of later evangelists, most early missionaries were ambivalent about Ottawa's insistence on imposing English on the residential school populations. Isaac Stringer, Anglican bishop of the Yukon, commented in his charge to his Synod in 1915, 'The Indian language is good and serviceable as a medium, but the Government has decided that Indian pupils must be taught English and perhaps that is the best policy in the end.'[34] The Oblate Vicar Apostolic in the territory of Grouard urged 'My dear Little Friends' who produced a newsletter at Blue Quills school 'to make more room in your "Moccasin Telegram" for your beautiful Cree language. It is your mother-tongue, so let no other one take its place on your lips and in your heart. Be proud of it. When you speak to Almighty God in your prayers and in your hymns, as well as when you speak and write to your dear parents, use the language that God has given your forefathers, as the most suitable expression of their thoughts and feelings.'[35]

And it was not just in the North that the Roman Catholics in particular thumbed their nose at Ottawa's will. The Oblate Provincial instructed the clerics at the Lestock school in 1909 that 'Il faudrait que les enfants apprennent les prières dans leur langue maternelle; les enfants sauteux en sauteux, and les enfants Métis français en français.'[36] At Spanish in 1935, the Jesuit principal acceded to his Provincial's instruction to resume teaching the children their prayers in Ojibwa, even though he was pretty sure that the policy 'would never meet the approval of the powers-that-be.'[37] And, while twentieth-century Protestant missionaries were less accommodating of Aboriginal languages than the Catholics, some of them clearly made little or no effort to extirpate the indigenous tongue. For example, one of the complaints that the Presbyterian principal reportedly levelled at the farm instructor at the Cecilia Jeffrey school in northwestern Ontario was 'that he could not recollect of one occasion that I had sent a pupil into his office for punishment for talking the Indian language.'[38]

In fact, it was in the praying and working areas of the schools, rather than the classroom, that Native languages were most likely to be heard, especially when the supervisors were themselves Native people. A Mohawk woman from Kahnawake recalled that the girls at the Daughters of the Heart of Mary school at Spanish particularly liked a Native woman classroom teacher and a Native woman laundry supervisor who treated them well.[39] At Wabasca in northern Alberta in 1961, the matron, who was also the wife of the principal, was 'often heard conversing with the children in a steady flow of Cree.'[40] Some school administrators, such as a remarkable principal, Earl Anfield, at the Anglican school at Alert Bay in the 1930s, understood the local Aboriginal language though he could not speak it, and dealt with the local community partially in their tongue during his tenure.[41] Although the Christian missionaries who operated the residential schools shared many of the ethnocentric attitudes towards Aboriginal peoples that bureaucrats, politicians, and Canadians at large held, their approach to linguistic assimilation was significantly different. In large part because their advocacy of assimilation was diluted by their preference for effective methods of proselytizing and by their close, daily contact with Native students in and around the schools, missionaries often were less oppressive about the use of Aboriginal languages than was the federal government.

Not only did the complex area of language in the residential schools reveal subtle differences of emphasis and approach between the state and its church partners, but the same area yielded ironic consequences. For example, Aboriginal groups who were being subjected to heavy pressure by the Indian Agent to abandon traditional practices, such as the Sun Dance, could use the statements of the exceptional courageous missionary, such as John McDougall, who spoke out publicly against such attempts at suppression on grounds of freedom of religion. Describing the Thirst Dance as 'a religious festival,' McDougall added that 'I altogether fail to see why in these days of our much boasted religious liberty anyone should interfere with a few Indians in the exercise of their faith.'[42] And on another occasion McDougall charged in a letter to the *Christian Guardian* that attacks on ceremonial dancing were a violation of commitments in the treaties that missionaries such as himself had helped persuade Plains nations to sign in the 1870s.[43]

Denominational competition between the various churches, most acutely in cases pitting a Roman Catholic mission against a non-Catholic one, encouraged some missionaries to be more accommodating of Aboriginal interests and sensibilities than they might otherwise have been. The concessions inspired by denominational rivalry ranged from the crass to the pedagogically defensible. Offering inducements – from assistance with transportation costs to a girl's dress to outright bribery of the parents – was common throughout western Canada.[44] Not all the beneficiaries were parents, however. At the Kamloops school, a former principal admitted in 1935, 'I paid the old Father LeJeune five dollars for every child who came from his missions. He was worth all that & more.'[45] According to Eleanor Brass, a graduate of the File Hills school in southern Saskatchewan, at least one Indian father exploited the competition between the Presbyterian and Roman Catholic schools in the region. 'Dad said that the principals of these schools used to bribe the parents to send their children to their schools,' she recalled. 'He thought his grandfather got paid for him to go to both schools but somehow he landed in the nearest one to the reserve, the File Hills Presbyterian boarding school.'[46] Rivalry could also push missionaries to be more accommodating on the use of Native languages. On the Poorman reserve in Saskatchewan, an Oblate missionary warned his Provincial it was vital to have a Cree-speaking missionary 'for recruiting purposes' so as to gain an advantage over the Anglican Gordon's school: 'the great & important need here is one who can speak *Cree*, to come where we have to compete with the other school.'[47]

This competition for souls could also force missionaries to make better provision, pedagogical and otherwise, for residential school children. For example, the Oblate principal on the west side of Vancouver Island was so concerned about keeping students from the Presbyterian institution at Ahousat that he urged his Provincial 'we must make the school attractive not by pandering to the children & parents but by giving them a reason to want to send their children. That is why I want a good carpentry & machine shop, a good carpenter & a good mechanic so the boys can learn how to build houses, do carpentry work, learn to repair engines, etc.'[48] First Nations leaders learned to exploit the rivalry, for example to secure a school closer to their reserve than otherwise might have been the case. A chief in the Battle River region of western Saskatchewan gave the Methodist church until the autumn to promise a school: 'If there was no prospect of a school, then they would have to put their children in the Roman Catholic School.'[49] A second example came from northwestern Ontario, where the Presbyterians were so desperate to satisfy the desire of the local Ojibwa band rather than see the field occupied by the Roman Catholics that they signed an agreement with Chief Red Sky committing them not to proselytize the children, block the children from participating in their traditional rites, or use the police to bring back runaways.[50] This Ontario case was exceptional, but it demonstrated boldly how First Nations that fortuitously found themselves in a cockpit of church rivalry and competition for students could exploit the situation in ways that stretched from bribes to toleration of Aboriginal spiritual practices.[51]

Another ironic aspect of the language issue was the fact that English frequently served as the *lingua franca* (pardon the pun!) at residential schools that drew their student body from the territories of First Nations who spoke more than one Aboriginal language. Redfern Louttit, who was to go on to be a distinguished Anglican cleric, journeyed far from his home in the James Bay region to Chapleau school, where he encountered Ojibwa-speaking students who did not understand his Cree.[52] In such situations, use of English was a linguistic common denominator for ethnically diverse school populations. In ethnic 'border' regions such as the stretch from Chapleau to Spanish in Ontario, or Beauval in Saskatchewan, the European language was frequently practical and efficient. British Columbia was an especially acute example of this because of the dozens of distinctive First Nations languages that were to be found there. In coastal regions, the development of 'trade Chinook,' or Chinook jargon, had been one early response to this situation. In the residential schools of the province, especially in the Interior, the common tongue would be English. As a French Oblate, John Duplanil, explained, 'In B.C. the children came from different Reserves. They spoke different languages and English was the only means of communication between children of different tribes. Those who came from the same tribe were not allowed to speak their dialect. Obvious reasons – no (one) group can be tolerated.'[53] As incidents of this sort clearly indicate, the issue of language in the residential schools and the missions with which they were associated was by no means a simple one, whether in its state–church or other aspects.

The troubled story of residential schooling for Aboriginal children in Canada reveals subtleties and complexities in the roles of state and Christian church that are often overlooked or downplayed. Part of the reason for scholarly commentators to place church–state differences in shadow is that observers fear running the risk of appearing to trivialize or dismiss the painfully real damage that these missions and schools often did. Let there be no mistake about it: whatever the subtleties of policies and practices on language in the schools, a very large majority of former residential school students recall their coerced acquisition of English as a scarring experience. No sensitive student of the history of residential schools is likely to forget that reality.

At the same time, a desire to be sensitive to such traumatic phenomena should not drive analysts into being insensitive or unjust towards the non-Native participants in the tale. The historical reality of residential schooling is not that it was a seamless and untroubled partnership between crown and altar against the interests and well-being of Aboriginal populations. There were important, if subtle, differences in objectives between government and church. For the state, the reduction and elimination of financial liability for status Indian populations, especially those in treaty, was the overriding preoccupation. However, for missionaries of all denominations, the schools represented not an opportunity to improve non-Native Canada's bottom line, but a chance, with governmental support, to save Aboriginal souls for Christ and assist Native society to make a successful adjustment to a world now dominated by non-Aboriginal people and their ways.

In the complex area of the history of relations between the state and the church, the residential schools that were inflicted on First Nations and some Inuit between the 1880s and the 1970s offer important insights. The history of residential schooling indicates clearly that apparent cooperation between throne and altar masked underlying tensions and differences. Although they could agree on the tool to be used, the missionaries and bureaucrats did not necessarily agree on objectives or other means. Both sought assimilation through schooling, but Ottawa's purpose was principally financial while the churches' goals were both religious and humanitarian. They hoped that imposing Euro-Canadian ways on Native society through the coercive schooling of their young would facilitate conversion both to Christianity and to the newcomers' ways of maintaining themselves economically. The underlying differences emerged over financial commitments and language policies. The history of church–state cooperation in Native residential schools is more complex and subtle than is generally realized.

Notes

1 The encounter was captured in a photograph now found in an album loaned by school officials to Professor John Dewar, University of Saskatchewan, who permitted me to have a copy made. Given the period of St Laurent's prime ministry, the photograph is probably from the early 1950s. The support of two Strategic Grants from the Social Sciences and Humanities Research Council of Canada is gratefully acknowledged.
2 On the residential schools and the bureaucrats' careful public relations campaign, see J.R. Miller, *Shingwauk's Vision: A History of Native Residential Schools* (Toronto: University of Toronto Press, 1996), 145–6.
3 Ibid., chaps. 2–3.
4 See, for example, the report of Indian Superintendent David Laird to the Minister of the Interior, 2 January 1878, in Records of the Department of Indian Affairs (RG 10), Black Series, vol. 3679, file 12,046, RG 10, National Archives of Canada (NAC).
5 House of Commons, *Debates*, 9 May 1883, 1107.
6 N.F. Davin, 'Report on Industrial Schools for Indians and Half-Breeds,' confidential, 14 March 1879, 12–5, Sir John A. Macdonald Papers, vol. 91, 35428, MG 26 A, NAC.
7 Margaret Connell Szasz and Carmelita Ryan, 'American Indian Education,' in *History of Indian-White Relations*, ed. Wilcomb E. Washburn, vol. 4 of the Smithsonian Institution's *Handbook of North American Indians* (Washington: Smithsonian Institution, 1988), 291.
8 *Statistics respecting Indian Schools with Dr. Ryerson's Report of 1845 Attached* (Ottawa: Government Printing Bureau, 1898), 73.
9 For a summary of these polices and their interrelatedness, see J.R. Miller, *Canada and the Aboriginal Peoples, 1867–1927* (Ottawa: Canadian Historical Association, 1997).
10 A.G. Harper, 'Canada's Indian Administration: Basic Concepts and Objectives,' *America Indigena* 5, no. 2 (April 1945): 127.
11 Roger L. Nichols, *Indians in the United States and Canada: A Comparative History* (Lincoln and London: University of Nebraska Press, 1998), 225–6;

Frederick E. Hoxie, *A Final Promise: The Campaign to Assimilate the Indians, 1880–1920* (Lincoln and London: University of Nebraska Press, 1984), esp. chap. 6.

12 *Constitution Act (1867)*, sec. 91 (24).

13 Memo of D.C. Scott to Acting Deputy Minister, 28 June 1892, Black Series, vol. 3879, file 91,833, RG 10, NAC.

14 Miller, *Shingwauk's Vision*, 390–2.

15 House of Commons, *Debates*, 9 May 1883, 1107.

16 E. Dewdney to Superintendent General of Indian Affairs, 14 February 1884, vol. 3674, file 11422–2, RG 10, NAC.

17 Annual Report of the Department of Indian Affairs for 1895, *Sessional Papers*, 1896, no. 14, xxii.

18 Records of the Presbyterian Church (PC), Foreign Mission Committee (FMC), Western Section (WS), Indian Work in Manitoba and the North West (IWMNW), box 4, file 68, Report of Synod's Commission on Indian Affairs, December 1904, United Church of Canada Archives, Toronto (UCA).

19 R.P. MacKay to M. Craig, quoting view of W.E. Hendry, 23 December 1910, Board of Foreign Missions (BFM), Correspondence with Women's Foreign Missionary Society (WFMS), box 1, file 25, PC.

20 Davin, 'Report on Industrial Schools,' 12–15.

21 Mark 16:15.

22 P.-F.-X. de Charlevoix, *History and General Description of New France*, trans. J.G. Shea, 6 vols. (1743; Chicago: Loyola University Press, 1870), 4:198. More generally, see Miller, *Shingwauk's Vision*, 54–5.

23 On the CMS Native church policy, see Jean Usher [Friesen], *William Duncan of Metlakatla: A Victorian Missionary in British Columbia*, Publications in History No. 5 (Ottawa: National Museum of Man, 1974), 18–21.

24 *Christian Guardian*, 27 January 1891, 51.

25 For example, A.G. Morice, O.M.I. See David Mulhall, *Will to Power: The Missionary Career of Father Morice* (Vancouver: University of British Columbia Press, 1986), esp. 20–1.

26 Parliament, Special Joint Committee of the Senate and the House of Commons on the Indian Act, *Minutes of Proceedings and Evidence 1947*, 952. The speaker was Joseph Dreaver of the Union of Saskatchewan Indians.

27 For a brief explication of the point, see Miller, *Shingwauk's Vision*, 408–9.

28 For example, on the west side of Vancouver Island. See J.L. Bradley, Supervisor of Indian Missions in the Diocese of Victoria, Report on West Coast Missions, March 31–April 28, 1944, 10–1, series 1, box 9, file 4, Archives of St Paul's Province of Oblates, Vancouver (Oblates-Vancouver).

29 Miller, *Shingwauk's Vision*, 390–2.

30 Copy of report of Special Joint Indian Commissioners, 1858, Manitoulin Island, 230, Rev. E. O'Flaherty Papers, file 'Hanipaux-Ferrard Report 1858,' Regis College Archives, Toronto; Rev. J. Paquin, S.J., 'Modern Jesuit Indian Missions in Ontario,' 181 and 195, ibid. It was not completely clear if the government instruction to use only English was inspired by opposition to the use of an Indian language or by the use of French along with some English in the Manitoulin Island schools.

31 Report of the Department of Indian Affairs 1894, *Sessional Papers*, 1895, no. 14, 248–9. The entire curriculum is in ibid., 246–9.

32 George Forbes, O.M.I., to Father Provincial, 4 August 1940, series 1, box 9, file 3, Oblates-Vancouver. Father Forbes continued, '(his "proof" was that the Blessed Virgin spoke to St. Bernadette in French, – which she didn't).'

33 *Acte Général de Visite des Missions Indiennes du Nord-ouest Canadien* (Rome: Maison Générale, 1936), 49, 52, 56, 93; *Acte de la Visite Générale de la Province du Manitoba* (n.p., 1941), 72, 77; *Acte Général de la Visite de la Province d'Alberta-Saskatchewan* (Montreal, 1942), 18–23; Donat Levasseur, *Les Oblats de Marie Immaculée dans l'Ouest et le Nord du Canada, 1845–1967* (Edmonton: University of Alberta Press/Western Canadian Publishers, 1995), 196–7.

34 *Report of the [Third] Synod of the Diocese of Yukon ... 1915* (n.p., n.d.), Anglican Diocese of Yukon Records, box 19, file 3, Archives of Yukon.

35 *Moccasin Telegram*, December 1938 and January 1939, HR 6618.C73R 1, (Blue Quills), Archives Deschâtelets (AD); letter of U. Langlois, O.M.I. Vicar Aspotolic of Grouard, 10 December 1938, ibid., 2–3.

36 Codex historicus for Lestock, 27 March 1909 ('Children should learn prayers in their mother tongue, the Saulteaux children in Saulteux, and the francophone Métis in French.'), L 531.M27C 1, AD.

37 F.F. Walsh, S.J., to Provincial, 4 February 1935, Ontario Indian Missions Papers, file 'Correspondence Spanish 1926–1936,' Regis College Archives; Charles Belanger to Walsh, 19 February 1936, ibid.

38 P.W. Gibson Ponton to R.P. MacKay, 1 February 1911, box 6, file 131, PC, FMC, WS, IWMNW. The dismissed employee denied the accusation. For the school language issue in general, see J.R. Miller, 'Owen Glendower, Hotspur, and Canadian Indian Policy,' *Ethnohistory* 37, no. 4 (Fall 1990): 398–9.

39 Tape-recorded answers to questionnaire by Margaret Mayo, 16 January 1990. The Native laundry room worker, who was from Manitoulin Island, told the students that she took the job at the school to be close to her daughter, a pupil.

40 Indian Schools Administration Newsletter, November 1962, GS 75–103, series 2–15, box 34, General Synod Archives.

41 Interview with Mrs M. Anfield, widow of Earl Anfield, Vancouver, 12 September 1990. See also Verna J. Kirkness, ed., *Khot-La-Cha: The Autobiography of Chief Simon Baker* (Vancouver and Toronto: Douglas and McIntyre, 1994), 41, 100–1.

42 *Winnipeg Free Press News Bulletin*, 27 November 1907, in Black Series, vol. 3825, file 60, 511–2, RG 10, NAC.

43 *Christian Guardian*, 8 July 1914, 19–20.

44 H.G. Cook to W.R. Adams, 5 October 1951, box 11, file 15, Anglican Diocese of Yukon Records; H.G. Cook to C.T. Stanger, 9 October 1951, (copy), ibid.; J.W. Russell to R.P. MacKay, 4 September 1901, Indian Work in British Columbia, box 2, file 32, UCA, PC, FMC, WS; H. McKay to R.P. MacKay, 9 January 1901, IWMNW, box 1, file 21, ibid.

45 J. Duplanil, O.M.I., to Joseph Scannell, O.M.I., 12 July 1935, series 1, box 10, file 1, Oblates-Vancouver.

46 Eleanor Brass, *I Walk in Two Worlds* (Calgary: Glenbow-Alberta Institute, 1987), 6.

47 Wm Moss, O.M.I., to Father Provincial, 13 June 1932, L 535.M27L 355, AD. Concerning Methodist complaints at the Catholics' effective use of Aboriginal languages in recruiting, see A.R. Aldridge to A. Sutherland, 18 March 1908, Alexander Sutherland Papers, box 7, file 135, UCA; A. Sutherland to Joseph H. Lowes, 28 July 1908, file 143, (copy), ibid.

48 George Forbes, O.M.I., to Provincial, 16 August 1938, series 1, box 9, file 3, Oblates-Vancouver. Father Forbes added: 'These & other things will help us fight the Presbyterian school at Ahousat.'

49 E.R. Steinhauer to A. Sutherland, 13 April 1909, Sutherland Papers, box 7, file 139, UCA; A. Sutherland to A. Barner, 20 April 1909, file 135, ibid.

50 Ibid., J.C. Gandier to R.P. MacKay, 14 January 1902, and 'agreement' of the same date, Manitoba and the North West, box 2, file 33, PC, BFM.

51 On this topic generally, see J.R. Miller, 'Denominational Rivalry in Indian Residential Education,' *Western Oblate Studies* 2 (1991): 147–54.

52 Taped response to research questionnaire by Canon Redfern Louttit, November 1989.

53 J. Duplanil, O.M.I., to Joseph Scannell, O.M.I., 12 July 1935, series 1, box 10, file 1, Oblates-Vancouver.

6

Missionaries, Scholars, and Diplomats: China Missions and Canadian Public Life

Alvyn Austin

In 1989 the Royal Ontario Museum (ROM) organized a blockbuster exhibit of its African collections, called *Into the Heart of Africa*. The exhibit was a cutting-edge, ironic show with a suitably postmodern focus: the transformation of an artefact from 'ritual object to missionary souvenir and finally to museum specimen.'[1] It invited viewers to analyse the museum itself as a 'text,' a 'fiction' created by the curator, the objects on display, and the visitor. 'Museums are often accused of being cultural charnel houses, full of the remains of dead civilizations,' curator Jeanne Cannizzo wrote in the catalogue, and are often 'charged with cultural vandalism, represented by their collections of decontextualized objects.'[2] Almost as soon as the exhibit opened, 'there was yet another transformation,' as the artefacts changed 'from museum specimen to political symbol.'[3] At a time of racial tension in Toronto, a group calling itself the Coalition for the Truth about Africa started picketing the museum, which led to police confrontations and abject apologies from the ROM.

For all its talk about contextualization, *Into the Heart of Africa* was disconcertingly ahistorical in its understanding of missionary motives. The 'deconstructing' of museum collections as a way of gaining insight into the imperialist ideology of those who collected them has been a small but important theme in postcolonial studies. But, as mission historians are discovering, in the complexities of the postcolonial world – at a time when scholars from Asia and Africa are coming to Canada to reconstruct their own past, because their own archives have been destroyed – a narrow focus on imperialism is a constricting lens through which to view the missions enterprise and, indeed, the deconstructing of missionary ethnology.[4]

Museums are assembled in bits and pieces, over a long period of time, and thus a city gets the museum it deserves. 'Toronto the Good,' the rich, imperialist, evangelical city of churches, headquarters of many mission societies, got the Royal Ontario Museum, which has become, for better or worse, a vast storehouse of missionary collections. The founder and first curator was a former missionary, Charles Trick Currelly, and its first acquisitions were the 'missionary cabinets' of the university seminaries. Since then, missionary collections have continued to come in. The Far Eastern Department, in particular, Textiles and Anthropology, are filled with artefacts from other lands: the African collections showcased in *Into the Heart of Africa*, the Kathleen and Roy Spooner collection of Sichuan blue and white textiles, Lewis Walmsley's snuff bottles. For years, a baleful stuffed panda, courtesy of Leslie Kilborn, stood at the entrance to the foreign mammalogy gallery. Occasionally a box of figurines and bound-feet shoes arrives from small-town Ontario, the last remains of some maiden aunt. And the collections keep coming: in 1997 Tyndale Seminary (formerly Toronto Bible College) cleared out its attic and sent the ROM a box or two of 'curios.'[5]

This chapter takes a historical approach in keeping with the theme of this volume: it attempts to trace, in museological terms, the trajectory of one aspect of Canada's Protestant missionary enterprise in public life from the late nineteenth century, when missions were at their height of influence, to the beginning of the twenty-first, when they have virtually become eclipsed. It examines a set of objects in the ROM, its world-famous Chinese collections, which, though with less publicity than its African, also made the transition from missionary collection to political symbol. Rather than concentrate on the objects themselves, the study uses them as signifiers of the three generations of Canadian missionaries and their children who collected, classified, donated, and displayed (or did not display) them. In the process, it suggests avenues for future research, not least of which is the question, how do museums, places of special authority as repositories of public memory, display and interpret *specifically religious ideas* which are no longer acceptable today to a diverse multicultural audience?[6] In the 1990s, the three collections I examine have been rehabilitated – 'reeducated' in Marxist terminology – to build bridges between Canada and Asia, as well as between Canadians of Asian ancestry and older Canadians – 'white liberals' and New Age seekers – who come to contemplate the serene and exotic 'Other.' In the process, the artefacts have been stripped of their original doubly religious (as idol and trophy) context.

The first two parts of this chapter examine three missionaries at the turn of the twentieth century out of many whose collections ended up in the ROM. Each collected for a different purpose: George Leslie Mackay tried to rescue the dying culture of Taiwanese aboriginals in the 1890s; Bishop William C. White, a man of dignity and power, was purchasing agent for a large public museum; and James Mellon Menzies, a quiet scholar, helped create the science of archaeology in China. Nevertheless, each collected for a religious purpose, and the artefacts assumed an almost devotional aspect in their lives as they delved deeper into Chinese culture. As their collections passed from private to public, they were decontextualized and deconstructed at each stage of their transformation, subjected to rigid taxonomies and Western aesthetics either to refute the theory of evolution or to prove it.

The final part of the chapter broadens the focus from the ROM to examine a circle of missionaries' children – the so-called mish kids – who affected Canadian public life after the Second World War as scholars and diplomats. Within the Department of External Affairs, a small group of 'old China hands,' who had been born and raised in China before the revolution, formed an élite cadre who tried to shape a distinctive Canadian foreign policy, conciliatory not confrontational, international, and humanitarian. Foremost among them was Arthur Menzies, son of James Menzies the archaeologist, who donated his father's oracle bones to the ROM and in his own right was appointed Canadian ambassador to the People's Republic of China in 1980. During the Cold War, after the Communist expulsion of missionaries from mainland China, the ROM collections became pawns between supporters of the People's Republic of China (PRC) and the Republic of China (ROC) on Taiwan. Curiously, the fate of the objects reflected the fate of the missions enterprise itself, as it was consigned to the back shelf of history.

The select group of 'mish kids' examined here for a variety of reasons did not opt to follow in the footsteps of their missionary parents, but in subtle ways continued to draw on their religious heritage as they moved into secular careers as teachers, professors, social workers, writers, and media people.

The First Generation

The Canadian Protestant foreign missionary enterprise started in 1844, when the Maritime Baptists sent Richard Burpee to Burma, and the

Presbyterians (Secessionist Synod) sent John Geddie and his wife Charlotte to the New Hebrides (now Vanuatu). Although Geddie worked in a Scottish field, he inaugurated a connection between Nova Scotia and the South Pacific that lasted into the twentieth century. There was a long tradition of missionaries collecting things from far away, seen, for example, in the natural history exhibits in the Jesuit *Collèges* in Quebec.[7] Geddie and two of his colleagues, Hugh Robertson and Joseph Annand, became avid collectors. Geddie's collection in the Nova Scotia Museum is fine and very early, collected before his death in 1871, at the moment when the native culture was encountering the West. It contains rare pieces of tapa (bark) cloth and carved wooden figures. It was exhibited for the first time in 1994 to celebrate the 150th anniversary of Geddie's departure.

Robertson and Annand, collecting twenty years later at the high tide of imperialism, were more professional, picking 'representative' examples of 'pure native art' uncontaminated by hybrid 'trade goods.' Because Robertson was a friend of William Dawson, principal of McGill University, who was building a museum for the university, he donated his spears and 'pudding bowls' – such a cosy Victorian notion, South Seas 'cannibals' eating 'pudding' – to the Redpath. There, like dinosaur bones and stuffed animals, they were arranged by type of objects – Fijian spears with Roman spears, Chinese pots and Greek pots – in order to distinguish societies on a scale from savage to civilized. This organization, Dawson believed, would disprove the theory of Darwinian evolution. The ethnology department languished after his death, its collections were dispersed, research declined, and public support waned, until it was closed for forty years.[8] Meanwhile, in Toronto, Joseph Annand performed the same function as Robertson for David Boyle, the provincial archaeologist who was assembling a museum at the Canadian Institute, which also passed into the ROM in 1915.[9]

In 1871, the Free Church Presbyterians of Ontario commissioned George Leslie Mackay, who had the double distinction of being the first missionary sent by a Canadian church to China and the founder of the first distinctively Canadian field.[10] He set out 'in Abrahamic ignorance' of his destination, and arrived in the island of Taiwan the following year. Taiwan was then to Westerners a largely unexplored frontier of malarial jungles surrounded by dangerous seas, an 'unruly dependency only peripherally bound to the Chinese Empire.' Immigrants from the mainland were using slash-and-burn agriculture to create rice paddies along the western coast, and pushing the aboriginals back into the mountains.[11]

Mackay was an extraordinary figure, nicknamed the 'black-bearded barbarian,' who 'went native,' in the parlance of the day, and married a Chinese wife. He reported phenomenal success, and organized a 'peripatetic school' of 'students' and 'helpers' who followed him everywhere. 'Under a tree or by the seashore, or in the chapels,' he wrote, 'they received instruction in geography, astronomy, church history, anatomy, physiology, etc., but chiefly in Bible truth.'[12] In addition to conventional educational and medical work, Mackay adopted several 'peculiar methods' such as the practice of amateur dentistry. He and the helpers would walk into a village, set up a table in front of the shrine of a village god, sing a few hymns, then offer to pull diseased teeth, which were endemic in tropical countries. Mackay claimed to have pulled 20,000 to 30,000 teeth and, as a result, became one of the best-known and most-travelled men on the island.

By the time of his death in 1901, Mackay had built a shoe-string mission infrastructure that was without parallel in China: two missionary couples, sixty churches, each with its own full-time preacher, two ordained Taiwanese ministers (one of whom was his son-in-law), and over 3,000 baptized adherents.[13] In 1895, Japan had seized Taiwan as spoils after the Sino-Japanese War and, as it systematically tightened its control over its colony, tried to create a distinct Japanese-speaking Taiwanese identity divorced from the mainland. It instituted Japanese education in all schools with one exception, Mackay's school, which was allowed to teach in Taiwanese, and thus became the 'only high school of any standing' for three million Chinese.[14]

In 1882 with great fanfare Mackay opened a boys' school named Oxford College after his native Oxford County, Ontario, and the following year a boarding school for aboriginal girls. He gathered in Oxford College a museum of, as he put it, 'globes, drawings, microscopes, telescope, stethoscope, camera, magnets, galvanic batteries ... There are idols enough to stock a temple, ancestral tablets and religious curios, musical instruments, priests' garments, and all the stock in trade of Chinese idolatry.'[15] In other words, Mackay's first goal of collecting was to teach the Taiwanese about themselves and their island. As his book *From Far Formosa* shows, he was like many of his contemporaries, a student of the natural world untroubled by the implications of Darwin's theories. For him, the revelations of science demonstrated the works of God on earth, which he sought to share with the Taiwanese. He was keenly aware of the value of studying the natural history of Taiwan both as part of his educational mission and as his contribution to scientific knowledge. Also, witnessing what he felt was the inevitable passing of the aboriginal people's way of life, he tried to record its history and preserve its material culture.

In 1894 Mackay brought some of his 'trophies' home – over 600 artefacts – which he donated to the 'missionary cabinet' in Knox College, presumably to teach aspiring seminarians the reality of idol worship. Little did they know that in actual fact Mackay's collection systematically represented the three cultures of Taiwan: little Chinese gods, each labelled in Mackay's own hand 'Worshipped 247 years'; textiles, jewellery, and tools from the various tribes of aboriginals, including some gruesome material from the 'truly savage headhunters'; and Japanese wood-block prints, propaganda pieces depicting marching Japanese soldiers and bowing Chinese officials, set amidst surreal pink cherry blossoms. Unexpected, but not surprising considering Mackay's interests, are hundreds of tiny matchboxes filled with samples of Taiwanese flora and fauna, insects, herbal medicines, and minerals.

We do not know in what way or how long Mackay's collection was displayed in Knox College, but by the time the Knox missionary cabinet was incorporated into the ROM in 1915, it had become an embarrassment to modern ethnology. Taiwan, neither pure Chinese nor pure Japanese, was seen as a provincial backwater, as 'folk art,' compared with the high art that was coming directly from the Chinese mainland. Mackay's little gods were consigned to storage, where they sat for 82 years until retrieved for a special academic conference in 1997 examining Mackay's work. The museum's changed attitude towards Mackay's artefacts also reflected the changing judgment of the mission leaders, who were beginning to repudiate Mackay's style of 'eccentric' individualists in favour of 'all-round' team players.

Mackay and his collection recently became political symbols of a different sort, since he has come into prominence as a national hero in the Republic of China. In the early 1990s Mackay had become of interest to Taiwanese nationalists with a stated political purpose, namely that being 'Taiwanese' did not consist in ancestry, a narrow definition that would exclude mainlanders, but rather in a willingness to identify with Taiwan as a homeland. Mackay thus not only became revered in his role as a Canadian missionary but has become part of Taiwan's discovery of its real, often suppressed past: before the Japanese, before the Kuom-intang. He is a genuinely popular hero – his eagle-eyed, black-bearded visage even appears on T-shirts – a symbol of Taiwan's future as a multicultural nation, a builder of bridges between mainlanders and native-born. He is even credited as being a saviour of the aboriginals.

Mackay's collection in the ROM is considered by the Taiwanese to be a national treasure, and it too has acquired a new political significance, not out of hostility but in gratitude that he saved these few objects before the Japanese destroyed indigenous Taiwanese culture. These artefacts will be returning for a major exhibit in 2001, the centenary of Mackay's death, to a well-endowed new museum in Taipei devoted to Taiwan's aboriginal people. In 1999, when two Taiwanese anthropolo-gists came to evaluate the collection, they were astounded by its breadth and quality. They were particularly impressed with the model of a boat for which there are neither extant models nor photographs.[16]

The Second Generation

The Royal Ontario Museum, which opened in 1914, came at the tail end of the first 'Museum Age,' from 1880 to the First World War, when national and civic museums were established throughout Europe and North America. As a department of the University of Toronto, the ROM's primary purpose was scholarly, not to attract the general pub-lic. As the university shifted its emphasis from the arts and theology to the physical sciences, it needed systematic collections of rocks, trees, dinosaurs, stuffed birds. The emerging human sciences too – ethnology, anthropology, and archaeology – were museum-based, with their 'emphasis on classification, typologies, and geographical distribution, [which] required methodologically gathered and well-documented collections for research.'[17] In other words, the intellec-tual basis for Dawson's rigid taxonomies, where a museum would only need representative examples of spears or pots from various cultures to disprove Darwin's theories, had given way to an im-perial vision, in which metropolitan museums needed representative examples of whole cultures – ancient Egypt, Greece, Rome, China – in line with theories of social evolution.

The founder of the ROM, and its outstanding showman, was Charles Trick Currelly, who called his memoirs, modestly, *I Brought the Ages Home*. In the introduction, Northrop Frye commented on Currelly's remarkable career: 'A graduate of Victoria College in a generation when so many of its most brilliant graduates became missionaries, Dr. Currelly was a cultural missionary. His converts were Canadians and his gospel was preached by all the world.' Publicly, Currelly moved far from his Methodist roots, yet according to Frye, privately he returned via science to a strong 'evangelical' faith that was both mystical and simplistic: the Bible was true because evolution and archaeology proved it. 'We've got one of Nebuchadnezzar's lions here in Toronto,' he would say, confounding religious sceptics. 'Nebuchadnezzar's in the Bible, isn't he?'[18]

After graduation in 1898, Currelly went to Manitoba for two years as a missionary-in-training. He decided against ordination in order to pursue a career as an archaeologist, working under Flinders Petrie, the famous Egyptologist. Encouraged by Chancellor Nathanael Burwash, with a minuscule budget Currelly started collecting for a proposed museum for Victoria College. He charmed, cajoled, and haggled in order to amass a wide assortment of artefacts for a fraction of their value. Later, as curator, he was supported by a small pool of benefactors who bankrolled his purchases, sight unseen, to the tune of $100,000 a year.

At the time when Mackay's little gods arrived in the ROM in 1915, Currelly wrote that Canadians' knowledge of China was 'pathetically small.' He had bought a few Chinese pieces in London, including a life-sized lohan (monk) from the Tang dynasty (600–900 CE), but the treasures of ancient China had not yet come on the market. In 1918 he engaged an English antiquities dealer named George Crofts as the ROM's purchasing agent in China. Crofts sent a 'flood of Chinese material' (today designated as the Crofts Collection) estimated by Currelly to be 'ten million dollars worth of material for about a tenth of the London prices.' Some shipments weighed up to 150 tons, containing hundreds of spectacular pieces: an imperial wardrobe, a Ming tomb, endless processions of funerary figurines. 'These were exciting days, as we never knew when something of this kind would turn up,' Currelly recalled in his memoirs.[19]

In 1924, when Crofts retired, Bishop William Charles White stepped in as the museum's agent. White had been a missionary for twenty-seven years, first in Fujian and, after 1910, as the Anglican bishop in Henan with a cathedral in Kaifeng, the provincial capital. Henan was the ancient heartland of Chinese civilization, and Kaifeng had once been capital of China. It had been a rich city, filled with treasures, but by the time of White's tenure it was poor, and ripe for the picking.[20]

White's first acquisitions were the relics of an orphan colony of Chinese Jews, who had lived in Kaifeng for 1,500 years. White brought Shanghai Jews to Kaifeng to lecture on the history of the Jewish nation, even as he tried to convince them that since Christianity was the successor to Judaism, the mission would be the best custodian of their relics. In 1919 White purchased the ruins of the synagogue, but when he tried to move the stone steles to the cathedral, he was accused of theft. Eventually he bought the stones 'with no condition as to their custodianship other than that they were never to leave the province.' A stone laver and a Hebrew-Chinese scroll made their way to the ROM and today are on long-term loan to the Judaica museum in Holy Blossom Synagogue in Toronto, where by virtue of their relocation they have acquired yet another political meaning.[21]

For art collectors, the 1920s was a 'now or never' decade, a window of time during which North China was stripped of its ancient treasures. The country suffered from famines and civil wars, making it easy prey to collectors. As well, roads and railroads levelled many ancient monuments and burial mounds. White was able to purchase a large number of Bronze Age vessels dating from the Shang (1766–1122 BCE) and Zhou (1122 to 220 BCE) dynasties, and ceramic tomb figures from the Han dynasty (220 BCE to 200 CE). He collected systematically, searching for the perfect bronze helmet and chariot fittings, since every object 'held within it some key to clarify another segment of early Chinese history.' White's collection made the ROM a world-class museum, because it complemented Crofts'. As Currelly put it, 'Crofts had got very little that was B.C. and White very little that was A.D.'[22]

White's collecting practices were always questioned. According to his biographer and successor, Lewis C. Walmsley, he made friends with shady 'curio dealers' who 'hired spies and informers' to ferret out new discoveries. The dealers would not allow him to visit the tomb excavations, since his presence drew attention, and so he never saw objects *in situ*, only after they had been cleaned and warehoused. Collecting came to overshadow White's religious vocation. 'It required ingenuity, imagination, and diplomacy,' Walmsley wrote diplomatically. 'It demanded patience, insight, and a quick alertness to what was happening in the Chinese archaeological world if one were to be first on the scene of each new discovery and procure its choicest treasures. Beyond that, it called for a man of position who could deal with unscrupulous officials.'[23] The ROM's official historian, Lovat Dickson, is less diplomatic: 'Reading through the hundreds of letters that passed between [White and Currelly], one sometimes has the eerie feeling of listening to the whispered conversation of conspirators.' When the Chinese government passed a law concerning the 'preservation of all antiquities and ancient relics' in 1930, White was indignant, blaming the legislation on the 'selfish and narrow anti-foreign attitude' of the government. Nevertheless, for four more years he managed to evade the officials and smuggle artifacts to the ROM.[24]

By 1934, Bishop White's work in China was done, and he named Lindel Tsen as his successor, the first Chinese bishop in the worldwide Anglican communion. White was sixty, and a lesser man would have retired to his study. Instead, he started his third career: keeper of the Chinese collection at the ROM and professor of Chinese archaeology at the University of Toronto. By this time, as Dickson points out, his religious vocation 'was subordinated to another element in his nature, ambition for fame.' He hoped to be recognized as the scholar who assembled, classified, and interpreted the world's greatest Chinese collection.[25]

In 1932 Canon Henry John Cody, White's former teacher at Wycliffe College, became president of the University of Toronto. The two had discussed a department of Sinology, but White envisioned something grander, an 'Oriental college or hall.' He argued 'that the Chinese collection should become the basis for a major program of Chinese studies – linked to the University of Toronto – that would make the city a leading centre for research and scholarship in Chinese art, archaeology, history and other related fields.' His memorandum stressed a variety of motives: economic (Canadian softwood exports to China); political (a 'gesture of friendliness and sympathy'); and, revealing his orientalist view, 'ethnological studies of the peoples of North China and their relationship with Europe.' A school, rather than a department, would receive greater recognition, White felt, and he, as director, would have a special relationship with the president of the university.[26]

Bishop White appears to have been an inspiring teacher, who took his students 'into another world. His enthusiasm carried a contagion,' one student recalled. His Friday afternoon lectures, 'A Pageant of Chinese Life and Culture,' filled the museum theatre during the Second World War. He wrote five scholarly books in ten years, based on the ROM collections.[27] His colleagues, however, found him 'impersonal' and imperious. He and Currelly, two autocrats under one roof, seldom spoke to each other. Because White would have 'all-out rows' with subordinates,[28] he staffed the school with former missionaries who could work under his regulations. One was Ruth Jenkins Watts, who taught Chinese language; she had been one of White's favourites in Kaifeng before she married Horace Watts, later Bishop of Caledonia, British Columbia. The Watts provide a bridge to the third generation: their son Ronald Watts, born in Japan, became a constitutional expert and principal of Queen's University.[29] Another of White's protégés from Henan was Francis Tseng, a Chinese pastor and student at Wycliffe College, who would become Lindel Tsen's successor as Bishop of Henan.

Despite a boost during the war, the School of Chinese Studies never really got off the ground. It could not decide whether its purpose was to prepare 'missionaries-in-training, men for the diplomatic service and for business for future work in China,'[30] on a par with the Canadian School of Missions, or to be an academic department like Slavonic Studies. If the former, why the over-emphasis on archaeology? If the latter, why were there so many missionaries? In 1948, when White retired, the school was redesignated as the Department of East Asiatic Studies. Significantly, included in the committee which decided to dissolve the school were 'the heads of Theological Colleges and the Secretaries of Mission Boards, together with the Director of the School of Missions.'[31] Apparently, the church and mission people no longer saw the School of Chinese Studies serving a theological purpose. White's retirement marked the end of an era, as China increasingly became a political question.

Essentially Bishop White had been an old-fashioned orientalist, a self-taught amateur. His collection, though scholarly, shows he picked exotic, spectacular pieces according to Western aesthetics to demonstrate the idea of 'progress.' At the University of Toronto, out of his depth in the new academic world, he was unsure of his credentials. He was, one colleague said, 'scared to death inside when anyone took exception to his views in this new specialty.' Meanwhile he was estranged from Canon Cody and the churchmen who felt he had abandoned religion altogether. As one observer put it, 'He now talked incessantly about Chinese bronzes and bones, their dating and significance, but I never once heard him mention theology or the church.'[32]

White's most tragic relationship was with James M. Menzies, who came in 1936 to do a Ph.D. in Shang culture, White's specialty. Menzies represented a new generation of missionaries who sought to understand Chinese culture from the inside, rather than as a variant on European history. Moreover, nine years younger than White, Menzies was already a recognized scholar, the first professor of Chinese archaeology: he needed Canadian credentials merely to confirm his scholarly stature.[33]

In 1910, with a B.Sc. in engineering and a theology degree from Knox College, Menzies had joined the Presbyterian mission in North Henan, across the Yellow River from White's diocese. In 1914 he found a few fragments of ancient bones with 'chicken scratches' on them. Chinese scholars knew about 'oracle bones,' divination tools from the Shang dynasty, which contained the earliest form of Chinese writing, but did not know where they came from. Menzies discovered the so-called Waste of Yin, site of the Great City Shang (c. 1400 BCE), which became the first major excavation by Chinese archaeologists.[34]

Menzies became the foremost non-Chinese to decipher the oracle bone script, a feat that required going back through the stages of Chinese writing to determine its original meanings. 'Some of us,' he wrote, have to 'school ourselves in Chinese thought, and ideas, so that we know something of the soul and mind of China as well as the outside form.'[35] He acquired a personal collection of 20,000 bone fragments, one-third of those in existence at the time, which he bought from Chinese peasants, who called him 'Old Bones' because of his obsession. In 1934, despite concerns from the mission board that archaeology was not real mission work, he inaugurated the first university course in Chinese archaeology at Cheeloo University.

Menzies considered his study of ancient China to have profound Christian implications. 'I have directed my life,' he wrote to Sidney Smith, president of the University of Toronto, 'endeavouring to convince the peasants, students and scholars of North China that there is no contradiction involved in being a true Chinese, proud of his cultural tradition, a true scientist searching for truth wherever it may be found, and a true Christian living a Christian life in his own Chinese society. This was but the expression of the three great passions of my life, my Sinophilia, my scientific bent, and my missionary purpose.'[36] His special study was the pictograph Di (or Shangdi), which appears on the oracle bones as the earliest name for God ('Lord on High'). Seventeenth-century Jesuits had suggested that Shangdi had, like the Hebrew God, been monotheist, and nineteenth-century Protestants used the pictograph to translate Jehovah. According to Menzies, the original pictograph showed a bundle of faggots, 'the burnt offering of wood on the altar to God.'[37] Thanks to Menzies and the Chinese scholars who worked with him, we know more about Shang religion than we do about other later, less-documented periods.

Menzies had helped Bishop White since the latter had first started collecting. White assumed that the relationship would continue once Menzies became a graduate student and research assistant. Unfortunately, Menzies was shy and self-effacing, and White's treatment of him, as Menzies recalled, was 'inhuman, for he seemed to take an unholy delight in forcing me to tell him what he would then pass off as his own "research." A dozen times a day and often for long stretches of time, he would question me on the objects on which he was lecturing to his classes.'[38] In 1940, in desperation, Menzies wrote Currelly asking him to stop White from publishing two monographs he had 'stolen' from Menzies' thesis.[39] Menzies graduated in 1941 with a dissertation on bronze axes, still hoping to return to China. Since White made him persona non grata at the museum, he spent the war at the American War Information Office in San Francisco as a China specialist, formulating plans for psychological warfare. In 1945 the ROM published White's most famous book, *Bone Culture of Ancient China*, and in 1956 his *Bronze Culture of Ancient China*.[40] Menzies, who died the following year, never published anything befitting his scholarship.[41]

The Third Generation

In 1949, when the communists 'liberated' mainland China, the ROM's Chinese collections became discredited symbols of cultural imperialism. The firestorm broke when Francis Tseng, the ROM assistant who was now Bishop of Henan, denounced Bishop White in the name of the Chinese church. In his words, it 'filled him with hatred to think that Dr. White, under the cloak of religion, had taken advantage of his position, stolen those treasures from China, and grown rich by so doing.'[42] The ROM responded with the standard line: White had bought everything on the open market at current prices. If he had not saved the objects, they would have been destroyed. Besides, he 'had received no commission from the museum and had made no profit.'[43] As White's 'pageant of Chinese history' became an anachronism, his collection – displayed in dusty glass cases, unchanged for decades – became a historic artefact, sealed in time.

Arthur Menzies, James Menzies' son, provides the link between the antiquarians and the cold war generation of activists. When James left China in 1936, he gave the bulk of his collection to Cheeloo University, where they are regarded as national treasures. He did bring to Canada about 2,600 oracle bones and other ancient artifacts, which, after his father's death, Arthur Menzies donated to the ROM. It is a scholar's private passion, meticulously documented and translated. If Crofts and White had given the ROM international prestige, Menzies' bones made it unique. As well, Arthur gave other artefacts to Cheeloo University.

It was only natural that as the Department of External Affairs (DEA) expanded during and after the Second World War it would recruit mish kids. Canadian missionaries had always acted as informal ambassadors, and as embassies were opened in Asia, Africa, and Latin America, a considerable amount of their activities concerned the safety of missionaries and humanitarian aid workers. The creator of Canada's modern civil service was O.D. Skelton, who by 1941, when he died in office, had built a professional bureaucracy of generalists, highly educated men of 'all-round ability, capable of performing in widely different assignments at short notice.' Among the mandarins were a number of minister's children, such as Lester Pearson, Hume Wrong, and Hugh Keenleyside, who in their youth had been deeply exposed to the missionary movement.[44]

The first mish kid hired for his foreign expertise was Herbert Norman, a Japanologist recruited by Skelton in 1939. Born in Japan, Norman had followed the career path familiar in the DEA: Victoria College, Cambridge University, and Harvard, where he did a doctorate in Japanese Studies. Norman is still respected in Japan as 'one of the very few genuine Japan specialists in the West,' whose books are taught in universities. He served Canada with distinction as a language officer in Tokyo, where he was interned after Pearl Harbor, and during the war in 'secret counter-intelligence work.' He returned to Japan in 1945 as a key adviser to General Douglas MacArthur during the American occupation, where he was instrumental in maintaining the Emperor system. By 1950 he was named Envoy Extraordinary and Minister Plenipotentiary, a position that gave him diplomatic status with other Allied missions.[45]

With the opening of a wartime embassy to China in 1942, the DEA recruited two men who would shape foreign policy for three decades: Arthur Menzies and Chester Ronning. Menzies started a Ph.D. at Harvard in Chinese Studies and International Relations, and joined the DEA after his marriage to Sheila Skelton, the daughter of the late O.D. Skelton. He moved quickly up the ranks in Ottawa to become head of Far Eastern and American relations, where he helped shape China policy at a time when (as W.L. Morton wrote in 1946) Canada 'cannot properly be said to have a positive Far Eastern Policy.'[46] In 1980, at the culmination of a distinguished career, he was appointed ambassador to the PRC, where he was welcomed as the son of the great scholar of ancient China, who gave his collection to the Chinese people.

Chester Ronning had a quite different career. Gregarious and fluent in English, Norwegian, and Chinese, he became legendary in the DEA for his ability to charm world leaders. His parents had been Norwegian-American Lutheran missionaries in China. He returned to China in the 1920s, as a teacher in his father's old school, where he witnessed the Chinese civil war. He joined the DEA in 1943 as a China language officer. Upon his arrival in Chongqing (Chungking), he made friends with a wide range of people, including missionaries and communist leaders like Zhou Enlai, future premier of the People's Republic of China. During the crucial years 1949–51, when the West was debating recognition of the PRC, Ronning was chargé d'affaires, a pivotal person because he was the best speaker of Chinese in the diplomatic corps. After the Korean War, he remained an important international contact between China and the West, such as at the Bandung Conference of 1954, the Asian summit conference where China and India created the concept of 'peaceful coexistence.' In 1966, at the height of the Vietnam War, President Johnson called on 'Canada's good offices,' and sent Ronning as his personal envoy to Hanoi and Beijing.[47]

Other China hands joined the DEA, most from the West China mission. Robert Edmonds, graduate of the Canadian School in West China and Harvard University, succeeded Menzies at the China desk. John Small, brother of York University's bursar, was trade commissioner in Hong Kong. Through the 1950s they were strategically stationed around the Pacific – in India and Pakistan, for example, where they could meet Chinese leaders informally.[48] Their influence increased significantly in the 1960s, when Canada started selling massive amounts of wheat to China.

In the United States, mish kids in the American State Department were purged from government and universities by the McCarthy 'witch hunts.' Even scholars like Kenneth S. Latourette, the missions historian, were accused of being 'communists and fellow travelers.'[49] That Ronning continued to work behind the scenes is a tribute to the quiet diplomacy within the DEA. McCarthy's one Canadian victim was Herbert Norman. 'Named' as a former communist in 1950 in McCarthy's United States hearings, his innocence was supported by Lester Pearson, but in 1957, worn out by repeated U.S. charges of disloyalty, Norman committed suicide.[50]

Canadian recognition of the PRC was another matter on which Canadians and Americans diverged. As Pearson knew, given Ameri-

can intransigence, there was no 'compelling popular mandate' to recognize Red China. Even in the 1960s Diefenbaker did not need its
recognition to sell wheat to China. In 1968, when Trudeau made diplomatic recognition one of the features of his successful election campaign, the mish kids had their moment of triumph. The negotiations
between the PRC and Canada were held in Stockholm, where Chester
Ronning was ambassador, and were conducted by Robert Edmonds.
Since Canada was the first Western nation to recognize the PRC and
withdraw recognition from the Republic of China (Taiwan) – six years
ahead of the United States – these men had to work out a 'Canadian
formula' that could be copied by others. According to the compromise,
the PRC 'reaffirmed' that Taiwan was 'an inalienable part' of China,
while Canada merely 'took note of this position.' Canada's first ambassador to the PRC in 1970 was Ralph Collins, who had been a YMCA
secretary in Chongqing in the 1940s. The second was John Small, and
the third Arthur Menzies, both sons of missionaries.

The cold war generation had a different agenda from their parents.
For White and James Menzies, museum work had been a continuation
of their religious vocation. For Arthur and his generation, a career in
External Affairs was a secular equivalent of the family tradition of service to humankind, a career that utilized their overseas expertise without the religious overlay. Coming of age in revolutionary China, many
became student radicals in Canada, well known in the ban-the-bomb
movement and other leftist causes. As they moved into careers, they
were recruited by universities, media, banks, and companies for their
language ability and international perspective. Their role in university
life was noteworthy, and it seemed every university had one or two
professors who had been born in China, India, or Japan. Queen's,
which had trained so many missionaries and civil servants, had
Ronald Watts in political science and Roy Spooner, late of West China
Union University (WCUU), in chemistry. At the University of British
Columbia, Ross Mackay, grandson of George Leslie Mackay and his
Chinese wife (and son of George William Mackay, who had been a
Canadian missionary in Taiwan during the Japanese occupation), was
a respected professor of geology – with an interest in the Canadian
Arctic, as far as imaginable from his tropical birthplace.

The mish kids were most visible at York University, which was built
in the 1960s as a self-proclaimed 'modernist' alternative to the 'classi-
cism' of the University of Toronto. The bursar who presided over
York's spectacular growth was William Small, son of Walter Small, the
'Mission Builder' of West China. Bill Small had been one of the bright

young recruits after the war, bursar of WCUU and, with Earl Willmott, a senior missionary of leftist politics, had been the last Canadian to leave Chengdu. He became bursar of the University of Toronto and then at York, where he hired Earl's son, Don Willmott, and Stephen Endicott, son of former missionary James Endicott, the outspoken leader of the anti-nuclear weapons movement in Canada.[51] Peter Mitchell, son and grandson of North Henan missionaries, inaugurated the scholarly study of missions as a historical phenomenon, in York's world-renowned East Asia Project.

Conclusion

These 'mish kids' in Canada were working in an environment where the relationship with China had come to differ markedly from the time of their parents and grandparents. The ROM's Chinese collections offer a point of reentry into the charged atmosphere. In 1974 the PRC organized an exhibit of 'recent archaeological finds' excavated since 1949. In China, archaeology is regarded as political propaganda, since the Chinese communist state has always claimed control over history, and the exhibit used terms like 'feudal' and 'class struggle.' The exhibit was originally scheduled to be shown only in Washington, London, and Paris, but the Canadian government, pleading its 'special relationship' with China, convinced the Chinese government to include the ROM. But when the ROM suggested incorporating its own artefacts and modifying the text, the PRC was adamant: no advertising could mention the ROM's own collection. Thus, two Chinese collections were in the same building – on separate floors, one originating in the new era of communist China, the other in the old world of the missionary – and the two had nothing to say to each other.[52]

In 1980 the entire ROM closed for renovations, and was reopened in stages starting in 1982. Among the last to open, in 1996, were the T.T. Tsui galleries of Chinese art. Further Asian exhibits were opened in 1999, including a Korean gallery with missionary collections, which was financed by the Korean-Canadian community. Today, beyond the obligatory pictures of the three founders – Crofts, White, and Menzies – the ROM's Chinese collections have been scrubbed clean of their colonial and missionary past, and even of any Maoist rhetoric.

Toronto has changed immeasurably since 1980, and is now one of the most diverse cities in the world. The ROM, like all cultural institutions, has been forced to reinterpret its collections according a new political mandate of multiculturalism; *Into the Heart of Africa*, with which this chapter began, was an early attempt. The Chinese collections are perfect symbols of the new multicultural Toronto, for they bring together the Chinese diaspora. Who would have imagined fifty years ago that Menzies' ancient bones would in some small way help pave the way for recognition of 'Red China'? Or that Mackay's 'little gods' would become symbols of an independent, democratic Taiwan? Even Bishop White, the old imperialist, might be surprised that one day Hong Kong money would pay for the sumptuous galleries to house his treasures (a reality which some Chinese might consider a new form of cultural imperialism).[53]

Thus, old missionary collections, frozen in time, can be dusted off and reinterpreted for an audience which has no connection with the missionary world. One could call it an updated 'Canadian formula.' Not only can such collections build bridges between immigrants and older Canadians, but also among the multicultural communities themselves. On weekends, the ROM is filled with Chinese Canadians – mainlanders, Taiwanese, Hong Kongans, Canadian-born – teaching their children, many of whom do not speak Chinese, about the pageant of 4,000 years of Chinese culture.

That too is the legacy of Canadian missions: not all missionary collections were imperialist loot, not all missionary stories are 'postmodern irony.' Just as there was no straightforward transition from ritual object to missionary souvenir, and from museum specimen to political symbol, Canadian missionaries and their children had no straightforward means of translating their dual heritage into the secular world. The natural heritage the missionaries left behind, which over time became repeatedly decontextualized and recontextualized according to the fiction of the public museums, continues to provide a link to China in Canadian religious and public life. In a different form, that link can also be seen in the lives of their children. 'The common denominator that runs through the careers of these men and women,' Peter Mitchell has concluded, 'cannot be found in their style or specific views, but in their acute interest in China.'[54]

Notes

1 Jeanne Cannizzo, *Into the Heart of Africa* (Toronto: ROM, 1989), 12.
2 Ibid., 62, 80, 84.

3 Linda Hutcheon, 'The Post Always Rings Twice: The Postmodern and the
   Postcolonial,' *Material History Review* 41 (Spring 1995): 4–23, quotation on 9.
   This is the best analysis of the exhibit, and blames its failure on the ambiguity of 'postmodern irony' without a 'postcolonial exposé ... I cannot help
   thinking that the problems at the Royal Ontario Museum ... stemmed in
   part, at least, from the difference between Canada's relation to Empire (as a
   settler colony) and that of African nations, invaded by European (and in
   this case, Canadian) powers and subjugated to them by military might or
   missionary evangelism,' p. 7. Disconcerting to missions historians, however, is the author's conflation of 'Canadian soldiers and missionaries ...
   missionaries and soldiers,' until it becomes a trope, without questioning its
   historical accuracy. Confirming the thesis of my paper, Hutcheon also
   makes no separate mention of religion. Robert Fulford, more understanding of the Canadian historical context, noted in 'Into the Heart of the Matter,' *Rotunda* (September 1991): 'old-time Christian missionaries are now
   almost beyond the range of human sympathy,' p. 19.
4 According to Douglas Cole, *Captured Heritage: The Scramble for Northwest
   Coast Artifacts* (Vancouver: Douglas & McIntyre, 1985), missionaries were
   minor players in acquiring museum artefacts compared with traders, government officials, and 'invaluable half-breeds.' Since I wrote this chapter, a
   conference entitled 'Missions and Canadian National Identity: Missions
   and Empires' was held jointly at York University, the University of Toronto,
   and the ROM on 31 March–1 April 2000, which devoted one day to missionary museum collections, including displays of the Annand, Mackay,
   and Menzies collections. The papers are cited as 'Missions and Empires.'
5 Similarly, in Quebec, public museums have become repositories for religious collections, such as the Musée de la Civilisation in Quebec City,
   which acquired the Montreal wax museum and the Jesuit Musée d'Arts
   Chinois. Notable among new missiological/museological scholarship is
   France Lord, 'La muette éloquence des choses: Collections et expositions
   missionnaires de la Compagnie de Jésuites au Quebec, de 1843 à 1946'
   (Ph.D. diss., Université de Montréal, 1999).
6 See for example Crispin Paine, ed., *Godly Things: Museums, Objects and
   Religion* (London: Leicester University Press, 2000).
7 Archie F. Key, *Beyond Four Walls: The Origins and Development of Canadian
   Museums* (Toronto: McClelland and Stewart, 1973), 109–15.
8 Barbara Lawson, *Collected Curios: Missionary Tales from the South Seas*
   (Montreal: McGill University Libraries, 1994).
9 The Annand collection is divided between the ROM and Mount Allison
   University, Sackville, New Brunswick. See Arthur Smith, 'Spears and

Pudding Bowls: Rev. Joseph Annand and Cultural Salvation in the New Hebrides,' 'Missions and Empires.'

10 In April 1997 a symposium was held at the University of Toronto entitled 'Celebrating Mackay 125: George Leslie Mackay and His Legacy in Taiwan and Canada,' which is expected to be published as *The Legend of the Black-Bearded Barbarian: George Leslie Mackay in Canada and Taiwan*. The papers are cited as 'Mackay 125.' For biographical sketches, see Alvyn Austin, *Saving China: Canadian Missionaries in the Middle Kingdom 1888–1959* (Toronto: University of Toronto Press, 1986), 32–4; and *Dictionary of Canadian Biography*, vol. 13, 654.

11 Graeme McDonald, 'Taiwan before Mackay,' in 'Mackay 125.'

12 R.P. MacKay, *Life of George Leslie Mackay, D.D., 1844–1901* (Toronto: Presbyterian Church in Canada, Foreign Missions Board, 1913), 24.

13 James Rohrer, 'The Development of Mission Theory in the Field,' in 'Mackay 125.'

14 Hamish Ion, 'Canadian Presbyterian Missionaries in Taiwan under Japanese Colonial Rule,' in 'Mackay 125.'

15 George Leslie Mackay, *From Far Formosa: The Island, Its People and Missions* (New York: Fleming H. Revell, 1895), 288–9. Murray Rubenstein, a Taiwan specialist, calls *From Far Formosa* 'the most valuable of the missionary works on Taiwan ... that best conveys the love of Taiwan,' 'Mackay 125.' The *China Post* (2 May 1996) recommended the book, which was reprinted in 1991, as 'essential reading' for newcomers seeking a 'solid orientation' to Taiwan.

16 Trudy Nicks, 'Headhunters and Little Gods: The Mackay Collection,' in 'Missions and Empires.'

17 Lawson, *Collected Curios*, 2.

18 Northrop Frye, introduction to Charles Trick Currelly, *I Brought the Ages Home* (Toronto: Ryerson Press, 1956), 2–3.

19 Currelly, *I Brought the Ages Home*, 244–5, 247.

20 White is the subject of an authorized biography by Lewis C. Walmsley, *Bishop in Honan: Mission and Museum in the Life of William C. White* (Toronto: University of Toronto Press, 1974), and is examined in a chapter in Lovat Dickson, *The Museum Makers: The Story of the Royal Ontario Museum* (Toronto: ROM, 1986). White and Herbert Norman, briefly mentioned later, are examined in Charles Taylor, *Six Journeys: A Canadian Pattern* (Toronto: Anansi, 1977). White's papers are divided among the ROM, the Anglican Church Archives, and the Thomas Fisher Rare Book Library, University of Toronto.

21 Walmsley, *Bishop in Honan*, 137–8; W.C. White, *Chinese Jews: A Compilation of*

Matters Relating to the Jews of K'aifeng Fu (Toronto: University of Toronto Press, 1942). Originally published in three volumes, it was reprinted in one volume in 1966 and is still in print.

22 Currelly, *I Brought the Ages Home*, 249.

23 Walmsley, *Bishop in Honan*, 141–2.

24 Dickson, *The Museum Makers*, 76–7.

25 Ibid., 79, 86.

26 Ibid., 79–81; Walmsley, *Bishop in Honan*, 165–7; Taylor, *Six Journeys*, 65.

27 Walmsley, *Bishop in Honan*, 168.

28 Dickson, *The Museum Makers*, 82–3, describes White's relationship with F.S. Spendlove, later curator of the Canadian department. Currelly's successor, Gerard Brett, demanded that Bishop White 'be retired before he took up his office,' p. 104.

29 Ruth Jenkins Watts' correspondence is in the National Archives of Canada, Jenkins family papers, MG 30, D 183. Her weekly letters are the best collection of personal correspondence from China, a high-spirited commentary on life in Kaifeng.

30 Jesse Arnup, Secretary of United Church Board of Overseas Missions, to J.M. Menzies, 13 February 1948, in possession of Arthur Menzies.

31 Ibid.

32 Walmsley, *Bishop in Honan*, 169–70.

33 Although there have been rumours for years, White's relationship with Menzies is documented for the first time by Linfu Dong, 'James Mellon Menzies: Missionary and Archaeologist' (forthcoming Ph.D. diss., York University). Here, I use his earlier paper, 'James Mellon Menzies: Sinology and Missionary Methodology in Canadian Presbyterian Mission in China,' conference of North Atlantic Missiology Project, Pasadena, California, May 1998. Menzies' papers are in various collections in China, and in Canada at the ROM, the United Church Archives, and in the Bishop White Papers in the Thomas Fisher Rare Book Library, University of Toronto.

34 J.M. Menzies, *Oracle Records from the Waste of Yin* (Shanghai: Yee Wen Publishing, 1917), quoted in Dong, 'James Mellon Menzies,' 8.

35 Ibid.

36 J.M. Menzies to Sidney Smith, President of the University of Toronto, 22 March 1948.

37 J.M. Menzies, *God in Ancient China* (Jinan, Shandong: Cheeloo University, 1936), 1.

38 Menzies to Smith, 22 March 1948.

39 Menzies, *God in Ancient China*.

40 Compared with White's effusive thanks to Menzies in earlier works, he writes Menzies out of both books while using Menzies' drawings and unacknowledged quotations.
41 Menzies published a few articles in English and Chinese before he left Cheeloo, and mimeographed copies of his lecture notes have circulated among Chinese archaeologists. *Oracle Bone Studies*, printed privately in 1933, is regarded by Chinese scholars as 'the most correct, detailed, and authoritative history' of the discovery of oracle bones. It was reprinted in 1995, as an official PRC acknowledgment of Menzies' pioneering scholarship.
42 Walmsley, *Bishop in Honan*, 191–3.
43 Ibid.
44 Pearson's cousin Newton Bowles served in West China, where he was a founder of WCUU. See John English, 'Lester Pearson and China,' in *Reluctant Adversaries: Canada and the People's Republic of China, 1949–1970*, ed. Paul M. Evans and B. Michael Frolic (Toronto: University of Toronto Press, 1991), 134. Wrong's sister Margaret from 1929 to 1948 was secretary of the International Committee on Chinese Literature for Africa, based in London, England. See Ruth Compton Brouwer, 'Margaret Wrong's Literary Work and the "Remaking of Woman" in Africa, 1929–48,' in *Journal of Imperial and Commonwealth History* 23, no. 3 (September 1995): 427–52.
45 Roger Bowen, *Innocence Is Not Enough: The Life and Death of Herbert Norman* (Vancouver: Douglas and McIntyre, 1986), 117.
46 Quoted in Peter M. Mitchell, 'The Missionary Connection,' in *Reluctant Adversaries*, 6.
47 Chester Ronning, *A Memoir of China in Revolution: From the Boxer Rebellion to the People's Republic* (New York: Pantheon, 1974). See also Brian Evans, 'Ronning and Recognition: Years of Frustration,' in *Reluctant Adversaries*.
48 See brief biographies of Edmonds and Small in *The Canadian School in West China*, ed. Brockman Brace (The Canadian School Alumni Association, 1974), 148, 180.
49 Robert P. Newman, *Owen Lattimore and the 'Loss' of China* (Berkeley: University of California Press, 1992).
50 Herbert Norman is still a cause célèbre in cold war espionage. In 1986 two opposing biographies appeared, Bowen's sympathetic *Innocence Is Not Enough*, and James Barros, *No Sense of Evil: Espionage, The Case of Herbert Norman* (Toronto: Deneau, 1986), which dismisses Norman's Japanese childhood as 'unexceptional,' without examining the influence of life as the son of missionaries. In 1999 the National Film Board released a feature documentary on Norman, *The Man Who Might Have Been*.

51 Stephen Endicott, *James G. Endicott: Rebel out of China* (Toronto: University of Toronto Press, 1980). James Endicott gave a collection to the ROM, including a ceramic money jar currently on display.

52 Dickson, *The Museum Makers*, 153. The exhibition was the most profitable in the museum's history, netting a profit of $600,000.

53 T.T. Tsui, a Hong Kong businessman, reportedly gave $1,000,000 to the ROM galleries and a similar sum to the Victoria and Albert Museum in London (an exquisite but smaller collection).

54 Peter M. Mitchell, 'The Missionary Connection,' in *Reluctant Adversaries*, 5, 33.

7

Continental Divides: North American Civil War and Religion as at Least Three Stories

Mark Noll

Unlike the 1982 Canadian Charter of Rights and Freedoms, which begins by evoking 'principles that recognize the supremacy of God and the rule of law,' the United States Constitution of 1789 begins with assertions about 'the people' and contains almost no mention of religion. An even more striking contrast exists between the American Declaration of Independence of 4 July 1776 and Father Miguel Hidalgo's *Grito de Dolores* of 16 September 1810, which, like the American Declaration, marked the beginning of armed rebellion against one of Europe's great imperial powers and, also like the American Declaration, gave to later countrymen the day on the calendar for celebrating Mexico's national independence. Where the American Declaration is religiously cool, with its Enlightenment appeal to 'nature's God,' Hidalgo's *Grito* was hot in calling for the independence of New Spain in the name of Our Lady of Guadalupe and of Jesus Christ.[1]

If visitors from Mars had only those four founding documents to read, they might come to the conclusion that Canada and Mexico would be countries with a pervasive religious tone to their public lives, while the United States would exhibit a quite secular history of public life. Our Martian friends might, therefore, be surprised to explore the results of the 1997 Angus Reid World Survey (see Table 7.1), to which we return in the conclusion, that suggested the God-honouring Canadians and the Christ-evoking Mexicans were less likely to identify themselves as active Christians than their American neighbours.

The extraterrestrials would also perhaps puzzle over other artefacts of comparative history. They might in fact discover that some Christian leaders in the early United States did not at all approve of the secular character of the American Constitution. Timothy Dwight, for example,

TABLE 7.1
Angus Reid World Survey, 1997

	Canada (%)	U.S. (%)	Mexico (%)
Type of Religion			
Roman Catholic	47	23	76
Non–Roman Catholic Christian	35	60	10
Jewish	1	2	0
Muslim	1	0	0
Other/none	17	14	13
Importance of Religious Faith			
Very	34	60	49
Somewhat	29	26	32
Not very	21	8	13
Not at all	14	6	7
Prayer			
Daily or more	39	62	50
Weekly or more	11	18	16
Monthly	4	4	4
Occasionally	30	10	19
Never	15	5	10
Attend Religious Worship			
More than weekly	8	19	12
Weekly	17	28	28
Few times per month	8	12	14
Monthly	9	5	10
Few times per year	21	16	18
Once per year	14	6	5
Never	22	14	13
"I have committed my life to Christ and consider myself a converted Christian"†			
Strongly agree	18	51	18
Moderately agree	27	22	47
Moderately disagree	27	17	16
Strongly disagree	23	8	19
Has the U.S. had a positive or negative effect on your country in the last five years?			
Positive	44	–	20
Negative	29	–	39
No difference	18	–	28
No opinion	9	–	12

†In Mexican: 'He dedicado mi vida a Cristo y me considero un cristiano convertido.' In French: 'J'ai consacré ma vie au Christ et je me considère comme un chrétien converti.'

who ruled New England's conservative Congregationalists from his position as president of Yale College, pronounced the following sober judgment in 1812 as the United States edged closer to war with Britain and its Canadian colonies: 'We framed our Constitution without any acknowledgment of God; without any recognition of his mercies to us, as a people, of his government, or even of his existence. The [Constitutional] Convention, by which it was formed, never asked, even once, his direction, or his blessing upon their labours. Thus we commenced our national existence under the present system, without God.'[2] Yet they would soon discover that Dwight's has become a very lonely voice indeed, all but drowned out recently by a flood of American books from the 1980s and 1990s insisting on the sturdy Christian character of the United States Constitution.[3]

Looking southwards, the visitors might be astounded to discover that only in January 1992 did the government of Mexico revoke draconian anticlerical provisions of the Mexican Constitution, which – though honored often in the breach – since 1917 had criminalized many forms of Christian organization. At the same time, north of that southern border, as elsewhere in celebrations throughout the United States on Sunday, 4 July 1976, American citizens of all sorts revelled in the cosy relationship they held their Declaration to have established between God and the nation.

The histories of Canada and Mexico are just as firmly rooted in European history as is the history of the United States. Both have witnessed the same combination of local development and absorption of non-European influences that made the history of the United States different from Europe. Again like the United States, both have also experienced the effects of vigorous religious activity, and both strikingly illustrate the dialectical give and take of ecclesiastical influence on society alongside social influence upon the churches. Beyond these general ways in which the histories of the three North American nations resemble each other, however, there are also immense differences.

Contemplating those differences across two different borders may be a useful exercise for a number of reasons. Bilateral comparisons too easily lapse into an exercise in romantic wish fulfilment, especially for Americans looking toward Canada. As Robin Winks once phrased it, Canada is all too often 'loved best for what it is not: not British, not French, not America.' That problem is exacerbated, according to Winks, since outsiders so often construct 'an idea' about Canada which requires the exercise of imagination. But in Winks' cautionary phrase,

'To imagine adequately, one must see in technicolor and think in two languages: the first is easy for American scholars, the second difficult.'[4] Adding yet a third national perspective, not to speak of a third language, forces harder work at understanding both parallel and discordant circumstances, as well as harder thought in figuring out what to make of them. For considerations of religion and public life, an effort to view Canada from the perspective of Mexico as well as the United States should, at the least, complicate blithe and easy comparisons. Such comparisons will now be able to take advantage of a growing literature relating the religious history of Canada to that of the United States,[5] but, alas, far less for comparing the histories of the United States and Mexico,[6] and virtually none for all three.[7]

It is useful to begin by noting salient differences among the religious histories of the three nations before going on to think about the kind of edification that might accrue to Canadians concerned about religion and public life in their own country and able to contemplate religion and public life in the United States and Mexico. Of many possibilities for addressing that theme, I would like to concentrate on the blessing Canadians have enjoyed by being spared religious civil wars, and the special blessings of that relief for the character of religion itself. The focus of this paper grows out of a continuing conviction that the relative absence of climactic internal warfare in Canadian history has bequeathed a different character to public life – and to the place of religion in public life – than obtains in either the United States or Mexico. This conviction first arose for me when, as an American only just beginning to take an interest in the broader outlines of Canadian history, I happened to be present in Canada for several years running on the First of July. Particularly striking to my family and myself was the relative absence on Canada Day – at least as observed through CBC radio and television, the *Globe and Mail*, and the *Vancouver Sun* – of religiously tinged patriotism of the sort that is so pervasive for the American Fourth of July. That observation was the seed that has sprouted as this paper.[8]

General Comparisons

Since contrasts are rarely pursed from this direction, it is helpful to enumerate main differences in the three nations' religious history from the angle of Mexico. In the first instance, the religious history of Mexico was stamped at its outset by the kind of comprehensive Roman

Catholicism characteristic of Southern European regimes of the late Renaissance and the Catholic Counter Reformation. Canada, by contrast, developed under the necessity of accommodating in one nation Quebec, a traditional Old World society with church and state linked together organically, and English-language societies in Upper Canada and the Atlantic provinces shaped by both British Protestant paternalism and the American separation of church and state. For its part, the United States carried Reformed Protestant tendencies towards voluntary action and democratic polity to their logical conclusions (and sometimes beyond).

The European Christianity brought to Mexico attempted to absorb the Native population. In Canada and the United States, by contrast, Native populations were mostly shunted aside, if they were not wiped out altogether, by European diseases, loss of land, and warfare. Canadian Christian outreach to Native populations achieved somewhat less malignant results than in the United States, but not by much.[9]

In all three societies race has been an ever-present social factor. But Mexican history does not match the American experience (black-white-Hispanic-other ethnicities) or the Canadian (French-English-other ethnicities). Rather, in Mexico, three kinds of lower orders (Indians, mestizos [mixed race Indians and Spanish], and blacks) have been incorporated into a larger society dominated by two kinds of superior orders (Spanish and American-born descendants of the Spanish, or creoles).

The tensions dominating the modern history of Christianity in Mexico are those characteristic of Roman Catholic Europe; they feature the clash between anticlerical liberal rationalism and ultramontane Catholic conservatism. In the United States, the tensions are mostly the result of differences over how best to apply modern individualism to church and society. In Canada a mixture of patrician conservatism and multicultural democracy has dominated religious history. One might suggest that in Mexico a mostly anticlerical democratic liberalism has battled the church, that in Canada a potentially secular democratic liberalism was for a long time relativized by the churches, and that in the United States a sacredly sanctioned democratic liberalism has embraced thoroughly and been thoroughly embraced by the churches.

Protestantism with enduring institutions did not exist in Mexico before the mid-nineteenth century; it was then only a small factor during the next century; at the end of the twentieth century, though the number of Protestant adherents and the diversity of Protestant churches are both growing rapidly, Protestants still play a relatively small role in public life.[10] In the United States and English Canada, by contrast, Catholics learned to survive as a minority, while the Catholic majority in Quebec has always had to take account of the surrounding Protestant dominance of the United States and English Canada.

The consequence of these systemic differences is that the history of religion and public life in Mexico and Canada has been quite different from each other and from the United States. These differences also arise from the character of cross-border interactions. The religious border between the United States and Mexico was defined by the antagonism that existed in the sixteenth and seventeenth centuries between the Iberian Catholic Hapsburgs and the English Protestant Tudors. The border between the United States and Canada was defined by the strife between Catholic France and Protestant Britain in the eighteenth century. Yet after Britain, with its Protestant institutions, completed the conquest of Canada, it set the stage for a much freer religious exchange between the United States and Canada than has existed between the United States and Mexico. The one exception to that generalization is the fairly recent flow of migration from Mexico to the United States, which also builds a bridge between the religious histories (Protestant as well as Catholic) of the two countries.[11]

The religious histories of Canada and the United States share more between themselves than either does with Mexico. Where the organic, society-wide Catholicism of traditional Quebec does resemble some aspects of Mexican Catholicism, at least for the period 1840 to 1960, Quebec enjoyed a much more tranquil history of Catholic dominance than did Mexico. It is also symbolic of New World differences that, while France and Spain are separated by only a single mountain range, in North America New France and New Spain were divided by the English colonies that became a sprawling continental nation.

The Peril of Religious Civil Wars

It is difficult for an American, and maybe also for Canadians, not to display a patronizing sympathy for Mexico when regarding the seemingly endless series of religiously inspired civil conflicts that began in New Spain and lasted far into the twentieth century. To be sure, the gaze from the north must be realistic. It is not as if Canadians, for instance, have been entirely spared either religious connections to armed conflict or religiously inspired violence. Religious tensions certainly exacerbated military conflict during the American invasions of 1775–6 and 1812–14, the aborted revolutions of 1837–8, and the Fenian debacle of 1866.[12] Catholic–Protestant violence leading to fatalities surrounded the lectures of the Italian ex-priest Alessandro Gavazzi in 1853, and rioting inspired by the Orange Order once had a surprisingly expansive reach in Ontario and Newfoundland.[13] The tragic career of Louis Riel also precipitated a violent crisis which though political was also thoroughly imbued with religion.[14] The bitter conflict fuelled by Riel's execution in 1885 following his second failed rebellion endured for a full decade and was assuaged only when Wilfrid Laurier successfully addressed the wounded sensibilities of both sides. And for many Canadians, religious enthusiasm certainly soothed the deadly traumas of the First World War and, to a lesser extent, the Second World War.[15] Especially the Riel episode shows how socially corrosive religiously infused violence can be, for while it was a relatively small-scale and mostly contained incident, it left a large wound.

But all Canadian religiously connected violence taken together is but a drop compared with the Mexican river.[16] When in the early nineteenth century the Napoleonic Wars undercut the rule of Spain over its vast New World colonial empire, turbulence in Spain led to corresponding turbulence in New Spain. On the question of whether to seek independence, the Catholic clergy was divided, with the higher clergy (mostly Spanish by birth) opposed to revolution, but many of the lower clergy (mostly creoles) behind the push for independence. When the creole priest Miguel Hidalgo y Costilla issued the *Grito de Dolores* in 1810, armed conflict was the result. After Hidalgo was executed the next year, his work was taken up by another priest, the mestizo José María Morelos, who inspired widespread support but who soon met the same fate as Father Hidalgo. It is indicative of the conservative character of New Spain that, for leading this political movement, Hidalgo and Morelos were accused of fomenting Lutheran heresy, were stripped of their clerical offices, and became the last two individuals condemned to death by the Mexican Inquisition, which had been established in 1571.

Despite the suppression of the two revolutionary priests, agitation for independence continued. In early 1821 several factions supporting the revolution united under the leadership of a creole general, Agustin de Iturbide. Iturbide was a convinced political liberal, but also a loyal adherent of the Catholic Church. His vision for Mexico was set out in a *Plan de Iguala* that contained three main provisions: (1) the preservation of Roman Catholicism, (2) independence from Spain, and (3) equality of Europeans and creoles in government. The Army of these Three Guarantees successfully occupied Mexico City in September 1821, and the church hierarchy, which originally opposed independence, supported Iturbide because his program did not contain the anticlerical elements that had by this time arisen in Spain.

There followed, however, several decades of turmoil in which the difficulties of accommodating a conservative state church in a liberal polity fuelled uncertainty. The basic clash was between the ideal of Catholicism as an effective agent of social cohesion for this racially and regionally diverse nation versus an ideology of republicanism that drove successive generations of liberals to seek greater separation between church and state. It did not help matters that the United States, with its entwined commitments to republicanism and Protestantism, exerted pressure on Mexico's trade, land, and national security.

In 1843 another new constitution once again proclaimed Roman Catholicism to be the exclusive national religion. Yet formal professions of loyalty to Catholic tradition were also attended by significant strain. Iturbide, who ruled briefly as the Emperor Agustin I, was a self-styled champion of the church, but he had been deposed in 1823 and none of Mexico's succeeding strongmen were as supportive. Tension between Rome and the new independent government of Mexico led to a period in the late 1820s when all bishoprics in the country were vacated, and to another episode in 1833 when a new liberal government confiscated the property and funds of the missions, turned parishes over to secular clergy, ceased collecting tithes for the church, repealed laws compelling the fulfilment of religious vows, assumed authority to make appointments to ecclesiastical posts, and forbade political activity by priests. An immediate outcry by the clergy led to popular opposition that in turn caused many of these measures to be overturned. Only in 1836 did the papacy then recognize the independence of Mexico.

The 1846–8 war with the United States affected the church only indirectly. American intervention contributed to Mexico's tangled political history, which witnessed rapid changes of government, local resistance to national authority, and much conflict among the Spanish and creole élites. The American war was also important for the ongoing struggle concerning the place of religion in Mexican society. At one point early in the war the liberal chief of state Gómez Farías proposed confiscating Roman Catholic property to finance the conflict, but this proposal was counterproductive when it led to a clergy-inspired revolt by part of the Mexican army.

The next stage of church–state developments in Mexico began in the 1850s during a period identified by the reforming efforts of Benito Juárez (1806–1872). While minister of justice and ecclesiastical affairs in 1855, this future president issued a decree known as the *Ley Juarez* that limited the jurisdiction of ecclesiastical and military courts. The army and the church united to protest. But for a time liberal sentiment prevailed. The next year the government promulgated the *Ley Lerdo*. It stipulated that churches must dispose of all property not used directly for purposes of worship. The stated intent of this law was to make large property holders sell to the middle and lower classes and so encourage economic growth through the distribution of real property. Government leaders also hoped that stripping the church of real estate would weaken its political power. Prior to the Reform, the church may have owned over a third of the land in Mexico and controlled agricultural activity through heavy mortgages.

A new constitution in 1857 enacted several provisions restricting the church, included the provision that the Roman Catholic Church would no longer be recognized as Mexico's official religion. Implicitly this meant the legalization of Protestantism. In response, church leaders threatened government officials with excommunication. A few Catholic clergy, however, sided with the government. From this group eventually emerged a dissident Catholic church, encouraged by the then president Juárez, that eventually established a relationship with the Episcopal Church in the United States. Popular support for the official Catholic Church remained very strong, however, and the split-away body did not flourish.

In December 1857 a military–clerical alliance, under the leadership of General Felix Zuloaga, declared war on the government of the new constitution. This alliance called for the restoration of church lands, income, juridical privileges, and official recognition as the sole religion of Mexico; it also appealed for the establishment of a monarchy or European protectorate in the place of the 1857 constitution. Three years of civil war (the War of the Reform) followed. The fact that this civil conflict took place on the eve of the American Civil War and with the same prominence of religion as displayed in the American war reveals a measure of similarity in the religious histories of the two nations. The great difference separating them is shown by the fact that religion figured in the American Civil War as part of the struggle to define a

'Christian republicanism,' while in Mexico it concerned a struggle over whether a European system of church–state integration could be restored.

During the War of the Reform, the Juárez government instituted the most extreme anticlericalism Mexico had ever seen. All church property was nationalized; religious communities were suppressed; a civil registration for births, marriages, and deaths was established; divorce was legalized; and cemeteries were secularized. The government also announced both a complete separation of church and state and official recognition of freedom of religion. As if to ensure that no one misread his intentions, in 1861 Juárez expelled Luigi Clementi, Rome's first apostolic delegate to Mexico.

To shore up the ancien régime, France, Britain, and Spain invaded Mexico. Soon the Spanish and British gave way and the European intervention became solely an affair of the French, who wanted to secure payment of debts owed its citizens and to expand the empire of Napoleon III. The French action was supported by the church hierarchy, which saw the restoration of European rule as a way to regain its own power. In 1864 the French invaders installed Maximilian, Archduke of Austria, as emperor of Mexico. Maximilian, a personable and relatively liberal thinker, failed to reach an agreement with the Vatican since Rome demanded a fuller restoration of power than Maximilian was willing to grant. In the event, this Thermidorean reaction soon failed. When the French, preparing for war with Prussia, withdrew their troops from Mexico in 1867, guerrillas fighting under Juárez quickly regained control, deposed Maximilian, and then put him to death.

In the wake of war, Mexico's formal constitution reaffirmed the liberal provisions of the 1857 constitution, and even added sections confirming the separation of church and state, declaring marriage a civil contract, making monastic vows illegal, and prohibiting religious organizations from acquiring real estate. As so often in Mexican history, however, official statement and actual practice diverged. Under the long-term presidency of the dictator José de la Cruz Profirio Díaz (1877–1910) restrictions against the church were not enforced.

At the end of President Profirio Díaz's rule, the inability to hand over power peacefully created tumult that led to revolution. Several factions, including powerful *caudillos* in northern Mexico (led by Alvaro Obregón), the former bandit Pancho Villa also in the north, and the leader of southern Indians, Emiliano Zapata, worked to overthrow the inherited government. Attitudes toward religion varied greatly among both revolutionaries and supporters of the old government. But in general, the violent anticlericalism of most northern *caudillos* and the stiff resistance of the Catholic Church to liberalizing reforms created more strain between church and state over the next quarter century than had ever before existed in Mexican history.

A complicated series of coups, wars, reprisals, and revolts finally led in 1917 to the ratification of a new revolutionary constitution. This document recognized freedom of conscience and freedom in the practice of religion (Article 24), but put restrictions on the functioning of religious bodies. Free practice of religion was limited to indoor services in government-owned buildings. Religious ministry could be regulated by the state, with local authorities having the power to set a maximum number of clergy. Churches were given no legal standing. Ministers were disenfranchised and could not participate in politics (Article 130). Churches lost all property rights, while the state controlled all property held by churches (Article 27). Religious associations and clergy were prohibited from engaging in education (Article 3), and the establishment of monastic orders was forbidden (Article 5). Moreover, only native Mexicans were permitted to be ministers.

The draconian anticlericalism of these measures remained mostly a dead letter for the next nine years, but then in 1926 President Plutarco Calles began to enforce them. In response, Archbishop Mora y del Rio announced that the church did not accept Articles 3, 5, 27, and 130 of the constitution and would fight against them, whereupon the Mexican government ordered the arrest and deportation of all foreign priests. In April, when Archbishop Mora y del Rio was arraigned on a charge of inciting revolt, he offered this defence: 'We have aided no revolution. We have plotted no revolution, but we do claim that the Catholics of Mexico have the right to fight for their rights by peaceful means first and with arms in an extremity.'[17] He and five other church leaders were immediately deported to the United States. In July the Mexican bishops issued a letter suspending all religious services requiring priests, in protest of the 'anti-religious laws of the Constitution.' War followed.

The intermittent Cristero War of 1926–9 saw Catholic citizens engage in protests, riots, and armed violence against the government, while most of the much smaller Protestant community maintained its support for the revolutionary government.[18] The most public act of violence was the assassination of a president-elect in 1928 by a zealous

Catholic who was acting independently of Church leaders or organizations. President Calles blamed the assassination on 'direct clerical action.'

Finally in 1929 a compromise was reached between the church and the state, which led to the resumption of formal services and the return of exited bishops, priests, and religious. Nonetheless, tensions remained high. In 1931 most of the Mexican states passed legislation that severely restricted the number of priests allowed to work in their jurisdictions, and a few of the states suspended public services altogether. In October 1932 Pope Pius XI issued an encyclical to the archbishops and bishops of Mexico in which he called for continued protests in the face of the government's effort at destroying the Catholic Church. Less than two years later the government responded by amending the constitution to specify that all education should be socialistic. Religious organizations were prohibited from operating any schools, even seminaries for the training of ministers. Mexican seminaries were forced underground, and some Mexican priests went to the United States to pursue their education. Protestants submitted to the law and closed mission schools, but Catholics protested that the socialistic education in the public schools was anti-religious. Bishops issued pastoral letters warning parents that it was a mortal sin to allow their children to remain in schools teaching socialism. Teachers in some states were required to make 'Ideological Declarations,' stating, 'I am an atheist, an irreconcilable enemy of the Catholic, Apostolic, Roman religion, [and] I will endeavor to destroy it.'[19] The next year, in 1935, all buildings used for the administration, propaganda, or teaching of religion were nationalized, including private homes used for religious services or illegal private schools, and distribution of religious literature by mail was prohibited. By the end of 1935 there were fewer than 500 Catholic priests serving the whole nation, of which fewer than 200 were legally registered with the government. Seven states lacked either Catholic or Protestant clergy. These perilous circumstances set the stage for one of the great English-language novels of the twentieth century, Graham Greene's *The Power and the Glory* (1940), the story of an outlaw priest who, despite many personal flaws, remained faithful to his ecclesiastical vocation. Normalization of relations between the Catholic Church and the Mexican state took place only in the early 1990s.

This recital of religious-connected civil strife in Mexican history, though truncated, is still exhausting. Its evil legacy has been the overwhelming tendency to reduce religion to a matter of power, with efforts at accumulating power, hoarding power, fearing power, escaping power, negotiating about power, or defining power threatening to fill the religious horizon almost completely. It is indicative of a general situation that a recent and quite helpful survey, entitled *Toward an Essential History of the Church in Mexico*, contains almost nothing on patterns of devotion, the writing of theology, worship practices, or social benevolences, but is, rather, focused almost exclusively on constitutional negotiations and evolving patterns of oppression.[20] It is not necessary to paint Canadian religious history in idyllic colours to conclude that Canadians have, by comparison, been blessed to live out religious lives without suffering as Mexicans have suffered because of armed conflict over power.

Canadians, it can also be argued, are fortunate in something like the same way by comparison to Americans. Here it is not so much an extended history of religion directly connected to social violence, though that history too is much more extensive in the United States than in Canada. I have in mind more the religious effects of the American Civil War, which for the churches were catastrophic in nearly every way. Scholarly attention to the religious character of the American Civil War is at last beginning to come into its own.[21] As that scholarship has developed, it confirms that the lead-in to the war and the conflict itself were disastrous for religion. The situation of the prewar decades has recently been summarized by Richard Carwardine in a remarkably thorough monograph, *Evangelicals and Politics in Antebellum America*: 'When during the climax of the campaigns of 1856 and 1860 ministers officiated with equal enthusiasm at revival meetings and at Republican rallies, it was clear that religion and politics had fused more completely than ever before in the American republic.'[22] Since this statement was as true for the South as for the North, it is also true that religion, especially evangelical religion, provided much of the impetus that led to the Civil War.

In the wake of the war, and in large part because of the religious energies that had led to the war, American Protestants were not only sundered North and South but also pathetically weakened as a spiritual force in both regions. In the North, varieties of formalist evangelicalism soon fell apart into quarrelling factions of fundamentalists and modernists, both of which regained only portions of earlier evangelical vigour. In the South, with largely antiformalist types of evangelicalism prevailing, there was no inner motivation to confront the sin of racism until forced to do so a century later by a singular combination of African-American evangelical prophecy and Big Government national intervention. In other words, the Protestant energies that led, again in Richard Carwardine's words, to 'the cultivation of regional demonologies,' were energies that in the end severely compromised the character of Protestantism itself.[23]

To simplify a complex picture, the religious history of the American Civil War shows that American Protestants were enmeshed in the toils of national conflict and then the activities of war. As a result of fifty years of political action climaxing in the 1860s, Protestants came close to winning all of America – they were the ones who provided the moral energy that sustained a very long and very bloody war. But the cost was very great, since winning America could mean losing their own souls – religion exploited to fuel conflict was religion almost bound to be exhausted by conflict. Strangely, only a few individuals who remained aloof from the churches, like Abraham Lincoln, could catch the sad irony of what it meant (as Lincoln put it in his Second Inaugural Address of March 1865) that 'both read the same Bible, and pray to the same God; and each invokes His aid against the other.'

For the sake of their religion, Canadians have been fortunate indeed to be spared such conflict. Hegemonies of discourse are one thing. Hegemony by bullet and club is quite another.

The reality of what Canadians were spared by not engaging in civil conflicts like the American War between the States is far from exhausted by considering what Northern Protestants lost when they won the war. The recent republication of Robin Wink's general history of Canada and the American Civil War along with the appearance of Greg Marquis' study of the Maritime Provinces during that same conflict underscore the importance of the American war for shaping Canadian attitudes toward religion and public life.[24] If most of that shaping took place as negative reactions against what Canadians perceived as the excesses in the United States, these reactions were nonetheless still important.[25] A preliminary survey of Methodist and Presbyterian Canadian religious periodicals during the years of the Civil War indicates, for instance, that Canadians drew at least two lessons from the American conflict: first, that boisterous nationalism was an offensive failing to which republican governments were excessively prone; second, that for adjudicating major issues of public morality it was foolish to think that detailed biblical exegesis by itself should play a determinative part in public policy.

The first reaction is illustrated by a report that Daniel Duff sent to the *Home and Foreign Record of the Canada Presbyterian Church* of a visit he paid to San Francisco from British Columbia at the Fourth of July, 1864. It is clear that Duff had taken offence at American boosterism on behalf of, as he summarized it, '"Our government" – "Our nation" – "Our principles" – "Our flag" – "the excelsior of the western continent"' and so forth. In Duff's opinion, 'The Apostle's prudent and practical admonition, "Let your moderation be known to all men," seemed to be taken with some exception when applied to love of country.'[26] Similar sentiments looking askance at the attitudes on public display in America can be found with some regularity among the Presbyterians. Thus, in 1865 the *Home and Foreign Record* reported a speech by Robert Burns of Knox College in which criticism was quite pointed about 'the boasted land of the brave and the free' clinging 'convulsively' to slavery until jarred loose by the bloody horrors of war.[27] The Church of Scotland's *Monthly Record* for the Atlantic provinces was reacting much the same way when it defined the United States' 'republican institutions' as 'believing in human equality, American greatness and the almighty power of the dollar,' or when it roundly denounced the 'boastful arrogance' displayed by fellow Presbyterians in the states.[28] Such expressions may do no more than illustrate the long-standing Canadian habit of criticizing the United States, yet their appearance at that time may suggest that differing experiences of warfare are at least part of what constitute Canadian–American differences more generally.

A second striking feature of how at least some Canadian Protestant journals treated the Civil War concerns reactions to the American debate over slavery. As is well known, religious figures in the South had been mounting a learned scriptural defence of slavery from the early 1830s.[29] A striking thing in Canadian responses to those arguments during the war itself is how little exegesis Canadians pursued in rejecting the biblical defence. To be sure, some American abolitionists also disdained responding in kind to the apologists for slavery, but very many Northerners – abolitionists and moderate opponents of slavery as well as those who agreed that the Bible did sanction slavery – laboured diligently to match text with text and learned exposition to learned exposition in taking up the Southern challenge.

Canadians, however, responded to these apologies differently, not because they deprecated Scripture but because they seemed to fold reliance on the Bible into a broader set of authorities that, for them, conclusively settled the issue. Thus, for Presbyterians it was enough to evoke 'these days of Christian light and liberty' or simply to name 'that moral nightmare slavery' as a way of refuting the pro-slavery biblical argument.[30] The *Christian Guardian* of the Wesleyan Methodist Church in Canada was just as disdainful of the South's recourse to Scripture. For that periodical, in order to answer the claim that the Bible justified slavery, it was enough to highlight 'the corrupting effect of the ideas and opinions of the churches produced by those who try to make religion harmonize with slavery,' to ask, 'What would Wesley and Asbury say to all that?' and to observe that 'Slavery has sapped the foundation of moral and religious principles in the North as well as in the South.'[31] The even more strongly abolitionist *Canada Christian Advocate* of the Methodist Episcopal Church in Canada was similarly content to find sufficient refutation of slavery in 'the equality and the inalienable rights of man' that 'Jehovah has written ... on the conscience of intelligent men, as well as along the pages of Revelation'; in the self-evident 'barbarism' of the Southern way of life; and in the equally self-evident 'sinful' character of 'slavery ... in itself.'[32] In early 1863, both of these Methodist papers responded with derision, rather than with counter-exegesis, when the *London Times* defended the South by trying to show that Scripture did not contradict slavery.[33] A singular case of Canadian disdain for pro-slavery biblical exegesis came from the Presbyterians' *Monthly Record* when in 1862 it ran a short article that combined extensive denunciation of the North with a curt dismissal of the notion that the Curse of Ham applied to Africans – that is, an article that defended the South but more or less simply assumed that slavery as practised in the South was opposed by Scripture.[34]

I am almost certainly trying to make too much of a single, focused circumstance, but it nonetheless may be the case that debate over slavery during the War between the States offers an unusually stark instance of a deeper Canadian–American religious contrast. Put in simplistic terms, that contrast lies between American exaltation of 'the Bible only' versus the Canadian tendency to incorporate biblical authority into other authorities when attempting to influence public life.

The larger point to be made from such comparisons is that civil conflict of the sort that has been experienced by both Mexico and the United States has (at least to the present) been largely absent in Canada. Since it is obvious that these civil conflicts have played a large role in shaping attitudes, practices, and images of religion and public life in those two nations, it would seem apparent that exploring what Canada has been spared will also illuminate distinctive features of Canadian religion as well as other spheres of Canadian life.

But now back to the polling data from the Angus Reid World Survey. The data from this survey show that Christian adherence and traditional religion practices are more widely spread in the United States than in either Canada or Mexico. The standard approach to such differences, which social scientists pursue with often excellent results, is to examine the contemporary social arrangements that either support or undercut religious practice. Even brief attention to the histories of these three countries, however, shows that long-standing patterns of religious engagement may, even at this late date, bear on the contemporary situation. In particular, a preliminary examination of the relative absence of civil war in Canada may be enough to pose a question: is it possible to ascertain if there are long-term results for religious observance in national situations characterized by the alternatives in Mexico, the United States, and Canada?

- Mexico: many civil wars, often fought between the church and secular forces (and so creating intense loyalties in majority religious communities and active antagonism in minority secular communities);
- United States: one grand civil war fought between two sides who both thought they were specially chosen of God (and so driving religion deep, but perhaps also superficially, into national self-consciousness); and
- Canada: no real civil wars, with no domestic war-inspired trauma to solidify religious or anti-religious allegiance (and so perhaps leaving religious attachments weaker by comparison with societies that have experienced religious civil wars).

At this point, with the absence of serious research comparing the religious histories of the three nations, such a question can lead only to speculation. Yet for those concerned about the place of religion in any of these three societies, it might not be an entirely foolish question.

The history of religion and public life in Canada is its own extraordinarily variegated and important story, which deserves every bit of the focused academic attention it receives. At the same time, it is as unimaginatively commonplace as it is necessarily true to remind Canadians that no one knows Canada who knows Canada alone. Extending the Canadian gaze, not only south of the border, but south of south of the border, will only make the resulting Canadian wisdom that much clearer, richer, and truer.

Notes

1 For recent astute commentary on this contrast, see Josefina Zoraida Vázquez, 'The Mexican Declaration of Independence,' *Journal of American History* 85 (March 1999): 1364.

2 Timothy Dwight, *A Discourse in Two Parts*, 2nd ed. (Boston, 1813), 24, as quoted in Harry S. Stout, 'Rhetoric and Reality in the Early Republic: The Case of the Federalist Clergy,' in *Religion and American Politics*, ed. Mark Noll (New York: Oxford University Press, 1990), 62–3.

3 Authors of these books include John Barton; Peter Marshall and David Manuel; Tim LaHaye; Francis Schaeffer; Gary Amos and Richard Gardiner; and John Whitehead. For an exasperated response to such writing, see Isaac Kramnick and R. Laurence Moore, *The Godless Constitution* (New York: Norton, 1996).

4 Robin W. Winks, 'Imaging Canada,' in *Northern Exposures: Scholarship on Canada in the United States*, ed. Karen Gould, Joseph T. Jockel, and William Metcalfe (Washington, DC: Association for Canadian Studies in the United States, 1993), 4.

5 For Canadian–American comparisons, there has been a growing surge of scholarly attention. See, for example, Robert T. Handy, 'Protestant Patterns in Canada and the United States,' in *In the Great Tradition*, ed. J. D. Ban and Paul R. Dekar (Valley Forge, PA: Judson, 1982); Phyllis D. Airhart, '"As Canadian as Possible under the Circumstances": Reflections on the Study of Protestantism in North America,' in *New Perspectives in American Religious History*, ed. Harry S. Stout and D.G. Hart (New York: Oxford University Press, 1998); William Westfall, 'Voices from the Attic: The Canadian Border and the Writing of American Religious History,' in *Retelling U.S. Religious History*, ed. Thomas A. Tweed (Berkeley: University of California Press, 1997); and Mark A. Noll, *A History of Christianity in the United States and Canada* (Grand Rapids: Eerdmans, 1992), 545–50 and passim. The outstanding general comparison remains Seymour Martin Lipset, *Continental Divides: The Values and Institutions of the United States and Canada* (New York: Routledge, 1990).

6 Works useful for thinking more generally about comparative U.S.–Latin

American religious histories include David Martin, *Tongues of Fire: The Explosion of Protestantism in Latin America* (Oxford: Blackwell, 1990); Edward Norman, *Christianity in the Southern Hemisphere: The Churches in Latin America and South Africa* (Oxford: Clarendon, 1981); and J. Lloyd Mecham, *Church and State in Latin America: A History of Politico-Ecclesiastical Relations*, rev. ed. (Chapel Hill: University of North Carolina Press, 1966).

7 A fairly extensive bibliographical search turned up no writing comparing religious developments in the three nations, and not a whole lot of other writing, NAFTA excepted, discussing the three at once.

8 As a way of honouring the late George Rawlyk, who continues to mean so much for my understanding of Canadian–American comparisons, I am pleased to label this effort a 'preliminary probe' in imitation of George's many efforts to say something interesting about large, unwieldy, but very important subjects.

9 Compare Henry Warner Bowden, *American Indians and Christian Missions: Studies in Cultural Conflict* (Chicago: University of Chicago Press, 1985); and John Webster Grant, *Moon of Wintertime: Missionaries and the Indians of Canada in Encounter since 1534* (Toronto: University of Toronto Press, 1984).

10 See Jean Pierre Bastian, *Protestantism y Sociedad en México* (Mexico City: Casa Unida de Publicaciones, 1983); and Lindy Scott, *Salt of the Earth: A Socio-Political History of Mexico City Evangelical Protestants, 1964–1991* (Mexico City: Editorial Kyrios, 1991).

11 The outstanding treatment to date of that development is Jay P. Dolan and Gilberto M. Hinojosa, eds., *Mexican Americans and the Catholic Church, 1900–1965* (Notre Dame: University of Notre Dame Press, 1994).

12 George A. Rawlyk, ed., *Revolution Rejected, 1775–1776* (Scarborough, ON: Prentice-Hall, 1968), passim; on the War of 1812, see David Mills, *The Idea of Loyalty in Upper Canada, 1784–1850* (Montreal and Kingston: McGill-Queen's University Press, 1988), 25–8; Colin Read and Ronald J. Stagg, eds., *The Rebellion of 1837 in Upper Canada* (Ottawa: Carleton University Press, 1985), passim; Allan Greer, *The Patriots and the People: The Rebellion of 1837 in Rural Lower Canada* (Toronto: University of Toronto Press, 1993), 233–9.

13 On Gavazzi, see Terrence Murphy and Roberto Perin, eds., *A Concise History of Christianity in Canada* (Toronto: Oxford University Press, 1996), 178, 298; and D.G. Paz, 'Apostate Priests and Victorian Religious Turmoil: Gavazzi, Achilli, Connelly,' in *Proceedings of the South Carolina Historical Association* (1985): 57–69. For one Orange-inspired incident in Newfoundland, see Paul Laverdure, 'The Redemptorist Mission in Canada, 1865–1885,' in Canadian Society of Church History *Historical Papers 1993*, ed. Bruce L. Gunther (n.p.: Canadian Society of Church History, 1993), 86–7.

14 See Thomas Flanagan, *Louis 'David' Riel: Prophet of the New World*, rev. ed. (Toronto: University of Toronto Press, 1996).

15 See the opening pages of Farley Mowat, *And No Birds Sang* (Toronto: McClelland and Stewart, 1979).

16 Helpful orientation to Mexican religious history can be found in a number of places, including *The New Catholic Encyclopedia*, s.v. 'Miguel Hidalgo y Costilla,' 'Mexico,' 'Colonial Mexico,' 'Modern Mexico,' 'Patronato Real,' and related subjects; Lino Gómez Canedo, 'Religion in the Spanish Empire,' *Scribner's Encyclopedia*, 1: 187–200; Edwin E. Sylvest, Jr, 'Religion in Hispanic America since the Era of Independence,' *Scribner's Encyclopedia*, 1: 201–22; Jean-Pierre Bastian, *Historia del Protestantism en America Latina* (Mexico City: CUPSA, 1990); and Enrique Dussel, *A History of the Church in Latin America: Colonialism to Liberation*, trans. Alan Neely (Grand Rapids: Eerdmans, 1981). The narrative that follows is taken from these general sources except where indicated.

17 Quoted in Mecham, *Church and State in Latin America*, 400.

18 James W. Wilkie, 'The Meaning of the Cristero Religious War against the Mexican Government,' *Journal of Church and State* 8 (Spring 1966): 214–33.

19 Mecham, *Church and State in Latin America*, 407.

20 María Alicia Puente Lutteroth, ed., *Hacia una Historia Minima de la Iglesia en México* (Mexico City: JUS/CEHILA, 1993).

21 See, for example, Randall M. Miller, Harry S. Stout, and Charles Reagan Wilson, eds., *Religion and the American Civil War* (New York: Oxford University Press, 1998).

22 Richard Carwardine, *Evangelicals and Politics in Antebellum America* (New Haven: Yale University Press, 1993), 322.

23 Ibid., 452.

24 Robin Winks, *Canada and the United States: The Civil War Years*, 4th ed. (Montreal and Kingston: McGill-Queen's University Press, 1998); Greg Marquis, *In Armageddon's Shadow: The Civil War and Canada's Maritime Provinces* (Montreal and Kingston: McGill-Queen's University Press, 1998).

25 See Craig I. Stevenson, '"Those Now at War Are Our Friends and Neighbours": The Views of Evangelical Editors in British North America on the American Civil War' (master's thesis, Queen's University, 1997).

26 *The Home and Foreign Record of the Canada Presbyterian Church* 4, no. 1 (November 1864): 12–13.

27 Robert Burns, 'The Aspect of the Times Practically Considered,' in ibid., 4, no. 8 (May 1865): 198–205, quotation on 201.

28 Report from a traveller, A.P., *The Monthly Record of the Church of Scotland in Nova Scotia and the Adjoining Provinces* 8 (February 1862): 40; 'The Presbyte-

rian Churches in the States, and the Civil War,' in ibid., 8 (August 1862): 188–90, quotation on 188.

29 For a general picture, see Mark A. Noll, 'The Bible and Slavery,' in *Religion and the American Civil War*, ed. Miller, Stout, and Wilson, 43–73.

30 *Home and Foreign Record* 3, no. 1 (November 1863): 22; *Monthly Record* 7 (May 1861): 119.

31 *Christian Guardian*, 9 January 1861, 6; 18 September 1861, 148; 23 October 1861, 167.

32 *Canada Christian Advocate*, 31 October 1860, 1; 14 August 1861, 1; 25 March 1863, 4. The *Advocate* did run an article contrasting slavery in Old Testament times with slavery in the South, but that article featured very little actual attention to the texts that pro-slavery advocates used to defend the institution; 6 March 1861, 2.

33 *Christian Advocate*, 15 April 1863, 2; *Christian Guardian*, 4 February 1863, 22.

34 *Monthly Record* 8 (September 1862): 203–4.

Part Three

Claiming 'Their Proper Sphere':
Women, Religion, and the State

8

Evangelical Moral Reform: Women and the War against Tobacco, 1874–1900

Sharon Anne Cook

The nineteenth century in North America was a period when 'Christian rhetoric, values and morals ... permeated public discourse, shaping the focus, content and limits of imaginable popular debate.'[1] Although curiously underresearched by historians, the waves of anti-tobacco ferment throughout the late nineteenth and early twentieth centuries bear the unmistakable imprint of evangelical 'rhetoric, values and morals.' The commanding authority of evangelical rhetoric reigned supreme for a relatively short period in the extended history of opposition to tobacco use. The underlying message, however, of the evangelical anti-tobacco analysis – that tobacco usage is fundamentally a *moral* issue – remains with us still. At stake, after all, are questions of individual freedom versus control of public space, access to expensive health-care services, and assumptions about self-restraint and the ethical treatment of others. Public discourse as expressed through media presentations profiling irresponsible smokers, municipal edicts that bar smokers from many public sites, and the complaints of disenfranchised smokers who style themselves the 'new lepers,' all continue to position tobacco users in our own era as lacking moral resolve. While the modern anti-tobacco movement privileges medical concerns, the moral basis remains. The moral focus has, however, shifted from the evangelical concern with the soul to the medical interest in the body.

Surprisingly, in spite of tobacco's close links to alcohol, little academic attention has been paid in temperance studies in Canada or beyond to the particular contours of anti-tobacco campaigns or education.[2] This neglect is especially striking when one surveys the consistent interest that temperance and prohibition have held for Canadian historians from the 1970s onwards.[3] That these historians should have bypassed anti-tobacco campaigns in their own right is all the more startling when one assesses the effectiveness today of anti-tobacco campaigns as opposed to the prohibition of alcohol. The fact is that Canadian society has been much more successful in reducing tobacco than alcohol use, especially among youth.[4]

In the late nineteenth century anti-tobacco and temperance crusaders were closely linked; indeed, they were often one and the same. Both groups shared the evangelical belief that evil was a matter of choice. Tobacco users were first encouraged to smoke while drinking (and vice versa); once alcohol was removed as a societal evil, tobacco would follow close behind. Tobacco and alcohol were both seen to corrode character, intellect, and body. Notwithstanding their well-documented aversion to alcohol, many temperance reformers regarded tobacco as even more dangerous because of its slower, more insidious health and moral effects. Where alcohol almost immediately unsettled the mind and spirit, tobacco could be taken for long periods without any discernible negative results. Thus it created a false sense of well-being.

Christian Smith argues that evangelicals consistently had difficulty in defining their public program in other than strictly moralistic terms. As is the case with most subcultures, such an approach inevitably pitched them into confrontation with the wider society. Their relationship with the state was, however, ambiguous. Although evangelicals saw the primary source of sound ethical behaviour and good health as the individual's soul, mind, and character, their analysis of social maladies such as tobacco use did admit to some role for the state. Once individuals had been brought to face the error of their ways, or children had been suitably educated so that they avoided such destructive habits in the first place, evangelicals expected the state would step in to formalize moral behaviour through appropriate legislation. To be sure, evangelicals took a variety of positions on the necessity, or even the utility, of legislation. Although it was less dependent on state action than current anti-tobacco lobbying, the evangelical sector's significant contribution at the turn of the century to defining a wider public policy must be examined.

In this chapter I will first explore the particular critique of tobacco use espoused by evangelicals and the symbolic significance of tobacco to two prominent evangelical groups of late-nineteenth-century Ontario: the Woman's Christian Temperance Union (WCTU) and the Salvation

Army. Through case studies, I consider the importance of religion, class, and gender in defining these groups' ideas and actions in anti-tobacco campaigns. Second, I examine in some detail the first phase of anti-tobacco ferment in the last third of the nineteenth century and the special and defining role of evangelical analysis within this phase, followed by a brief examination of its more muted presence in the movement's second phase from 1900 to 1920.[5] I conclude that even though the period during which evangelical thought dominated anti-tobacco rhetoric is relatively short, the analysis forged by evangelical authorities on tobacco use remains influential, if uncredited, to the present day.

The Evangelical Critique of Tobacco Use

Evangelical fears of tobacco were situated in two complementary movements: 'social purity' and 'respectability.' Social purity campaigns of the late nineteenth century linked physical and moral purity in a vast program calling for adherents to avoid known pollutants to the body and soul.[6] Most purity advocates were also self-improvers, who sought respectability while at the same time negotiating admission to the developing middle class. However, those seeking 'respectability' were not necessarily also social purity advocates, but rather were intent on finding a route (through formal education, for example) to improved status and material standing. These two linked movements rejected tobacco use for different, but mutually supportive, reasons.

The Salvation Army, founded in 1882 in Canada, and the Woman's Christian Temperance Union, founded in 1874, were implacably opposed to tobacco. The Salvation Army held to a strict social purity model throughout the nineteenth century;[7] only after the First World War did Salvationists develop some interest in issues of respectability.[8] Commanding attention through colourful marching bands complete with uniforms and banners, 'Hallelujah lasses' with tambourines, and enthusiastic evangelism, the Salvation Army, rather than seeking middle-class respectability, set out to attract converts by stressing its affinity with, indeed its celebration of, working-class culture. The Army appealed most readily to single, young, working-class women who helped to establish its reputation of egalitarianism, good works, and evangelism among slum-dwellers.[9]

The WCTU, on the other hand, was motivated by questions of respectability as it developed its many-faceted educational program in support of abstinence from both alcohol and tobacco. This is not to say that it did not advocate mainstream social purity concerns; it did indeed do so, and vociferously on occasion, but the rhetorical weight of its message to young men was on the side of self-betterment. Concerned primarily with shaping self-discipline to ensure the survival of temperate behaviours, the WCTU poured a good measure of its energies into childhood and youth education. It intended its public program of education both to facilitate upward class mobility for its own lower-middle-class members and to ensure the survival of societal norms based on evangelical Christian ideals.

Despite their common aversion to tobacco use, the WCTU and the Salvation Army contrasted in many respects. The Salvation Army was proudly working-class; the WCTU, upwardly mobile and middle-class. The WCTU was resolutely women-centred; the Army was egalitarian and welcoming of female officers but imbued with a masculine ethic that stressed spiritual and moral warfare. The Salvation Army remained revivalist long after the WCTU had abandoned boisterous meetings; the objective of most of its work and writings was to bring adherents to Christ, and tobacco use was inconsistent with its vision of a saved soul. In general, the WCTU was more interested in public programs to effect institutional changes.

Founded as a revivalist women's single-issue group focused on alcohol abstinence, the WCTU had early broadened its mandate to include many other issues. Thus, it developed its particular calling by supporting public and extracurricular education in temperance, anti-narcotics (including tobacco), youth literacy, domestic and industrial arts training, youth and adult healthy 'lifestyles,' and instruction in social purity for young people. It accomplished its goals through a network of youth and adult groups, contests and pamphlets, public and private lectures, journals, and study and discussion groups. While less committed to childhood education than the WCTU, the Salvation Army also offered literacy training and job-related education, anti-tobacco clubs, and published *The Young Soldier* and *The Little Soldier* as well as special columns for youths in its adult periodical *The War Cry*.

Both groups subscribed to a mainstay of evangelical thinking on the use of tobacco that might be termed the 'slippery slope' argument, in which tobacco's power inevitably led to both the physical and moral corrosion of a person's constitution, as well as to adoption of the 'twin evils' of alcohol and foul language.[10] Evangelical texts also often associated gambling with tobacco, alcohol, and crude language. The physical danger of tobacco, temperance advocates argued, was that its users acquired an 'unnatural' appetite for stimulants that would drive them, particularly young people, into alcohol and drug use and thus away from God. 'The tobacco road, though reeking with smoke and the filthiest kind of filth, is the broadest, and by all means the shortest and most direct route to that river of death, Alcohol.'[11]

Evangelical anti-tobacco campaigns of the first two-thirds of the nineteenth century targeted all men, especially mature men. By the last third of the century, however, evangelicals identified young men as the most worthy recipients of anti-tobacco rhetoric. Both the WCTU and Salvation Army fully expected young men to lead the next generation; neither assumed that women, young or old, used tobacco. They reasoned that if the reduced prospects attendant upon tobacco use and the terrors held by this signal impurity could be impressed upon future male leaders while they were still children, young men, in self-interest, would see the merits of an abstemious life. Not until the 1920s, after evangelical leadership of the movement had been lost, were women, young or mature, seen as prey by tobacco interests.

In spite of their dependence on young men to carry the anti-tobacco message into the next generation of families, both the Salvation Army and the WCTU had difficulty in finding effective means to appeal to this resistant sector of the unchurched, and often hostile, population. The Salvation Army firmly held to an anti-tobacco program at a time when tobacco was – and remains – a defining component of male working-class culture. Male youths, defined by the Salvation Army both as 'earnest young Christians who failed to find satisfying outlets for their energies in the regular churches'[12] and as the local toughs,[13] were far more difficult to reach than women. The WCTU, too, habitually complained that its youth groups, including the Bands of Hope and Loyal Temperance Legions, were dominated at all levels by female members. It could accomplish a certain amount 'through the influence and companionship of the young women'[14] of the Young Woman's Christian Temperance Union, but in the arena of tobacco use, it struggled to find routes directly through to young men. The strategy it hoped to employ was for mothers to train young men so that 'when they grow up they shall be ours in sympathy, ours in pure habits, and ours as the coming leaders of the future in State and philanthropic work.'[15] The amount of ink devoted by WCTU members in the union minute books to their frustration in reaching this goal, however, illustrates the enormity of the challenge.

Evangelicals prohibited the use of any product that compromised a person's health or ability to engage in conversion, the work of the soul. At least part of the danger presented by products like tobacco was that people, particularly male youths, quickly became habituated to their use, ceasing to devote necessary attention to spiritual growth. Efforts to break the habit were similarly distracting; bad habits had to be broken wilfully and permanently. In the view of the Salvation Army: 'To break off gradually is only to tamper with the serpent and intensify the appetite. Come to Jesus! He will break the galling yoke of bondage, and liberate you from a habit so destructive to spiritual and physical health.'[16] The WCTU noted that '[b]oys who use tobacco almost invariably begin a practice of deception, which robs them of integrity of character.'[17] In addition, the sinner would experience the dreadful physical destruction attendant on tobacco use. Worse, he did so with a lost soul and certitude that death would result from his untrammelled slide into evil.

Both organizations took up the theme that friends played a vital role in influencing an individual towards either good or evil. The Army's paper, *The War Cry*, was explicit about the pivotal role of friends in abetting young men's moral backsliding through tobacco:

> The invitation of a friend often induces young converts to take just 'one smoke,' and on the impulse of the moment, they forget the vows they made to God, forget the good resolutions they made at the foot of the Cross, never to use tobacco again ... He tries to convince himself there is no harm in a smoke, reasons the matter over, but feels condemned, as he hands back the pipe to his friend, resolves in his mind never to give way to the temptation again; but instead of coming to God for pardon and Deliverance From The Very Desire, tries in his own strength to 'fight the foe' ... The terrible appetite is now fully aroused, and feeling unable (in his own strength) to battle with the enemy, he again yields to the temptation, and the 'tobacco fiend' with grip like steel, holds him in its loathsome embrace, fastens its poisonous fangs so tenaciously around him that escape seems impossible, and he begins to realize His Peace With God is Broken.[18]

The hopelessness of fighting the 'tobacco fiend' alone was clear: one needed strong friends to weld one's 'peace with God.' Hence, both the Salvation Army and the WCTU resolved to offer such a supportive network to young men. The Army provided fellowship through rallies, revivals, and entertainments. The WCTU sought to create a supportive system for weakened young men through the influence of women's

groups, particularly the YWCTU, whose young women would reinforce their male friends' determination to avoid tobacco.

The evangelical position was characterized more by efforts to
achieve personal commitment to behavioural change than by reliance
on anti-tobacco public campaigns to declare the vice illegal – although
the WCTU did argue for this at various times.[19] The emphasis in social
issues often remained on *personal* redemption and responsibility rather
than on wholesale public reform. Female activism defined as personal-
ized pressure was an effective weapon in the fight against tobacco: the
Newmarket WCTU recording secretary, for example, noted in the minutes of one meeting that 'the WCTU means business' and that 'it was
suggested that ... members ... fairly [besiege] the [tobacco] inspector
until he does his duty in order to get peace.'[20] The tobacco inspector
would be convinced to do his duty not through formal edict alone,
which could be all too easily ignored, but through the moral suasion of
WCTU women to do what he knew in his heart was his responsibility.
Thus, the state could help in the war against tobacco, but it could not
be trusted to do so unless evangelical women remained vigilant,
watchful, and insistent.

Phase One of Anti-Tobacco Activism: 1804–1900

North American anti-tobacco campaigns progressed through several
fairly distinct phases, of which only the first two are discussed in this
paper. The first, spanning most of the nineteenth century, saw anti-
tobacco interests pitted against the presumed therapeutic value of
tobacco. The specifically evangelical critique in this era dominated for
about the last third of the nineteenth century and centred on the spiritual erosion accompanying the physical damage wreaked by tobacco.
Although evangelicals figured prominently in anti-tobacco activism
only during this first phase, this formative period defined many of the
issues that came to shape the modern debate about tobacco use.

In the nineteenth century, tobacco was consumed in a variety of
forms: as snuff; chewed in plugs; and smoked in pipes, cigars, and
some cigarettes. Advocates posited that tobacco had much to offer to
the over-burdened men of the world: 'as a narcotic it absorbs and
removes all sorts of natural obstructions and malignities that trouble
man, and as a stimulant it is of use and delight in calling forth new
forces of life and activity.' Pro-tobacco literature of the time commonly
argued that tobacco operated as a catalyst for summoning renewal and

creativity, and employed the imagery of *expansion*, a widening of life view and possibilities to meet the challenges of a new era: 'A sociable smoke opens the flow of soul where frozen dullness reigned before. It makes men take larger, loftier views of principles and persons. It induces patience and mutual forbearance, generosity and general good feeling.'[21] Such maxims, probably targeting equally working and middle-class men, presented the values of the 'progressive' male-centric nineteenth-century world. This panegyric – characterized by conviviality, tolerance, and nimble-wittedness – directed the tobacco user to the product's value for his 'soul,' a term that here had a quite different meaning from its evangelical connotation.

As a bonus, tobacco was declared to be especially beneficial to digestion by stimulating the secretion of saliva and gastric, pancreatic, and intestinal juices. It presumably also saved on nervous energy, reducing the disintegration of muscular tissue, served as an alternate source of nutrition in times of privation, soothed overly weary workers and promoted civilized discussion and social interaction among men.[22] Thus, tobacco could lay claim to more than personal benefits: all of civilization found advantage in the male tobacco user's harmless diversion.

Rhetorically, this position was difficult for anti-tobacco forces to discredit. The high and optimistic ground seemed fully occupied by those calling for a benign relaxant for dutiful leaders, those most heavily burdened with society's cares. In opposition to these bucolic notions of tobacco's benefits ranged the anti-tobacco forces, who insisted that the use of the nicotine narcotic resulted in systematic and cumulative poisoning of the body. Dr Benjamin Waterhouse had first put this hygienic argument to the American public in 1804. He condemned tobacco use because it was 'unnatural,' causing 'muscular indolence,' impaired senses, damaged teeth, and 'consumptive' afflictions.[23] By mid-century, temperance advocates and the broadly based evangelical community assumed leadership of the anti-tobacco forces. Giving the hygienic approach a moral twist, they reshaped the message and methodology of anti-tobacco rhetoric to put the case to young men more effectively, and to address their own interests. By the early twentieth century, the evangelical argument had reached its mature form, as illustrated in the Salvation Army's *The Young Soldier*:

> The charm of a cigarette to a grown person lies in its soothing effect, they say, on the over-wrought nerves and fagged brain. Now, however lawful this excuse may be for a man who has spent his days in hard, physical, or

mental labour, every boy will understand that for a healthy lad to need a soothing drug at any time, even at night, is ridiculous. If he wants soothing let him buy a baby's dummy at the chemist's or ask his mother *To Rock him to Sleep!*[24]

To deliver this message, youth-oriented popular literature and school curricula were developed during the 1880s and 1890s, especially after Ontario's Department of Education mandated Scientific Temperance Instruction courses for public school children. In addition to compulsory physiology courses, both the WCTU and the Salvation Army taught formal oratorical skills in their youth groups. Children typically committed to memory moral tales and anti-tobacco poetry for public competitions. The WCTU also provided large quantities of tailor-made curricula and pamphlets to Sabbath School Superintendents in the hope that anti-tobacco literature would be adopted in that setting. Similarly, the Salvation Army's 'Young Soldier Anti-Tobacco Legions' offered young men pledge cards, activities, and companionship. Boys in these youth groups sang special anti-smoking songs with melodies that mimicked popular working-class tunes.

This broad anti-tobacco literature adopted a consistent form, modelled on the familiar structure of the conversion narrative. Even avowedly secular texts, such as school textbooks, were strongly influenced by conversion structures. If the conversion trope represented a point of similarity underpinning anti-tobacco literature, the major difference between Salvation Army and WCTU literature was located in the gender and qualities of the narrator who brings the sinner safely through doubt and pain to a tobacco-free life. An essay by Methodist revivalist H.T. Crossley, who often spoke at WCTU functions, provides one example:

In conversation with a Methodist, I asked, 'When did you begin to use tobacco?' He replied, 'When I was fifteen.' 'You remember Paul said, "when I became a man, I put away childish things." Having been so childish as to begin to use tobacco, when a boy, why don't you now, as a man, put away the habit?' He answered, 'I have often *tried* to do so, but failed every time.' I remarked, 'Certainly persons who only *try* to stop fail, but those who firmly resolve, "I'll quit," have success.' Grasping my hand, he said, 'I'll quit now, and never chew or smoke again.'

Two weeks later I asked him, 'How goes the battle?' He replied, 'There

has been no battle. That night I renewed my vow to God, and asked Him
to help me; and from then till now I have had no desire to smoke or chew.
Christ gave me the victory without a struggle.'[25]

The form of such anecdotes parallels the evangelical conversion process: confronted with sin, the victim undergoes a spiritual catharsis similar to conversion, with the support of a Christ-like example and
temporal aid from other saved Christians. The message is strongly rem-
iniscent of temperance literature, in which victims of alcoholic sub-
stances or untoward ideas are confronted with their sin. After a weak
defence of his benighted behaviour, the sinner readily capitulates to a
stronger, temperate moral force, often in the person of a spunky temperance worker. The sinner resolves to mend his ways by taking up a clean
life, and is loyally supported through various trials by the same temperance worker, who is thus able to report on the reformed life. In keeping
with evangelical Arminian theology, the battle is won because of the
support of a superior person, who works as the agent of divine grace.
  Such an intermediary, who also implicitly serves as an agent of middle-class respectability, is not, however, present in the Salvation Army
anti-tobacco trope modelled on the evangelical conversion narrative.
Consider this example of an Army song:

Tobacco
By Lieut. Jas. Forman
Tune – *Gird on the armor*

I have read of men of health,
But this weed has caused their death,
Who now beneath the sod are lying;
When the thought it comes to me,
Can a victim be set free,
From a thing so terribly degrading?

Chorus
Oh, yes, there is freedom,
And cleansing for you,
It matters not whether you smoke or chew,
If you will but come and bow,
At the Cross of Calvary now,
Jesus can set you free forever.

There are many would delight,
Could they prove the practice right,
That to all men it was a blessing.
But the thing it is impure,
And the Lord has brought a cure,
Come to Jesus now for cleansing.

There's salvation now for you,
From the filthy stuff you chew;
Vain it is to think it makes you stronger.
If you will for Jesus fight,
You yourself must first be right,
Come to Jesus now, wait no longer.[26]

Sung with other young men in one of the Army's youth groups, this song demonstrates how the theology and language of conversion have been popularized into the victory over tobacco. The middle-class reformer has been replaced by the sinner personally fighting against the power of darkness in the form of tobacco chewing.

The Salvation Army's internal reporting left no doubt about the cosmic connection between tobacco and moral perdition, as well as the possibility of holiness and freedom from all 'inbred sin.' In 1889 *The War Cry* reported on a Salvation Army meeting:

We have laboured faithfully the past week and have seen results ... on Friday night at the holiness meeting a dear brother gave up the pipe and tobacco and all inbred sin, and the very God of Peace sanctified him wholly, and we pray God 'that his whole spirit, and soul, and body be preserved blameless unto the coming of the Lord Jesus Christ' ... There are a large number here convicted for the blessing of holiness but are letting their friends come between them and God ... Every soldier is blood-and-fire and do all they can to bring souls to Jesus and the Lord does His part; so if sinners will only do their part they shall be saved.[27]

In late-nineteenth-century WCTU anti-tobacco literature, the Christian helper is almost always a mother, pure and unblemished, who reminds the penitent of his own mother. Typically, the WCTU mother figure encounters the tobacco-using (young) man through her distribution of temperance materials. In being provided with an opportunity to talk seriously about these matters, 'mother' and 'son' move to ever-deeper levels of conversation during which the young man demonstrates a hunger for this mother's high regard and spiritual guidance. Frequently, the mother in return extracts a promise of reform from the wayward youth, and immediately receives it.[28]

In contrast, the literature of the Salvation Army, which had welcomed women into its ranks as leaders, provides no such honoured role for the mother, or for women generally. While also utilizing the conventions of the conversion narrative, Salvation Army anecdotes portray women as being as likely to use tobacco and alcohol as their menfolk. In one report from a 1910 *War Cry*, 'Old Joan' is presented as both a drinker and a smoker, habits which had made 'horrible her very appearance,' even '[b]eyond redemption.' After the Army 'opened fire' on the town, a recently converted young man promises to pray for Joan, offering her the validation she needs. 'Can it be true that someone really thinks enough of me to pray for me?' she wonders incredulously. Indeed, only a few days later, Joan, 'the despair of the town, knelt at the penitent-form and learned to pray for herself.'[29]

In keeping with the WCTU's emphasis on respectability, H.H. Seerley at the turn of the century surveyed the costs of tobacco to the young man's physical welfare in his pamphlet *The Tobacco Habit and Its Effect upon School Work*, featured in the National WCTU Signal Lights series. Boys were told that if they took up the tobacco habit before reaching maturity, they would face stunted growth, indigestion, impaired taste, defective eyesight, dull hearing, 'nervous affections,' and heart disease. Worst of all, however, smokers lost the ability to concentrate, remember, or comprehend their studies: 'The faculties of a boy under the influence of the narcotic seem to be in a stupor, and since depraved nerve power stultifies and weakens the willpower, there is but little use for the teacher to seek to arouse the dormant, paralyzed energies, or to interest and foster the fagged desire.'[30] In such educational literature, the WCTU's relationship to the state comes to the fore, and the gradual shift from religious morality to scientific hygiene begins to take shape.

To demonstrate this relationship, one must look to the structure and message of school texts used for teaching hygiene and Scientific Temperance Instruction during this first era of anti-tobacco activism. By the time anti-tobacco lessons were first mandated in the Ontario curriculum in the 1890s,[31] the list of the physical ravages of tobacco was lengthening, and becoming increasingly terrifying. Effects were said to include 'faintness, nausea, vomiting, giddiness, delirium, loss of power of the limbs, general relaxation of the muscular system, trembling, complete prostration of strength, coldness of the surface, with cold, clamming perspiration, convulsive movements, paralysis, and death.' But the real dangers, one textbook notes, were not physical distress or intellectual torpor but rather one's 'powerlessness to improve the character or promote the welfare of the person' using tobacco.[32] The fundamental danger, then, was damage to a young man's character. Though less sharply focused than the evangelicals' discourse, the textbooks largely adopted the evangelical analysis of the core danger of tobacco, which lay in its soul-destroying properties. This emphasis on character in the anti-tobacco educational literature helped set the stage for the second period of activism.

Phase Two: 1900–1920

A second era of anti-tobacco activism occurred between 1900 and 1920. Mindful of the rigours of the First World War, some public perceptions held that fighting men needed restorative pastimes, and that tobacco was a relatively benign choice for this necessary diversion. The anti-tobacco authorities in this period were scientific researchers who investigated the link between physiological stamina and smoking, by now the major way in which tobacco was consumed. The contested terrain therefore shifted from issues of medical and spiritual welfare to those associated with physiological 'efficiency.' Where the evangelical community had been central to the campaigns during the first period, it was marginalized in almost all respects in the second. Yet, echoes of the earlier evangelical analysis were still present in the second period, especially in moralisms contained in school texts and in popular literature.

The most important single textbook of the late nineteenth century, and the one that endured longest in hygiene and Scientific Temperance Instruction courses, was Dr William Nattress' *Public School Physiology and Temperance*. Nattress' text is especially interesting because it foreshadows the blend of pre- and post-1900 hygiene textbooks. His medicalization of tobacco represents the dominant discourse in educational materials in the second phase of the anti-tobacco movement in the 1910s and 1920s. At the same time, Nattress' treatment harkens back to the evangelical assumptions that had grounded earlier literature on tobacco use. For example, after a scientific summary of the skeletal system, Nattress notes in his conclusion that both alcohol and tobacco use stunt skeletal growth. He ends this discussion with an illustration that

recasts the old evangelical stress on moral responsibility into eugeni-
cist rhetoric:

> One physician reports a child five years of age, who measured only two
> feet three inches, and weighed twenty-two pounds; and he says further,
> that he has known such children to live to twenty and over, and still
> remain permanent infants. Such are examples of a species of degeneracy,
> and are evidences of the visiting of the sins of the fathers upon the chil-
> dren, which may extend even unto the third and fourth generations.[33]

In his *Domestic Hygiene and Rational Medicine*, a home-care book
prominently featured in the popular press during this period, J.H.
Kellogg quotes another textbook author, Dr Richardson, who summa-
rizes the effects of tobacco on the heart. Here again is a presumably scientific analysis of tobacco's dangers, but the contours of the
evangelical approach can still be discerned in Richardson's approach
to the impact of moral contagion on the heart, source of physical and
spiritual health:

> overburdened with blood, and having little power left for its forcing
> action, [the heart] is scarcely contracting, but is feebly trembling as if, like
> a conscious thing, it knew its own responsibility and its own weakness. It
> is not a beating, it is a fluttering heart; its mechanism is perfect, but each
> fibre of it to its minutest part is impregnated with a substance which
> holds it in bondage and will not let it go.[34]

In short, as this quasi-scientific literature indicates, the evangelical
analysis of this first period seems to have found general societal acceptance. Certainly, fears about unrestricted tobacco use found a hearing
among legislators, who outlawed the selling of tobacco to minors in
most provinces after 1890.[35] The comparable legislation at the federal
level was the Tobacco Restraint Act, passed in 1908, which made it illegal to sell, give, or furnish cigarettes or cigarette papers to persons
aged sixteen or under.[36]

After 1900 the authoritative voices in the anti-tobacco movement
were more centrally located in the scientific community, eventually in
league with professionalizing medical interests, and in formal legislation. As a social, as opposed to a political, movement, temperance –
and thus evangelical anti-tobacco activity – had lost its preeminent
position by 1900.

In the nineteenth century, anti-tobacco campaigners had attempted to demonstrate tobacco's harm through the recitation of shocking anecdotes. These testimonials were a staple of temperance meetings and literature, combining evangelical notions of personal awakening, conversion, and salvation with classic nineteenth-century beliefs in self-help. But when the burden of proof shifted in the new century from examining individual instances of personal salvation to surveying controlled subject groups in scientific experiments, the evangelical moral message was subsumed in scientific rationalism. Instead of the earlier staple of horrifying case studies, large groups of young people in American colleges were now studied to demonstrate that tobacco use reduced athletic and intellectual performance.[37] The central fear of tobacco use became physiological 'inefficiency' rather than incremental poisoning or loss of salvation.[38] Yet, whether targeting the soul or the body, the moral tones of anti-tobacco rhetoric have never really been lost, but have emerged time and again, and most powerfully in our own age. Evangelical activists built the foundations for this moralistic fervour – now expressed in very different terms – well over a century ago.

Notes

1 Christian Smith, *American Evangelicalism: Embattled and Thriving* (Chicago: University of Chicago Press, 1998), 4.

2 For American examples, see Philip J. Pauly, 'The Struggle for Ignorance about Alcohol: American Physiologists, Wilbur Olin Atwater, and the Woman's Christian Temperance Union,' *Bulletin of the History of Medicine* 127, no. 5 (Fall 1990): 366–92; and Jonathan Zimmerman, '"When the Doctors Disagree": Scientific Temperance and Scientific Authority, 1891–1906,' *Journal of the History of Medicine* 48, no. 2 (April 1993): 171–97. For Canada, see Sharon Anne Cook, '"Educating For Temperance": The Woman's Christian Temperance Union and Ontario Children, 1880–1916,' *Historical Studies in Education/Revue d'histoire de l'éducation* 5, no. 2 (1993): 251–77; and '"Earnest Christian Women, Bent on Saving Our Canadian Youth": The Ontario Woman's Christian Temperance Union and Scientific Temperance Instruction, 1881–1930,' *Ontario History* 86, no. 3 (1994): 249–67.

3 See Jan Noel, *Canada Dry: Temperance Crusades before Confederation* (Toronto: University of Toronto Press, 1995); Wendy Mitchinson, 'The WCTU: "For God, Home and Native Land": A Study in Nineteenth-Century Feminism,'

in *A Not Unreasonable Claim*, ed. Linda Kealey (Toronto: Canadian Women's Educational Press, 1979), 151–68; and Graeme Decarie, 'The Prohibition Movement in Ontario, 1894–1916' (Ph.D. diss., Queen's University, 1972).

4 See, for example, Michael S. Goodstadt and Margaret M. Willett, 'Opportunities for School-Based Drug Education: Implications from the Ontario Schools Drug Surveys, 1977–1985,' *Canadian Journal of Education* 14, no. 3 (1989): 338–51.

5 By the third period, from about 1920 to 1950, the evangelical analysis was all but extinguished. Anti-tobacco activism continued from the scientific community, sometimes working in tandem with the medical establishment in an uneasy alliance. During much of this period, and most particularly during the Second World War, tobacco was understood in mainstream society to be an essential ingredient of male social bonding, allowable if used in moderation. Social icons, from political leaders to movie stars to sports figures, were frequently shown smoking. The fourth period opened with the publication of the American surgeon general's report in the early 1960s, which officially approved and disseminated research linking incontrovertibly cancer, heart disease, and tobacco use. The medical community took leadership of the anti-smoking forces, injecting a new urgency into the medically based discussion and tapping into the moralistic rebellious spirit of the '70s flower children against the culture of their parents. The last twenty years of the twentieth century might be seen as a further and fifth phase, though still directly linked with the health hazards now proved with tobacco use. In this final period, coming full circle, the question of health dangers has again been defined as a moral issue, imbuing the debate with emotion and energy not seen since the late nineteenth century. And while the North American media during this period have had no difficulty in identifying the morally reprehensible chicanery of the tobacco cartels' marketing campaigns on this continent, anti-tobacco reformers have yet to take on the tobacco companies' peddling of their products to the developing world. See especially Richard Kruger, *Ashes to Ashes: America's Hundred-Year Cigarette War, the Public Health, and the Unabashed Triumph of Philip Morris* (New York: Alfred A. Knopf, 1996).

6 Social purity advocates involved themselves in a wide range of nineteenth- and early-twentieth-century issues, including prostitution, the 'white slave trade,' properly ventilated classrooms and appropriately equipped school playgrounds, dress and food reform of a variety of types, and homeopathy. See, for example, Sharon Anne Cook, '"Do Not ... Do Anything That You Cannot Unblushingly Tell Your Mother": Gender and Social Purity in Canada,' *Histoire sociale/Social History* 30, no. 60 (1997): 215–38.

7 Phyllis D. Airhart, 'Ordering a New Nation and Reordering Protestantism, 1867–1914,' in *The Canadian Protestant Experience, 1760–1990*, ed. George A. Rawlyk (Burlington, ON: Welch, 1990), 119.

8 Lynne Marks, *Revivals and Roller Rinks: Religion, Leisure, and Identity in Late-Nineteenth-Century Small-Town Ontario* (Toronto: University of Toronto Press, 1996), chap. 6.

9 David Bebbington, *Evangelicalism in Modern Britain: A History from the 1730s to the 1980s* (Grand Rapids: Baker, 1989), 174.

10 Sharon Anne Cook, *'Through Sunshine and Shadow': The Woman's Christian Temperance Union, Evangelicalism, and Reform in Ontario, 1874–1930* (Montreal and Kingston: McGill-Queen's University Press, 1995), 175.

11 See ibid., 54. See also Geoffrey Giles, '"I Like Water Better": A Comparative Study of Temperance Materials for Children in Britain, France and Germany' (paper presented to the International Congress on the Social History of Alcohol, London, Ontario, 1993).

12 John Webster Grant, *A Profusion of Spires: Religion in Nineteenth-Century Ontario* (Toronto: University of Toronto Press, 1988), 196 and 211.

13 Marks, *Revivals and Roller Rinks*, 163.

14 Ida C. Clothier, *Is a Y.W.C.T.U. a Necessity?* Y.W.C.T.U. Department Leaflet No. 58, WCTU Collection, Archives of Ontario (AO).

15 *Woman's Journal*, 1 January 1901, WCTU Collection, AO.

16 'The Tobacco Devil,' *The War Cry*, 18 February 1889, 6, Salvation Army Archives (SAA).

17 Helen I. Bullock, *The Tobacco Toboggan*, National W.C.T.U. Leaflet No. 32, WCTU Collection, AO.

18 'The Tobacco Devil,' 6.

19 For example, the Dominion WCTU used 'petitions, memorials and deputations' to 'besiege' the House of Commons during the debate in 1900 on the federal tobacco bill. S.G.E. McKee, *Jubilee History of the Ontario Woman's Christian Temperance Union, 1877–1927* (Whitby: G.A. Goodfellow, 1927), 50.

20 Minute Books of the Newmarket W.C.T.U., 4 February 1896, WCTU Collection, AO.

21 An Old Smoker, *Tobacco Talk: Giving the Science of Tobacco, Its Botany, Chemistry, Uses, Pleasures, Hygiene, Etiquette, History and Ethnology* (Toronto: Carswell, 1894), esp. 34–46.

22 No parallel product was identified for women; tobacco producers ignored this marketing opportunity until the 1970s with the marketing of 'Virginia Slims.'

23 John C. Burnham, 'American Physicians and Tobacco Use: Two Surgeons

General, 1929 and 1964,' *Bulletin of the History of Medicine* 63, no. 1 (Spring 1989): 5.

24 'Why a Boy Should Not Smoke,' *The Young Soldier*, 7 October 1905, 15, SAA.

25 H.T. Crossley, *Practical Talks on Important Themes* (Toronto: Wm. Briggs, 1895).

26 'Salvation Songs,' *The War Cry*, 25 January 1890, 8, SAA.

27 'A Volunteer and a Tobacconist,' *The War Cry*, 6 April 1889, 2, SAA.

28 *Somebody Is Praying for You*, n.d., WCTU Collection, AO.

29 'Does He Pray for Me?' *The War Cry*, 6 March 1910, 6, SAA.

30 H.H. Seerley, *The Tobacco Habit and Its Effect upon School Work*, Signal Lights Series (n.p., n.d.).

31 From 1883, Ontario teachers were encouraged to give 'familiar lectures' on temperance, but in 1887 a textbook was first authorized in that province, and Scientific Temperance Instruction was added to the formal course of study. By 1893 a textbook was mandated for compulsory use.

32 Benjamin Ward Richardson, *The Temperance Lesson Book: A Series of Short Lessons on Alcohol and Its Action on the Body: Designed for Public Schools* (Toronto: Grip Printing and Publishing, 1887), 98–100.

33 William Nattress, *Public School Physiology and Temperance* (Toronto: William Briggs, 1893), 38.

34 Richardson, quoted in J.H. Kellogg, *The Home Hand-Book of Domestic Hygiene and Rational Medicine* (Battle Creek: Health Publishing, 1887), 511.

35 New Brunswick passed a law prohibiting the sale of tobacco to minors under age 16 in 1890 and then strengthened it in 1893 by providing prison sentences for those who ignored the statute. *Acts of the General Assembly of Her Majesty's Province of New Brunswick*, 1890, 1893. British Columbia passed legislation prohibiting the sale or giving of tobacco or opium to minors under the age of 15 in 1891. *Statutes of the British Columbia Legislature*, 1891. Ontario passed similar legislation for youth under 18 in 1892. *Statutes of the Province of Ontario*, 1892. The Northwest Territories passed similar legislation in 1896. *Ordinances of the North West Territories*, 1896. In Nova Scotia a law was passed in 1900 to prevent the 'use of Tobacco and Opium by Minors' and was strengthened a year later. *Statutes of Nova Scotia*, 1900 and 1901. Prince Edward Island enacted a very stiff law in 1901 to control the sale and possession of tobacco, and providing for the imprisonment of minors found with 'cigarettes, cigars, or tobacco in any form' on their person. *The Acts of the General Assembly of P.E.I.*, 1901.

36 James R. Robertson, Law and Government Division, Library of Parliament, Legislative Summary 'Bill C-111: The Tobacco Sales to Young Persons Act,' 1993?

37 See, for example, M.V. O'Shea, *Tobacco and Mental Efficiency* (New York: Macmillan, 1923). Although this book was published after 1920, its style and research base place it in the earlier period. The book's three subsections are: 'Data Derived from Observation, Introspection, and Biography,' 'Data Derived from School and College Records,' and 'Data Derived from the Psychological Laboratory.'

38 See, for example, M. Mac Levy, *Tobacco Habit Easily Conquered: How to Do It Agreeably and without Drugs* (New York: Albro Society, 1916).

9

Religion and the Shaping of 'Public Woman': A Post-Suffrage Case Study

Mary Kinnear

Over the centuries religion has comforted and inspired as well as oppressed women.[1] While there is no dispute that it sustained women during the nineteenth-century women's movement in Western society, religion seems to have disappeared from the historiography of twentieth-century women who entered public life by the thousands after enfranchisement.[2] Modernizing rhetoric has dominated historiography and has blocked out questions as to whether the lives of individuals have indeed become divorced from religion in its various forms. The received view has become that secularization is part of modernization, and that the power of the churches has evaporated as the state increasingly determines the context of people's lives.[3] More recently, however, some historians of religion have questioned this view. They argue that if the evidence regarding women's presence, rather than men's absence, is comprehensively evaluated,[4] the declension, feminization, and secularization of churches 'never happened.'[5]

In this chapter I consider the cultural expectations for Canadian middle-class women of the post-suffrage generation. I examine the experience of six prominent interwar Canadian women who used their new legacy of citizenship to involve themselves in public life. I provide brief accounts of religion's influence on their politics and show that they continued to engage with religion in the first generation after enfranchisement. Finally, I offer an analysis of the features they shared in common. I conclude that their participation in public life was, for them, a manifestation of religious faith. Religion inspired and justified their desire to make the post-suffrage political order a Christian Canada.

My analysis must be general and provisional because the evidence for individuals' engagement with religion necessarily involves resources that at present are rare. The most direct source material is auto-biographical and biographical, yet until recently it was uncommon for women to write their own lives, and there are few deposits of personal and business letters of public women in accessible archival collections.[6] I have drawn evidence for the women considered here from letters, memoirs, speeches, interviews and biographies. From Parliament I examine Agnes Macphail, MP, and Cairine Wilson, the first woman senator. From Manitoba politics I consider Margaret McWilliams, elected repeatedly as a Winnipeg city alderman. From women who provided a rhetorical and cultural context for the first generation of enfranchised women I consider Nellie McClung, writer, suffragist, and reformer; Charlotte Whitton, the most famous social worker in Canada of the time; and Beatrice Brigden, religious and political activist. I do not ask what contribution these women made to religious sensibility. Rather, I examine the extent to which religion was a significant part of their involvement in public life, and I look to their own testimony for evidence.

I

Cultural expectations for educated middle-class women at the end of the nineteenth century already included an obligation of service to community. Women as well as men shared the 'ideological consensus' that society must protect women because of their special role as moth-ers and the guardians of future generations.[7] The powerful women's organizations of the interwar period – national and local councils of women, university women's clubs, and farm and labour organiza-tions – gave voice to this maternalist notion.[8] 'Protection' in this context was a contested concept, but it included the commitment of educated, privileged women to help those less fortunate than themselves,[9] a role that neatly coincided with the New Testament requirement to love one's neighbour and serve as a Good Samaritan. Maternalism was an acceptance of Christian and civic responsibility.

Frances Willard, president (1880–98) of the Woman's Christian Tem-perance Union in the United States, understood well the concept of neighbourly obligation. The WCTU was the first mass organization among women devoted to social reform, saving souls with social work. Willard's 'Do Everything' policy involved a multifaceted program to combat the effects of alcohol and obliged members to advocate women's suffrage as a means to bring reform through legislation. By the early 1890s Willard saw socialism as a way to apply her faith.[10] The passionate evangelical fervour of WCTU conventions and chapter meetings sustained thousands of women left cold by the more intellectual literary meetings of early suffrage groups. In Canada the WCTU had approximately 16,000 members by 1914, mobilized for action 'in the name of God and home and humanity.'[11] Theirs was a powerful maternalism, justifying public action in order to protect home and family. As Letitia Youmans, founder of the WCTU in Canada, wrote: 'It is not the clamour of ambition, ignorance or frivolity trying to gain position. It is the prayer of earnest, thoughtful Christian women in behalf of their children and their children's children ... to advance God's Kingdom beyond the bounds of our homes.'[12]

The link between religion and public life also served to empower concerned female youth throughout the country.[13] Young women dedicated to ideals of Christian citizenship were an integral part of the cultural context of the interwar years. Their purpose, epitomized by the credo of the Canadian Girls in Training (CGIT), was to 'cherish health, seek truth, know God, serve others and thus, with his help, become the girl God would have me be.'[14] While accepting that most young women would take on traditional roles, the church-run CGIT also cultivated 'world-mindedness' and cooperative social collaboration with others, claiming to put forward 'Jesus's specifications for those who would be citizens of the Kingdom of God.'[15] Among members of the United Church of Canada and other Protestant denominations, up to 20 per cent of female teenagers belonged to the CGITs during the interwar period.[16] Among young women at university, the Student Christian Movement inspired with a 'burning sense of the great problems of the world' those who wished to create a new Jerusalem.[17]

Women in both Canadian and international organizations took Christianity for granted as a beneficent force, a belief that on occasion had the effect of minimizing the credentials of women of other faiths. Except for a few Roman Catholics and Jews, most members of these ostensibly ecumenical organizations were indeed Protestant Christians. For that generation of educated middle-class women, Protestantism facilitated the expansion of their life chances.

II

Before the interwar years, thousands of women across Canada were already involved in public life. Building on earlier religiously inspired institutions like Toynbee Hall in London and Jane Addams' Hull House in Chicago, women involved themselves in social welfare organizations that sought to ameliorate individual suffering and effect reform. Many worked for the churches as missionaries to remote communities, overseas and in Canada.[18] Some became prominent in emergent professions, such as journalism and social work, which did not yet have an embedded patriarchal history to impede women's advance. After enfranchisement in 1918, however, the women most in the public eye were those who for the first time were eligible to serve in electoral office. Hundreds became school trustees. Fewer were elected as city councillors, fewer still as members of provincial legislatures, and those who served in Ottawa can be counted on the fingers of one hand.[19] The one woman member of Parliament, Agnes Macphail, said women at that level were considered freaks, and, observed statistically, so they were.[20]

Agnes Macphail (1890–1954) was the first woman elected to Parliament, sitting as an independent from 1921 to 1940. A populist with radical social democratic values, she advocated women's rights, prison reform, and pacifism, though in 1939 she reluctantly supported the war. After her electoral defeat in 1940, she was returned to the Ontario legislature in 1943 as a Co-operative Commonwealth Federation (CCF) member.[21]

Macphail was raised a Presbyterian, but in her youth boarded with relatives who were members of the Church of Jesus Christ of Latter Day Saints and so joined that church. Her inspiration to public life came during a Bible class as she studied the Book of Job, an experience that made her determined to seek ways to right some of the social wrongs that disturbed her.[22] She became the candidate of the United Farmers of Ontario, a party arising out of agrarian revolts that cannot be fully understood, says Richard Allen, except as 'religious phenomena seeking to embed ultimate human goals in the social, economic and political order.'[23]

There is little direct evidence regarding Macphail's religious beliefs. She frequently underlined passages in the Bible, especially in the Old Testament, relating to taxes, deliverance, and the need for strength in the midst of the fray,[24] and she used biblical references in her speeches. In support of her party's opposition to the tariff, she said in 1921: 'I believe in the theory as set forth in the Book of Books that no nation can live unto itself, and if it does, it dies.'[25] Her papers in the National Archives do not display a woman forthcoming on religious matters, although she kept a torn-out page from a 1939 issue of *Nautilus* magazine, devoted to 'Self-help Through Self-knowledge,' which listed quotes about religion under the title 'The Force and How to Use It.'[26]

The most formative influence on Macphail's development came from J.S. Woodsworth, a former Methodist minister who entered the House of Commons as a Labour MP in 1921. He was, she thought, 'a man of the deepest integrity, the greatest vision, and most formidable industry.' Nonetheless, she took her time before finally embracing his socialism.[27] Judged by the values of his own time, Woodsworth's politics were a living testament to his belief that 'all manner of social and cultural existence was penetrated by Christian feeling and purpose.'[28] When Woodsworth established the Labour Church in Winnipeg in 1919, Macphail travelled in to give an address.[29] Once in Parliament she continued to respect him. During the 1920s Macphail participated in Woodsworth's Ginger Group of radical MPs whose approach 'sharpened' religious hopes for political action.[30]

A liberal feminist, peace activist, and humanitarian particularly interested in the resettlement of Jewish refugees, Cairine Wilson (1885–1962) was the first woman senator appointed by Prime Minister Mackenzie King after the Persons Case of 1929 established their eligibility. Wilson was first and foremost an active and loyal Liberal. She continuously supported women's access to career opportunities, equal pay, welfare measures for working and poor mothers, and the liberalization of divorce laws.[31] She was frequently lauded also as the wife of a wealthy Liberal donor and mother of eight children. The celebration of women's traditional role was not lost on commentators, who saw her patronage appointment as a cynical insult to advocates of women's equality. They had expected the first woman senator to be selected from among the women who had worked so hard to render women eligible for the Senate.

As a young woman Wilson was involved in volunteer work for the Presbyterian church and continued to contribute to publications of the Women's Missionary Society (WMS).[32] She also worked for the Young Women's Christian Association. Her involvement with the League of Nations Association gave rise to the Canadian National Committee for Refugees, perhaps her most significant achievement.

Wilson was a staunch Presbyterian who, according to Franca Iacovetta, 'viewed politics as a way of performing God's work on earth ... Her Christianity and her liberalism ... fuelled her commitment to maternal feminism.' Wilson was convinced that 'a liberal democratic tradition, infused with Christian precepts, would endure conservative and radical attacks against it,' and observed in 1957 that the 'relation between Christianity and self-government has long been recognised.'[33] Wilson always credited her faith as her mainspring. She said in 1930, 'there is no more stabilising influence in life, nothing that gives it a deeper and sweeter significance than religion.'[34]

Ten years older than Wilson, Margaret McWilliams (1875–1952) was a founder and first president of the Canadian Federation of University Women. During the 1930s she served four consecutive terms as Winnipeg's second woman alderman and became chair of the important Health and Unemployment Relief committees. In 1943 she chaired the subcommittee on the postwar Problems of Women, part of the federal Advisory Committee on Reconstruction.[35]

In her public language McWilliams frequently used religious terminology. She urged a Christian ethic of service to one's neighbours in order to promote what she expressed as the ideals of Jesus, which she connected with nation-building. 'By an ... ardent pursuit of the great ethical ideals of Jesus our country might become a great moral force,' she wrote in 1920. Twenty-five years later her language had become more, not less, religious. At the end of the Second World War, she urged the local Council of Women: 'Realising that we stand as equals, let us accept our responsibilities, renew our spirits, renew our vows to God, and trust in His divine Will.' Accepting the 'one clear way of life taught by Jesus,' she wrote in 1947, meant 'we must work unceasingly, patiently and tolerantly to remove want and disease and, above all, fear from our people.' As late as 1950 she espoused the 'great enterprise' of making Canada Christian.[36]

McWilliams' ideas reflected her University of Toronto education. Her professors were imbued with the philosophy of T.H. Green, whose civic idealism considered 'the life of citizenship ... a mode of divine service ... The life most worth living found its nurture and its sphere of realisation in that supreme institution, the organized State.'[37]

McWilliams' maternal grandmother was Presbyterian and her parents, who were both dead by the time she was ten, became Plymouth Brethren. When she married Roland McWilliams, a Congregationalist minister conducted the ceremony. The McWilliamses attended a Presbyterian church, and their minister in Winnipeg was the Reverend Charles Gordon, also known as novelist Ralph Connor. In her local parish McWilliams took her share of female hospitality chores, but preferred to take part in temperance and public welfare work rather than the traditional female power base of the WMS. She was inclined to be dismissive of such work until she visited China in 1932, when she met many missionaries and was impressed by their intensive health and educational networks.[38]

Identification as a Christian was always important in McWilliams' political career. Visiting Bolshevik Russia in 1926, she expressed critical admiration for a new social experiment, but was apprehensive of the threat she saw to Christianity from Leninism and feared the diminution of individual initiative and moral responsibility.[39] In 1937, the visit to Winnipeg of General Evangeline Booth of the Salvation Army convinced McWilliams to declare her beliefs explicitly, and publicly. 'It is only by example and testimony that others can be truly helped,' she said a year before her death.[40] Her husband Roland wrote that the couple 'shared deep religious convictions, even though not always orthodox. We had supreme confidence in a future life, the character of which will depend on the life lived in this existence.'[41]

The Christian gospel provided McWilliams with a model of equality in diversity. Souls were equal in the sight of God, and individuals had different gifts to use in his service. The image of the church as a corporate body, with each part contributing its own necessary and particular function, similarly supported the idea of a society with different groups, divided by class, ethnicity, and gender, working for the common good.

McWilliams was a Christian who believed her duty was to help in the moral regeneration of this present world. She was able to balance her concern for individual moral responsibility with the notion of an expanded state providing social services as a power for good. Not against private charity, she nevertheless considered the state to be more efficient and even-handed. She believed in the beneficence of a state whose function was to create the environment in which individuals could pursue the objectives of a Christian democracy.

Charlotte Whitton (1895–1975), whom McWilliams called 'one of the ablest women in Canada,'[42] shared McWilliams' objective of a Christian democracy. Whitton worked with the new Social Service Council of Canada from 1918 to 1922 and directed the Canadian Welfare Council from 1922 to 1941. Subsequently she worked as a lecturer and journalist, and was elected mayor of Ottawa five times between 1951 and 1964. She served as city controller until 1972.[43]

Whitton was an Anglican who resented her church's marginalization of women in leadership. Her father was raised a Methodist and her mother a Roman Catholic, but as a child of thirteen Charlotte insisted on confirmation as an Anglican.[44] At Queen's University, Whitton was socialized into the legacy of Principal George Grant,[45] who urged graduates to serve their country through a Christian mission united with social service. He challenged students 'to bring their religious convictions to bear ... on every individual in society, on social problems, and on the duties of the voter and the political leader in relation to social problems.'[46] Whitton believed the state should interfere minimally in the lives of people, but at the same time it should maintain satisfactory living standards for its citizens.[47]

Whitton's model of womanhood included spirituality, and her view of the world predicated a divine plan: 'it can only be the result of very superficial thinking on humanity to imagine that mankind has so far come upon this road without some predestined purpose in an enduring plan ... there must be some setting of the life of the individual and the raising into accord with some underlying divine harmony.'[48] Just as it was important for women to educate themselves as informed citizens, it was also women's spiritual imperative to develop a well-formed conscience.[49]

In her speeches and writings Whitton frequently used religious language. In 1936 she devised a social worker pledge that ended with the invocation: 'I ask my God to give me knowledge of truth, faith in goodness, and the power to do good in His service.'[50] She thought people had an obligation to contribute to society and, in her view, obligation was infused with religious duty. 'The educated informed member of a State who withholds himself from an active citizenship within a community, is equally culpable with the person who more flagrantly abuses his privileges as a member of a civilised, organized state ... Citizenship ... is a high and well-nigh sacred thing,' she said.[51]

Of the six women considered here, Whitton was the least optimistic about individuals and society. In 1945 she wrote to an Anglican clergyman: 'I am convinced that nothing but a revitalizing of spiritual power will save our Christian civilisation.'[52] Looking back on her life, in 1960 Whitton noted she had 'held certain basic beliefs and values to be immutable and inexorable, and sought their application in a Christian social order.' However, to her deep dismay, she was now 'no longer positive as to what constitutes a Christian order, and no longer certain as to what is required of one to be an Anglican.' Revealingly, she wrote to an Anglican official that it would be better 'for me to keep the practice of my faith, like so many of our finest prayers and hymns, "chiefly for personal use."'[53]

A founding member of the Winnipeg Political Equality League, Nellie McClung (1873–1951) put her impressive communication skills to the service of suffrage, temperance, and liberal causes. For five years she served as an MLA in Alberta and joined with four other women in the Persons Case, which in 1929 pronounced women to be persons and therefore eligible for appointment to the Senate.[54]

McClung was raised by a strict Calvinist Presbyterian mother and an 'out-and-out Methodist father,' and married the son of a Methodist clergyman.[55] After unification of the Methodists and Presbyterians in 1925, McClung committed herself to the reform of the United Church and was prominent in the movement to have women ordained.[56] She deplored the coldness of official church attitudes towards women in positions of leadership. 'The Church of Christ should have championed the woman's cause; it should have led all the reform forces in bringing liberty of soul and freedom of action to women. It has not done so,' she said.[57]

Religion was a 'central unifying category for [McClung's] life and work.'[58] She did not describe herself as a theologian, but observed: 'I believe we all know enough to live by. It is not so much spiritual food we need as spiritual exercise.'[59] McClung exercised her own kind of comprehensive Christianity in her fiction, her polemical writing, and through her explicit statements of belief. Randi Warne's analysis of McClung's fiction demonstrates that her female characters serve as 'peacemakers, judges and nurturers whose responsibilities as agents of God transcend institutional boundaries.'[60]

Along with her fiction, McClung's 1914 feminist polemic *In Times Like These* was informed by an understanding of the social gospel in the lives of women. Strongly influenced by Charlotte Perkins Gilman and Olive Schreiner, McClung reproduced much of their socialist idealism in her own work and eventually became committed to 'a Christian socialism in the best sense of that much abused word.'[61] McClung was an optimist concerning the power of human beings to construct a new and better world.[62] She required sympathizers to act: 'God demands our love, not just our amiability ... if we love humanity we must hate humanity's enemies ... Toleration when applied to weeds, germs, dirt, mad dogs and racial poisons, ceases to be Christian virtue. It becomes indifference and cowardice.'[63]

McClung's sense of humour and common touch brought her work before many women – and men – attracted by melodrama and sentiment. A reviewer in 1943 claimed that McClung's didactic enthusiasm had marred her art. 'Some of her stories are sermons in the guise of fiction. There is the flavour of the Sunday School hymn and the Foreign Mission Board in some of her work.' McClung denounced his condescension with the retort: 'I would be very proud to think that I had even remotely approached the grandeur of a Sunday School hymn.' Despite her criticism of religious institutions and leadership, she recognized 'what Christianity has done for women. It has an absolute hold on us,' she said. 'Its appeal is irresistible.'[64]

While McClung's communication skills served her well in her public speaking and writing career, Beatrice Brigden (1888–1979) worked behind the scenes. Brigden was a Methodist church worker in the department of Social Services and Evangelism; after 1919 she worked for the Labour Church. An unsuccessful parliamentary candidate in 1930, she joined the CCF and was a community activist for the Labour movement.[65]

Brigden's mother came of Quaker stock, but in their western Manitoba homestead the family worshipped in the Methodist church on the preaching circuit of the young J.S. Woodsworth.[66] As a member of the young people's Epworth League, Brigden discussed temperance, socialism, missions, immigration, and the 'social concerns of the city,' as well as the requirements of 'intelligent and loyal piety' using Woodsworth's books *Strangers within Our Gates* and *My Neighbour* as texts. At church summer schools she met social gospel proponents William Ivens, A.E. Smith, and Salem Bland and took inspiration from their religious passion.[67]

One of Brigden's biographers, Valerie Regehr, claims that throughout her life Brigden's religious ideas remained constant while the institutions in which she practised religion changed.[68] Her formal affiliation with religion moved from the Methodist Church, to the Labour Church, through no formal church affiliation, and then after the Second World War to a Quaker meeting. In the 1930s Brigden left the organized church and became strongly committed to the new CCF, but like many other Christian socialists in the CCF, she did not deny her continuing faith. Christianity demanded solidarity with the powerless, she thought, and when the church failed to align itself accordingly, she pursued these goals on her own. Jesus was the clearest example of commitment to the ideal of equality, she said in an address to the Labour Church. 'Jesus kindled a light and we have been following that gleam ever since.'[69]

True faith meant following Jesus' example and for Brigden it meant working on behalf of women, and 'the common people.' Religion was not just a guide for individual spiritual development, it was a clarion cry to political action. 'Politics is working together to fulfill the need of others as you would have them fulfill yours ... it describes my religion as much as it does my politics,' she said at a conference on the Social Gospel in 1974.[70]

III

For the public women considered here, protestant Christianity was not a perfunctory prop but rather an organizing principle, to greater or lesser degrees, in each of their lives. Religion for these interwar public women was an 'engine of social action,' impelling them into a public culture that could promise social justice as well as a larger voice for women like themselves.[71]

These women shared more than religious faith. Although only one was born into a rich family, all were well-educated, confident, and assured. Demographically, they were privileged and middle-class, all of Anglo-Celtic stock. Three were single (Macphail, Whitton, Brigden) and self-supporting. Of the three married women, one had a wealthy husband (Wilson), one earned a living from her own pen (McClung), and the third (McWilliams) always worried about money. Only two had children (Wilson and McClung).

Their common Christianity, however, did not result in common politics. Some stressed individual responsibility, others cooperation. Some were cautious about expanding the power of the state in people's lives, others enthusiastic. While Macphail, McClung, and Brigden thought Christianity demanded a socialism of sorts in politics, McWilliams was more cautious, Wilson remained a loyal Liberal, and Whitton was in favour of state social policy only under limited conditions. Wilson was concerned about alleviating individual suffering while Whitton emphasized individual responsibility. McWilliams wanted to see the state undertake more social programs, but she insisted too on the moral responsibility of individuals to care for themselves and their neighbours. Not all viewpoints were unanimous: Whitton and Wilson, for example, publicly disagreed on immigration. Whitton played a significant role in preventing refugee Armenian and Jewish children entering Canada at the same time that Wilson worked to provide a refuge for children from fascist Europe.[72]

Religion was not the only force propelling these women towards public action. Macphail entered politics, she said, to clean up public affairs 'along the lines of honesty, economy, truthfulness,' in a Parliament 'unbiased, free from malign influence and wholly bent on doing the people's will.'[73] McWilliams wished through her public work to repay society for the gifts she had inherited. By extension she felt all university-educated women, who in her day were few and far between, should take leadership roles as 'pilgrims of peace abroad and pilgrims of understanding at home.'[74] With the exception of Whitton, none of the women discussed here appeared to place a premium on her personal advancement, even though there is evidence that all enjoyed a position in the public eye.[75]

Brigden, McClung, and McWilliams were linked by a commitment to temperance. Brigden admired the WCTU: 'it was the best organized women's group of that time.'[76] McClung joined the organization as a young teacher and through her writing became a major propagandist for prohibition.[77] 'We believed,' she said, that 'we could shape the world nearer to our heart's desire if we had a dry Canada and that, we felt would come, if and when women were allowed to vote.'[78] McWilliams was one of the few women members of the Public Welfare committee of her church, and demanded it send telegrams to Ottawa 'in support of total prohibition' in 1918. During the 1920s she said she was 'working overtime speaking in the interests of prohibition.' When she became hostess at Government House in Winnipeg, she never served liquor, offering nonalcoholic punch or hot tomato juice to her guests.[79]

The period between 1900 and 1940 has been described as the apogee of the cultural authority of the mainline Protestant churches. They envisioned their mission ambitiously as the complete Christianization of Canadian life and saw good Canadians and good Christians as synonymous.[80] Like novelist Ralph Connor's Prairie missionary in the novel *The Foreigner*, the churches wanted to 'make [children] good Christians and good Canadians, which is the same thing.'[81] This vision was a heaven-sent opportunity for women who could use religion and patriotism in their own, as well as others', interests. Women could turn the expansion of religion into politics into a useful sanction of what might otherwise have been deemed importunate or nonfeminine behaviour. That is not to say the faith of these women was insincere. Rather, participation in public life itself was a manifestation of their religious faith. They carried out the tenets of philosophical idealism, as disseminated by intellectuals at Queen's University and the University of Toronto, and as displayed in the life of J.S. Woodsworth.

Their commitment to serve the state as a synonym for service to God helped veil motivations of self-aggrandizement or ambition – attributes still considered inappropriate for women. Through the embodiment of religious feeling, Christianity could permeate public life. Through work for others, an individual could find salvation for herself. And through community and political action, the structures of society could be improved for the poor and powerless. As Whitton said in a speech to the graduating class of Ottawa Ladies College in 1936, 'You will be caught up in this tendency today to think it smart to live without a God; you will not truly live, though, if you close the door on the greatest of human experience.'[82]

These six women, among the first generation of female citizens, self-consciously contributed to the development of a Christian Canadian nation. They inhabited a version of feminism that was not hampered but informed and enlivened by religion. Alone among the six women, Whitton eventually concluded that public life in this world was not the site of the new Jerusalem. Before her disillusion, however, she had joined the other five in a brave attempt. These women did not abandon religion, but, in Ruth Brouwer's words, redirected it into new channels that could not be contained within the institutional churches.[83]

Notes

1 Gail Malmgreen, ed., *Religion in the Lives of English Women, 1760–1930* (London: Croom Helm, 1986), 8. For the religious oppression of women, see Mary Daly, *The Church and the Second Sex. With a New Feminist Postchristian Introduction by the Author* (New York: Harper and Row, 1975); Rosemary Ruether, *Religion and Sexism: Images of Woman in the Jewish and Christian Tradition* (New York: Simon and Schuster, 1974); Olwen Hufton, *The Prospect before Her: A History of Women in Western Europe*, vol. 1, *1500–1800* (New York: Harper Collins, 1995), 25–40. For the religious empowerment of women, see Sabina Flanagan, *Hildegard of Bingen: A Visionary Life* (London and New York: Routledge, 1989); Jo Ann Kay McNamara, *Sisters in Arms: Catholic Nuns through Two Millennia* (Cambridge: Harvard University Press, 1996); Eileen Power, *Medieval English Nunneries, 1275–1535* (Cambridge: Cambridge University Press, 1922); Natalie Zemon Davis, 'City Women and Religious Change,' in *Society and Culture in Early Modern France* (Stanford: Stanford University Press, 1975), 65–96; Merry Wiesner, *Women and Gender in Early Modern Europe* (Cambridge: Cambridge University

Press, 1993); Deborah M. Valenze, *Prophetic Sons and Daughters* (Princeton: Princeton University Press, 1985); Cecilia Morgan, *Public Men and Virtuous Women: The Gendered Languages of Religion and Politics in Upper Canada, 1791–1850* (Toronto: University of Toronto Press, 1996); Glenna Matthews, *The Rise of Public Woman* (New York: Oxford University Press, 1992).

2 Sandra Stanley Holton, Alison Mackinnon, and Margaret Allen, 'Introduction: Between Rationality and Revelation: Women, Faith and Public Roles in the Nineteenth and Twentieth Centuries,' *Women's History Review* 7, no. 2 (1998): 163–4; Susan Hill Lindley, '*You Have Stept out of Your Place': A History of Women and Religion in America* (Louisville: Westminster John Knox Press, 1996), 385; Kenneth D. Wald, *Religion and Politics in the United States*, 3rd ed. (Washington: Congressional Quarterly Press, 1997), 6–7, 17–20; Harry S. Stout and Catherine A. Brekus, 'Declension, Gender and the "New Religious History,"' in *Belief and Behavior: Essays in the New Religious History*, ed. Philip R. Vandermeer and Robert P. Swierenga (New Brunswick, NJ: Rutgers University Press, 1991), 16.

3 Yolande Cohen, 'From Feminine to Feminism in Quebec,' in *Toward a Cultural Identity in the Twentieth Century*, ed. Françoise Thebaud, vol. 5 of *A History of Women in the West*, ed. Georges Duby and Micelle Perrot (Cambridge: Harvard University Press, 1994), 548–66.

4 Marguerite Van Die, '"The Marks of a Genuine Revival": Religion, Social Change, Gender, and Community in Mid-Victorian Brantford, Ontario,' *Canadian Historical Review* 79, no. 3 (1998): 557–62; Cynthia Grant Tucker, *Prophetic Sisterhood: Liberal Women Ministers of the Frontier, 1880–1930* (Bloomington: Indiana University Press, 1994), 1, 234. See also Randi R. Warne, 'Toward a Brave New Paradigm: The Impact of Women's Studies on Religious Studies,' *Religious Studies and Theology* 9, nos. 2 and 3 (1989): 35–46.

5 Ann Braude, 'Women's History *Is* American Religious History,' in *Retelling United States Religious History*, ed. Thomas Tweed (Berkeley: University of California Press, 1997), 96.

6 Margaret Conrad, '"Sundays Always Make Me Think of Home": Time and Place in Canadian Women's History,' in *Rethinking Canada: The Promise of Women's History*, ed. Veronica Strong-Boag and Anita Fellman, 2nd ed. Toronto: Copp Clark Pitman, 1991), 100–1; Carolyn G. Heilbrun, *Writing a Woman's Life* (New York: Norton, 1988).

7 Nancy Christie and Michael Gauvreau, *A Full-Orbed Christianity: The Protestant Churches and Social Welfare in Canada, 1900–1940* (Montreal and Kingston: McGill-Queen's University Press, 1996), 120.

8 Linda Kealey, introduction to *A Not Unreasonable Claim: Women and Reform in Canada, 1880s–1920s* (Toronto: Women's Press, 1979), 7–10.

9 Alice Kessler-Harris, Jane Lewis, and Ulla Wikander, eds., introduction to *Protecting Women: Labor Legislation in Europe, the United States and Australia, 1880–1920* (Urbana: University of Illinois Press, 1995), 1–28.
10 Barbara Leslie Epstein, *The Politics of Domesticity: Women, Evangelism and Temperance in Nineteenth-Century America* (Middletown: Wesleyan University Press, 1981), 115–46.
11 Sharon Anne Cook, *'Through Sunshine and Shadow': The Woman's Christian Temperance Union, Evangelicalism, and Reform in Ontario, 1874–1930* (Montreal and Kingston: McGill-Queen's University Press, 1995), 7; Wendy Mitchinson, 'The WCTU: "For God, Home and Native Land": A Study in Nineteenth-Century Feminism,' in A *Not Unreasonable Claim*, Kealey, 157.
12 Mitchinson, 'The WCTU,' 159.
13 M. Lucille Marr, 'Church Teen Clubs, Feminized Organisations? Tuxis Boys, Trail Rangers, and Canadian Girls in Training, 1919–1939,' *Historical Studies in Education* 3, no. 2 (1991): 249; Brian Clarke, 'English-Speaking Canada from 1854,' in *A Concise History of Christianity in Canada*, ed. Terrence Murphy and Roberto Perin (Toronto: Oxford University Press, 1996), 287–90.
14 Margaret Prang, '"The Girl God Would Have Me Be": The Canadian Girls in Training, 1915–39,' *Canadian Historical Review* 66, no. 2 (1985): 163.
15 Ibid., 175.
16 Ibid., 180.
17 Editorial in *Canadian Student* (1924), quoted in Elizabeth Anderson, 'Women and the Student Christian Movement in Canada,' unpublished paper (1980), 10, United Church Archives, Victoria University, University of Toronto.
18 See Ruth Compton Brouwer, *New Women for God: Canadian Presbyterian Women and India Missions, 1876–1914* (Toronto: University of Toronto Press, 1990); Rosemary R. Gagan, *A Sensitive Independence: Canadian Methodist Women Missionaries in Canada and the Orient, 1881–1925* (Montreal and Kingston: McGill-Queen's University Press, 1992); W.L. Morton, ed., with the assistance of Vera Fast, *God's Galloping Girl: The Peace River Diaries of Monica Storrs, 1929–31* (Vancouver: University of British Columbia Press, 1979).
19 See Ramsay Cook, introduction to *The Woman Suffrage Movement in Canada*, by Catherine Cleverdon (Toronto: University of Toronto Press, 1974); Sylvia B. Bashevkin, *Toeing the Lines: Women and Party Politics in Canada* (Toronto: University of Toronto Press, 1985); Linda Kealey and Joan Sangster, eds., *Beyond the Vote: Canadian Women and Politics* (Toronto: University of Toronto Press, 1989).
20 Joan Sangster, *Dreams of Equality: Women on the Canadian Left, 1920–1950* (Toronto: McClelland and Stewart, 1989), 103.

21 Macphail was MP for South-East Grey in Ontario (supported by the United Farmers of Ontario), and later served as a CCF member for York East in the Ontario provincial legislature 1943–5 and 1948–51. During the 1930s she supported Senator Cairine Wilson's initiatives for refugees. As a CCF member she supported equal-pay legislation for women and formed an Elizabeth Fry society for the rehabilitation of women prisoners. See Terry Crowley, *Agnes Macphail and the Politics of Equality* (Toronto: James Lorimer, 1990); Doris Pennington, *Agnes Macphail: Reformer* (Toronto: Simon and Pierre, 1989); and Margaret Stewart and Doris French, *Ask No Quarter: A Biography of Agnes Macphail* (Toronto: Longmans Green, 1959).

22 Crowley, *Agnes Macphail*, 21.

23 Richard Allen, 'Religion and Political Transformation in English Canada: The 1880s to the 1930s,' in *From Heaven Down to Earth: A Century of Chancellor's Lectures at Queen's Theological College*, ed. Marguerite Van Die (Kingston: Queen's Theological College, 1992), 134.

24 Crowley, *Agnes Macphail*, 212 n. 20.

25 Ibid., 42.

26 Macphail Papers, vol. 4, file 17, National Archives of Canada (NAC).

27 Crowley, *Agnes Macphail*, 73.

28 Christie and Gauvreau, *A Full-Orbed Christianity*, 244.

29 Valerie Regehr, 'Beatrice Brigden: Her Social Gospel Theology in Its Historical Context' (master's in Theological Studies, Associated Mennonite Biblical Seminaries, 1989), 50.

30 Richard Allen, *The Social Passion: Religion and Social Reform in Canada, 1914–28* (Toronto: University of Toronto Press, 1971), 349; Crowley, *Agnes Macphail*, 75–6.

31 Wilson was appointed for her Liberal Party work, which culminated in her work for the National Federation of Liberal Women. Moved by the predicament of individuals fleeing fascist Europe in 1938, she vainly urged a more welcoming immigration policy for Canada. See Franca Iacovetta, '"A Respectable Feminist": The Political Career of Senator Cairine Wilson, 1921–1962,' in *Beyond the Vote*, ed. Kealey and Sangster, 63–85; Valerie Knowles, *First Person: A Biography of Cairine Wilson, Canada's First Woman Senator* (Toronto: Dundurn Press), 1988.

32 Iacovetta, 'A Respectable Feminist,' 67.

33 Ibid., 65, 68.

34 Knowles, *First Person*, 164.

35 Margaret McWilliams began her career as a public woman in 1910 on her arrival in Winnipeg. In 1898 she was the first woman to graduate with a degree in political economy from the University of Toronto, where a class-

mate was Mackenzie King. For five years she earned her living as a journalist before her marriage to a barrister and Liberal Party supporter. Working in women's organizations like the Women's Canadian Club and the local Council of Women, she was also the first vice-president of the International Federation of University Women. She was a historian, producing a book of women's history, *Women of Red River*, in 1923, a book on her impressions of Russia in 1927, a history of Manitoba in 1928, a blueprint for Canadian social and economic reform in 1931, and a book on the political institutions of Canada in 1948. During the 1940s, when her husband was appointed lieutenant-governor of the province, she helped revitalize the Manitoba Historical Society, serving as president when it sponsored research into ethnic communities. For over thirty years in Winnipeg she maintained classes for women, her biweekly 'current events' classes, which provided continuing education in politics. See Mary Kinnear, *Margaret McWilliams: An Interwar Feminist* (Montreal and Kingston: McGill-Queen's University Press, 1991).

36 Mary Kinnear, 'Margaret McWilliams and *Her* Social Gospel,' *Manitoba History*, no. 22 (Autumn 1991): 30–5.

37 John McCunn, *Six Radical Thinkers* (London: Edward Arnold, 1910), 220, 243–4, 262.

38 Kinnear, 'Margaret McWilliams and *Her* Social Gospel,' 33.

39 Margaret McWilliams and R.F. McWilliams, *Russia in 1926* (Toronto: J.M. Dent and Sons, 1927), 48, 49–52.

40 *Winnipeg Tribune*, 23 October 1937; Kathleen Strange, 'Margaret McWilliams of Manitoba,' *Canadian Home Journal*, August 1951.

41 Kinnear, 'Margaret McWilliams and *Her* Social Gospel,' 33.

42 Margaret McWilliams to Catherine Cleverdon, 1 October 1946, Cleverdon Papers, NAC.

43 Whitton made a major contribution to social work training and to the standardization of child welfare practice and policy across Canada. She was appointed as an assessor then as a delegate to the Child Welfare Committee of the League of Nations. She enjoyed strong professional and personal friendships with British and American reformers like the Labour cabinet minister Margaret Bondfield, and in the United States with Frances Perkins and Edith and Grace Abbott, all leaders in the first generation of professional social workers. See P.T. Rooke and R.L. Schnell, *No Bleeding Heart: Charlotte Whitton, A Feminist on the Right* (Vancouver: University of British Columbia Press, 1987).

44 Rooke and Schnell, *No Bleeding Heart*, 6.

45 Frederick Gibson, *Queen's University*, vol. 2, *1917–1961* (Montreal and Kingston: McGill-Queen's University Press, 1983), 4.

46 Hilda Neatby, *Queen's University*, vol. 1, *1841–1917*, ed. Frederick Gibson and Roger Graham (Montreal: McGill-Queen's University Press, 1978), 234.

47 Rooke and Schnell, *No Bleeding Heart*, 82.

48 Ibid., 80, 103.

49 Ibid.

50 Ibid., 100.

51 Ibid., 113.

52 Charlotte Whitton to Dean Waterman, 22 January 1946, Whitton Papers, vol. 22, NAC.

53 Charlotte Whitton to Leonard Hatfield, 12 August 1960, Whitton Papers, vol. 22, NAC.

54 McClung, who was born in Ontario and raised in Manitoba, was inspired by her mother-in-law to write fiction. She early became a best-selling author and celebrity speaker. In Alberta, she briefly (1921–26) represented the United Farmers of Alberta in the provincial legislature. In 1936 she was appointed the only woman member of the board of governors of the Canadian Broadcasting Corporation, and in 1938 she was appointed a Canadian delegate to the League of Nations. See Veronica Strong-Boag, '"Ever a Crusader": Nellie McClung, First-Wave Feminist,' in *Rethinking Canada*, ed. Strong-Boag and Fellman, 271–84; Mary Hallett and Marilyn Davis, *Firing the Heather: The Life and Times of Nellie McClung* (Saskatoon: Fifth House, 1994).

55 Hallett and Davis, *Firing the Heather*, 5.

56 Mary E. Hallett, 'Nellie McClung and the Fight for the Ordination of Women in the United Church of Canada,' *Atlantis* 4, no. 2 (Spring 1979): 2–16; Valerie Korinek, 'No Women Need Apply: The Ordination of Women in the United Church, 1918–1965,' *Canadian Historical Review* 74, no. 4 (1993): 473–509.

57 Nellie L. McClung, 'The Awakening of Women,' in *Proceedings of the Fifth Ecumenical Methodist Conference, London, England, 1921* (Toronto: Methodist Book and Publishing House, 1921), 258.

58 Randi R. Warne, *Literature as Pulpit: The Christian Social Activism of Nellie L. McClung* (Waterloo: Wilfrid Laurier University Press, 1993), 6.

59 Nellie L. McClung, *Be Good to Yourself* (Toronto: Thomas Allen, 1930), 130.

60 Warne, *Literature as Pulpit*, 23.

61 Hallett and Davis, *Firing the Heather*, 299.

62 Nellie McClung, 'Dedication II,' in *In Times Like These* (1915; reprint, Toronto: University of Toronto Press, 1972), 4, and the introduction by Veronica Strong-Boag.

63 Hallett and Davis, *Firing the Heather*, 188.

64 McClung, 'The Awakening of Women,' 259.
65 Brigden was a woman who played a significant role in the Social Gospel. Training for work in the Social Services and Evangelism department of the Methodist Church, she included two months of study at Hull House with Jane Addams. As a salaried employee of the church she followed a similar path to Woodsworth, who found himself unable to support the institutional church at the time of the Great War. For Brigden the breaking point came not with pacifism but with the 1919 Winnipeg General Strike. When her local Methodist minister, A.E. Smith, resigned from the Methodist Church to join a People's, or Labour Church in Brandon, she joined him and started to work for the new congregation. After 1922 she organized an annual 'Women's Social and Economic Conference,' which considered peace concerns, health and unemployment insurance, and reform of the justice system. In 1930 Brigden ran as a Farm-Labour candidate in the dominion election. She attended the founding conference of the national Commonwealth Co-operative Federation and was a founder of the Manitoba CCF. She was an active member of the Women's International League for Peace and Freedom, worked for refugees, helped to run a Women's Labour Conference, and during the Second World War was employed by the Unemployment Insurance Corporation. See Beatrice Brigden, 'One Woman's Campaign for Social Purity and Social Reform,' in The Social Gospel in Canada, ed. Richard Allen (Ottawa: National Museums of Canada, 1975); Allison Campbell, 'Beatrice Brigden: The Formative Years of a Socialist Feminist, 1881–1932' (master's thesis, University of Manitoba, 1991); Joan Sangster, 'The Making of a Socialist-Feminist: The Early Career of Beatrice Brigden, 1888–1941,' Atlantis 13, no. 1 (1987); Regehr, 'Beatrice Brigden.'
66 Brigden, 'One Woman's Campaign,' 39.
67 Ibid., 43–4.
68 Regehr, 'Beatrice Brigden,' 88–9.
69 Ibid., 99.
70 Brigden, 'One Woman's Campaign,' 57.
71 Malmgreen, Religion in the Lives of English Women, 8; Elizabeth Gillan Muir and Marilyn Färdig Whiteley, eds., 'Putting Together the Puzzle of Canadian Women's Christian Work,' in Changing Roles of Women within the Christian Church in Canada (Toronto: University of Toronto Press, 1995), 16; Kathryn Kish Sklar, Florence Kelly and the Nation's Work: The Rise of Women's Political Culture, 1839–1900 (New Haven: Yale University Press, 1995), xiv.
72 Rooke and Schnell, No Bleeding Heart, 71.
73 Pennington, Agnes Macphail, 29.
74 Winnipeg Free Press, 18 April 1936.

75 Rooke and Schnell, *No Bleeding Heart*, 65.

76 Brigden, 'One Woman's Campaign,' 40.

77 Nellie McClung, *Clearing in the West* (Toronto: Thomas Allen, 1964), 344; Strong-Boag, introduction to *In Times Like These*, McClung, xviii.

78 Nellie McClung, *The Stream Runs Fast* (Toronto: Thomas Allen, 1965), 180.

79 Kinnear, *Margaret McWilliams*, 139.

80 Christie and Gauvreau, *A Full-Orbed Christianity*, xii; Marguerite Van Die, *An Evangelical Mind: Nathanael Burwash and the Methodist Tradition in Canada, 1839–1918* (Montreal and Kingston: McGill-Queen's University Press, 1989), 193–5.

81 Ralph Connor, *The Foreigner* (Toronto: Westminster, 1909), 253; Phyllis D. Airhart, '"As Canadian as Possible under the Circumstances": Reflections on the Study of Protestantism in North America,' in *New Perspectives in American Religious History*, ed. Harry S. Stout and D.G. Hart (New York: Oxford University Press, 1997), 116–37.

82 Message to the Graduating Class, Ottawa Ladies College, 10 June 1936, Whitton Papers, vol. 82, NAC.

83 Ruth Compton Brouwer, 'Transcending the 'Unacknowledged Quarantine': Putting Religion into English-Canadian Women's History,' *Journal of Canadian Studies* 27, no. 3 (1992): 54.

Part Four

Religion's Redefinition of the Role of the State:
The Example of Prairie Populism

10

Young Man Knowles: Christianity, Politics, and the 'Making of a Better World'

Eleanor J. Stebner

Volumes could be written analysing the long public career and countless parliamentary actions of the Reverend Stanley Knowles. First elected as a Winnipeg city alderman in 1941, Knowles found his niche in 1942 when he became the member of Parliament for Winnipeg North Centre. Knowles represented this constituency for over thirty years, first as a member of the Co-operative Commonwealth Federation (CCF) and then as a member of the New Democratic Party (NDP).[1] In public life, Knowles quickly became known as the 'conscience of Parliament and crusader for the rights of the working person.'[2] Former colleagues have said of his political commitments that he 'epitomize[d] the struggle of the CCF-NDP for social justice.' Politicians of various party stripes acclaimed him as 'Mr. Parliament – rules expert, relentless debater, [and] champion of pensioners.'[3] Prior to his death in June 1997, schools, streets, and buildings had already been named for him and two biographies had been written on him.[4] He had become a political legend even in his own time.

This chapter does not examine Knowles' public career, but focuses instead on matters central to the theme of this book, namely, how Christianity and politics coalesced to shape the thought and career of a well-known Canadian public figure. Knowles' theological and political ideals were based on the formation he received as a young man coming of age in the 1920s and 1930s. His understandings of the implications of Christianity, however, compelled him to leave the formal ministry and become a career politician. In making this decision, he considered himself completely faithful to what he held to be the central purpose of Christianity: to reform society by working to improve the economic and social conditions of all people.

This study considers Knowles' life and thought until 1940, the year he resigned as minister of the Kildonan United Church in Winnipeg. By exploring his early sermons and writings and his personal history – the influence of his father; his experiences at Brandon College and United Colleges; his involvement in the Student Christian Movement (SCM), the Fellowship for a Christian Social Order (FCSO), and the United Church – we can identify the religious roots of his political vision. Knowles' goal was to provide leadership and service, and work towards establishing the ideals of God's realm within the very structures of the Dominion of Canada. Like other Christian reformers throughout Western history, he believed that Christianity was useless without applications that resulted in a more just physical world. Intensely individualistic and idealistic, Knowles incarnated the middle – or progressive – social gospel tradition in Canada.[5]

For Knowles, Christianity required political and social reform. The irony of this demand, of course, was that while his formation within Christianity grounded his political perspective and commitment, it also led him out of the institutional church into the civic arena. Knowles did not as a politician utilize overtly Christian language in the manner of his contemporary Ernest Manning, or some of the politically active women a generation or more older than himself examined elsewhere in this volume.[6] But his political commitments were based on and shaped by his understanding of Christianity, and his Christianity was shaped by his political commitments. Knowles became the 'conscience of Parliament' because his foremost allegiance was to a prophetic ideal of reform that few people – and possibly no religious or political movements – could sustain.

Born on 18 June 1908, in Los Angeles, California, Knowles was the son of Canadian expatriates Margaret (Murdock) and Stanley Ernest Knowles. Knowles and his younger brother were brought up in an ambitious working-class family. From an early age, Knowles exhibited the serious nature and an intellectual capacity that would characterize his adult life. When his mother died of tuberculosis in 1919, Stanley Ernest took his boys on an extended trip to visit relatives scattered thoughout Canada and the eastern states. In 1924 they returned to the west coast, where the 15-year-old Knowles received his high school diploma – and training as a printer. After high school graduation he set off on his own trip to visit relatives in Manitoba, the Maritimes, and Massachusetts. He planned to end his trip by staying in New York City and starting studies at the King's College of Columbia University. But he was miserable in New York City and departed within the first month.

Knowles had been brought up in a religiously Christian household, and his family was active in the Methodist Episcopal Church. The Knowles' home and church environment upheld moral behaviour and hard work, but perhaps more important, it upheld the centrality of living one's life in service to both God and humanity. The Methodist heritage shaped Knowles' perception of the purpose of life, as did the close relationship he developed with his father. Knowles was also influenced by his father's sister, Lois, who was a Baptist missionary in India. Aunt Loie (as she was affectionately called) had encouraged her young nephew to become a missionary, a calling he adamantly refused to consider as a child. But in 1924, after dropping out of university and returning to Los Angeles, Knowles experienced a conversion event. He proudly wrote to his extended family about his call to be a missionary; they were elated.[7]

Knowles enrolled in his first year of Arts at the evangelical California Christian College, a school founded and operated by the Christian Church denomination, but also associated with the southern branch of the University of California. On the surface, life was going well. He studied and worked nights as a printer to earn money. But his father had remarried and the relationship between stepson and stepmother was trying. Through his travels and letter-writing, he had become close to his father's sister and her family in Manitoba. Knowles decided to move to Canada. Part of his decision to relocate was based on the fact that a college affiliated with the Baptist Union in Canada existed not too far from his relatives' farm.

Knowles entered Brandon College in the fall of 1927, stating his career objective as 'Christian Ministry (Missionary).'[8] He excelled academically and participated in numerous student groups, including the Ministerial Association, the Student Volunteer Band, the Student Christian Movement Executive, and the Student's Association. As with other classmates planning to enter a form of church ministry, he spent Sundays preaching at various churches scattered throughout the Prairies. The summer following his first year at Brandon, Knowles was appointed to a home-missionary position by the Alberta Baptist Conference and served a rural pastoral charge in Hairy Hill, Alberta. During these months, he finalized paperwork confirming his decision to join the Student Volunteer Movement for Foreign Missions upon graduation. But in the summer of 1929 Knowles attended a western student conference sponsored by the Student Christian Movement in Jasper National Park.

The Jasper SCM conference was pivotal for Knowles. Its theme focused on the power of God and how this power was to be expressed through prayer, study, and service and claimed within Canada and the world. At a later conference hosted by Brandon students, Brandon College Professor Harris L. MacNeill gave the major address on the subject of 'The Idea of the Kingdom.' Student delegates were asked to consider the theme 'Jesus' Faith in Man' and speculate on how the kingdom was present in Canada and the world. Students were convinced that the kingdom was present in Canada and that they had a 'large part to play in making this kingdom'; world problems, most significantly that of war, could be solved by an internationalism that upheld the importance of 'personality, [the] brotherhood of Nations, and corporate responsibility.' Such conferences 'opened up a new vision, a new world, a new challenge,' and persuaded students to understand themselves as the 'makers of tomorrow.'[9]

These conferences, along with three years at Brandon College, changed Knowles' theology, his understanding of ministry, and ultimately, the direction of his life. Professor MacNeill was important in modelling to Knowles a combination of religious devotion and a non-literal interpretation of Scripture. The writings of American theologians such as Walter Rauschenbusch and Harry Emerson Fosdick expanded Knowles' understanding of the Christian tradition and its purpose in the world. Writing as a member of the Ministerial Association at Brandon College, he said: 'A growing realization of the tremendous problems, yet wonderful opportunities, facing the modern minister, and a growing conviction that the pure and simple message of Jesus of Nazareth contains the seeds for a better world, has characterized the Ministerial Association during this past year.' As president of the SCM at the college, Knowles wrote that participating in such a national organization connected all students in a 'quest for worthwhile things in life.'[10] As historian Robert A. Wright observes, the SCM was the 'most liberal organization in Canadian Protestantism in the 1920s, practically celebrating scientific inquiry and humanizing Jesus unabashedly ... [while striving] for full democracy.'[11] Knowles would have wholeheartedly agreed.

Even as a young minister, Knowles preached not what people wanted to hear, but what he thought they needed to hear. He came to hold tremendous confidence in his own particular interpretation of Christianity. His theology upheld the centrality of Jesus and the sacrifice of Jesus for all humanity. The Jesus he preached was kind and tough, intolerant of injustice. This Jesus called his followers to engage in voluntary self-sacrifice so that the kingdom could be achieved in this world. Knowles' Christology is apparent in a sermon first preached in 1930 entitled 'The Light of the World.' The world needed more light, he argued, the light given in Jesus that revealed the dangers of the world and awakened others by showing the light of 'lives sacrificed.' Arguably, Knowles came to believe that his personal sacrifice – or calling – was to expose and confront the 'dangers of the world.' Unlike most evangelical Protestants, he did not understand these dangers as related to personal morals or inner struggles. Rather, they were the economic, political, and social systems, which at their worst caused people to fall into poverty and parochialism and resulted in hopelessness, passivity, and even violence. At their best, they caused people to perpetuate unjust systems and self-righteousness.

By the spring of 1930, as a result of his changing theology (which was now closer to his own Methodist roots), Knowles had decided to enter the ministry of the recently formed United Church rather than the Baptist denomination. Encouraging this decision – and providing the affirmation needed for Knowles' changing theological understandings – was his father. The relationship between father and son was one of emotional intimacy, mutual admiration, and constant encouragement. They exchanged scores of letters that kept one another current on family happenings, but perhaps more important, provided a forum in which they discussed major theological issues. Knowles provided his father with synopses of his sermons and detailed descriptions of his changing theology. His father responded with pride, self-identification, and almost total agreement. 'Your last two sermon letters have been above the average in thot [sic] and expositions and revelation of the real spirit of Christ,' he wrote in the fall of 1929. 'I do not say this to praise unduly, tho [sic] I appreciate all you have written, but I have read quite widely and have heard a great many widely known preachers ... and yet I have never heard one who had such a practical insight to the real life and purpose of Jesus and his purpose for his followers ... I do not say this to puff you up, if I thot [sic] it would I would keep silent, but I think you have humility and sense enough not to get a big head.'[12]

Knowles senior had unfulfilled – and largely hidden – ambitions of becoming a preacher himself and was thrilled that his son was carrying the 'torch of a new life linked up with God on earth by following the teachings of Jesus of Nazareth.' He too had experienced a theological transformation, but had never previously – prior to his son's revelation – discussed it. 'I am glad that you have acquired this new concept of the mission and teachings of Jesus,' Knowles' father wrote, 'and it is what I have been trying to grasp and formulate in words for more than twenty years, but lacking ability and knowledge to express it.'[13] His father had also been a long-time supporter of Henry George and the so-called single tax. Numerous times he encouraged his son to read George's best-selling book *Progress and Poverty* (1879). He suggested that while his son might not completely agree with George's economic ideas, he would most certainly appreciate the 'spiritual vision that [George] had of a race of men devoted to the higher things of life, and not to the greed and gain of commercialism.'[14]

The relationship between Knowles and his father reflects the findings of American historian William R. Hutchison in his exploration of why some male religious leaders between the years 1875 and 1914 became religiously 'liberal' while others became religiously 'conservative.'[15] Hutchison found that those individuals who became Protestant liberals shared significant relationships with their fathers or uncles in which the younger men developed a strong Christian identity but also knew that changing their theology would not 'explode [the] orthodoxy' of their familial roots. This pattern is discernible in the letters between Knowles and his father. 'To some people the casting away of old religious forms and phrases is the casting away of all religion,' Knowles senior wrote, 'when in reality it is only throwing away the shell and holding on to the real meat inside the shell.'[16]

Knowles' father was concerned, however, about the denominational affiliation of his son, and had urged him to return to the United States and become a Methodist minister: 'Of course you have to choose for yourself, but I could wish that you would find it in God's plan for you to be affiliated with the church of your childhood and of your father and also of your native country.' Prodding his son, he continued, 'I have written on this point before, but you have not answered me yet.'[17] Perhaps Knowles was tardy in responding to his father on this issue because he knew that he would not return to the United States; Canada had become his adopted home. Father and son did come to agree, however, that the Baptist denomination would not be the best choice for Knowles' future ministry. The senior Knowles was concerned that it would not support his son's theology and understanding of a personal and social gospel, and he feared that it would circumscribe his son's 'usefulness.'[18] The most logical choice for Knowles was the recently formed United Church of Canada, whose roots included Methodism.

Historian Richard Allen has noted that the formation of the United Church in 1925 was 'among other things, a triumph of the social gospel.'[19] The United Church, however, faced numerous challenges in the late 1920s and 1930s, not the least of which were the needs to establish a church organization in the midst of a national economic depression and to direct scarce financial resources to maintain programs and personnel. Church feasibility was especially challenging on the Prairies, where severe social tension existed due to drought and depression, immigration and migration, and the discord of labourers and farmers. United Church leaders mulled over how their church was to be active in these issues, which affected both religious and civic life. Disagreements regarding member and/or formal church endorsement of labour, pacifism, and socialism – not to mention temperance, suffrage, and the ordination of women – were often controversial and sometimes ecclesiastically disruptive. By the very nature of its union – and its self-perception as a national public church – the United Church encompassed the spectrum of theological beliefs and political views.[20]

How much Knowles knew about the United Church in 1930 is questionable.[21] While his decision to join it was likely based on a desire to appease his father and maintain some tie to Methodism, personal connections also played a role, as his Brandon classmate Duncan Wilkie and his SCM friend Lloyd Stinson both intended to enter the United Church ministry. But Knowles was not dedicated to any particular form of denominationalism; what he wanted was a base from which to propagate his understanding of the gospel as a prophetic element within the world at large. By the time Knowles graduated – with highest academic honours – from Brandon in June 1930, he had decided to pursue ordination in the United Church and theological studies at the United Colleges in Winnipeg. The college was at that time experiencing a kind of revival. Faculty, students, and staff were all excited about what they saw as the 'world standing on the verge of a great spiritual awakening.'[22]

Knowles' theology was encouraged and deepened by studying for his Bachelor of Divinity at United. Being in Winnipeg itself – the city of the Great Strike of 1919 and the social gospel leadership of J.S. Woodsworth and Salem Bland, not to mention William Ivens, founder of the short-lived Labour Church – provided personal incentive to Knowles. Living during the depression – observing the continuing economic hardships, labour disputes, and struggles of new immigrants – provided him with a practical dimension to his intellectual and theological interpretations. Theological students visited city missions to 'see the needs of those at our very doors' and the efforts being made within the United Church 'to meet those needs.' Faculty such as Principal John MacKay encouraged students to be active in 're-making the world.' In later reflection Knowles said, 'most of us [at United Colleges] in those days and my kind of United Church Minister at the time [were] just completely convinced that [the social gospel] was the main purpose of the Christian message.'[23]

As a theology student, Knowles busied himself with his studies, participated in student affairs, and worked in ministry positions. During his first two academic years at United, he found part-time employment as church school superintendent at the First Baptist Church, and during the summer of 1931 he was student minister at a United Church in Winnipeg Beach. In 1932, he and a fellow student split ministerial duties at the Central United Church, the congregation that called him in 1933 to be their sole minister. But before Knowles could become a United Church minister, he needed to become a member of a United Church congregation that would be willing to sponsor him as a candidate for ministry. He therefore joined Young United Church, a formerly Methodist congregation not far from the downtown college campus, and preached before this congregation several times as a ministerial candidate.

Knowles' extracurricular energy was exerted writing for the student newspaper, *VOX*, and participating in several high-profile debates. In his writings of the period, he discussed what he understood to be the purpose of the Christian church and, more specifically, the purpose of ministry. In one article, Knowles argued that the purpose of theological education was to equip students to provide 'definite and visionary leadership.' He challenged educational institutions 'to foster less of mere technical training and far more of creative living.' He wanted theological courses to emphasize the 'way of life which Jesus sought to impart' and the practical dimensions of it within the 'complexities of economic, social and political orders.' 'Surely education cannot be content as a mere reflection of its environment,' he wrote. 'The essential part which it is hers to play is that of leadership.'[24]

Three years later Knowles wrote about the challenges faced by the church during the 'social crises' of his day. He suggested that the criticisms received by the church relating to its failures, its perceived conservatism, and 'subservience to the *status quo*' were positive signs showing that people expected the church to live up to its teachings. Such judgments were good, he argued, because they forced the 'church to re-think her teachings in terms of our social and economic structure.' Knowles applauded the fact that the church was 'discovering, or perhaps rediscovering,' that 'human welfare comes ahead of the sanctity of systems.' He applauded the emphasis the church placed on the equality of all people and its rediscovery of the 'necessity of destroying the value of wealth as an end in itself, as something to be sought, acquired and held.' He was excited that 'in no small section of organized Christianity there is already being offered definite leadership in the task of economic reconstruction.'[25]

As a student minister at Central United, Knowles' sermons emphasized the social aspects of Christianity. One of his sermons was taken almost directly from his prepared script for a debate that called on Knowles and his teammate to argue affirmatively for the resolution that the 'Western World Must Travel the Moscow Road.' Knowles was not a communist, but his sermon – like the content of his debate – condemned capitalism and advocated economic reorganization.[26] In a sermon entitled 'Is Capitalism Doomed?' Knowles preached that the church must not grant to capitalism a sacredness it did not inherently possess. Like the church, capitalism was responsible for the economic, social, and moral well-being of humanity. 'If Capitalism is unable to serve these needs, if Capitalism is doomed to defeat the very purposes of Christianity,' he continued, 'it is the solemn duty of the Christian Church, in the name of mankind, and in the sight of her God, to demand that the whole system be thoroughly revised, or completely overthrown ... Economic systems are made for men, and not men for economic systems.'

Knowles not only wrote, debated, and preached his ideas, but also organized his ministry goals around them. In the fall of 1932 he started Sunday evening forums, which attracted mostly nonchurch members. Susan Mann Trofimenkoff, Knowles' biographer, suggests that in organizing these forums Knowles unknowingly revived a tradition of the short-lived Labour Church movement.[27] But in January 1933 Knowles launched at the Central Church the Winnipeg portion of the Movement for a Christian Social Order, showing that he understood the forums as connected to a wider network within the United Church. Later renamed the Fellowship for a Christian Social Order (FCSO), this organization had been started in Toronto in 1931 by United Church clergymen and professors. Its ultimate purpose was to call the church away from maintaining the political, economic, and social status quo to claiming the revolutionary resources of Christianity that affirmed the 'faith of the prophets and of Jesus as a disturbing, renovating force' in the world. A socialized economic system, a prophetic church emphasizing the equality of all people, and a theistic theology aiming to 'convert human society into a divine commonwealth of righteousness and love,' were central tenets to the FCSO. Radical clergy, liberal academics, and former SCM participants found it attractive. Not surprisingly, historian John Webster Grant identifies the FCSO as one of the best examples of the radical left within 1930s Protestantism.[28]

Knowles supported the movement because it addressed the gap between labour and the church specifically, and between the civic and religious realms generally. It showed that the 'ideal of a "Kingdom of Heaven upon Earth" ... [has] much if not everything in common' with the 'dream of a "Classless Society."' Moreover, it responded to the 'pressing problems of the modern world,' which Knowles believed were the responsibility of the church as well as of labour. It gave labour a voice in the official courts of the United Church by presenting resolutions at the Annual Conference. Knowles continued his involvement in the FCSO and later became active in the Alberta School of Religion, whose leaders were affiliated with the organization.[29]

United Colleges' classmate Lloyd Stinson wrote that Knowles 'became known as a radical preacher, champion of the poor and unemployed' because of his preaching and forums.[30] While Knowles may have developed a following in parts of the city, the board members of Central United did not warmly receive his ideas and actions. Although they had called Knowles to be their full-time minister in the summer of 1933, they did so hoping that their young pastor would lessen the social focus of his ministry. When he did not, the board requested that Knowles discontinue the forums. He complied, but then decided to utilize radio broadcasts to preach his message. These radio sermons attracted even more listeners than did the forums. Again the board was not pleased. One board member asked him, 'How many souls are you saving with all these activities?' While Knowles acknowledged both an individual and social message within Christianity, he declared that during the economic and social dislocation of the 1930s – and in his own particular ministry – the social aspect of Christianity must be emphasized.[31]

Knowles' early years in ministry paralleled his initial formal political involvements. In 1934, he joined the CCF. Founded just two years previously as an alliance between farmers, labourers, and socialist reformers, it quickly achieved wide support by United Church people on the left and ardent opposition from people on the right.[32] At its first national convention in 1933, J.S. Woodsworth was elected president and the federation adopted its political program. The so-called Regina Manifesto contained elements that Knowles wholeheartedly supported, including the establishment of a 'planned [and] socialized economic order,' the nationalization of essential industries and services, and the establishment of 'freely available' health services.[33] Knowles became active in promoting the CCF platform. He preached at his church on Sunday mornings, on Sunday afternoons he spoke at CCF events, and in the evenings he often did radio broadcasts. To appease his board, he tried to distinguish between his political and ministerial activities. Ultimately he was unable to do so; Knowles' political platform became a way to implement his theological vision of establishing God's reign on earth.

In the spring of 1935 Knowles was asked to let his name stand for nomination in the upcoming federal election. He described his decision to run for Parliament as 'as distinctly a call as anything I ever experienced.'[34] A number of factors contributed to his affirmative response. In April of that year he had become a naturalized citizen, so he was eligible to run.[35] His working relationship with the Central United board had not improved, and that situation, combined with the likelihood that the church would be forced to close due to the inability to finance necessary building repairs, also contributed to Knowles' decision to resign his ministerial position at the end of June 1935. As with all his important decisions, Knowles also had the full support of his father. To Knowles' surprise, however, he lost the election.

More personally unsettling than electoral defeat was the death of his father less than two weeks before the election. Knowles came to believe that his father's death due to cancer was related to his unfair dismissal from employment just two years earlier. The death now provided an underlying personal motive for Knowles' devotion to social change.

With his, albeit unsuccessful, entry into the political process, Knowles had discovered his vocational direction. Nevertheless, he was to remain in the United Church ministry for the next five years. He accepted appointment at the MacLean Mission. Located in the north-central area of Winnipeg, this mission provided worship and community services. It had a hard time 'attracting and keeping a minister,' partly because it could not pay a very good salary.[36] Like many other city missions, however, its consistent leadership was provided by female deaconesses, not by male ministers.

The deaconess at MacLean when Knowles arrived was Vida Cruikshank, who had been there since 1930. A bright and outgoing woman – and a daughter of a prominent Anglican Winnipeg family – Cruikshank was a 1927 Bachelor of Arts graduate from the University of Manitoba, where she excelled as a member of the women's track and co-ed basketball teams.[37] After graduation, Cruikshank served as a missionary-teacher on a Native American reservation in Saskachewan, directed girls' programs at the YWCA, and wrote for a newspaper. Because her primary interest was religious education, she then decided to complete the one-year deaconess program at United Colleges. When she graduated in 1930, she won numerous awards for her academic work, including top honours for an essay contest involving all students – female and male – in theological colleges of the United Church in western Canada. Her essay, entitled 'The Contribution of the New Canadian to Canadian Life,' would have prepared her well for the work at MacLean.[38]

Three years older than Knowles, much more experienced in community work, and excelling in community networking, Cruikshank taught her future husband much about practical ministry matters. She helped him form his sermons and, later, his political speeches. Because she was also a well-known leader in the neighbourhood, it is likely that many of Knowles' political votes in 1942 were cast for his wife as much as for him. At least initially, it appeared that Knowles and Cruikshank were a good match; they were intellectual peers and equally committed to the ideal of service.[39]

With their upcoming marriage, Knowles needed a position that would pay a married minister's salary. He accepted a call to serve as minister of the Kildonan United Church. This working-class congregation was very supportive of Knowles and his ministry. Like other parish pastors, Knowles conducted worship services, weddings, funerals, and baptisms. He also resumed his Sunday evening radio broadcasts, which continued in a social gospel vein. In one sermon entitled 'Whither Canada,' preached in 1937, Knowles argued that the 'supreme need in Canada today is to organize, *intelligently* [emphasis mine], into the actual machinery of life in this Dominion, the good-will, the human kindness, and the well-wishing, the hoping and the dreaming, of which we are possessed in our abundance.' Knowles believed that Christians needed to address the economic, democratic, and international aspects of life in Canada. He posed the question, 'Where does religion come in all this?' His response was simple: 'This is religion. True Christianity has always had one aim, the making of a better world.' Knowles identified the Christian religion – understood intelligently – as the prime motivator for public action.

Despite all the rhetoric and advocacy of Knowles and people of sim-ilar theological and political persuasion, however, the world was not becoming better. Knowles' pacifism, which had been shaped by the SCM and furthered by the FCSO, was firm by the 1930s. In 1934, he wrote to the United Church journal *New Outlook*, stating that he would endorse civil disobedience in the event of war.[40] In 1938 the United Church passed a resolution that condemned war in the solving of international problems and upheld individual conscience in choosing pacifism, but reached no consensus on when war could be deemed legitimate or illegitimate.[41] When war was declared by Canada on 10 September 1939, Knowles objected. Along with over sixty other United Church men and women – many of whom were active in the FCSO – he signed 'A Witness against the War,' a document published a month later in the *United Church Observer*.[42] While acknowledging that other United Church clergy and members supported the war, the sign-ers of the letter declared that the 'nature of modern war is such that it is and must be incompatible with the Christian spirit and aims.' It reminded readers how the church lost authority due to its support of the First World War and declared that at 'no point has Christendom departed so radically from the mind of Christ and its own original faith as in its acceptance of war.' The document became highly contro-versial within the United Church and many of the clergymen who signed it faced dismissal by their congregations.[43]

Knowles himself was not reproved by the Kildonan Church for his public pacifist position. The failure of the United Church to condemn the war officially, however, may have confirmed his decision to resign from Kildonan and seek public office: he had become convinced that he could accomplish more reform as a politician-minister than just as a minister. The church board accepted his resignation at the end of June 1940, at which time he ran for the federal election. He lost that election, as well as a provincial one a year later. He was then elected a city alderman in 1941. When J.S. Woodsworth died in 1942 and a by-election was held in Winnipeg North Centre, Knowles was elected to Parliament.[44] While he lacked 'Woodsworth's authority or charisma,' Knowles did share the 'same single-minded devotion to service and the same commitment to reform and social change.'[45]

Some scholars may be tempted to interpret Knowles' entry into the political arena as an example of secularization.[46] But such an interpretation does not recognize the intricacy and connectedness of Knowles' theology and political commitments at a time when many considered Christian moral values to have profound implications for public life. Like other United Church clergy during this period, he believed that economic restructuring was necessary in order to make the world a better place. Influenced and supported by his father, shaped by Brandon and United Colleges, and encouraged by the dedication upheld by the SCM and the FCSO, Knowles simply undertook the next logical step: he left the church to build the kingdom. As did the Hebrew prophets – and in his interpretation, as did Jesus himself – Knowles rationally and calmly protested against the injustices perpetuated by the powerful against the weak. He became the 'conscience of Parliament.'

Notes

1 Knowles ran in thirteen reelection campaigns in Winnipeg North Centre between the years 1945 and 1980, losing only in 1958. Between 1958 and reelection in 1962, he served as chair of the National Committee forming the New Democratic Party. See his *The New Party/Le Nouveau Parti* (Toronto: McClelland and Stewart, 1961).

2 *Winnipeg Free Press*, 28 February 1999.

3 See Lloyd Stinson, *Political Warriors: Recollections of a Social Democrat* (Winnipeg: Queenston House, 1975), 59–60.

4 Susan Mann Trofimenkoff, *Stanley Knowles: The Man from Winnipeg North Centre* (Saskatoon: Western Producer Prairie Books, 1982); and Gerry Harrop, *Advocate of Compassion: Stanley Knowles in the Political Process* (Hantsport, NS: Lancelot, 1984).

5 See Richard Allen, *The Social Passion: Religion and Social Reform in Canada, 1914–1928* (Toronto: University of Toronto Press, 1971), for the three-strand theoretical framework of the social gospel in Canada, a theory first proposed by C.H. Hopkins in *The Rise of the Social Gospel in American Protestantism, 1865–1915* (New Haven: Yale University Press, 1940).

6 See David Marshall's and Mary Kinnear's contributions to this volume.

7 Lois Knowles to Stanley Knowles, 6 September 1918 and 11 February 1925, Stanley H. Knowles Fonds, vol. 390–2 and 390–3, National Archives of Canada (NAC).

8 Student Registration and Transcript, vol. 490, NAC. See my article, 'The Education of Stanley Howard Knowles,' *Manitoba History* 36 (Autumn/Winter 1998–9): 41–51, for a more in-depth treatment of Knowles' years at Brandon College and United Colleges.

9 See Stinson, *Political Warriors*, 62f.; and personal papers of David Stanley Knowles, Western Student Conference of the SCM, 20–7 June 1929, pamphlet. See also *The Quill* (published by the Students Association of Brandon College) 10, no. 2 (21 October 1929).

10 Brandon College *Sickle*, 1928–9, 46.

11 Robert A. Wright, 'The Canadian Protestant Tradition 1914–1945,' in *The Canadian Protestant Experience, 1760–1990*, ed. George A. Rawlyk (Burlington, ON: Welch, 1990), 146. See also Margaret Eileen Beattie, *A Brief History of the Student Christian Movement in Canada* (Toronto?: [1975]).

12 Stanley E. Knowles to Stanley Knowles, 15 September 1929, vol. 500–2, NAC.

13 Stanley E. Knowles to Stanley Knowles, 11 August 1929 and 27 August 1928, vol. 500–2, NAC.

14 Stanley E. Knowles to Stanley Knowles, 11 August 1929, 15 September 1929, 10 September 1933, vol. 500–2 and 500–4, NAC. For an analysis of George's place within the social gospel movement, see Paul T. Phillips, *A Kingdom on Earth: Anglo-American Social Christianity, 1880–1940* (University Park: Pennsylvania State University Press, 1996).

15 William R. Hutchison, 'Cultural Strain and Protestant Liberalism,' *American Historical Review* 76, no. 2 (April 1971): 386–411.

16 Stanley E. Knowles to Stanley Knowles, 11 August 1929, vol. 500–2, NAC. See also letters from vol. 500–4, dated 9 June 1929, 20 and 28 September 1930.

17 Stanley E. Knowles to Stanley Knowles, 16 June 1929, vol. 500–2, NAC.

18 Stanley E. Knowles to Stanley Knowles, 28 July 1929, vol. 500–2, NAC.

19 Allen, *The Social Passion*, 256.

20 For an analysis of these 'years of crisis,' see John Webster Grant, *The Church in the Canadian Era* (Burlington, ON: Welch, 1988), chap. 7; Ben Smillie, *Beyond the Social Gospel: Church Protest on the Prairies* (Toronto: United Church Publishing House, 1991), chap. 6; and Michiel Horn, ed., *The Dirty Thirties: Canadians in the Great Depression* (n.p.: Copp Clark, 1972), esp. 390f.

21 Knowles knew about the union when he still lived in Los Angeles, for he cut out and pasted into his scrapbook a multipaged article entitled 'Canada Leads the World in Church Union.' Private papers of David S. Knowles, scrapbook no. 3.

22 As expressed by the principal of Manitoba College, the Rev. John MacKay, in a lecture given to the Manitoba Baptist Convention, which Knowles covered as a student reporter. *Western Baptist* 23, no. 6 (July 1930): 4. See also Joint Executive Board, Minutes, 7 October 1926 to 12 November 1937, Minutes of the United Theological Faculty of Manitoba and Wesley Colleges, UC-3–2, University of Winnipeg Archives. For a historical survey of United, see A.G. Bedford, *The University of Winnipeg: A History of the Founding Colleges* (Toronto: University of Toronto Press, 1976).

23 See United Colleges student newspaper, *VOX* 6, no. 1 (December 1932): 14f.; John MacKay, graduation speech, *Brown and Gold* (University of Manitoba, 1933), 139; interview between Stanley Knowles and Brian McKillop, 3, University of Manitoba Archives. See also Kenneth McNaught, *A Prophet in Politics* (Toronto: University of Toronto Press, 1959); Allen Mills, *Fool for Christ: The Political Thought of J.S. Woodsworth* (Toronto: University of Toronto Press, 1991); Benjamin Smillie, 'The Woodsworths: James and J.S. – Father and Son,' in *Prairie Spirit: Perspectives on the Heritage of the United Church of Canada in the West*, ed. Dennis L. Butcher et al. (Winnipeg: University of Manitoba Press, 1985); Richard Allen, 'Salem Bland and the Spirituality of the Social Gospel: Winnipeg and the West, 1903–1913,' in *Prairie Spirit*; and Vera Fast, 'The Labour Church in Winnipeg,' in *Prairie Spirit*. For an overview of the decade, see *The Dirty Thirties in Prairie Canada*, ed. R.D. Francis and H. Ganzevoort (Vancouver: Tantalus Research, 1980).

24 'A Question or Two,' *VOX* 4, no. 1 (December 1930): 31–2.

25 'The Church in the Social Crises,' *VOX* 6, no. 2 (March 1933): 8–9, 11.

26 Private papers of David S. Knowles, Imperial Debate: 'Resolved That the Western World Must Travel the Moscow Road,' sponsored by the National Federation of Canadian University Students, Civic Auditorium, 10 November 1932; pamphlet, 'Is Capitalism Doomed?' a sermon preached in Central United Church, 4 December 1932, as part of a sermon series on the Church and Economic Reconstruction.

27 See Mann Trofimenkoff, *Stanley Knowles*, chap. 4, for an excellent interpretation of Knowles' experiences in pastoral ministry.

28 R.B.Y. Scott and Gregory Vlastos, eds., *Towards the Christian Revolution* (Chicago: Willett, Clark, 1936), ix and 50. (This was the handbook of the FCSO.) See also Roger Hutchinson, 'The Fellowship for a Christian Social Order: 1934–1945,' in *A Long and Faithful March: Towards the Christian Revo-*

lution, 1930s/1980s, ed. Harold Wells and Roger Hutchinson (Toronto: United Church Publishing House, 1989), 20; and Grant, *The Church in the Canadian Era*, 140f. For a feminist analysis, see Marilyn J. Legge, *The Grace of Difference: A Canadian Feminist Theological Ethic* (Atlanta: Scholars Press, 1992), 40f.

29 Private papers of David S. Knowles, 'Movement for a Christian Social Order – Basis, Aims, Program'; pamphlet, The Alberta School of Religion, 27 July to 6 August 1937, meeting with Knowles listed as devotion leader.

30 Stinson, *Political Warriors*, 65.

31 Mann Trofimenkoff, *Stanley Knowles*, 40f.

32 See Brian Clark, 'English-Speaking Canada from 1854,' in *A Concise History of Christianity in Canada*, ed. Terrence Murphy and Roberto Perin (Toronto: Oxford University Press, 1996), 344.

33 Pamphlet, Co-operative Commonwealth Federation Programme, adopted at the First National Convention, Regina, Saskatchewan, July 1933.

34 Quoted by Mann Trofimenkoff, *Stanley Knowles*, 38.

35 Certificate of Naturalization, issued 26 April 1935, vol. 486, NAC.

36 Mann Trofimenkoff, *Stanley Knowles*, 48.

37 *Brown and Gold* (1927), 20.

38 *VOX* 3, no. 3 (June 1930): 9, 25.

39 Private papers and interview with Donna Cruikshank Friesen, Winnipeg. The Knowles had one son, David, and one daughter, Margaret. With Knowles' entry into federal politics – and the need for him to travel and spend much of his time in Ottawa – the relationship between wife and husband deteriorated. Not unlike some other women of her generation, Mrs Knowles also began to suffer from depression and anxiety. Although they remained married until her death in 1978, they led virtually separate lives from the 1950s. Before her death, she became a known artist in the city of Winnipeg.

40 *New Outlook*, 21 November 1934, 1033, quoted by Thomas P. Socknat, *Witness against War: Pacifism in Canada, 1900–1945* (Toronto: University of Toronto Press, 1987), 153f.

41 Grant, *The Church in the Canadian Era*, 150.

42 *United Church Observer*, 15 October 1939, 21.

43 Socknat, *Witness against War*, 200–11.

44 Knowles was nominated as CCF candidate in the Winnipeg North Centre riding only after Woodsworth's widow declined the candidacy. Vertical file, United Church Archives (Winnipeg).

45 David Lewis, *The Good Fight: Political Memoirs, 1909–1958* (Toronto: Macmillan, 1981), 199f.

46 Allen, *The Social Passion*; Ramsay Cook, *The Regenerators: Social Criticism in Late Victorian English Canada* (Toronto: University of Toronto Press, 1985); David B. Marshall, *Secularizing the Faith: Canadian Protestant Clergy and the Crisis of Belief, 1850–1940* (Toronto: University of Toronto Press, 1992). For an argument against these understandings of secularization theories, see Nancy Christie and Michael Gauvreau, *A Full-Orbed Christianity: The Protestant Churches and Social Welfare in Canada, 1900–1940* (Montreal and Kingston: McGill-Queen's University Press, 1996).

11

Premier E.C. Manning, *Back to the Bible Hour*, and Fundamentalism in Canada

David Marshall

In 1960, one of the most perceptive observers of the Social Credit movement in Alberta, John Irving, wrote a retrospective article in *Saturday Night* magazine asserting that 'the challenge of Christianity suffuses the whole being of the Premier of Alberta.'[1] Although the article referred to Ernest C. Manning, the leader of the Social Credit Party and premier of Alberta from 1943 to 1968, the same could be said for Manning's predecessor and mentor, William Aberhart. Both of these successful Alberta political leaders were fundamentalist lay preachers, driven by the call to spread the Christian gospel.[2] From 1935, when Aberhart's Social Credit Party swept into power in Alberta, to 1968, when Ernest Manning stepped down from the premier's chair, politics and government in Alberta were dominated by men who were heard weekly over the radio preaching that the Bible was the inerrant Word of God and that the Second Coming of Christ was imminent. Manning in particular spearheaded a popular religious movement that was typical of post–Second World War evangelical fundamentalism.[3] He expanded the Alberta-based radio ministry he inherited from Aberhart into a well-organized network of broadcasts with a national following, and during the 1950s and 1960s *Back to the Bible Hour* was broadcast across Canada.

Aberhart and Manning were different from other fundamentalist leaders in North America in one important respect: they were not on the margins of society. They held political power and enjoyed a large political following outside their immediate fundamentalist constituency. Nevertheless, what struck and also troubled many was that neither Aberhart nor Manning kept their religious faith private. For both, religion and politics were indivisible. According to Manning's reading of Scripture, God led truly born-again Christians 'into fields of public service' in the same way that others were led 'to the mission field and to the pulpit or into business or into any other sphere where He wishes them to be as His witnesses in the midst of an ungodly world.' Manning continually stressed in letters and speeches that anyone who has 'experienced a supernatural spiritual new birth cannot divorce the effects of the new birth from any issue or activity.'[4]

While we know a great deal about Aberhart, little is known about his successor.[5] Neither Ernest Manning nor his *Back to the Bible Hour* broadcasts have received attention from historians of religion in Canada. The only scholarly studies of Manning largely ignore his religious faith.[6] Yet in terms of the history of popular religion in Canada, Manning and the *Back to the Bible Hour* broadcasts played an important role on the national stage.

Back to the Bible Hour and its brand of fundamentalist religion translated across Alberta's borders with the central message of the inerrant King James Bible and dispensationalism, a distinctive form of premillennial biblical interpretation. Manning encountered difficulties in the face of CBC regulations and political suspicions that his evangelistic broadcasts mixed his religion with his political life. Critical and attentive listeners of *Back to the Bible Hour* discerned that Manning provided biblical sanction for the Social Credit Party through the quotation and explication of the prophetic passages of the Bible. Nevertheless, his religious broadcasts were popular, had a national audience, and were able to weather the political storms of their day. The transcendent role of religion in Manning's private and public life was at the heart of his conviction that he could carry on his radio ministry while fulfilling the role of premier. As premier of Alberta, he forged a unique and controversial way of dealing with the classic conundrum that confronted all Christians – of engagement with the world and separation from it.

Ernest Manning was born in Carnduff, Saskatchewan, in 1908. In 1925, at the age of seventeen, he bought an Emerson radio set. After installing the aerial on the farmhouse roof, he began 'twirling the dials to see how many stations he could pick up' in an effort to break the isolation of rural Prairie life. One Sunday afternoon, he happened to catch Calgary radio station CFCN, known as the 'Voice of the Prairie' because it had the strongest signal in western Canada. William Aberhart was delivering an impassioned radio sermon that was, as Manning recalled, 'responsible for changing the whole course of my life.'[7] The young Manning continued to listen to Aberhart's broadcasts every Sunday and learned of the radio preacher's plans to build a Bible school.

The Calgary Prophetic Bible Institute opened its doors in September of 1927. Ernest Manning was the first student to enrol. Like many other Bible colleges that were emerging in North America, the curriculum at the Calgary Institute featured personal holiness, evangelization and missionary work, and Bible study with an emphasis on dispensational-ism.[8] In the summers, Manning returned to Saskatchewan. While working on the farm, he drove the tractor from sunup to well after sundown. As he explained, the furrows were long and the tractor slow, so he could read many passages of Scripture before having to lift his gaze from the Holy Book to turn the tractor around. At the end of the day, he returned to the bunkhouse, where he would 'pore over the Scriptures, often till 1:00 or 2:00 in the morning – just fascinated.'

Manning was the first to complete the three-year curriculum at the Prophetic Bible Institute. He was a young man of quiet manner and serious dedication with steady and thorough work habits. Aberhart recognized his young student's managerial skills, considerable devotion, and ability to work long hours. In the fall of 1929 he asked Manning to stay on at the college and assume some office responsibilities, including looking after the management of the radio broadcasts. During the 1930s and 1940s Manning became well known to Albertans as Aberhart's trusted lieutenant in the Social Credit movement and government. He often took over the weekly broadcasts from the Calgary Prophetic Bible Institute when Aberhart's schedule was too busy.

It would be a mistake to assume that Manning merely carried on Aberhart's legacy in the premier's office and in the radio ministry. Their differences became apparent soon after Aberhart's death, as Manning emerged from his mentor's dominant shadow. Some of their differences reflected the basic tension in fundamentalism. Whereas Aberhart was sectarian, separatist, and insistent on doctrinal purity, Manning was more in tune with the revivalist heritage in fundamentalism; his evangelicalism was designed to reach out to as many people as possible. Both men stressed biblical prophecy in their radio ministries, but Manning also encouraged his listeners to be 'born again' and stressed the need for revival much more than did Aberhart. He did not engage in the doctrinal battles of his predecessor that had led to strained and broken relations with other fundamentalists and evangelicals. In fact, Manning established contacts with numerous American fundamentalists, such as W.E. Houghton of the Moody Bible Institute, and institutions, such as the Christian Business Men's Committee, which was interested in promoting a spiritual awakening. Perhaps the most influential contact he made was with Charles E. Fuller,[9] whose *Old Fashioned Revival Hour* pioneered the extension of radio ministries through an independent network of radio stations. Manning may have been inspired to reconsider many elements of the radio ministry by this popular American radio evangelist.

Manning quickly placed his own imprint on his mentor's radio ministry when he inherited it in 1943. He changed the format of the show to make it more appealing for radio audiences. Instead of combining the Sunday school class for children, Bible study for adults, worship service from the Prophetic Institute, and the gospel tunes and sermon of the radio ministry into one five-hour broadcast, Manning split up these different elements. The gospel tunes and Bible talk were packaged into a one-hour program called *Back to the Bible Hour*. The Sunday school for children was separately broadcast as *Radio Sunday School*. Similarly, the Bible class became *Family Altar Bible Class*. Manning's greatest innovation was his decision to extend the territory of the broadcast. In December of 1948, sometime after Fuller's revival tour in Alberta, he began to establish an informal network of radio stations to broadcast *Back to the Bible Hour*. CFRN of Edmonton, CKWX in Vancouver, and CKCK in Regina became part of a network of broadcasters. As he expanded the territory of his radio ministry, however, he began to encounter difficulties with Canadian Broadcasting Corporation regulations.

In Canada, as in the United States, there were suspicions about the controversial nature of religious broadcasting sponsored by movements or institutions that were outside the denominational mainstream.[10] The anti-Catholic religious broadcasting of the Jehovah's Witnesses in the late 1920s prompted government regulation in Canadian broadcasting. The Broadcasting Act of 1936 supported the interests of the major denominations and favoured the churches; only ordained clergy had access to the CBC's impressive array of religious programming. Church services could be broadcast over the CBC network on Sunday free of charge as a public service. The National Religious Advisory Council, comprised of clergy from the major denominations, invited representative ministers from churches across Canada to conduct *Church of the Air* and *Religious Period*. Local ministerial associations scheduled the weekday CBC broadcast *Morning Devotions*.[11]

Since the CBC relied upon the mainline churches in determining policy or religious broadcasting, the Calgary Prophetic Bible Institute had no influence on the regulations concerning any program with religious content. Furthermore, CBC advertising regulations made it difficult for Manning to raise the funds necessary to air the show. With the exception of mentioning the name of a sponsor, advertising or commercial spot announcements on Sundays were prohibited. Thus, Manning was forced to develop highly innovative ways to make his radio ministry's dependence on donations absolutely clear without advertising or soliciting for funds directly over the airwaves. He announced the creation of a Radio Club during the 25 September 1949 program. Those individuals who donated $5.00 and those families who donated $10.00 became regular members. Sustaining members were 'those who covenant to give $100.00 per year to sustain the radio Broadcasts already in existence [and] to help in spreading the Gospel of Grace through additional stations, as far across Canada as possible.' Within the first month seventy-seven members had enrolled in the Radio Club. The funds raised were used to add stations in Grande Prairie, Alberta, and Vernon, British Columbia.[12] Manning invested additional funding in further expanding the number of stations broadcasting *Back to the Bible Hour*. By the mid-1950s, nine stations, from Winnipeg to Halifax, were added to the network. On any Sunday in the 1950s, at least three different *Back to the Bible Hour* broadcasts were aired.

The major responsibility for fundraising rested with Manning; any donation was entirely voluntary and, in large measure, a response to his preaching. Raising funds for this ambitious radio ministry proved to be one of Manning's greatest challenges. He took time from his busy schedule as premier to respond to many of the contributors' letters. No doubt this was a way to build a sense of a *Back to the Bible Hour* community and to keep the correspondence and donations flowing. In this correspondence to listeners he frequently touched on the evangelical and premillennial themes of the show. He expressed his hope that through the radio ministry 'many of the unsaved may hear the Word and accept the Lord Jesus Christ as their personal Saviour while there is time yet.'[13] On some occasions he was much franker about the value of the contribution. 'We are happy to learn that you are enjoying the *Back to the Bible Hour* programs,' he wrote to a listener from Halfway Lake in Alberta. 'In addition to broadcasting from Edmonton at a cost of $15.00 each week, we are sending the program over the radio station in Prince Albert, Saskatchewan, and they charge $26.00 each week.'[14]

Manning's constant appeals for support met with some criticism from devoted listeners. One long-time listener complained that she was tired of hearing appeals for funds to aid the radio ministry. It was time, she thought, that the gospel be heard 'free of charge.' This critic, who obviously took Manning's preaching about prophecies to heart, encouraged him to choose a parcel of land near Edmonton, preferably near Leduc, and then she would 'pray earnestly that the mighty God will send 3 gushers of oil to carry on the work.'[15]

The constant necessity of raising funds from listeners ultimately placed *Back to the Bible Hour* in conflict with CBC broadcasting regulations. According to Regulation 5(g), no radio station could broadcast an appeal for monetary donations or subscriptions unless the appeal was for churches or permanent religious institutions 'serving the area covered by the station.' The regulation did not forbid local religious organizations from making appeals over local radio stations. Thus, there was no problem in fundraising for *Back to the Bible Hour* over the Calgary or Edmonton stations because the show originated from those two cities. But for radio stations outside Alberta, the CBC denied any requests for appeals for funds to be broadcast on the show on the grounds that the station submitting the request was some distance from where the Calgary Prophetic Bible Institute was located and the broadcast originated.[16] Herein lay the potential problems for *Back to the Bible Hour* with respect to CBC regulations. The tapes of the original show recorded in Calgary or Edmonton and originally broadcast over Alberta radio stations contained requests for support. These tapes, unedited, were sent outside Alberta to the other stations broadcasting *Back to the Bible Hour*. Clearly, this practice went against CBC regulations and rulings. Manning's ability to raise funds from across Canada would be seriously hindered if this practice were discovered and the regulation strictly enforced.

In 1953, CBC regulations were stiffened in a manner that seemed even more specifically directed at *Back to the Bible Hour*. In the wake of the Royal Commission on National Development in the Arts, Letters and Sciences (Massey Commission), the Special House of Commons Committee on Broadcasting debated a number of new regulations proposed by the CBC's Board of Governors. One proposal was particularly disturbing to Ernest C. Hansell, the Social Credit representative on the broadcasting committee and MP from the constituency of Macleod in Alberta. Hansell had a long association with both Aberhart and Manning.[17] What concerned him was the proposal that no radio station shall 'broadcast any appeal for donations or subscriptions in money or kind on behalf of any person or organization.' The proposed exceptions were charitable institutions and universities, but not churches or religious organizations. There was particular unease about transcribed or tape-recorded shows which, as Davidson Dunton, the chair of the CBC's Board of Governors explained, 'might put forth a very appealing religious or Bible program and which might also appeal for funds ... but which did not help the cause of religion very much.' This concern was directed at American radio preachers who were suspected of drawing money away from Canadian charitable and religious institutions. Although the intent of this regulation was consistent with the CBC's protective nationalist mandate, it clearly could be applied to a Canadian show like *Back to the Bible Hour*. Hansell was particularly alarmed by the suggestion that the CBC would determine what was 'desirable or undesirable' in religious broadcasting.[18] It seemed clear to him that while the CBC would grant a local church permission to make direct appeals for funds over the air, nondenominational religious organizations and lay ministries, such as *Back to the Bible Hour*, were suspect and would likely be denied.

CBC regulators raised serious questions concerning Manning's fundraising practices in 1955. They did not confront him directly but instead put pressure on local stations outside Alberta that were unauthorized to broadcast any appeals for funds in support of *Back to the Bible Hour*. Radio CKOY in Ottawa, under the watchful eyes of parliamentarians, was particularly vulnerable. It was instructed by a CBC official to delete the appeals for support that were on the tapes. Comments made by Manning, such as 'This program is supported by your free will offerings' and 'Please pledge your interest and support' contravened CBC regulations. Subtler, indirect appeals, such as 'In order to receive help through prayer you must become generous,' 'It is through your letters each week that I remain on this great radio station,' and 'Your letters are the lifeline of this broadcast,' were also considered to be in violation of the spirit and intent of the regulation.[19]

Walter Kerr, Manning's radio agent and manager, took a hard line with respect to these attempts to censor the contents of *Back to the Bible Hour*. He attacked the CBC for hiding behind local radio stations instead of addressing Manning personally. He also disputed the charge that appeals specifically for 'money' were made during the broadcasts and suggested that the CBC's regulations would not stand up in court. 'After all,' Kerr wrote, 'it must be admitted that Mr. Manning is not the

type of person who would use money for his own purposes or working down on back-street methods.'[20]

In the end, Manning needed to find ways for *Back to the Bible Hour* to
skirt around CBC regulations. To remain safely inside the Broadcasting
Act and still be able to raise funds from across Canada, he had to be
sure that he did not mention money. Typically, he would instead mention the fact that *Back to the Bible Hour* was 'supported entirely by free-
will support.' He would also ask the listeners to send cards or letters
explaining how much they enjoyed the show. Sometimes he would
hold special campaigns, such as the Christmas remembrance campaign
of 1951. During this broadcast, he asked listeners to write or send a
card of greetings. He never mentioned money, but entreated the audience not to disappoint and promised a copy of *Prophetic Voice*, which
included summaries of his *Back to the Bible Hour* addresses, in exchange
for a letter.[21] Occasionally, when donations were lagging, his appeal
was even more direct: 'Look, we're going to have to drop a few stations
if we don't get some more support.'

During the early to mid-fifties, Manning was embroiled in a potentially more serious controversy. Concern was expressed in the House
of Commons Committee on Broadcasting that Manning was mixing
politics into his *Back to the Bible Hour* addresses. Contrary to the concerns of the committee, however, Manning was more likely to mix religion with his political broadcasts than insert politics into his religious
broadcasts. For example, he routinely mixed his religious beliefs with
cold war politics. On New Year's Day 1951 he counselled Albertans
that 'we are not fully prepared to meet the threats of godless materialism, irrespective of the sphere in which the attacks may come until
individually and as a people we have acknowledged the sovereignty
of the Almighty God, whose omnipotent arm is our strongest defence
and whose Divine providence affords security and peace to all who
will put their trust in Him.'[22] While in the premier's office, Manning
constantly promoted the necessity of spiritual renewal – which he
defined in explicitly evangelical and biblical terms – in order to meet
the dangers of the age.

Ernest Hansell assured his colleagues on the House of Commons
Broadcasting Committee that Manning was fastidious about ensuring
that political commentary did not enter his religious broadcasts. But privately, in letters to some *Back to the Bible Hour* listeners, Manning was
quite open about the connections he saw between religion and politics.
He wrote approvingly to one listener in Cutknife, Saskatchewan, about

her prayers for Christian candidates to be nominated for election. There was a direct link, he explained, between Christianity and Social Credit: 'We can make much progress if the Christians will lead and stand with those who believe in Social Credit principles and march forward together. We can do no better than to let our light shine, for in the past many Social Creditors have been led to Christ through the Christians in the Movement and we pray and trust that more will follow.'[23] He claimed on numerous occasions that the principles of Social Credit were the same as the basic principles of Christian life. Writing to a radio listener in Halifax, Manning asserted: 'Social Credit stands for the physical abundance of God's material world being made available to His people and not being kept from them by man-made financial restrictions.'[24] This classic Social Credit doctrine and rhetoric conjured up images of the financial conspirators identified as responsible for the problem of 'poverty amongst plenty.' Little wonder, then, that there was continuing suspicion that Manning, like his mentor, used his religious broadcasts as a veil to raise money for political purposes.

In defending Manning in the debates of the House of Commons Committee on Broadcasting, Hansell had to admit his surprise that during *Back to the Bible Hour* broadcasts Manning signed on and off as 'premier.' Still, he insisted that the great difficulty simply was that Manning happened to be premier of Alberta. He challenged his colleagues to consider whether the same issues would be raised if another premier's background and previous experience happened to be the 'titular head of a theological college.' He invited members of the broadcasting committee, which included M.J. Coldwell of the CCF as well as John Diefenbaker and Donald Fleming of the Progressive Conservatives, to consider the question: 'should a man, just because he is in public office, be penalized from carrying on what he believes to be his religious convictions regarding the Bible?'[25] Hansell was particularly troubled that while CBC regulatory activity seemed intent on limiting religious broadcasts such as *Back to the Bible Hour*, it allowed broadcasts advocating ideas that destroyed faith in the Bible and the living God. It appeared that the CBC tolerated ideas giving 'comfort to the enemies of Christian democracy' while certain expressions of Christianity were seriously limited by CBC regulations.[26]

Manning was able to weather all of these storms. Despite considerable financial challenges and real regulatory obstacles, he was able to build and sustain a trans-Canada radio ministry. By the late 1950s *Back to the Bible Hour* was broadcast every Sunday over twenty-six radio stations.[27] Quebec and the Far North were the only parts of the country out of range. One indication of the extent of the show's audience can be gained from the radio surveys of the Board of Broadcast Measurement (BBM). During the week of 13–19 March 1961, *Back to the Bible Hour* was the number one–rated show during its time slot in only one city, Halifax. In other centres, where there were more radio stations and stiffer competition, *Back to the Bible Hour* was the third- or fourth-ranked radio show. In the markets of Vancouver, Edmonton, and Winnipeg, the number one–rated program drew at least two or three times the listenership of Manning's program. By contrast, in Calgary and Ottawa, the difference in number of listeners between the number one–ranked radio program and *Back to the Bible Hour* was marginal. More important and impressive was the total number of households tuned into the show. On any Sunday, approximately 20,000–25,000 households in major metropolitan areas across Canada tuned in.[28]

The style and substance of Manning's broadcasts lay at the very root of *Back to the Bible Hour's* appeal. Like many of the other highly successful radio evangelists from the 'golden age of radio,' Manning understood the medium's potential as a new technology that could achieve the age-old objective of proclaiming the Word of God. Radio was a potentially powerful and far-reaching pulpit that could expand the evangelists' congregation. Manning's preaching style was not dramatic. He spoke in serious and measured terms in a calm and steady voice. Despite this plain style, he was an effective preacher on radio and in person, coming across the airwaves as a man of deep, sincere, and clear conviction. The program had an informal air that made it seem as if he was speaking directly to every member of the radio audience. Typically, he would end a talk with the following request: 'we call you, whoever and wherever you are in this vast Canadian homeland of ours ... Get back to the Bible today, back to God through the open door of the Lord Jesus Christ. Come to Him in faith believing, bow and confess Him as your Redeemer and your Lord.'

Manning's oratorical style, which demanded reflection and reverence for each word, was most appropriate for a radio ministry that was based on the fundamental belief that every word in the Bible was the Word of God. Manning's religious faith and his radio ministry were primarily shaped by this belief. In his opinion, the Bible was under siege in North American culture as never before. He was particularly saddened and alarmed by the implications of modernist scholarship; claims that the Bible was primarily a text for moral guidance undermined its divine authority and reduced Christianity from a living faith to a set of abstract ideas. Manning was most concerned over the status of the King James Bible; he was firmly convinced that only the King James Version was 'the verbally inspired and divinely preserved infallible word of the living God.' Any other translation was a 'corruption.' He rejected the pragmatic position of many evangelicals that the new translations of the Bible should be supported if they made it easier to understand and consequently helpful in gathering souls.[29] The only result of the explosion of biblical translations that Manning could see was widespread confusion and doubt. And confusion and doubt about the Word of God contributed to the 'wholly materialistic and secular creed' that dominated contemporary society.[30] In his steadfast opposition to more recent biblical translations, such as the 1952 Revised Standard Version, Manning was in the same camp as the most committed and perhaps militant fundamentalists.[31] The perceived threat to the King James Bible bolstered Manning's resolve to make his radio ministry an 'unchanging spiritual oasis where week after week men and women can feast on unadulterated Bible truth drawn from the King James Authorized Version.'[32]

Not only was the low status of the Bible in contemporary society a cause of current problems; according to Manning it was also a sign of how deeply society had sunk into the abyss of atheism and materialism. The signs of decline and imminent Second Coming were abundant; the 'collapse of civilization' was near at hand. As the lines of the cold war were drawn, events only confirmed his dispensationalism.[33] The decline of Christianity, the rising apostasy within the churches, the rising number of people in the throes of dictatorship, as well as the fact that the Jews had never been so persecuted and were on an exodus to Palestine were all clear signs that 'Christ's personal return must be very near at hand.'[34] With respect to the Holocaust, Manning's views were characteristic of the deeply 'ironic ambivalence' about Judaism that characterized dispensationalism. While deploring the persecution of the Jews, dispensationalists like Manning greeted their persecution as a harbinger of the Second Coming. The rebirth of Israel, in particular, was considered a key sign that God was fulfilling his prophecies as outlined in Scripture.[35] Russia's emergence as the great military threat to democracy, free enterprise, and Christianity also demonstrated to Manning the veracity of his dispensational reading of the Bible. Soon the Antichrist would assume the throne of Russia, which would become his base to destroy the world.[36] Despite the bleak interpretation of contemporary events, Manning's message was a hopeful one. Many of his listeners were reassured that God still controlled human history.

In a series of nine talks entitled 'Things Which Must Shortly Come to Pass,' broadcast in September and October of 1958, Manning outlined the sequence of events that the prophetic Scriptures foretold. He paid particular attention to describing the Four Horsemen of the Apocalypse, as they symbolized what the world would be like in the wrath to come. In these addresses, Manning subtly integrated his Social Credit ideology with his apocalyptic religious theology and, for careful listeners, provided classic Social Credit doctrine with a clear biblical sanction. The third horseman of the Apocalypse, riding a black horse and carrying a pair of balances, would bring famine, want, and regimentation, 'the just recompense to a society that rejects the power of God but puts unlimited power in the hands of materialistic godless men.' Here again was a reference to the deeply rooted Social Credit beliefs that a conspiracy of unscrupulous forces sought absolute control of wealth, resources, and power in order to destroy Christianity.[37] To meet the growing menace of totalitarianism, which would usher in the end of the world, Manning stressed a platform of Social Credit, Christianity, and democracy.

Manning's reading of the Old Testament Mosaic Law and the teachings of Jesus made it clear to him that there was a 'collective responsibility for morality and spirituality.'[38] But he was deeply suspicious of using the state to achieve Christian ends. Indeed, he was critical of the tendency of many Christians 'to rely on man-made laws and prohibitions to curb expressions of ungodliness.' He dismissed suggestions that his government introduce legislation expanding religious exercises and instruction in schools beyond the current practice of simply reciting the Lord's prayer and a passage of Scripture, because he saw this to be beyond the state's responsibility. 'There is a tendency today,' Manning explained, 'to hold that the State, through the public schools, should attempt to provide children with the religious instruction which properly they should receive in their own homes and through the activities of the churches and Sunday Schools of their communities. No amount of religious instruction in school can possibly take the place of a proper Christian home environment.'[39] Such a proposal would also set a dangerous and unworkable precedent in a modern civil society, he thought. 'After all,' he wrote, 'individual worship is the most sacred of all individual rights and for this reason the majority of people are very sensitive to any religious influence being brought to bear on their children without their consent and which might contain religious viewpoints differing from their own convictions.'[40] On this explosive question, he demonstrated his appreciation of the need to be accommodating and tolerant in a modern pluralistic society. Although it was declared *ultra vires*, the Manning administration introduced a Bill of Rights in 1946 that included religion as a basic freedom guaranteed to all Albertans. Manning led his government according to the cardinal principles of religious tolerance. He was able to purge the Social Credit Party in Alberta of its anti-Semitic fringe and also build a base of support with the Mormons, a religious people considered anathema to many evangelicals.[41]

Recognition of the limits of legislation in religious, ethical, and many social matters was at the root of Manning's opposition to reliance on the state. His Social Credit government introduced a number of welfare programs, including the Public Welfare Act of 1960, which dealt with mothers' allowances, pensions for widows and disabled persons, child welfare, and the building of homes for the aged. However, in Manning's estimation the building of the welfare state was simply another indication of how close civilization was to its end. If society were Christian, he thought, state social welfare measures would not be necessary. The government's motive in introducing such measures was to help save individuals from a godless, uncaring, and overly materialistic society. It was yet another indication of the continuing decline of morality and Christianity.[42] Manning concluded that the deplorable conditions of contemporary society were a direct result of the modern tendency of Christian believers to isolate themselves from public responsibilities.[43] In his view, any distinction between a secular public sphere and a private religious sphere, with neither imposing upon nor intermingling with the other, was deeply unchristian and a false dichotomy.

The transcendent role of religion in Manning's private and public activities was at the heart of the difficulties he encountered with respect to his religious broadcasting. Many liberals also blended their religious faith with public life in their advocacy of the social gospel–inspired welfare state, while evangelicals did the same in calling for legislation to create a Christian moral order. These positions were within the mainstream of reform-minded public discourse and the heritage of the historic churches in Canada, and therefore were not met with charges that such advocacy somehow breached the boundaries between religion and politics.[44]

Rather than calling for Christian-inspired legislation, however, Manning sought to convert people. More specifically, during the *Back to the Bible Hour* broadcasts he constantly encouraged people to be 'born again' before the imminent Second Coming. It was one thing for clergy to advocate Christian-inspired reform but quite another for a premier to engage with the public in the most private of matters by making appeals to their personal faith and inquiring into the state of their souls. The manner in which Manning mixed religion with his public life and the fact that he maintained and expanded a radio ministry while he was Social Credit leader and premier caused difficulty. His appeal for funds in order to sustain his radio ministry only muddied the waters and raised more serious questions. Was *Back to the Bible Hour* a religious broadcast or was it a combination of religion and Social Credit political commentary for the purposes of raising funds? For Manning this dichotomy was a false one, because he could not separate religion from politics. For his critics these were troubling issues. Few listeners of *Back to the Bible Hour*, however, seemed to be disturbed by questions about whether Manning was inappropriately mixing religion and public life. For the dedicated radio audience what mattered was that he was showing the way out of the dark, confusing, and fearful times by guiding them 'Back to the Bible.'

Notes

1 John Irving, 'Social Credit in Alberta after 25 Years,' *Saturday Night*, 9 January 1960. Irving's *The Social Credit Movement in Alberta* (Toronto: University of Toronto Press, 1959) remains one of the most sensitive portrayals of the appeal of Social Credit and Aberhart among Albertans.
2 Many Canadian historians have gone out of their way to reject the applicability of fundamentalism in a Canadian context. See especially John G. Stackhouse, Jr, *Canadian Evangelicalism in the Twentieth Century: An Introduction to Its Character* (Toronto: University of Toronto Press, 1993). But if we adopt George Marsden's view that fundamentalists are a subgroup in a larger evangelical mosaic distinguished by dispensational theology, strict adherence to biblical infallibility, and separatism, then Manning is best understood as a fundamentalist. See George Marsden, *Understanding Fundamentalism and Evangelicalism* (Grand Rapids: Eerdmans, 1991), 1–6.
3 Joel Carpenter, *Revive Us Again: The Reawakening of American Fundamentalism* (New York: Oxford University Press, 1997), passim.

4 Manning to Reimer (Mennonite Brethren College, Winnipeg) 13 February
   1963, fd. 395a, Public Archives of Alberta, Accession #77–173, (hereafter
   Manning Papers).
5 On Aberhart, see David Elliott and Iris Miller, *Bible Bill: A Biography of
   William Aberhart* (Edmonton: Reidmore Books, 1987). On issues related to
   religion and public life, see David Elliott, 'Antithetical Elements in William
   Aberhart's Theology and Political Ideology,' *Canadian Historical Review* 59,
   no. 1 (March 1978): 38–58.
6 Alvin Finkel, *The Social Credit Phenomenon in Alberta* (Toronto: University of
   Toronto Press, 1989). Insightful comments about Manning's religion and
   how it shaped his politics are provided by Bob Hesketh, *Major Douglas and
   Alberta Social Credit* (Toronto: University of Toronto Press, 1997), passim. For
   a journalistic exploration that takes Manning's religion seriously, see Lloyd
   Mackey, *Like Father, Like Son: Ernest Manning and Preston Manning* (Toronto:
   ECW Press, 1997).
7 The following account of Manning's conversion experience and his
   experiences in the late 1920s while enrolled at the Calgary Prophetic Bible
   Institute is based on interviews he gave in the early 1990s. The transcripts
   are in the University of Alberta Archives, Ernest Manning Fonds, Accession
   #81–32, May 1982, 19–20.
8 Virginia Brereton, *Training God's Army: The American Bible School, 1880–1940*
   (Bloomington: Indiana University Press, 1990), passim.
9 See the correspondence between H. Roye (Public Relations Officer *Old-
   Fashioned Revival Hour*) and Premier Manning, 16 July, 16 August, and
   5 September 1946, fd. 1179, Public Archives of Alberta, Accession #69–289
   (hereafter Premiers' Papers). See also Manning to J. Blackmore, MP, 17 January 1958, on his relationship with Fuller.
10 Quentin Schultze, 'Evangelical Radio and the Rise of the Electronic Church
   1921–48,' *Journal of Broadcasting and Electronic Media* 32, no. 3 (Summer
   1988): 289–306.
11 Canadian Broadcasting Corporation, *Annual Report*, 1947–48, 27.
12 *Prophetic Voice* (October 1949).
13 Manning to R.E. Henning, 2 April 1948, fd. 1862, Premiers' Papers.
14 Manning to Mr Honsberger, 19 March 1948, fd. 1862, Premiers' Papers.
15 Mrs W. Buttery to the Premier of Alberta and Mrs Manning, 7 July 1953, fd.
   1852, Premiers' Papers.
16 House of Commons, *Special Committee on Broadcasting, Minutes of Proceedings and Evidence* (Ottawa, 1953), no. 3, 14 April 1953, 82.
17 For Hansell's religious background see 'Sermon by Rev E.G. Hansell,'
   26 April 1926, and 2 May 1926, Hansell Papers, box 1, fd. 1, Glenbow

Archives, M 471. See also E.G. Hansell, 'Four Simple Rules for a Successful Christian Life,' *Prophetic Voice* (April 1952). On Hansell's relationship with Aberhart, see Elliott and Miller, *Bible Bill*, 74–9.

18 House of Commons, *Special Committee on Broadcasting, Minutes of Proceedings and Evidence*, no. 3, 14 April 1953, 70–1, 73–6.

19 Correspondence dated 4 April 1955; 29 July 1955; and 3, 5, 9, 15 August 1955, fd. 1852, Premiers' Papers.

20 Walter Kerr to Manning, 4 April 1955; Walter Kerr to J.C. Morris (National Broadcast Sales), 4 April 1955, fd. 1852, Premiers' Papers.

21 Audio recordings of the Special Christmas broadcasts of December 1950 and 23 December 1951, RED 5, Glenbow Archives.

22 'New Year's Day Message by Premier Manning over C.J.C.A.,' 1 January 1951, fd. 1825, Premiers' Papers.

23 Manning to Mrs Ole Pederson, 10 December 1947, fd. 1862, Premiers' Papers.

24 Manning to Rev. G. Wilson, 18 April 1962, fd. 394B, Manning Papers.

25 House of Commons, *Special Committee on Broadcasting, Minutes of Proceedings and Evidence*, no. 3, 14 April 1953, 83–4.

26 See House of Commons, *Debates*, vol. 2 (1951), Drew, 9 November 1951, 890–5; Blackmore, 13 December 1951, 1869–72; vol. 2 (1952–3), Fleming, 27 January 1953, 1364. See also 'Religious Censorship and the CBC,' *Maclean's Magazine*, 1 January 1952; Frank W. Peers, *The Politics of Canadian Broadcasting, 1920–51* (Toronto: University of Toronto Press, 1973), 433–7.

27 Data on the network can be compiled from the radio schedules in fds. 796 and 1852, Manning Papers.

28 Board of Broadcast Measurement, *Radio Station Report, Spring 1961 Survey* (13–19 March), Ryerson University Library. A random sampling of the statistics for other weeks does not reveal a wide variation in results. The week of 13 March 1961 was selected because it was one of the first surveys providing sufficiently detailed data and it was closest to the 1950s, the chronological focus of this paper.

29 Billy Graham held this more tolerant view. See George Martin, *A Prophet with Honor: The Billy Graham Story* (New York: William Morrow, 1991), 219–20; George Marsden, *Reforming Fundamentalism: Fuller Seminary and the New Evangelicalism* (Grand Rapids: Eerdmans, 1987), 136–7.

30 *Prophetic Voice* (September 1960).

31 Marsden, *Reforming Fundamentalism*, 136–7.

32 Global Outreach Mission, E.C. Manning, transcript, #945, 'The Effectual Word,' n.d.

33 Manning's dispensational thought falls within the broad outlines of

twentieth-century premillennial thought. See Timothy P. Weber, *Living in the Shadow of the Second Coming: American Premillennialism, 1875–1882* (Chicago: University of Chicago Press, 1983); and Paul Boyer, *When Time Shall Be No More: Prophetic Belief in Modern American Culture* (Cambridge: Harvard University Press, 1992).

34 Carpenter, *Revive Us Again*, 71.

35 See especially Weber, *Living in the Shadow of the Second Coming*, 185–215. The term ironic ambivalence comes from Weber, who provides the most extensive treatment of premillennialism, Judaism, and the question of anti-Semitism. See also Boyer, *When Time Shall Be No More*, 217–24.

36 *Prophetic Voice* (July 1945). These ideas were first outlined by Manning in a play he co-wrote with Aberhart and performed in 1931. See 'Branding Irons of the Antichrist,' reprinted in L.P.V. Johnson and Ola MacNutt, *Aberhart of Alberta* (Edmonton: Co-op Press, 1970), 231–9; and David Elliott, ed., *Aberhart: Outpourings and Replies* (Calgary: Historical Society of Alberta, 1991), 1–9. For Manning's postwar views, see Hesketh, *Major Douglas and Alberta Social Credit*, 221.

37 Hesketh, *Major Douglas and Alberta Social Credit*, 193–4, 202–10, 220–1. Manning's understanding of the conspiracy changed as the cold war emerged. He was less inclined to point to financiers and bankers, and instead, communists, socialists, and labour leaders were seen as the evil forces conspiring to create a huge centralized bureaucratic state to control wealth and enslave people. See also Finkel, *The Social Credit Phenomenon in Alberta*, 86, 106, 109.

38 Manning Interviews, 4 July 1980, 30–5, University of Alberta Archives.

39 Manning to Stauffer, 3 February 1947, fd. 1853, Premiers' Papers.

40 Manning to Phibbs, 4 February 1949, fd. 1860A, Premiers' Papers.

41 There has been some suggestion that Manning vacillated in purging his Social Credit Party of its vehement anti-Semitism. His personal views, strongly influenced by his dispensationalism, were clear: 'I am convinced that the [anti-Semitic propaganda] *Protocols of the Elders of Zion* are spurious and are a diabolical device on the part of the powers of evil that are seeking to establish a dictatorship of godless materialism to turn Christians and unbelieving Gentiles against the Jews and the Jews against the Christians [with the result that they] will destroy each others influence and the powers of evil are left free.' Manning to M.W. Sharp, 17 March 1948, fd. 1860A, Premiers' Papers. See also Hesketh, *Major Douglas and Alberta Social Credit*, 232–5. Billy Graham is an example of an evangelical who had difficulty working with Mormons. See Martin, *A Prophet With Honor*, 218.

42 Manning Interviews, 29 March 1982, University of Alberta Archives.

43 Manning to L.C. Fritz, 24 July 1958, fd. 2187; and Manning to Mrs Gough, 11 March 1964, fd. 395A, Premiers' Papers.
44 See J.R. Mutchmor, *The Memoirs of James Ralph Mutchmor* (Toronto: Ryerson, 1965), for the activities of a prominent clergyman within this mainstream 'liberal evangelical' tradition during the 1940s and 1950s.

Part Five

Matters of State: Redefining the Sacred
in Public Life, 1960–2000

12

Catholicism's 'Quiet Revolution': *Maintenant* and the New Public Catholicism in Quebec after 1960

David Seljak

Much has been written about the public face of Catholicism in Quebec before the 1960s. Because the church dominated the fields of education, health care, and social services and because Catholicism served as the 'civil religion' of French Quebeckers, historians and social scientists have studied in detail the public functions of the church and its relations with the state from 1840 to 1960.[1] Studies of public Catholicism after the Quiet Revolution that resulted in some separation of church and state in the 1960s have been far fewer in number. Guided by theories of secularization, most scholars have assumed that public Catholicism had mostly been relegated to the 'private' sphere and was no longer of consequence in the 1960s and 1970s.

What has not been documented sufficiently is the emergence of a new type of public Catholicism, one reconciled to modern society, the new state, and democracy. In this chapter, I look at the new form of public religion[2] in Quebec – and how it came to replace the province's pre-1960 Catholicism. I do so by examining the history of *Maintenant*, an experimental Catholic journal launched by the Dominican Order in 1962 to inspire a democratization of the internal structure of the church by fostering cooperation between lay Catholics and clerics. The order also hoped to redefine the church's relationship to state and society in order to make it more relevant to modern Quebec. The successes and failures of the *Maintenant* experiment tell us much about the nature and limitations of public Catholicism in Quebec. While it was the bishops who finally decided the shape of the new public Catholicism in Quebec, the intellectuals who wrote for *Maintenant* were particularly influential in closing the door on two options the church faced in the early 1960s: a return to the public Catholicism of the 1950s and the privatization of religion.[3]

Public Catholicism before 1960

In Quebec, Catholicism was an integral part of public life since the founding of New France, a colony in which the government's administrative units were parishes. After the conquest of the colony by the British in 1759, the French political and economic élite returned to France, leaving the church as the largest public institution controlled by the *canadiens*. In the 1840s, following the failed rebellion of 1837–8, the church again stood as the most credible public voice for French Canadians. This historical development coincided with the rise of ultramontanism, a militant, conservative Catholicism in Europe that would serve as the basis for French-Canadian nationalism. From 1840 to the 1920s, as Roberto Perin has noted in an earlier chapter, the Catholic Church, even more than the state, provided the 'public space' in which French Canadians could exercise autonomy.

From the 1920s on, the Quebec state took on a more important role in providing such a space, but still needed the cooperation of the Catholic Church. The provincial government, headed by Maurice Duplessis' Union Nationale from 1944 to 1960, supported the church financially and declared Quebec a Catholic province. In return, the church helped to legitimate the state, particularly the several governments of the Union Nationale. In charge of education, health care, and social services for francophone Quebeckers, the church, which boasted some 45,000 nuns, brothers, and priests in 1961, was a powerful public institution.[4] Like many countries where a local population was distinguished from a dominant élite by religion and ethnicity, religion and nationalism fused in Quebec.

The Quiet Revolution and the New Public Catholicism

When Jean Lesage's Liberal Party was elected in 1960, it began an ambitious program of political modernization later dubbed the Quiet Revolution. The goal of this 'revolution,' frequently reduced to the slogan 'l'état, c'est nous,' was to make the state the motor of the national liberation of French Canadians. Studies in the 1950s and 1960s showed that the Quebec economy was dominated by capital controlled by English Canadians, Americans, and British subjects. Furthermore, anglophones also dominated managerial positions in private enterprises. Given this situation, the Liberals believed that only by exercising state power could French Canadians have a real presence in the economy or access to management opportunities in business. By nationalizing the hydroelectric system, investing in crown corporations, and making investment capital available to Quebeckers, the government sought to increase the participation of French Canadians in the economy.[5]

While the new nationalism promoted by the Liberals was not ideologically anticlerical, it was adamantly secular and contested the traditional nationalism that had guaranteed the church's privileges. The Liberals expanded and reformed the state bureaucracy and took control of those functions formerly performed by the church, especially regarding education, health care, and social services. Some leading Quebeckers sensed that the province's church-run public institutions seriously lagged behind their secular counterparts in Ontario and the United States. The concern for 'bureaucratic competence' gave rise to a mild form of anticlericalism in Quebec, based not on any deep hatred for the clergy or the church, but on the sense that the clergy monopolized positions of authority without merit.[6]

The immediate impact of the government's policies was a renegotiation of the alliance worked out between church and state from 1840 to 1960. Conservative Catholics insisted that the Liberals' reforms were illegitimate and argued that the church should take an intransigent position, especially on the issue of control over education. The Quebec City–based Catholic daily newspaper l'Action; the Jesuit journal Relations; the nationalist journal l'Action nationale; Monde Nouveau; the journal of l'Institut Pie XI, a learning centre affiliated with le Grand Séminaire in Montreal; and a host of conservative political parties demanded the restoration of the old order and the church's privileges. The provincial wing of the Social Credit Party and other Catholic parties even advocated political independence from Canada in order to protect French Canadians from what they saw as the secularizing effects of the federal government's policies.[7]

Despite the protests of conservative Catholics, it was clear to many progressive Catholics that the church would have to redefine its role in the new Quebec. This new position required a double movement on behalf of Catholic leaders: a rejection of both the semi-established position of the church and the relegation of all religion to the 'private life' of individuals, as prescribed by modern liberalism. Support for this position came largely from two groups. The first consisted of activists from the worker movements in the church's Catholic Action network. Given that the Union Nationale had severely curtailed the power of unions, it was natural that Catholic workers' groups, such as the Mouvement des travailleurs chrétiens,[8] Jeunesse ouvrière catholique, and the Centre de pastorale au milieu ouvrier, supported the progressive policies of the Liberal Party. The second group consisted of Catholic intellectuals, especially former members of the Jeunesse étudiante catholique, and university-educated professionals working in the social bureaucracy controlled by the church. Many of these, like Claude Ryan, editor of the Montreal-based daily paper *Le Devoir*, believed that the Catholic Church should withdraw from public life in the name of democracy. Others, including many Dominicans, became progressive voices in society and in the church, calling for a democratization of both. Just as the Jesuits identified with resistance to the new Quebec, so the Dominican Order identified with this progressive option.

The *Maintenant* Experiment

In 1962, the year that marked the opening of the Second Vatican Council, the Dominicans launched *Maintenant*, a monthly journal that supported both the political modernization of Quebec and the religious renewal symbolized by the Council. The congruence of the Council with the Quiet Revolution meant that Catholics could criticize the old religion and the old Quebec but remain loyal in their dissent. *Maintenant* openly aligned itself with a number of dissenters: Frère Untel, a brother who had just published a series of stinging criticisms of the church-run school system; *Cité Libre*, a journal critical of the old Catholicism and Quebec in the 1950s; Fathers Dion and O'Neill, two priests who had publicly censured the corrupt politics of the Union Nationale in the 1950s; Radio-Canada, the public broadcasting system that had become a haven for progressive thinkers; and *Le Devoir*, the daily Montreal newspaper that had become alienated from the traditional nationalism.[9] By placing itself in this tradition of dissent, *Maintenant* announced its intention to challenge authoritarianism both in the church and in Quebec society, which were seen as interconnected. Consequently, the definition of a democratic public Catholicism required an internal critique of the antidemocratic structures and culture of the church – and vice versa.

The journal was immediately successful and influential. Three years after its launch, it had close to 11,000 subscriptions and an estimated readership of 50,000. Given that the population of francophone Quebec at the time was approximately five million and that a relatively small portion of those were university educated, the figure was impressive. The structure of *Maintenant* expressed the Dominicans' commitment to challenging the old order and to experimentation. While the order financed the journal, and a Dominican, Père Henri-M. Bradet, was given editorial control, the Dominicans allowed *Maintenant* a great deal of autonomy and freedom of expression. This was the first time that a religious order had sponsored a publication without controlling its content. Bradet went even further. While he officially had total control over the journal's content, he shared his power with those who most regularly contributed. He organized these volunteers into an editorial 'team' composed equally of Dominicans and lay Catholics, a structure that challenged the traditional clericalism of Quebec Catholicism.

The first issue of *Maintenant* made clear its departure from traditional Catholicism. In the editorial, Bradet announced the journal's rejection of the 'otherworldly' spirituality of the old Quebec, one that favoured the spiritual and a heavenly paradise over this material world. Catholics, he argued, had to take this world seriously and dedicate themselves to improving it in the present (hence the journal's title). For Bradet, this was the message of the Second Vatican Council. Once the church entered the real world, it had to admit that it was not in sole and serene possession of the whole truth. The first consequence of that admission was a shift in method; no longer could the hierarchy announce truth from on high. The second consequence was that the church had to adapt to the reality of pluralism and the necessity of dialogue.[10]

Similarly, the editorial team of *Maintenant* rejected the dualism that defined the clergy as superior to the laity.[11] Bradet argued that this dualism had legitimated the clergy's control of Quebec society and its monopolization of leadership positions. *Maintenant* was to be a place where priests, nuns, brothers, and lay Catholics could meet as equals.[12]

These rather abstract debates had real implications. Nowhere was this more readily seen than in the debate over the Liberal Party's decision to reform the school system and create a Ministry of Education.[13] For conservatives, this decision was a betrayal of the rights of the church and the rights of parents to educate their children as they saw fit. Conservatives saw the Parent Commission, the government's inquiry into the education system, and Bill 60, the law that created the

Ministry of Education, as signs that the centralizing, bureaucratic state apparatus was intent on destroying the Catholic fabric of Quebec and replacing it with what the Jesuit Richard Arès called 'la démocratie totalitaire.'[14]

In contrast, the Catholics of *Maintenant* supported the creation of a Ministry of Education and the modernization of the school system. Adopting the slogan 'L'état, c'est nous,' the writers of *Maintenant* protested against the mistrust of the state that marked traditional nationalism and ultramontanism.[15] They argued that Bill 60 actually conformed to the principles of Catholic social teaching. Accusations that the creation of a Ministry of Education would lead to a dictatorship, they wrote, were exaggerations.[16]

In the 1960s the education question was symbolic of many debates around the issue of liberty. At *Maintenant* the consensus was that the people of Quebec were caught in a state of infantilism, marked by conformity and an automatic submission to authority. The barriers to liberty were many: political, economic, social, cultural, religious, psychological, and spiritual. The writers of *Maintenant* attacked them all. Despite the still-conservative culture of Quebec in the early 1960s, there were no issues the magazine would not discuss: changes in theology, birth control, abortion, sexual morality, feminism, anticlericalism, interreligious dialogue and ecumenism, relations with atheists and socialists, Quebec separatism, the deconfessionalization of schools, censorship, and papal authority. The journal approached each question beginning with the lived experiences of real people and moved inductively towards higher principles. This approach was a self-conscious challenge to traditional theology, which starts with first principles and then moves down to applications in ordinary life.

The journal's readiness to discuss any issue and to apply this inductive method precipitated its first crisis. In July 1965, Bradet received notice from the provincial superior, Thomas-M. Rondeau, that the Dominican superior in Rome, Aniceto Fernandez, had removed Bradet from his post as editor. While the head of the Dominican Order gave no reasons for this action, it was widely assumed that *Maintenant* had scandalized the religious establishment by departing from the official ban on all forms of birth control and suggesting that the Catholic position take as its starting point the lived experiences of married people.[17]

Fernandez's decision was devastating. The news came out of the blue, without consultation, opportunity to respond to charges, or right of appeal. Bradet complained that he was given no explanation for his removal and had not even been allowed to see the contents of the letter from Fernandez.[18] While *Maintenant* enjoyed the support of the Dominican provincial council, the provincial superior, and even Montreal's cardinal, Paul-Émile Léger, Bradet was still subject to his superiors.[19] He obeyed the order and *Maintenant* ceased publication. The future of the experiment was in doubt.

In the new Quebec, however, Catholics were not as powerless as they once were. Bradet and the editorial team took their story to the press. Despite the fact that they did not hold official positions, the contributors of *Maintenant* 'resigned' in open letters released to the press, and 'l'affaire Bradet' was born. Claude Ryan, editor of *Le Devoir* and a respected Catholic thinker, criticized the Dominicans for their handling of the affair and especially their callous disregard for the opinions and rights of the lay contributors.[20] Catholic papers in Canada, England, the United States, France, and Germany picked up the story. The Quebec publishing house Éditions du Jour even published a small book on it.[21] Besides worrying about the bad publicity, Rondeau had to appreciate the fact that the journal was widely read in influential circles. Moreover, many Dominicans supported *Maintenant* and did not want to see it disappear.

The Dominicans met with the editorial team to negotiate a settlement. While the superior in Rome had the power to remove Bradet, only Rondeau had the power to name his successor or shut down the experiment. The team was defiant: there was to be no change at *Maintenant*, either in tone or in mission.[22] The Dominicans organized an extraordinary public consultation with the lay contributors and the public and went even further by consulting with the contributors before Rondeau named Bradet's successor, another Dominican, Père Vincent Harvey. A new 'charter' for the journal that guaranteed it continuing funding and autonomy was written and published.[23] Finally, the journal maintained the editorial team structure of power-sharing: two Dominicans, Paul Doucet and Harvey, were matched with two lay Catholics, Hélène Pelletier-Baillargeon and Pierre Saucier.

Maintenant under Vincent Harvey: Catholicism, Socialism, and Nationalism

Père Harvey would become the spiritual and intellectual anchor of *Maintenant* from 1965 until his death in 1972. Under his leadership, *Maintenant* was even more openly critical of the authoritarianism of the old public Catholicism. Harvey told Catholics not to panic over the so-called death of the churches, the decline of their former public power; this was really the death of Christendom, of the Constantinian 'infection' of the church, and of the church's role in legitimizing an antidemocratic social order.[24] He was even more critical of any public Catholicism that violated the liberty of individual conscience. In 1968 *Maintenant* expressed disappointment with *Humanae Vitae*, Pope Paul VI's encyclical on sexual morality and the use of birth control. The editorial team argued that the encyclical was a sign that the preconciliar ecclesiology, a 'top-down' model in which the clergy dictated moral truths from first principles, was not dead.[25]

While the Dominicans might have expected Harvey to follow Bradet's lead on church matters, they did not expect the politicization of *Maintenant* that occurred under his leadership. Bradet always acknowledged that there were barriers to liberty in the wider society, but he tended to focus on those inside the church. But by 1965, the secularizing effects of the Quiet Revolution had already changed the nature of Quebec society and the sources of authority and oppression. Moreover, in 1966 the Quiet Revolution seemed to have stalled when the Union Nationale returned to power. The forces of progress, according to Harvey, had been dealt a severe blow. *Maintenant* reacted to the change by widening its field of vision. It adopted a more sophisticated social scientific analysis to identify and dismantle these barriers to liberty. According to Harvey, this shift was inspired by questions of economic inequality and Quebec's sovereignty.[26]

In the August–September 1967 issue, 'Un Québec libre à inventer,' *Maintenant's* editorial team announced its support for socialism and Quebec's independence from the rest of Canada.[27] Laissez-faire capitalism, they argued, dictated against an interventionist state in the name of a free-market economy. Likewise, federalism inhibited the development of this interventionist state because the British North America Act gave to the federal government many of the powers that the Quebec state needed. Consequently, *Maintenant* saw both capitalism and federalism as obstacles to the Quiet Revolution's promise to make French Quebeckers 'masters in their own house.'

While *Maintenant's* writers were not willing to define in precise details the character of either this independence or of the socialist 'projet de société,' they were clear on the point that socialism had to inform Quebec nationalism and vice versa. They argued that this 'participatory democratic socialism that has yet to be defined' could not be a simple application of an abstract theory or formula; it would have to be defined by the concrete context in which the Quebec people lived and be 'faithful to the most authentic historical aspirations' of French Quebeckers.[28] The writers were similarly open-minded about the goals of Quebec nationalism. Whether sovereignty were exercised in a loose confederation or an independent republic would be decided by a constituent assembly; the final form was open to debate.[29]

The position of the *Maintenant* team was paradoxical, a clear commitment both to socialism and sovereignty married to a refusal to identify the precise structures and program that would guarantee the liberty promised by this commitment. This position was rooted in the writers' understanding of the proper relationship between nationalism, socialism, culture, and religious commitment. The writers of *Maintenant* were greatly influenced by French political theology, especially as articulated by Dominicans such as Christian Duquoc, who wrote for the journal while he was at the Université de Montréal. For Duquoc, the eschatological imagination fostered by Christianity meant that Christians could not be fully loyal to any human system, party, regime, or ideology. Only the reign of God that would be ushered in by Christ at the end of time was perfect. Consequently, Christians were called to a kind of 'permanent revolution,' always criticizing injustice and exclusion in every human society.[30] Without this critical imagination, the progressive Christians' commitment to political action would degenerate into a clericalism of the left or a sacralization of socialism.

Maintenant, Inc.: *Maintenant* after the Dominicans

The journal's newfound political interests precipitated the second great crisis in the *Maintenant* experiment. In the federal election of 1968, won by the Liberal Party and its French-Canadian leader, Pierre Elliott Trudeau, *Maintenant* supported the New Democratic Party, a social democratic party that had only recently made inroads in Quebec. Many Dominicans were unhappy with the fact that the journal had publicly supported a political party that the majority of Dominicans did not support. Catholics, they complained, might well believe that *Maintenant*'s support of the NDP and its position on sovereignty were the official positions of the order.[31] On 18 November 1968 the provincial council of the Dominican Order voted to discontinue all financial support for the magazine.

Again the decision came as a shock to the writers of *Maintenant*.

Again they turned to the public press. Harvey himself alerted two of Montreal's largest daily papers, *La Presse* and *Le Devoir*, to the Dominicans' decision. In response to the press reports, fifty-three professors at the Université de Montréal signed a petition calling for continued support for the journal.[32] These efforts, and support from within the order, brought concessions from the Dominicans. They agreed to fund the journal for three more months and to allow Harvey and his fellow Dominican, Père Yves Gosselin, who had replaced Père Doucet on the editorial team, to continue their work.[33]

The withdrawal of financial support meant that the journal was now free from any control by the Dominicans. It also meant that *Maintenant* faced almost certain bankruptcy. The main contributors incorporated independently as 'Maintenant, Inc.' and found a white knight in Pierre Pélardeau, president of Québecor, who guaranteed them an annual contribution of $10,000, a handsome sum in 1969. Pélardeau allowed the editorial team complete editorial control and liberty.[34]

In 1971 *Maintenant* gave itself a real editorial team, comprising some of the best-known social scientists and secular thinkers in Quebec. The committee included Robert Boily, a lawyer and political scientist at the Université de Montréal; Fernand Dumont, a Université Laval social scientist (now recognized as Quebec's most important sociologist); Jacques Grand'Maison, a priest, well-known social activist, and theologian at the Université de Montréal; Pierre Harvey, an economist; Jacques-Yvan Morin, a lawyer, specialist in international constitutional law and nationalist activist; Guy Rocher, another well-known sociologist; Claude Saint-Laurent, a psychiatrist; and Pierre Vadeboncoeur, a labour lawyer and widely published essayist. Less influential in the church because of the loss of the Dominicans' sponsorship, *Maintenant* still attracted a wide audience with its mixture of socialism, nationalism, and spirituality. While subscriptions declined in the early 1970s, magazine stand sales increased; when the journal folded in 1974, it still sold 10,000 copies a month.

In 1968, the same year the Dominicans withdrew their support for the journal, René Lévesque, who had left the Liberal Party over its commitment to Canadian federalism, merged his Mouvement souveraineté-association with several indépendantiste groups to form the Parti Québécois (PQ), a coalition dedicated to the sovereignty of Quebec. Almost immediately, *Maintenant*'s writers and readers supported the party. Several factors pushed the writers into the PQ camp. First, the PQ, which had begun as a coalition between conservative and progressive indépendantistes, became more coherently social democratic. Second, like many Quebec nationalists, the editorial team was infuriated by the Union Nationale's Bill 63, which guaranteed the right of parents to choose the language of their children's education. Third, in 1970 the federal government invoked the War Measures Act in response to the kidnappings of the British trade commissioner and a member of the provincial cabinet by members of the Front de libération du Québec (FLQ), a small radical Marxist group that believed that the independence of Quebec could be secured only by violent revolution. While it rejected the violence of the FLQ, *Maintenant* became a vehicle for many critics of the federal government's suspension of civil liberties and for supporters of the hundreds of people arrested under the act. The whole episode further alienated the *Maintenant* team from the federal order. Finally, in 1971 the federal NDP rejected a resolution recognizing the right of Quebeckers to self-determination. The decision crushed the hopes of the editorial team; if the most progressive party in English Canada could not recognize the nationalist aspirations of French Quebeckers, they felt, then all hope for federalism was lost.[35]

After 1968, *Maintenant* supported the PQ as the true heir of the Quiet Revolution's promise to make French Canadians 'maîtres chez nous.'[36] They denounced the provincial Liberals (reelected in 1970) for supporting the twin structures of capitalism and federalism. In both the 1970 and 1973 provincial elections, the journal supported the PQ and lamented the victory of the Liberal Party.[37] While *Maintenant* writers claimed to be nonpartisan, they consistently depicted the Liberal leader Robert Bourassa as a traitor to the Quiet Revolution, a technocrat, and the archetypal 'unidimensional man' who offered all of Quebec to the highest bidder. Trudeau, the French-Canadian prime minister of Canada, received the same treatment.[38]

Maintenant's writers did not see their support for the PQ as compromising the prophetic distance from all human projects and institutions that their 'eschatological imagination' demanded. Rather, they argued that gospel values demanded that individuals become responsible citizens, dedicated to building an open and participatory society. The PQ, at its best, was a tool for building that society; as such it deserved their 'provisional' support. *Maintenant*'s commitment to the PQ, argued Hélène Pelletier-Baillargeon, who became the editor after Vincent Harvey's death in 1972, was sincere but not absolute. The editorial team wrote that they wanted to defend humanity above any ideology, economic system, or political party.[39] Indeed, they developed a critique of

Quebec nationalism that went beyond their criticism of the PQ. Nationalism had to promote participation by the largest number of people from all sectors in society. When nationalism legitimated ethnic chauvinism or masked differences between classes in Quebec, it was unacceptable. Consequently, according to *Maintenant*, its best expressions were in the popular movement in Quebec, groups representing women, workers, farmers, residents of the regions, and the urban poor.[40] It called upon the new public Catholicism to support the legitimate elements of participation and freedom in the new nationalism and to criticize its excesses and limitations.

Conclusion: *Maintenant* and the Search for a Public Catholicism

In the 1960s, *Maintenant* had two goals: to democratize the internal structures of the church and to define a public Catholicism that respected democracy, pluralism, and civil liberties. In terms of the former, only a little ground was gained. Much more was achieved on the second issue. In 1962, few people could have imagined that the critical acceptance of the new Quebec promoted by *Maintenant* and others would become the official position of the Catholic Church only a decade later. But, in the early 1970s, the Dumont Commission on the status and role of lay people in the church took on the task of redefining the relationship of the Catholic Church to the new state and society. Fernand Dumont and Jacques Grand'Maison, both regular contributors to *Maintenant*, penned the report's first and most important volume, *L'Église du Québec: Un héritage, un projet*. Released in 1971 and 1972, the six-volume report argued that the church had to reform both its internal structures and its relationship to society in the name of participatory democracy; it had to be as democratic as possible, actively searching out ideas from the grassroots; and finally, it had to declare itself resolutely in favour of the poor, the oppressed, and the marginalized in society. As Quebeckers made their way into the future, the church had to act as a supportive fellow traveller but also as a critic or prophet.[41]

Although the bishops of Quebec never fully adopted the Dumont Report's recommendations on democratizing the internal structures of the church, they did agree with its critical affirmation of the new Quebec.[42] Whatever its failures and shortcomings, the Dumont Commission helped to close the door on two options that faced the Quebec church in the 1960s: the return to the public Catholicism of the 1950s and the privatization of religion prescribed by modern liberalism. This orientation has been evident in the Quebec bishops' social teaching since 1970 in which they have consistently affirmed democracy, pluralism, and civil liberties but have been very critical of the state and society when they have neglected the suffering of Quebec's weakest inhabitants.[43]

Though many others who rejected the public Catholicism of the 1950s could see no legitimate role for the church in Quebec public life, the writers of *Maintenant* refused to abandon Catholicism to what they called the 'no man's land' of private religion. First, they argued, the church had done much in the past to legitimate the economic and political structures that had marginalized francophone Quebeckers; now it must commit itself to their liberation. Second, the church had to make this commitment not only for French Quebeckers but also for its own sake. Inspired by the new papal teaching and political theology, *Maintenant*'s writers believed that the gospel called people to be the authors of their own development. Consequently, if the church did not take the issue of participation seriously, both in society and its internal operation, then it was missing the essential message of the gospel. Finally, a public Catholicism could add a necessary spiritual and humanist element to the projects of social development and national liberation. For the writers of *Maintenant*, the danger of the Quiet Revolution was that, in the search for rapid modernization, Quebeckers would disown their heritage, cutting themselves off from the sources of their own particular genius and creativity. Since Catholicism played such an important role in that heritage, the absence of the church in public debates would allow Quebec society to evolve into a purely technocratic state, a carbon copy of the United States. By outlining the necessity of maintaining a public role for the church, *Maintenant* was instrumental in helping it accept the Quiet Revolution while feeling that it still had an important role to play in the new Quebec.

Despite the optimism surrounding the democratization of the church prevalent in the 1960s, public Catholicism remained very much a preserve of the hierarchy: the bishops and the religious orders. Since publication was an expensive and time-consuming task, only those groups that controlled sufficient resources were able to debate and influence the public position of the church.[44] Moreover, the media and public still tended to see the hierarchy as the 'official' church, whereas the opinions of Catholic individuals were usually perceived as subjective, idiosyncratic, and sometimes incompetent.[45]

In 1974, *Maintenant* faced its final crisis. A newsprint shortage increased the cost of producing the journal dramatically. Pélardeau refused to increase his subsidy and in December 1974, the last issue of the journal hit the newsstand. It appeared three more times in April, June, and December of 1975 as a Saturday supplement to *Le Jour*, the indépendantiste daily newspaper founded by René Lévesque, Jacques Parizeau, and Yves Michaud. In the pages of *Maintenant*, Catholic intellectuals, especially university professors and journalists, were able to overcome both the financial and cultural barriers to lay participation in the debate over the new public Catholicism. That time, it seems, had passed. With the current shortage of priests, nuns, and brothers, however, it may see a new day in the next century.[46]

Maintenant made a major contribution to the shift in public Catholicism and, in the early 1960s, was its most influential voice. However, the democratization of the church's relationship to society had also increased the desire for a democratic culture *within* the church itself. This created a new contradiction between recently acquired democratic values and the largely unreformed ecclesiastical structures. The tensions arising from this contradiction guaranteed that in the end the *Maintenant* experiment would only be partially successful.

Notes

1 In a province of about seven million inhabitants today, 86 per cent of all Quebeckers still identify themselves as Catholics, even though only less than 20 per cent attend Mass regularly. Among French Quebeckers, 95 per cent identify themselves as Catholics. A note on terminology is needed. One of the effects of the Quiet Revolution was a redefinition of the 'imagined community' (to use Benedict Anderson's term) of French Quebeckers. Before 1960, they thought of themselves as 'French Canadians,' part of an ethnic group that stretched across Canada. Because the Quiet Revolution focused people's attention on the state apparatus of Quebec, many French Quebeckers began to call themselves 'les Québécois,' a term previously reserved for the inhabitants of Quebec City. The writers of *Maintenant* used the term 'Canadiens français' until 1970 and then used the term 'Québécois,' by which they meant French Quebeckers. Only after the election of the Parti Québécois in 1976 did French Quebec nationalists begin to use the term 'Québécois' to refer to all citizens of the province.

2 For a useful discussion of public religion, upon which my definition of

'public Catholicism' is based, see José Casanova, *Public Religions in the Modern World* (Chicago: University of Chicago Press, 1994).

3 'The privatization of religion' and 'private religion' are technical terms used by sociologists to describe the relationship of a religious community to the state. Its opposite, public religion, does not imply that religion ceases to have a private, personal, intimate dimension. See Casanova, *Public Religions in the Modern World*.

4 Jean Hamelin, *Histoire du catholicisme québécois. Le XXe siècle*, vol. 2, *De 1940 à nos jours* (Montreal: Boréal Express, 1984), 173, table 13.

5 Kenneth McRoberts, *Quebec: Social Change and Political Crisis*, 3rd ed. (Toronto: McClelland and Stewart, 1988), 131–9. Earlier editions were by Kenneth McRoberts and Dale Postgate.

6 Hubert Guindon, 'The Social Evolution of Quebec Reconsidered,' in *Quebec Society: Tradition, Modernity, and Nationhood*, ed. Roberta Hamilton and John H. McMullan (Toronto: University of Toronto Press, 1988), 24.

7 For the rejection of the Quiet Revolution by Catholic conservatives, see David Seljak, 'The Catholic Church's Reaction to the Secularization of Nationalism in Quebec, 1960–1980' (Ph.D. diss., McGill University, 1995), chap. 5.

8 The Ligue ouvrière catholique (LOC) was transformed into the Mouvement des travailleurs chrétiens (MTC) in 1964.

9 Henri Dallaire, O.P., 'Mon oncle!' *Maintenant*, no. 4 (April 1962): 150.

10 H.-M. Bradet, O.P., 'Nouveau départ,' *Maintenant*, no. 1 (January 1962): 1–2; 'Le Concile: Scandale nécessaire!' editorial, *Maintenant*, no. 24 (December 1963): 263–4; 'Plutôt à l'accélérateur qu'au frein,' editorial, *Maintenant*, no. 14 (February 1963): 37–40.

11 H.-M. Bradet, O.P., 'Heure des laïcs, horloge des clercs,' editorial, *Maintenant*, no. 23 (November 1963): 325–8.

12 H.-M. Bradet, O.P., 'Nouveau départ,' *Maintenant*, no. 1 (January 1962): 1–2.

13 The Catholic Church's privileges in the school system were one of the remaining vestiges of the state-supported, public Catholicism of the pre-1960 period. This arrangement, enshrined in Article 93 of the British North America Act, has now been undone. Until 1997, the state-funded school system was organized along confessional lines, with a large Catholic system beside a smaller Protestant one. In the Catholic system (which included 185 of the 217 school commissions), the church participated in the creation of the content of Catholic education and usually provided some kind of pastoral presence. In 1997 the PQ government reorganized the school system along linguistic lines. Individual schools maintain confessional status,

and Protestant and Catholic religious education or nonconfessional moral education is offered as an option in all but a handful of schools.

14 Richard Arès, S.J., 'Le Bill 60 et la démocratie totalitaire,' editorial, *Relations*, no. 279 (March 1964): 65–6.

15 Pierre Saucier, 'L'État, c'est nous,' *Maintenant*, no. 21 (September 1963): 266–7.

16 'Famille, Église, État,' *Maintenant*, no. 21 (September 1963): 260–1.

17 From an interview with Hélène Pelletier-Baillargeon, 27 July 1999. See also Jules Leblanc, 'Forcé de quitter *Maintenant*, le père Bradet déclare au *Devoir*: 'C'est l'affrontement de la droite et de la gauche et c'est la droite qui a gagné,'' *Le Devoir*, 17 July 1965, 1.

18 Jules Leblanc, 'Forcé de quitter *Maintenant*,' 1.

19 Ibid.

20 Claude Ryan, 'Le renvoi du directeur de *Maintenant*,' *Le Devoir*, 19 July 1965, 4; 'Nouveau propos sur l'affaire Bradet,' *Le Devoir*, 29 July 1965, 4.

21 Yolande Chêné, *L'Affaire Bradet* (Montreal: Éditions du jour, 1965).

22 Vincent Harvey, O.P., Pierre Saucier, Pelletier-Baillargeon, and Paul Doucet, O.P., 'Après l'entracte,' editorial, *Maintenant*, nos. 45–8 (Fall 1965): 257–60.

23 See 'Nouvelle "charte,"' *Maintenant*, nos. 45–8 (Fall 1965): 278.

24 Vincent Harvey, O.P., 'La mort des églises,' editorial, *Maintenant*, no. 77 (15 May–15 June 1968): 131–3.

25 'Humanae vitae,' editorial, *Maintenant*, no. 79 (August–September 1968): 195–6. This editorial was reprinted in *Le Devoir*.

26 Vincent Harvey, O.P., 'Centième numéro de *Maintenant*,' editorial, *Maintenant*, no. 100 (November 1970): 279–81.

27 Vincent Harvey, O.P., et al., 'To Be or Not to Be,' editorial, *Maintenant*, nos. 68–9 (August–September 1967): 234–7.

28 My translation of 'socialisme démocratique de participation qui est à inventer' and 'fidèle aux plus authentiques aspirations historiques.' Pierre Saucier and Vincent Harvey, O.P., 'Le statu quo particulier: "bread and butter,"' editorial, *Maintenant*, no. 71 (November 1967): 331.

29 Saucier and Harvey, 'Le statu quo particulier,' 237.

30 Christian Duquoc, 'Christianisme et politique,' *Maintenant*, no. 81 (November-December 1968): 259–62.

31 See Georges Perrault, O.P., 'Les dominicains et la revue *Maintenant*,' *Le Devoir*, 5 December 1968, 5. At first, the Order claimed that the reasons for its actions were purely financial. Its own large deficit meant that it could no longer afford to subsidize the journal. The Dominicans also worried about the pastoral effectiveness of the journal, given that other projects were vying for the same funds. While the financial question was an issue, the

political question, in the end, was decisive according to Perrault. See Jean-Pierre Proulx, 'La revue *Maintenant* menacée de disparition,' *Le Devoir*, 27 November 1968, 2.

32 'Des universitaires lancent un appel pour la survie de *Maintenant*,' *Le Devoir*, 14 December 1968, 2.

33 Pierre Saucier and Yves Gosselin, O.P., 'L'Affaire *Maintenant*,' *Maintenant*, no. 82 (January 1969): 7–9.

34 Jean-Pierre Proulx, '*Maintenant* reparaît grâce à l'appui financier de Pierre Pélardeau,' *Le Devoir*, 8 January 1969, 3.

35 From an interview with Hélène Pelletier-Baillargeon, 27 July 1999.

36 See Robert Boily, 'Un état fort et efficace dans une démocratie de participation,' *Maintenant*, no. 94 (March 1970): 74–87.

37 'Faut-il pleurer, faut-il en rire,' editorial, *Maintenant*, no. 96 (May 1970): 146; 'Il s'agit de notre propre pouvoir,' editorial, *Maintenant*, no. 129 (October 1973): 6–7.

38 'Il s'agit de notre propre pouvoir,' *Maintenant*, no. 129 (octobre 1973): 6–7; see also Gabriel Gagnon, 'L'économie à la Bourassa: De la Baie James à O'Bront,' *Maintenant*, no. 129 (October 1973): 20–3.

39 'Vincent Harvey disparu, que devient *Maintenant*,' editorial, *Maintenant*, nos. 120–1 (December 1972): 4. For a fuller explanation of this 'stratégie du provisoire,' see the posthumously published article by Vincent Harvey, 'Agir ici et maintenant,' *Maintenant*, nos. 120–1 (December 1972): 35.

40 The work of Jacques Grand'Maison was especially important on this issue. See his 'Jonas et le nationalisme de Baptiste,' *Maintenant*, no. 82 (January 1969): 43–6; 'L'Église québécoise face aux défis politiques,' *Maintenant*, no. 85 (April 1969): 116–20; and 'Les ruses populaires,' *Maintenant*, no. cahier 2 (21 June 1975): 5.

41 See the commentary on the report by Gregory Baum, *The Church in Quebec* (Ottawa: Novalis, 1991), chap. 2. In fact, Grand'Maison had already outlined the report's final position in the pages of *Maintenant* in the late 1960s and early 1970s. Naturally enough, the writers of *Maintenant* voiced their support for the Dumont Report's general orientation in a special issue dedicated to the report. See Vincent Harvey, O.P., 'Le Rapport Dumont,' *Maintenant*, no. 112 (January 1972): 3–6.

42 For evaluations on the impact of the Dumont Report, see Julien Harvey, S.J., 'Le rapport Dumont, à court terme et à long terme,' *Sociologie et sociétés* 22, no. 2 (October 1990): 127–32; Baum, *The Church in Quebec*, 63–5; and Fernand Dumont, 'De l'absence de la culture à l'absence de l'Église,' *Relations*, no. 447 (April 1979): 121–7.

43 For the evolution of the social justice statements of the Assemblée des

évêques du Québec, see Gérard Rochais, dir., *La justice sociale comme bonne nouvelle: Messages sociaux, économiques et politiques des évêques du Québec 1972–1983* (Montreal: Bellarmin, 1984). For an analysis of their acceptance of the new Quebec and its new nationalism, see David Seljak, 'The Catholic Church's Reaction to the Secularization of Nationalism,' 439–67, and 'Religion, Nationalism and the Break-up of Canada,' in *Religion and Nationalism, Concilium: The International Review of Theology*, no. 6, ed. John Coleman and Miklós Tomka (1995), 68–76.

44 A number of small journals have existed as exceptions to this rule. One was *L'Autre Parole*, a feminist Christian journal that folded in the 1990s. The other major journal controlled by lay Catholics, *VO: Le Magazine de Vie Ouvrière*, was until recently supported by the Oblate Order.

45 Jacques Grand'Maison, *Nationalisme et religion*, vol. 2, *Religion et idéologies politiques* (Montreal: Beauchemin, 1970), 398.

46 A sign of things to come may well be the hiring of a lay Catholic woman, Carolyn Sharp, as the editor of the Jesuit journal *Relations* in 1993.

13

The Christian Recessional in Ontario's Public Schools

R.D. Gidney and W.P.J. Millar

Did twentieth-century Ontario have a religion 'by law established,' a set of doctrines and beliefs that were not only widely shared by its people but incorporated into the legal framework of the state? In the schools it certainly did.* Here, Christianity was privileged by law, required to be taught 'by precept and example,' and integrated into the curriculum in both formal and informal ways. To the extent that it formed an integral part of the school system, moreover, the propagation of Christian belief was underwritten financially by the state itself. Was all of this little more than a lingering nineteenth-century archaism, doomed in a more modern age to an early death by desiccation? Rather the reverse, we think. The centrality of Christian doctrine in Ontario's public schools, albeit in a nondenominational Protestant form, was alive and well in the mid-twentieth century; still alive, though less well, as late as the mid-1960s; and, even in the last third of the century, finally ousted only through a prolonged, contested process.[1]

The governance of public education in Ontario rests upon a mixture of statute law, regulations, and policies. The education act sets out the basic structure and gives the minister of education (or the cabinet) wide powers to make regulations or to fashion policies, both of which have much the same legal force as the law itself.[2] Consider, then, the place of Christianity within this skein of law, regulations,

---

*This is true for both public and Roman Catholic separate schools; in this chapter, however, we are focusing on the public schools alone. For stylistic reasons, we will occasionally use the word 'religion' to mean the Christian religion or as a substitute for 'Christianity' or 'the Christian religion.'

and policies – not in Egerton Ryerson's day, or in 1910 or 1920, but as recently as 1960 or 1965, just four decades ago.

The education act itself contained only a handful of relevant passages. One enjoined on teachers the duty 'to inculcate by precept and example respect for religion and the principles of Christian morality and the highest regard for truth, justice, loyalty, love of country, humanity, benevolence, sobriety, industry, frugality, purity, temperance and all other virtues.'[3] Another provided that clergymen could act as 'school visitors' and, in that capacity, attend school exercises, examine the pupils and the state of the school, and 'give such advice to the teachers and pupils ... as they deem expedient.'[4] A third specified the days that could be designated school holidays; among others, these included a Christmas vacation, the period from Good Friday to the weekend following Easter, and a day appointed for Thanksgiving.[5] More general sections of the statute conferred broad powers upon the minister of education to decide what was taught in the schools and what books were to be used as texts, and to make regulations with regard to every aspect of school organization, administration, and government, including the power to determine the nature of opening exercises and religious instruction.[6] Students had the legal right to receive religious instruction if their parents so wished, though they also could be withdrawn from any religious exercise or study by parents who objected to it.[7]

The details of this legislation were spelled out in a series of regulations and policies that shaped practices in every public elementary and secondary school in Ontario – or at least set out those practices that were required as a matter of law. Every elementary school, for example, was required to hold daily opening or closing exercises that featured reading the Scriptures and repeating the Lord's Prayer (or other prayers authorized by the department of education), and could also include hymn singing. In addition, religious instruction of a noncontroversial and nonsectarian nature was to be given by the teacher, in accordance with the authorized program, during school hours for two half-hour periods a week.[8]

The program of studies put these policies into practice. In both its content and its underlying assumptions, it embodied the central role of the school in imparting and sustaining Christian teachings. For the elementary schools the pertinent aspects of the curriculum were to be found in two overlapping manuals. The first, entitled the *Programme for Religious Education*, contained detailed instructions on how both the opening exercises and specific religious instruction were to constitute 'two phases' of the same course of study,[9] whose purpose was to establish an avowedly Christian framework within which the child would pursue all learning. The exercises were 'not merely ... an opening ceremony, but ... a preparation for the day's work, the influence of which will be felt throughout all the activities of the school.' The first minutes of the school day were intended to provide food for the child's intellectual as well as spiritual growth: 'The Scripture reading should normally be taken from one or other of the two great English versions, since it is in the highest degree desirable to familiarize the children with the beauty of diction and rhythm of these priceless literary masterpieces.' Preparation for the opening exercises occupied other moments throughout the day: readings and prayers, to be clear and most effective, might be studied beforehand, and require 'coaching' by the teacher; hymns 'should be learned and practised in class beforehand' to 'assist the instruction and enhance the religious value of hymn singing during the religious exercises.'

In those periods specifically allocated for religious instruction, 'systematic study of the Scriptures' constituted the core of the curriculum.[10] Fully half the manual listed 'suggested daily Bible readings,' grade by grade, throughout the school year. Other activities might be undertaken at particular grade levels, such as listening to Bible stories, making pictures and models, reciting Bible passages in unison, memorizing them, and preparing for religious celebrations. One section included prayers for general use (such as the Protestant version of the Lord's Prayer), for specific occasions (such as Christmas and Thanksgiving), and on specific themes (for Christian missions, for example, including one that implored the Heavenly Father, 'for all who do not know of Thy love, both at home and in other lands, Grant that through the work of our missionaries they may be led to know Jesus Christ as their Saviour, and serve Him truly at all times'). Complete lesson outlines were provided in the 'Teachers' Guides to Religious Education,' including the particular Scripture passage to be studied, 'background notes' to 'furnish the teacher with historical and other information regarding the setting of the Scripture story,' and suggestions for related activities such as 'further readings from the Bible, choral reading and verse speaking, memory work, written work, discussion, dramatization, drawing, and handwork of various sorts.'[11]

Religious instruction, however, was not to be confined within the two designated periods. Such instruction, the manual intoned, 'will be sterile and uninspiring unless all the teaching through the school is infused with an appreciation of goodness, beauty, and truth. Religious Instruction must aim to set up ideals, to build attitudes, and to influence behaviour, as well as to teach Scriptural facts and Biblical text.' Values and character were to be taught throughout the day by precept and example: 'The personal reverence, both outward and inward, of the teacher is of immeasurable importance. The wakening and guidance of the spiritual sense in the children is the first factor in creating the finest fruit in individual character, and consequently in the happiness and right development of the race. The responsibility of the teacher for the spiritual growth of the child is as great as for the intellectual and physical, because education is one and indivisible.'

The second pertinent manual was the *Programme of Studies for Grades 1 to 6*; originally introduced in 1937, it remained in force, with only minor revisions, until the late 1960s. Conventionally known to a generation of teachers as the 'little grey book,' this was the document that told elementary school teachers what subjects and topics they were to cover in each grade. In tone, content, and direction, it underlined the centrality of Christianity in the school. The introduction asserted that the whole purpose of education in Ontario was 'to [prepare] children to live in a democratic society which bases its way of life upon the Christian ideal.'[12] Thus one of the main tasks of the school was 'to lead the child to choose and accept as his own those ideals of conduct and endeavour that a Christian and democratic society approves.' To achieve this end, it was necessary that Christianity infuse the curriculum: 'Religious teaching cannot be confined to separate periods on the timetable,' the guide went on, echoing the religious education manual. 'It will affect the teaching of all subjects, and the wise teacher will be anxious, in the various departments of school activity, to bring home to the pupils, as far as their capacity allows, the fundamental truths of Christianity and their bearing on human life and thought.' Throughout the program of studies, themes and topics for each grade reflected that admonition and often drew unselfconsciously upon common assumptions of a shared Christian culture. The subjects taught, to be sure, were overtly secular. Still, for example, under the general topic of 'Our Family' in grade 1 social studies, the guide listed such commonplace activities as 'seeing mother at work in the home,' 'hearing stories told by mother and father,' and 'going to church and Sunday School.' Secular topics were illustrated by biblical references. Learning about 'Family Life' was to focus on 'good family relationships that present patterns of desirable social behaviour' such as stories about 'the baby Moses, the infant Jesus, Miriam and Moses, the infant Samuel, Told from time to time throughout the year.' Similarly, in grade 4, Ontario students learned, in the social studies unit called 'getting food from the soil,' about 'how men learned to farm in the long ago' and 'keeping flocks and herds'; suitable illustrations were to be drawn, among other examples, from 'stories of early Bible times.'

Some of the texts authorized for use in the elementary schools revealed similar assumptions of a shared Christian heritage. Although the English readers no longer routinely included religious literature to the extent they had up until mid-century, there were still books as late as the mid-1960s that contained explicit references to Christian custom and belief. As one analysis notes, citing a selection entitled 'David and Susan Go to Church,' the subtext was that 'all students are church-going Christians.' In another passage, father's donation to the collection plate each Sunday to support 'missionaries who teach the Christian faith to people in other lands' is likened to the way in which 'Christian men and women in France' supported missionaries 'to the first Canadians, the Indians.'[13]

The presence of Christianity was less overt in the high school program, and yet its teachings, its history, and certainly its language pervaded much of what was absorbed, consciously or otherwise. As in elementary school, some of this was governed by regulation. Opening exercises that included 'systematic reading of the Scriptures' and the Lord's Prayer were mandatory. Religious instruction by a clergyman during the school day for up to one hour a week was permitted, at the discretion of each school board. As well, school principals could 'suggest Bible passages to be memorized by the pupils.'[14]

Particularly in some subjects, such as English and history, every student grappled with texts from the Bible, or Christian writers or commentary. Curriculum outlines and compulsory examinations ensured that this material would be studied in depth. Students preparing for the grade 13 departmental examinations of 1957–8, for example, were required to study three 'longer poems,' one of which was Milton's 'Ode on the Morning of Christ's Nativity,' a poem steeped in Christian belief, and rich in allusions to a culture impenetrable to those outside the Christian pale. While no good teacher would intentionally exploit the opportunity to turn such literature into a Bible lesson, the message could hardly go unnoticed. The theme of the poem, scribbled one student in the margins of his text, was 'the moral significance of Christ as a symbol of truth which can banish the errors typified in the mass of pagan deities.'[15] Similarly for history. In grade 11, for example, *every* student was introduced to the highlights of Western civilization from caveman to the Renaissance, including the rise of Christianity, its centrality and achievements in the following centuries, and its legacy in literature, philosophy, and art.[16]

From the perspective of 1960, much of the emphasis on Christian indoctrination was of recent vintage, most notably the Drew regulations of 1944. Introduced during wartime by a new Conservative government as a response to both the perception of moral decline in a time of national crisis and the desire to augment religious teaching in the schools, their main innovation was to make religious instruction compulsory in the elementary schools during the school day.[17]

The Drew regulations were only the culmination of a movement that had been underway since the 1920s to increase the amount of direct religious instruction, in the elementary schools especially, and to make the Christian ambience of the school more pervasive.[18] But even with these qualifications, the fact remains that in law, regulation, and ambience, the schools had always been expected to reflect Christian beliefs, values, and practices. Clergymen had always had the right to visit the schools and to instruct children of their own faith, though only after school hours. Students had always possessed the legal right to receive such instruction. Opening exercises had long had a religious element. Texts and readers had always contained at least allusions to Christianity, and sometimes more. And beyond the purview of law, regulations, and official policies, there were the seasonal rhythms of school life in accordance with the Christian calendar: the universal Christmas concert with its explicitly Christian emphasis, the preparations before Thanksgiving and Easter holidays, the Christian hymns and Scripture readings that accompanied Remembrance services. Throughout most of the twentieth century, as in earlier decades, Christianity was taught 'by precept and example,' accorded a place of privilege in Ontario's schools by custom as well as by law.[19]

One can argue, and one might be right to do so, that even at mid-century (and certainly by the early 1960s) there was a substantial gap between formal injunction and actual practice. One can also point to open dissent, especially about religious education during the school day.[20] Still, at mid-century compliance was widespread if not universal, and the principle of religion as an integral part of schooling had a high degree of legitimacy. Certainly it received benediction from the Hope Commission, appointed in 1945 to investigate the general state of education in Ontario and reporting five years later. Widely representative of élite and progressive opinion, the commission formulated the premise that 'there are two virtues about which there can be no question – honesty, and Christian love.'[21] Furthermore, the school was key, for 'patterns of behaviour which are based on Christian ideals, and are acceptable to society, can be realized only through the cooperative efforts of the home, the school, and the church.'[22] In that mutual endeavour, it was the school's role to ensure that children received the proper preparation: 'The moral and spiritual lessons of the Scriptures should deeply influence the conduct and behaviour of children in their daily lives.'[23] Thus 'religious education should be included as a subject of study in the curriculum of the ... public elementary schools. The present regulations,' added the Hope Report, 'seem to be eminently satisfactory.'[24]

Between the late 1950s and the early 1970s, nonetheless, both the premises that underpinned that comfortable consensus and its embodiment in law and regulation were substantially compromised.[25] Like so much else in Ontario education, discontent found its focus, and revisionism its voice, in the late 1960s.[26] Asked in 1965 by William Davis, the minister of education, to review the place of religion in the schools in the light of the circumstances of a new age, the Mackay Committee consulted, pondered, and then submitted a report in 1969 which called for the full-scale disestablishment of Christianity in the province's schools. Almost certainly its authors would take exception to that assessment of their work: they were neither anti-Christian nor anti-religious, and their report did not envisage the introduction of a thoroughly secularized system of public education. But its entire thrust pointed in that direction.

The committee was firmly agreed on 'the importance of the role that religious faith has played, and continues to play, in the life of the people of this province.'[27] But in the schools, which particular religion? That was the rub, 'for indeed we have seen that our society has been altering greatly in recent decades, and is continuing to change rapidly.' Given that fact, Ontario schools required a new approach to the 'means by which character building, ethics, social attitudes and moral values and principles may best be instilled in the young.' With a bow to the prevailing educational discourse, the report concluded that in a democratic society every adult, and every young person, has the right to choose freely the spiritual and moral values he wishes, or, indeed, to reject them. A central object of education is to further the search for truth, and to enable the learner to make informed judgments. Thus we hope it will be through true education, and not through any kind of indoctrination, that he will be encouraged to choose the religious and moral values that will hold as good for his time as those which we ourselves prize so highly have held good in ours.

Teaching the tenets of a specific religion was indoctrination; learning moral values separated from any particular religious teaching was not. By these standards, the current program of study in Ontario schools was not only outdated but offensive. Using subject material that was 'definitely Christian and Protestant in content,' it was 'a vehicle leading to religious commitment rather than to true education.' 'Christian indoctrination' began in kindergarten with Bible stories and hymns, and continued in each grade. It was an affront to adherents of other faiths. It implied superiority where none existed, as though Christianity stood at the apex of a hierarchy of beliefs. In no uncertain terms, the Mackay Report proceeded to recommend an end to this sorry state of affairs.

On the issue of opening exercises, the committee took exception to the primacy of Christian symbols: therefore 'the most significant change we recommend ... is the cessation of Bible readings.' But 'religion does indeed play a vital part in our life and ... the holding of opening exercises therefore exposes the child to a valuable learning experience in relation to the whole community in which he lives.' Thus the committee thought the solution would be 'the singing of the National Anthem and a prayer, either of universal character appealing to God for help in the day's activities, or the Lord's Prayer.' A 'sensitive and intelligent teacher' could also seize the opportunity to recognize days of national import like Remembrance Day, and 'significant religious days of all faiths such as Easter, Hanukkah, Christmas, or Passover' (those outside the Judaeo-Christian fold were not mentioned). Though exemption from participation even under these new conditions was, it felt, discriminatory, the committee nevertheless reluctantly accepted that as a necessary evil.

It also recommended the repeal of the regulation allowing clergymen to be official school visitors, as well as the establishment of an optional World Religions course in grades 11 and 12 which would focus on the 'systematic and detailed study of the various religions of the world' to provide 'knowledge about and insight into the bases of religious doctrines, creeds, liturgical practices.' But the most radical proposal was yet to come. The report recommended complete abolition of the existing religious education program for the elementary schools, as well as of Regulation 45, which permitted the teaching of religion in secondary schools for two periods a week. Instead, citing the need to 'join the mainstream' in North American schooling, the committee opted for a pervasive system of 'moral education' in which 'the high duty of public education to foster character building ... should be discharged through a clearly understood, continuously pursued, universal program pervading every curricular and extra-curricular activity in the public school system from the beginning of elementary to the close of secondary education.'

The new program was to convey information *about* moral values, divorced from confessional teaching and particular beliefs or doctrines. Relying on the 'discussion technique,' teachers were to engender discussion in 'an unobtrusive but quietly guiding way,' using 'situational anecdotes involving moral conflict.' These discussions, integrated through every part of the curriculum and at every level, would allow students to evaluate situations and conflicts, weigh results, and rationally arrive at a personal moral standard.[28]

It was a clarion call for change, and one that paralleled, and was intended to parallel, the more wide-ranging review of the school system being conducted by the Hall-Dennis Committee, which was attempting to disestablish the premises and practices traditional to Ontario education generally. Like Hall-Dennis as well, the Mackay Committee did not work in a vacuum or signal the commencement of reform; rather, it reflected a thrust already taking shape within the ministry of education. For years, the ministry had turned a blind eye to boards that were not implementing the mandatory religious program; after the mid-1960s, it implicitly condoned such neglect, allowing the religious manual to lapse by not reprinting it.[29] This stance was, however, more than passive acquiescence; it reflected policy preferences within the ministry itself. In the late 1960s the ministry began to rewrite the elementary school program of studies – to replace the 'little grey book' with a document more congruent with the educational fashions of the age. Still unprepared to abandon the formulary of the 1937 program, the new interim guideline reiterated earlier phraseology about preparing children 'to live in a democratic society that bases its way of life upon the Christian ideal.'[30] It did not, however, reproduce two key sections: first, a passage containing references to the detailed suggestions for religious instruction found in the 1949 guide and the *Teachers' Guides to Religious Education*; and second, a paragraph on the necessity of infusing the entire program with 'the fundamental truths of Christianity and their bearing on human life and thought.'[31] It also omitted all the small references to biblical stories and examples that had been part of 'the little grey book.' While the regulations were left intact, in other words, Christianity was effectively excised from the curriculum of the elementary school.

The final version of the new program of studies, published in 1975, completed this work by dropping all mention of the related regulations (even though technically they remained in force) and of the goal of preparing students for living in 'a democratic society' based on the 'Christian ideal.' The new formulation simply stated that the child was 'to develop the moral and aesthetic sensitivity necessary for a complete and responsible life.'[32] The key resource document that accompanied the guideline expounded on this cryptic notion at greater length, defining values as 'those qualities of life that the individual and/or society considers important principles of conduct and major aims of existence,'[33] and devoting several paragraphs to explaining how teachers could help pupils develop a 'value system.'[34]

Other tentative steps the ministry took in this direction were to fund research throughout the 1970s into moral education and, in 1974, to distribute to school boards a booklet, entitled 'Moral Education in the Schools,' for review and recommendations.[35] A similar trend characterized the attempt, beginning in the same decade, to formulate a new set of 'goals' for the education system. One statement announced, for example, that 'education should encourage individuals to develop an appreciation of the ethics of their society and the conduct prescribed by such ethics,'[36] and a later version included, among the goals of the school, that of developing 'values related to personal, ethical, or religious beliefs and to the common welfare of society.'[37]

In the high schools, the new World Religions course was intentionally comparative and nonconfessional in approach, but at least Christianity had a recognized place. The course, however, proved a weak reed for entirely contingent reasons. Introduced at a moment when the entire program of studies was being optionalized, it had to compete against a welter of other subject choices and it was largely marginalized for that reason alone.[38] At the same time, history became an optional subject as well, and the coherent grade 11 and 12 course in Western Civilization ceased to be a mandatory part of every graduate's cultural baggage. For a variety of reasons,[39] it also became less likely for students in English literature to be exposed to prose or poetry specifically Christian in reference or context.

Even the most mundane housekeeping details in the education system seemed to conspire against the traditional verities. In the 1970s the second term in the school year was changed to end, not with the peripatetic feast of Easter, but with 'the March break,'[40] an innovation that gave gladness to the hearts of all winter-weary Ontarians and that resolved the vexing (to administrators and teachers) uneven length of terms, but that swept away the indirect but potent symbolism of 'Easter holidays.'

It was one thing, however, to introduce shifts in emphasis in the program of studies – shifts which largely took place outside the public eye, and which, in any case, had a certain cachet among the cognoscenti, including many practising Christians. It was quite another to confront, head-on, the more tangible symbols that privileged Christianity in law. Thomas Wells, minister of education for most of the 1970s, was apprized of that political reality early on, and in no uncertain terms. Unveiling what he and his officials surely believed would be the most uncontroversial of measures – a huge, highly technical, and very complex revised and consolidated education act – Wells was caught totally off-guard by the reaction to one proposed change that would have deleted the word 'Christian' from the phrase that enjoined teachers to uphold the principles of 'Christian morality.' The news created an uproar. Over the next few months, more than 7,000 letters poured in to the ministry 'expressing concern about the deletion of the clause.'[41] Quickly reacting to what might better be described as 'outrage,' the ministry backed down; though not all the way, adding the word 'Judaeo' to 'Christian' morality.[42]

That was not the first sign of disapprobation, nor was it to be the last. From the outset the Mackay Committee had heard from a substantial number of people who wanted to see religious education in the schools retained, or even enhanced.[43] Similarly the reformulated 'goals of education' were attacked as nebulous and incomprehensible. As one acerbic critic would put it, 'Hitler, Idi Amin, Pol Pot and Stalin all developed values related to personal religious and ethical systems; they would have met Ontario's values criterion.'[44] The moral education movement drew reactions that ranged from scepticism to outrage. What exactly was it to consist of? How was it to be implemented independent of any religious framework? And what dangers did it pose in the hands of well-meaning but naive practitioners?

It may well have been the case, in other words, that by the late 1970s or early 1980s, the mid-century consensus about the place of Christianity had substantially collapsed under the weight of increasing secularization, materialism, pluralism, and so on – all the 'first causes' contemporaries fell back on when they wanted to explain their own society to themselves. But pluralism *included* large numbers of folk, great and small, who believed that the schools should continue to exhibit distinctly Christian affinities, and that the symbolic links between the state and the Christian faith should not be abandoned. That view even reached the floor of the legislature in 1982 with a private member's resolution calling for observance of the clauses on religion in the education act and regulations, and, more radically, for the *repeal* of the section that allowed school boards to receive exemption from offering religious instruction – a resolution that was carried by a vote of 56 to 22.[45]

Given this uncertain climate, it is not surprising that politicians ducked and parried. Studies were commissioned without noticeable outcome. The pertinent legislation remained in place, while ministry guidelines talked of values, or, in blithe disregard of its own regulations, announced that religious education could be an *optional* area of study in the grade 7 and 8 course.[46] The ambience of the era was perhaps best exemplified by an incident in 1979 resulting from an amendment to the regulation on opening exercises. In recognition of the diversity of faiths in the new Ontario, that amendment had allowed the substitution of 'other suitable' readings and prayers for the Scriptures and the Lord's Prayer. When the Toronto Board of Education proposed, however, to include a 'moment of silence' instead of a prayer, the politicians, reacting to a 'storm of protest from bedrock Christian Ontario,'[47] came down with a heavy foot. Bette Stephenson, the minister of education, informed the board that a moment of silence, even for 'silent meditation,' contravened the education act. Rejecting the notion entirely, Premier William Davis averred that 'the Lord's Prayer establishes a common respect for a society where morality, humility and faith in God are important pillars of stability and the social norm,' and that its retention was 'an important part of the moral values of Canadian society.'[48] His outburst prompted the *Globe and Mail* to comment wryly that, unlike the present premier, 'Education Minister William Davis knew that "the social norm" in Toronto and Ontario includes adherents of many religions other than Christianity, as well as non-religions,' when he appointed the Mackay Committee.[49]

Nor would the issue go away. It smouldered throughout the 1980s, catching fire every time some related issue fanned it, most notably the bitter warfare over full funding for Catholic high schools. As Rosemary Speirs, then the acute Queen's Park reporter for the *Toronto Star*, would summarize it in 1987, the ministry of education found itself

> under pressure from many quarters: from Roman Catholic educators who want religious education to be worth more credits towards a high school diploma; from Protestant church leaders who argue that Roman Catholicism has been given special status and are demanding equal time; from principals in the public high schools who say they could halt the drain of students to the separate system if they could just offer Catholic religious teachings in the public system; and from other private religion-based schools which are demanding funding and credits for courses in religion.[50]

The cross-pressures were intense enough in the late 1980s, indeed, to provoke yet another ministry review of the place of religion in the schools. Its public hearings attracted an enormous response and elicited stacks of briefs and letters – far more than the Hope Commission had received on the same subject.[51] The depth of passions roused by the issue may be judged from this account of the scene at a hearing in Sault Ste Marie: 'In a standing-room-only auditorium, members of Ontario's Bible Belt demanded that local schools have the right to teach Christianity. "Let's keep the country Canadian. Let's keep the country Christian," said one spokesman for a local group called Citizens for Christian Values.'[52]

Even in the late 1980s, then, the place of Christianity in the schools was still at issue. Despite the clamour for an end to this 'anachronism' in public education, despite the substantial revisions which marginalized it in the curriculum, despite the fact that, with ministry connivance, the regulations were ignored in large numbers of schools, much of the traditional structure remained in place. The education act was the same as it had been in 1960. The Drew regulations, forty years old, were still in force. Nor was the intent of the law and regulations merely an empty shell. Utterly abandoned by some school boards, Christian practice still had a place in others. In many schools there were still opening exercises featuring the Lord's Prayer. In a few boards at least, there was still (or in revived form) religious education in the elementary schools.[53]

What resolved the issue was not a uniformly secularized public opinion increasingly indifferent to the traditional role of Christianity in the schools. Opinion indeed was deeply divided. Substantial numbers of those who supported Ontario's public schools continued to form their vision of the good school within a Christian context. Others, though less committed to that view, were reluctant to sunder public education entirely from the outward symbols of the faith. What really pried the lid open was the passage, by the federal Parliament, of the Canadian Charter of Rights and Freedoms, and two crucial court cases that followed from it. There are thorough accounts of these court decisions elsewhere and we will not reiterate the details here.[54] But altogether, the courts ruled that both the religious portion of opening exercises and the Drew regulations on religious education violated the Charter guarantees of freedom of religion. Thus were the politicians (and the ministry as well) taken off the hook: they could now claim, with a good deal of justice, that laws and policies had to change regardless of the divisions in public opinion. And change they did. Within months, policies were put in place that ended the privileged place of the Lord's Prayer and Scripture reading in opening exercises, and that eliminated compulsory religious instruction of any kind. The new formulary was, in essence, this: one could teach *about* religion but one must not give primacy to any one faith in doing so, or indulge in any activity which might be construed as indoctrination, or confessional instruction.

Vestiges remain. According to the education act, teachers must still inculcate 'Judaeo-Christian' morality. Students must still, by law, be allowed to receive religious instruction – though this is perhaps meaningless for non–Roman Catholics, since the right is 'subject to the [new] regulations.'[55] Clergy may still offer religious instruction outside of school hours, though this now depends on the acquiescence of the local school board, and equal time must be given to all religious groups. In their official capacity as school visitors, clergy may still attend the schools, but they can no longer 'give advice.' The curriculum still allows teaching about Christian beliefs, but only if other faiths receive equal attention.[56] Opening exercises *may* include Christian prayers and readings, but again, only if other religious literature *and* 'secular writings' are given equal weight.[57] Specifically Christian holidays such as Christmas or Good Friday may appear to remain privileged; but even that has been contested, the courts deciding that these are not religious holidays but 'secular pause days' equivalent to any other secular holiday.[58] And in the schools themselves, traditional 'Christmas' celebrations have increasingly become 'winter festivals' or 'festivals of light.'

Unlike some critics of the schools, we are not arguing that the Christian recessional was necessarily 'a bad thing.' Ontario, and especially urban Ontario, is now a very different society than it was fifty years ago, and the schools, like other public institutions, reflect that reality. What cannot be at issue, however, is the magnitude of the changes. Beginning in the 1960s Ontario's public schools were gradually stripped of their specifically Christian characteristics. The state ceased to finance or legislate Christian teaching in them. In this particular part of the public arena – and no one should need reminding that the public school touches individuals in a way, and to an extent, that few other public institutions do – Christianity has not only been disestablished but banished, at least as an animating force, in both the ceremonial and the mundane activities that inform its daily life.

Notes

1 For a fine introduction to recent controversies over religion and schooling across Canada, see Lois Sweet, *God in the Classroom: The Controversial Issue of Religion in Canada's Schools* (Toronto: McClelland and Stewart, 1997). Ontario, like some other Canadian provinces, has both state-funded Roman Catholic ('separate') schools, and nondenominational (or latterly, secular) 'public' schools. Roman Catholic separate schools have always had the right to offer denominational religious instruction, and in this respect they have a history distinct from that of the public schools. Generally, see Franklin A. Walker, *Catholic Education and Politics in Ontario: From the Hope Commission to the Promise of Completion (1945–1985)*, vol. 3 (Toronto: Catholic Education Foundation of Ontario, 1986).

2 A consolidated education act was introduced in 1974. It supplanted all the pertinent legislation which before that date was found in several different statutes.

3 *The Schools Administration Act, 1962*, s. 22 (c). All the statutes cited in this paragraph had been repeated in virtually the same words in successive enactments from the beginning of the twentieth century or even earlier.

4 *The Public Schools Act, Revised Statutes of Ontario (R.S.O.)*, 1960, chap. 330, as amended 1960–1, 1961–2, 1962–3, s. 8. Certain other officials, such as MPPs and judges, could also be school visitors.

5 *The Schools Administration Act, R.S.O.*, 1960, chap. 361, as amended 1960–1, 1961–2, 1962–3, ss. 3, 4. Easter and Christmas were statutory holidays for the schools from well before the turn of the century.

6 *Department of Education Act, R.S.O.*, 1960, chap. 94, as amended 1961–2, 1962–3, ss. 10, 12.

7 *The Public Schools Act, R.S.O.*, 1960, chap. 330, as amended 1960–1, 1961–2, 1962–3, s. 7.

8 *Elementary and Secondary Schools – General*, Regulation 339/66, as amended 1967 and 1968, s. 44. Individual teachers could be exempted from this task, but substitutes had to be found; in such cases, the school board was authorized to appoint one or more clergymen or lay representatives, of any denomination, to take over religious education in the school.

9 *Regulations and Programme for Religious Education in the Public Schools*, 1949, 10. Quotations in this and the following two paragraphs are from various pages, 8–31.

10 Since 'Scriptural interpretations' were to be 'confined to those expressions of the Christian faith upon which all Christian denominations are in substantial agreement,' such study avoided, it was felt, any sectarian taint in the public schools.

11 Adapted from the English Teachers' Guides, these are described in W.D. Edison Matthews, 'The History of the Religious Factor in Ontario Elementary Education' (D.Ped., University of Toronto, 1950), 193–5. Guides for grades 1 to 6 were produced for the 1944–5 school year; the grade 7 and 8 guides were published as late as 1959 and 1961: see *Religious Information and Moral Development: The Report of the Committee on Religious Education in the Public Schools of the Province of Ontario*, 1969 (Mackay Report), 13.

12 *Programme of Studies for Grades 1 to 6 of the Public and Separate Schools, 1960* (Ontario Minister of Education, 1960), 5 (a reprint of the 1955 edition with minor revisions). The following quotations in this paragraph are from ibid., 7, 68–9, 73.

13 Garnet McDiarmid and David Pratt, *Teaching Prejudice: A Content Analysis of Social Studies Textbooks Authorized for Use in Ontario* (Toronto: OISE, 1971), 99.

14 *Elementary and Secondary Schools – General*, Regulation 339/66, as amended 1967 and 1968, s. 45. Unlike the elementary schools, the regulations for high school opening exercises specified only the Lord's Prayer. Like the elementary schools, however, an exemption clause was included.

15 Text in the possession of the authors.
16 See, for example, one of the two authorized texts: John H. Trueman, *The Enduring Past: Earliest Times to the Sixteenth Century* (Toronto: McGraw-Hill Ryerson, 1964).
17 Religious instruction remained optional in the high schools; opening exercises were compulsory.
18 For the details, the most accessible source is Matthews, 'The History of the Religious Factor,' esp. 163–93. Ontario appears to be unique in North America in moving to *compulsory* religious instruction in 1944 (elsewhere, when allowed at all, it was most commonly a local option). This peculiarity of the Ontario case deserves more analysis than it has yet received. For comparisons, see Matthews, 'The History of the Religious Factor,' chap. 10; Andrew G. Blair, *The Policy and Practice of Religious Education in Publicly-Funded Elementary and Secondary Schools in Canada and Elsewhere* (Toronto: Queen's Printer, 1986); B. Edward McClellan, *Schools and the Shaping of Character: Moral Education in America, 1607–Present* (Bloomingdale, IN: ERIC Clearinghouse for Social Studies/Social Science Education and the Social Studies Development Center, Indiana University, 1992), chap. 3; *The Report of the Ministerial Inquiry on Religious Education in Ontario Public Elementary Schools* (Watson Report), 14–19.
19 Commenting on the 1998 movie *The Prince of Egypt*, one journalist noted that *Time* magazine's review of it first had to describe and explain the Bible story for its readers; in contrast, when Cecil B. DeMille's *The Ten Commandments* was produced in 1956, 'everyone who saw it already knew who Moses was, along with the basics of his story,' partly 'because at school we had Bible readings each day.' Rick Salutin, 'We've Come a Long Way ...,' *Globe and Mail*, 17 December 1998.
20 See, for example, Mackay Report, 13–14.
21 *Report of the Royal Commission on Education in Ontario, 1950* (Hope Report), 28.
22 Ibid., 163.
23 Ibid., 166.
24 Ibid., 126.
25 For an assessment of how these changes were expressed in the broader Canadian society, and especially in the role of the churches, see John Webster Grant, *The Church in the Canadian Era*, updated and expanded (Burlington, ON: Welch, 1988), chap. 9. For a brief summary of the U.S. situation, see Edwin S. Gaustad, 'The Pulpit and the Pews,' in *Between the Times: The Travail of the Protestant Establishment in America, 1900–1960*, ed. William R. Hutchison (Cambridge: Cambridge University Press, 1989), 40–3.

26 For the context and the parallels in this and the paragraphs that follow, see R.D. Gidney, *From Hope to Harris: The Reshaping of Ontario's Schools* (Toronto: University of Toronto Press, 1999).

27 Mackay Report, xv. The quotations in this and the following three paragraphs are taken from the report, various pages, vii–74.

28 For an assessment of the moral education movement in the United States, see McClellan, *Schools and the Shaping of Character*, esp. chap. 5, on the influential theories of Lawrence Kohlberg and others. For an example of a local curriculum guide for such a program, see London Board of Education, *Moral Education Manual*, Kindergarten–Grade Eight, 1978.

29 *London Free Press*, 7 February 1972; note that the regulations, incorporated into the school law, remained intact.

30 Ontario Ministry of Education, *Curriculum P1J1, Interim Revision, Introduction and Guide, 1967*, 5.

31 *Programme of Studies for Grades 1 to 6 of the Public and Separate Schools, 1960*, 7.

32 Ontario Ministry of Education, *The Formative Years*, 1975, 4.

33 Ontario Ministry of Education, *Education in the Primary and Junior Divisions*, 1975, 5.

34 Ibid., 20.

35 Watson Report, 13. This response came well after various school boards had taken the initiative in developing moral education programs, however. A ministry committee established in 1978 to review religious education recommended continued exemptions for boards from teaching the program, while also asking for support documents from the ministry; ibid., 13.

36 'Goals of Education: Providing an equal opportunity for all,' *New Dimensions* (May/June 1973): 5.

37 Ontario Ministry of Education, *Ontario Schools, Intermediate and Senior Divisions, Grades 7–12/OACs: Program and Diploma Requirements (OSIS)*, 1984, 4.

38 In 1980, about 1 per cent of high school students were taking it: see Blair, *The Policy and Practice of Religious Education*, 20.

39 These include not simply the larger forces at work in society such as growing pluralism, but endogenous shifts within the school system itself, including changes in pedagogical fashions. See, for example, Don Gutteridge, *Stubborn Pilgrimage: Resistance and Transformation in Ontario English Teaching, 1960–1993*, with a teaching unit by Ian Underhill (Toronto: Our Schools/Our Selves, 1994).

40 *Elementary and Secondary Schools – General*, Regulation 546/73, s. 2 (3).

41 *Ontario Education Dimensions* (February 1974): 4.

42 *The Education Act*, 1974, s. 229, 1 (c).

43 Walker, *Catholic Education*, 223–4, describes the impassioned arguments both for and against religious education.

44 Mark Holmes, quoted in George Radwanski, *Ontario Study of the Relevance of Education and the Issue of Dropouts* (Ontario Ministry of Education, 1987), 32.

45 No action followed, however: see Watson Report, 20. More than a decade later, an all-party vote in the Ontario legislature endorsed the return of prayers in the public schools, despite the changes of the intervening years; see *Toronto Star*, 11 May 1996. Again, no action followed.

46 *OSIS*, 14.

47 The phrase is from Rosemary Speirs' assessment in the *Toronto Star*, 7 February 1987.

48 *London Free Press*, 14 September 1979.

49 *Globe and Mail*, 17 September 1979, editorial. Many boards, including Toronto, ignored Davis' statement: *Toronto Star*, 7 February 1987.

50 *Toronto Star*, 7 February 1987 (Rosemary Speirs).

51 Compare Hope Report, ix, and Watson Report, 5.

52 *Toronto Star*, 22 September 1989.

53 See for example *Toronto Star*, 7 June 1988 and 7 January 1989; *Globe and Mail*, 27 September 1988; *London Free Press*, 1 March 1989.

54 The two cases were *Zylberberg et al. v. Sudbury Board of Education*, heard in the Ontario Divisional Court in 1986 and in the Ontario Court of Appeal in 1988, and *Corporation of the Canadian Civil Liberties Association et al. v. Ontario (Minister of Education)* (Elgin County), heard in the Ontario Divisional Court in 1988 and decided on appeal in the Ontario Court of Appeal in 1990. For the judgments, including much of the history, see *Ontario Reports*, 2nd series, vol. 64 (64 O.R. 2nd), 577–619, and vol. 65 (65 O.R. 2nd), 641–719. Generally, see John S. Snowden, 'The *Charter*, the Courts and Religion in Ontario's Public Schools' (M.Ed. thesis, University of Western Ontario, 1993).

55 Unlike other public school boards, Roman Catholic separate school boards have the legal right to offer religious education in their schools.

56 For the regulation, see *The Education Act, 1998*, regulation 298, 4 and 28–9; for the ministry resource document, see Ontario Ministry of Education and Training, *Education about Religion in Ontario Public Elementary Schools*, 1994.

57 See Ontario Ministry of Education and Training, *Opening or Closing Exercises for Public Schools in Ontario*, 1993.

58 Sweet, *God in the Classroom*, 203.

14

From a Private to a Public Religion: The History of the Public Service Christian Fellowship[1]

Don Page

In both Canada and the United States, the 1960s witnessed the beginning of an outpouring of conservative Christian concern about the loss of familiar cultural values in the face of a growing liberalism in social and economic values that was supported or at least tolerated by governments.[2] Sociologist José Casanova has characterized this period as one of 'deprivatization' of religion as it took part in the process of contestation and legitimization of religiously inspired morality in civil society.[3] In both nations, conservative Christians were increasingly dissatisfied with the political response to such issues as the sanctity of life, a perceived degeneration of sexual mores, and the intrusion of government into the lives of believers and their churches. To varying degrees, on both sides of the border conservative Christians believed that their nations had been founded on biblical values, beliefs, and morals now so undermined that only direct intervention accompanied by a spiritual repentance and revival could restore moral propriety.[4] The strategies used in the United States and Canada to respond to this perceived threat were, however, quite different.

In the United States a massive organization of the right began to bring direct pressure on the American government through well-financed political lobbying and campaigns to elect congresspeople who would support the right's values. The rebirth of Protestant fundamentalism or the Christian Right, as this organization was often labelled, formed the well-publicized Moral Majority, Christian Voice, and Religious Roundtable. In Washington, members of Congress and their staffs were the targets of the Christian Right, while bureaucrats played virtually no role in advancing this moral agenda.[5]

Their Canadian counterparts also decried the changing moral landscape, but, with the exception of the occasional outburst emanating from Renaissance Canada, they were not comfortable with what they perceived to be the more brazen tactics and strident voice of the American religious right.[6] Most sought a quiet way of preventing the government's encroachments on their biblical morality, rather than seeking to impose it on the nation by political means. They generally eschewed any organized proactive political involvement in the public affairs of the nation.[7] There was, however, in the 1970s an awakening of an evangelical social voice that joined with like-minded believers from the mainline Protestant and Catholic communities to influence the morality of Canadian society in the face of increasing secularization.[8] A combination of a small but well-organized group of federal bureaucrats and their allies in the House of Commons used their influence to uphold conservative cultural values and to encourage the organization of like-minded public interest groups to provide the needed public support for their activities. How this unique combination of multidenominational Christians converged in an effort to make a difference through their prayers and organization in Ottawa in the 1970s and 1980s is the subject of this chapter, one that has remained largely unexplored to date. As one of the network's charter members, the author was an active participant, and his religious convictions shape the account that follows.

Although there were several independent Christian fellowship groups functioning within the government before the mid-seventies, there was no coordination among them and little interest shown by any of them in taking a position on government policy. The oldest such group, the Military Christian Fellowship, traced its roots back to before the Second World War. By 1980 it had grown to 800 members, meeting in groups on virtually all military bases and at the National Defence Headquarters in Ottawa. Its mandate was to help people in the military to grow in their private spiritual maturity, to support each other through the trials of repeated military postings, and to encourage the work of military chaplains.[9]

Much better known was the group on Parliament Hill. In 1962 the national leader of the Social Credit Party, Robert Thompson, disappointed with what he perceived to be the continuing partisan wranglings on Parliament Hill, began to speak about the need for Christians of all parties to unite in transcending their differences in order to find a statesmanlike way of bringing civility into politics and offering an alternative Christian perspective. Knowing that such a move would

require more than a minority voice, Thompson enlisted the cooperation of Walter Dinsdale, a fellow Christian and Conservative member
from Brandon, Manitoba, to begin a weekly Parliamentary Prayer
Breakfast for members and senators.[10] In 1964 a National Prayer Breakfast was launched to invite Christian leaders from across the land,
regardless of their political or religious affiliations, to join with parliamentarians, judges, the diplomatic corps, and other Ottawa dignitaries, 'in the spirit of Christ to express their spiritual values and reflect
on the spiritual heritage of Canada.'[11] The breakfast was an opportunity for Christians from across party lines to meet regularly and to provide encouragement for those who were bold enough to speak out on
the basis of their Christian faith.

At first, the group seemed to be an exclusive gathering of those who
shared Thompson's fundamentalist beliefs. Later, under the leadership
of Jake Epp and Ursula Appollini, the group expanded to include a
broader section of interested, but not necessarily committed, parliamentarians. Although it was never spoken of publicly, these regular
meetings did provide a means for drawing together members who
could work together on legislative tactics outside of the maelstrom of
their partisan activities.

Within the public service a few Christians had come together informally to study the Bible for personal spiritual encouragement. Such
groups had existed at various times in the National Research Council
and the Department of Health and Welfare. From 1971 a more consistent group had been meeting weekly for the same purpose in the
Department of the Environment. In 1975 a new form of Bible study and
prayer group emerged in the Department of External Affairs. Its focus
was work-related for both Bible study and prayer. Through church connections with the people at External Affairs, a similar group started in
the Department of Trade and Commerce; a total of sixteen such groups
had formed by 1979. What made these groups different from their pre-
decessors was that most of them followed a specific Bible study outline
prepared by the leader at External Affairs. The thrust of these studies
was to encourage the individual pursuit of Christian values in the
workplace. Participants were also committed to praying for their minister and senior leadership in accordance with the apostle Paul's admonition 'to pray for those in authority over you' (1 Timothy 2:2).

In 1971 a religious revival swept across western Canada, led by the
Sutera Twins, Ralph and Lou, from Mansfield, Ohio. They went on to
hold crusades in many cities under the auspices of the newly formed

Canadian Revival Fellowship. In the spring of 1979 the Suteras went to Ottawa at the invitation of a large local church. Night after night at their rallies, many Christians who worked for the government came forward to recommit their lives to God. Realizing the potential in these government workers, the Suteras challenged them to organize so that they could become effective witnesses for conservative Christian values within the government. An organizing committee, comprising Christians who worked for fourteen different departments, was struck. They chose Ray Robinson, an assistant deputy minister at Environment Canada, and the author, Don Page, as co-chairmen to organize a conference to begin the Public Service Christian Fellowship (PSCF) in Ottawa.

On 24 November 1979 nearly 400 public servants from across Ottawa and Hull came to hear Christian members of Parliament Robin Richardson and Jake Epp; assistant deputy minister in Veteran Affairs, Nick van Duyvendyk; Colonel Ferdinand Braun from National Defence Headquarters; and the co-chairmen of the conference share their dreams for making Canada a better country through the moral influence of Christianity. This gathering was diverse in nature. Catholics, Baptists, Presbyterians, Anglicans, Canadian Reformed, Pentecostals, anglophones and francophones, men and women, members of Parliament and clerks, all sought to work towards the same end: a discernible Christian presence in the Public Service of Canada. Two months after this conference, which brought together members of the Military Christian Fellowship (MCF), the PSCF, and the Parliamentary Prayer Breakfast, thirty-five groups were functioning throughout the public service,[12] reflecting, as the *Ottawa Citizen* reported, 'an international trend towards greater interest by society in religion and greater emphasis towards evangelism and learning more about the Bible.'[13] Similar groups began to organize in the provincial governments of Ontario, Manitoba, Alberta, and British Columbia.

While the various groups retained autonomy in their actual operations, they shared a common executive selected by those attending the initial meeting of the PSCF. Because of the informal nature of the organization, this group was never voted into office but became self-perpetuating with the support of the constituent groups. The members of this executive became the primary spokespersons for the PSCF, publishing a monthly newsletter aimed at inspiring members to fulfil their mission of 'learning and applying Christian principles in all areas of public service' through aspiring 'to work worthily, honorably, heartily, lovingly, and diligently.'[14] Any group of like-minded public servants could select a leader and seek the endorsement of the PSCF executive. Because anyone could join a group, the membership tended to be more broadly based than the group leaders and executive, who tended to come from the evangelical wings of their denominations, which espoused conservative beliefs and cultural values.

As senior public servants, the leaders of the PSCF did not want to be perceived by their colleagues as having an agenda. They were careful never to identify themselves with the agenda of the religious right or the Moral Majority in the United States, protesting vehemently when the media tried to make that connection.[15] They were sufficiently politically astute to know that such identification, even if they did share some of the same concerns and interests, would destroy their credibility to work effectively with other decision makers in Ottawa. In typical Canadian fashion, they preferred to support each other through networking behind the scenes in order to influence the levers of power on issues around which they felt deeply. Christian clerical workers, for example, played a key role in curbing violence during a clerical strike in the public service in 1978, and lobbied to restrict official travel on Sundays so that they could worship with their families.

The groups encouraged inclusivity. As Jean Blaquière, the francophone leader of the group in the RCMP, pointed out:

We are quite diverse and in this diversity we grow in love, understanding and faith about the things that are in heaven. We are neither French nor English, neither catholic nor protestant. Instead of trying to come together on points that already set us apart, we try to focus on the person of Jesus Christ and strive to improve our relationship with our Father in heaven ... Our mission is simple. 'We are a chosen generation, a royal priesthood, a holy nation' (1 Peter 2:9). This makes us ambassadors of the Kingdom of God and ministers of the Word.[16]

While the ecumenical spirit of acceptance worked well in the public service, the PSCF was not without its problems. Strains developed over the participation of Mormons in one group, who wanted to use the group to proselytize, which was contrary to public service regulations, and the group had to suspend its activities temporarily. It was also learned that because of the latent memories of religious conflict in Quebec, francophone Catholics and Baptists would not attend groups led by someone from the other side. Periodically, there were complaints that government notice boards or rooms denied to other religious groups were used for PSCF purposes.

The PSCF, like other conservative Christian groups in the United States, united its prayers around the challenge of 2 Chronicles 7:14: 'If my people, who are called by my name, will humble themselves and pray and seek my face and turn from their wicked ways, then will I hear from heaven and will forgive their sin and will heal their land.'[17] This verse was the theme of the organization's first conference in 1979. Members prayed regularly that their leaders in government would have wisdom to discern between good and evil (1 Kings 3:9), that they would develop common sense and good judgment (Proverbs 4:7), that the counsel of the Lord would stand (Proverbs 19:21), and that they would not become weary in well-doing (2 Thessalonians 3:13). To these and other scriptures they added specific issues in the belief that 'Righteousness exalteth a nation: but sin is a reproach to any people' (Proverbs 14:34). PSCFers distributed thousands of copies of the leaflet 'Praying for Our Nation and Those in Authority over Us' to churches across Canada. The leaflet was also published in the *PSCF Newsletter* in March 1986.

In the late 1970s its American parent organization persuaded Campus Crusade for Christ of Canada to begin a nationwide Great Commission Prayer Crusade (GCPC) in Canada. Staff workers in various cities launched the GCPC with the mandate to pray for a spiritual awakening in the nation and its leaders. This last part of the mandate brought the GCPC into an informal working relationship with the PSCF. Together, over a period of several years, they offered workshops to hundreds of churches and denominational conferences.

To facilitate the transmission of prayer requests and link these various prayer ministries together, the Executive Ministries of Campus Crusade for Christ of Canada sponsored a National Prayer Leadership Conference in Toronto in November 1982. Among the speakers calling for a national prayer movement were MPs Jack Murta (chairman of the Parliamentary Prayer Breakfast), the Honourable Jake Epp, and Jack Burghardt. Representing the PSCF were Diane Scharf (from the Prime Minister's Office and the leader of the PSCF group for staffers on Parliament Hill) and Don Page as co-chairman of the PSCF. The primary outcome of this conference was the decision to launch a National Telephone Prayer Chain. By this means, a prayer request originating in Ottawa, usually from Christian MPs or the PSCF, could be sent across the country to those who had committed themselves to pray for such requests. The GCPC facilitated and paid for the organization of the prayer chain. In its first year of operation, prayer chains operated in forty cities in nine provinces and could reach over 100,000 people by telephone within twenty-four hours. To be transmitted, the prayer request had to be of 'a national nature involving legislation, a speech by a Christian MP on an issue of specific concern to Christians, or a national emergency.'[18]

Ironically, not all of the PSCF groups could agree on the wording of the requests and the prayer chain movement functioned better across the country than within the PSCF itself. As a result of concerns expressed by the group at the Canadian Radio-Television and Telecommunications Commission (CRTC) at a meeting of the PSCF executive, the requests were reworded so as to state the issue for which prayer was requested but without any direction as to how to pray. The CRTC group did not feel comfortable in passing on requests that suggested a desirable outcome or had an implicit political connection attached to the passing of a piece of legislation.

Soon after the launch of the national prayer chain a National Prayer Committee of church leaders and representatives was established to promote citywide interdenominational Concerts of Prayer for Canada and its leaders. Other groups began to promote prayer for Canada: Prayer Canada out of Surrey, British Columbia; Intercessors for Canada out of Fort Erie, Ontario; and Canadian Revival Fellowship out of Regina, Saskatchewan. The daily television ministry *100 Huntley Street* embraced the call to prayer in the nation through regular broadcasts of prayer requests and invited guests from the PSCF, MCF, and Parliamentary Prayer Breakfast. A representative sample of requests included: the inclusion of a reference to God in the Constitution; a ruling outlawing the production of a film in Canada that portrayed Jesus as homosexual; an amendment to Bill C-10 involving the Non Profit Corporation Act, which would exclude churches from certain government-imposed fiduciary controls; the defeat of Bill C-53 to amend the Criminal Code to allow acts of gross indecency between consenting adults in privately owned establishments; the hiring of a Christian on the prime minister's personal staff; the outlawing of lotteries wishing to operate in sports arenas; protection for the charitable status of certain Christian organizations that had been critical of government policies; arrangements for evangelist Billy Graham to have a private meeting with Prime Minister Trudeau; and provisions for Bible college students to deduct their tuition fees on their income tax returns.

In most cases, prayer was directed to efforts being made by PSCF members and Christian MPs to effect changes to, stop, or amend legislation regarded as potentially threatening to the work of the churches or detrimental to conservative Christian values. For example, when the Equality for All Report (1985) recommended amendments to Section 15 of the Charter of Rights and Freedoms, successive ministers of justice hinted that they would introduce amendments to include sexual orientation as a basis for nondiscrimination. Conservative Christians in Ottawa, with the support of their praying partners across the land, organized a letter-writing campaign in opposition and then arranged meetings with the justice minister, his legal staff, and Prime Minister Mulroney to protest.[19]

The PSCF mounted another major campaign of prayer and influence over the inclusion of a reference to God in the new Constitution. Prime Minister Pierre Elliott Trudeau had made it known publicly that he was not in favour of such an inclusion; his Liberals had defeated an opposition amendment to that effect.[20] The PSCF persuaded like-minded organizations to join with them in campaigning for a reference to the sovereignty of God in the Constitution. The reference, they felt, would provide a basis on which to appeal to those in authority should they experience the state's interference with Christian principles. Prayer requests went out, meetings were held, and 300,000 Christians across many denominations were persuaded to express their dismay over the lack of a reference to the sovereignty of God in the Constitution in both prayer and by writing to the Prime Minister's Office. Since the government would not listen to the official opposition, PSCF members lobbied sympathetic Liberal MPs to pressure the prime minister. Trudeau, who was anxious to get on with repatriating the Constitution, relented and agreed to allow an amendment acknowledging the sovereignty of God.

Another event that brought a focus to religion and the PSCF in public life flowed, in part, from the conclusion of this debate over the Constitution. The Reverend David Mainse of *100 Huntley Street* organized a great prayer pilgrimage across Canada in June 1981. The seventeenth city in this 'Salute to Canada' was Ottawa, and the PSCF and MCF were at the heart of a local committee planning the event on Parliament Hill. Suitable anglophone, francophone, and Aboriginal spokespersons, representing a wide spectrum of denominations, as well as the leaders of the PSCF, the MCF, and the Parliamentary Prayer Breakfast were to be part of the program. But Mainse wanted Trudeau and the leader of the opposition, Joe Clark, to participate as well.

Invitations to Trudeau and Clark had been delivered weeks before-hand, but neither responded. At first, the Prime Minister's Office indicated that the prime minister would not participate because it would break a long-standing practice of not participating in public religious events that might show favouritism to any religious organization. As Salute to Canada began to move across the nation, momentum and a following began to build. Guests on the show included denominational leaders, mayors, members of Parliament and provincial legislative assemblies, and the lieutenant-governors of Alberta, Saskatchewan, and Manitoba. The projected North American audience for the Ottawa broadcast and its subsequent rebroadcast was estimated at 10 million viewers, and there would be an estimated 2,000 people on Parliament Hill for the live broadcast. As interest in the broadcast grew, Clark announced that he would release a prerecorded statement for the broadcast and the Prime Minister's Office reversed its position and quickly followed suit. Both offices turned to the PSCF for a draft speech.[21]

Trudeau's speech acknowledged the debt Canadians owed to their forbears, whose 'golden thread of faith is woven throughout the history of Canada from its earliest beginnings up to the present time.' 'Faith,' he concluded, 'played a large part in the lives of so many men and women who have created in this land a society which places a high value on commitment, integrity, generosity and, above all, freedom. To pass on that heritage, strong and intact, is a challenge worthy of all of us who are privileged to call ourselves Canadians.' Clark as well acknowledged the value that religion added to Canadian society. 'That support of faith,' he added, 'is as important today, in modern times, as it ever was, and even more so, because the forces of cynicism and doubt are so much more strong today ... We pray today that God's sovereignty over our Canada continues to bless and to guide us.'[22]

Christian concern for public life in Canada was also tied into electoral politics. From the early 1970s onwards, groups of conservative Christians became more active in local politics in an effort to have like-minded politicians elected to the House of Commons. Many of these MPs became vocal about the need for Christians to join with others in making their views known in the shaping of public policy. It was an auspicious time for interested Christians to increase their involvement in public policy issues. Since the late 1960s the Trudeau government had encouraged the public to express their views to the government as part of an increasing effort to overcome citizen alienation from govern-

ment through 'participatory democracy.'[23] Conferences were organized to publicize the role of religion in public life. One of the most
noteworthy was held in Ottawa in April 1984. Speakers included the
Honourable Jake Epp; Dr John Redekop, the moderator of the Canadian Conference of Mennonite Brethren Churches; and business con-
sultant and religious broadcaster Preston Manning.

Because of the national publicity given to the work of the PSCF and
the national prayer movement, the organization found itself functioning as a network for conservative Christian interest groups and individuals seeking to influence the federal government or its many
agencies. Working together from the inside, PSCF members in many
departments and a handful of supportive MPs connected petitioners
with sympathetic power brokers and activated the levers needed for
favourable decisions. Before long, many like-minded Christian groups
were asking the PSCF in Ottawa to give seminars for churches, para-
church organizations, and denominational conferences, not only on
how to pray and what to pray for, but also on how to influence government policies through activities like lobbying and letter writing. An
average of three dozen such seminars were offered each year outside of
Ottawa by the PSCF and supportive MPs.

This was also a time when major moral issues were being decided.
Christians were encouraged to influence the government's proposed
course of action through their network. During the abortion debate of
1988–9, for example, Christian MPs arranged for prominent pro-lifers
to meet with the prime minister, and PSCF members briefed the delegation on how to make an effective presentation to him. Individuals
wrote pro-life letters from churches, and Christian doctors and lawyers
testified for the sanctity of life from conception in strategically managed debates in parliamentary committees and the Conservative caucus. Even though the House of Commons passed Bill C-43 before
losing the bill through a tie vote in the Senate, this public pro-life concern over abortion was an example of the growing deprivatization of
religion in Canada.[24] Similar integrated campaigns were mounted over
issues pertaining to divorce legislation (1985); sexual orientation
(1986); rights of the unborn (1986); child care (1987); the Fraser Royal
Commission on Pornography and Prostitution's recommendations for
the decriminalization of prostitution, the legalizing of brothels, and
antipornography legislation (1987); and the reinstatement of capital
punishment (1987).

The 1980s were the high point of conservative Christian activity in the public service, as believers went public in their advocacy of moral righteousness in the country. The PSCF peaked in 1983 with 38 groups. By 1989, however, that number had shrunk to 26 groups with a total of approximately a thousand members.[25] While the PSCF, MCF, and the Parliamentary Prayer Breakfast continued into the 1990s, their focus changed as newer ministries took their place in the nation's business. The more political activities of the PSCF spun off in 1988 into a new organization known as the Christian Network, which sought a more proactive and strategic means of influencing cabinet members without endangering the positions of apolitical public servants. It sought to inform and mobilize Christians in every federal constituency to become more aggressive and professional in their direct lobbying for changes in government regulations and legislation. It published and distributed information packets on how to lobby persuasively and effectively. These packets, under the title of 'Christian Networking: Building A Constituency,' were widely used by Christians lobbying to have Christian values reflected in the Canada clause or preamble to the 1992 Charlottetown Accord.[26] The first issue of the *Canadian Christian Activist* was published in December 1989, but the organization was unable to build the needed support in the constituencies to continue publication. More lasting has been the Centre for Renewal in Public Policy, developed in the early 1990s by former PSCF members who recognized the need to present a well-researched conservative perspective on public policy issues through its Ottawa office.[27]

The Great Commission Prayer Crusade changed its name to Prayer Alert and, following the 1988 federal election, tried to organize its prayer chains on an electoral riding basis in order to have more direct and local impact. While prayer captains were found for most constituencies, the movement became overextended and could not sustain itself. The original financial backers who had supported the staff to maintain the prayer chains and publish *Prayer Alert*, the organization's prayer sheet, were unwilling to support the extra cost of the new organization, and the anticipated donations from those involved in the ridings' prayer chains did not materialize. Moreover, those involved lost interest. Gradually, Prayer Alert took on less of a national focus and reverted to its original purpose of supporting the ministry opportunities of Campus Crusade.

The Christian Embassy, meanwhile, worked closely with a small group of Christian MPs, primarily from the Conservative Party, who participated in the Embassy's evangelistic ministry to government officials and diplomats in other countries. In Ottawa, successive Embassy directors devoted more attention to foreign diplomats, a move that lessened their contact with PSCF members and the power brokers in Ottawa, especially after the 1992 federal election, which brought a new group of Christian MPs to Parliament Hill through the Reform Party. In order to be effective in its primary, nonpartisan evangelistic ministry, the Christian Embassy chose to avoid any direct association with controversial public policy issues.

Social justice issues, while not ignored by the PSCF, were secondary in its efforts to influence government policy because there were already well-established channels operating for religious and government officials to interact on these issues. Representatives of the mainline denominations continued to make their representations directly to cabinet ministers on issues pertaining to social welfare, unemployment, international development assistance, disarmament, peace, and human rights, but there were now more evangelical denominations and individual congregations joining with them to express their views. In the 1980s the government, on its own initiative as part of participatory democracy, organized regular consultations with religious groups on disarmament and human rights.[28] PSCF members were not needed to facilitate such interaction with these special interest groups, which now had well-established and officially sanctioned channels to the bureaucracy. Consequently, the PSCF focused on moral issues and on enabling the more evangelical newcomers to enter into participatory dialogue with the government.[29]

Once Christian organizations had established their own channels to the levers of government power, they no longer needed the PSCF and Christian MPs to open doors for them. This was particularly true for the largest and most outspoken group, the Evangelical Fellowship of Canada (EFC) and its very active Social Action Committee. Its new executive director, the Reverend Brian Stiller, quickly learned through PSCF tutoring how to access various levels of government, including the Prime Minister's Office. Representing over 100 evangelical organizations and 28 denominations, Stiller came to speak for an estimated 2.5 million evangelicals. As editor of the largest subscriber-driven religious magazine, *Faith Today*; host of a weekly television show known as the *Stiller Report*; and a presenter of a popular public seminar, 'Understand Our Times,' Stiller brought a powerful voice for righteous government to Ottawa.[30] Through its publications *National Alert* and *Sundial*, the EFC had the means of generating its own prayer support and informing Christians across the country about government actions – municipal and provincial as well as federal – followed by instructions on how to make their views known strategically. The EFC organized the presentation to parliamentarians that became the basis for including Christian values in the draft preamble to the Charlottetown Accord.[31] The EFC later opened its own permanent office in Ottawa to lobby the government and to orchestrate interventions in cases before the Supreme Court.

At the close of the 1980s, as the EFC and other smaller groups of Christians made their appeals directly to the government, the PSCF focused more on their original mandate of Bible study and prayer for strengthening their individual and private witness as Christians within the bureaucracy. Christian MPs continued to interface as speakers with the PSCF, but there was no longer a need for a coordinated network for public ministry. An era had passed. The most activist-oriented leaders of the PSCF retired or left Ottawa, and those who succeeded them had the same intent but rotated through the leadership every couple of years, thereby depriving the movement of consistency in leadership. There were new Christian newspapers and other channels for getting information to possible prayers, and the Chrétien government was much less interested in facilitating the participatory democracy that Trudeau had championed.

The PSCF enabled conservative Christians to come out of the woodwork and to gain respect from their political masters for how they worked and what they stood for in public affairs. By no means were all of their cultural values enshrined in legislation, but their perspective on these matters and those of social justice did make it onto the table for decision making. Unlike the American religious right, which sought to organize for political warfare, supporters of conservative cultural values and righteousness in government in Canada had found a more direct method for influencing their government through a sympathetic group of networked Christians within the bureaucracy. At the end of the 1990s, the influence and interaction continue, but through less conspicuous and more diverse channels. Perhaps one of the greatest legacies from this period was the bridging through the PSCF of the historical gap between those conservative Christians who focused on social concerns and influencing governments and those who focused on personal piety and evangelism. The PSCF always drew support from across the multitude of denominational connections of its members. The three most prominently represented denominations among its members were three very theologically different denominations: Catholics, Pentecostals, and Baptists.[32] Because of their efforts, there seemed to be a greater respectability accorded by church leaders and government officials to those who boldly expressed their Christian concerns in the public square. And thousands of Christians were now better informed about the workings of government on their behalf and their means for influencing matters of state.

Notes

1 I am grateful to have had the input of many of the main actors in this story, who graciously read this chapter and offered their insights. Readers included Herm Braunberger, Benno Friesen, Steve Hill, Andy Kolada, Diane Scharf, John Reimer, Nick Van Duyvendyk, and Clarence Zimmerling.

2 See Robert Wuthnow, *The Restructuring of American Religion* (Princeton: Princeton University Press, 1988), 65; and John G. Stackhouse, Jr, *Canadian Evangelicalism in the Twentieth Century: An Introduction to Its Character* (Toronto: University of Toronto Press, 1993), 201.

3 See José Casanova, *Public Religions in the Modern World* (Chicago: University of Chicago Press, 1994), 65–6.

4 See James Davidson Hunter, *America Evangelicalism: Conservative Religion and the Quandary of Modernity* (New Brunswick, NJ: Rutgers University Press, 1983), 113–14. While evangelical Americans emphasized that their nation was founded on Christian principles, Canadians could make no such historic claims and chose to focus on the Christian principles of its leading figures who influenced the morality of Canadian public life and legislation. For the best example, see Paul Knowles, ed., *Canada: Sharing Our Christian Heritage* (Toronto: Mainroads, 1982), 9, 11.

5 See Matthew C. Moen, *The Christian Right and Congress* (Tuscalosa: University of Alabama Press, 1989), 65–80.

6 While one could find examples of James Skillen's seven categories of political approaches found in the United States, it could not be said that any of them is prominent enough to warrant independent recognition in influencing any substantial number of Canadian Christians whose political clout would be recognized in Canada. See James W. Skillen, *The Scattered Voice: Christians at Odds in the Public Square* (Grand Rapids: Zondervan, 1990). The group that was closest to the Moral Majority in Canada was Ontario-based Renaissance Canada, led by the Rev. Ken Campbell, but it

was disregarded in Ottawa because of the harshness of its advertisements attacking major political figures. Jerry Falwell of the Moral Majority visited Campbell in Canada in 1979 and wrote the preface to Campbell's book, *No Small Stir: A Spiritual Strategy for Salting and Saving a Secular Society* (Burlington, ON: Welch, 1980).

7 In this sense Canadians did not fit the four postures of the political rebirth of Protestant fundamentalism in the United States. See Casanova, *Public Religions*, 157. For how differently organized Canadian evangelicals responded, see Stackhouse, *Canadian Evangelicalism*, 170. There was, however, the Christian Heritage Party, which was formed in the late 1980s in response to the challenges to traditional morality, but it failed to make any significant mark on the electoral landscape.

8 See Brian C. Stiller, *From the Tower of Babel to Parliament Hill: How to Be a Christian in Canada Today* (Toronto: HarperCollins, 1997), 68–71, for the main reasons for this change in outlook and cultural participation by evangelical groups. See also John Webster Grant, *The Church in the Canadian Era* (Burlington, ON: Welch, 1988), 231–4.

9 See Bob Fletcher, 'History of the Military Christian Fellowship (MCF) of Canada,' *PSCF Newsletter*, March 1980, 4–5; and 'Military Christian Fellowship,' *PSCF Newsletter*, January 1986, 3–5.

10 See Robert N. Thompson, *A House of Minorities* (Burlington, ON: Welch, 1990), 123.

11 Ibid., 124.

12 See Ray Robinson, 'Public Service Christians Join in Worship,' *PSCF Newsletter*, March 1980, 2–3.

13 See Leslie Dutton, 'In Government Bible Groups, Even Opposites Attract,' *Ottawa Citizen*, 17 May 1980, 43.

14 According to its own literature, 'The Public Service Christian Fellowship is an organization of ambassadors for Christ in the public service. It is open to all who seek to find and make Jesus Christ Lord of their lives. As Christ's ambassadors, its members seek to reflect Christian attitudes and principles in their work. Believing that the Bible is the standard for working and living, the PSCF promotes Bible study, prayer and Christian fellowship directed toward the application of Christian principles in their workaday world in a way which will always glorify Christ.' 'Report on the Prayer and Business Meeting,' *PSCF Newsletter*, March 1983, 1.

15 See the letter to the editor on 'Salute's spiritual message ignored,' by Roy Rowe, who signed a protest letter written by the PSCF (2 July 1981, 6) in response to Jacquie Miller's article on 'More than 2,000 crowd Hill to see TV preacher's Canada salute,' *Ottawa Citizen*, 22 June 1981, 24.

16 See Jean Blaquière, 'Greetings from the Mounties,' *PSCF Newsletter*, June 1981, 5. For a more extensive discussion of the PSCF's influence on government operations, see the unabridged conference paper in possession of the author.

17 Although the message and the scriptural basis were the same, especially calling on the promise of 2 Chronicles 7:14, Canadians were not beholden to their American friends for their inspiration or activities. For a parallel American version, see James Davidson Hunter, *America Evangelism: Conservative Religion and the Quandary of Modernity* (New Brunswick: Rutgers University Press, 1983), 113; and Moen, *The Christian Right and Congress*, 38.

18 See 'National Prayer Chain Operating,' *PSCF Newsletter*, November 1982, 1.

19 Interview with John Reimer, Langley, British Columbia, 3 June 1999.

20 See John Gray, 'Tories Dragging of God into Patriation Row Detestable: PM,' *Globe and Mail*, 25 April 1981, 12. See also Robert Sheppard, 'Tory Plan Would Put God, Family in Preamble,' *Globe and Mail*, 22 January 1981, 15. The PSCF carried a lengthy excerpt from the debate in its newsletter under the banner, 'God keep our land glorious and free!' *PSCF Newsletter*, February 1981, 3–6.

21 The author recalls being contacted by telephone by separate requesters from both Clark's office and from the PMO to write draft speeches. Having written both, he handed the draft texts to the requesters in person and was in the audience when Trudeau and Clark gave their respective speeches.

22 Both statements were reprinted in the *PSCF Newsletter*, September 1981, 1–3, and can be found in the Global Network broadcast, 'Salute to Canada,' 20 June 1981.

23 See Richard Gwyn, *The Northern Magus: Pierre Trudeau and Canadians* (Toronto: McClelland and Stewart, 1980), 18 and 271.

24 See House of Commons, *Debates*, 28 July 1988, 18153–62, for how the pro-lifers voted on the pro-life amendment. For an earlier attempt by the Clark government to limit abortion, see House of Commons, *Debates*, 30 November 1979, 1916–21, when a private member's bill was talked out.

25 See David Scanlon, 'Community Leader Takes up New Post in British Columbia,' *Ottawa Citizen*, 27 May 1989, H4.

26 See Don Page, 'Participating in Constitutional Debate,' in *Shaping a Christian Vision for Canada: Discussion Papers on Canada's Future*, ed. Aileen Van Ginkel (Toronto: Faith Today, 1992), 77–80.

27 The possibility of such a research centre had been discussed at length by PSCFers Phillip Bom, Ian Shugart, and the author in the early 1980s. Its first two full-time employees, Paul Racine and Greg Pennoyer, were former members of the PSCF group on Parliament Hill, and two of its early direc-

tors were former co-chairmen of the PSCF. The PSCF as an organization, however, was not connected to the Centre. Because of its connections and that of one of its principal sponsors, former MP Benno Friesen, the Centre was able to work directly with the offices of MPs rather than through the PSCF.

28 See Robert Matthews and Cranford Pratt, eds., *Church and State: The Christian Churches and Canadian Foreign Policy* (Toronto: Canadian Institute of International Affairs, 1982). PSCFers also participated in these discussions.

29 One group that worked equally hard on moral as well as social justice issues was Citizens for Public Justice, whose public affairs director, Gerald Vandezande, was at the forefront of several coalitions of diverse Christian lobbyists. Vandezande was equally at home with the General Council of the Evangelical Fellowship of Canada, the social activists of the mainline denominations, both Protestant and Catholic, and the PSCF. See Vandezande, *Christians in the Crisis: Toward Responsible Citizenship* (Toronto: Anglican Book Centre, 1983); and *Catalyst*, the magazine of Citizens for Public Justice.

30 The fervour of his appeals can be seen in the book by Brian C. Stiller, *Don't Let Canada Die by Neglect and Other Essays* (Markham, ON: Faith Today, 1994); and *Critical Options for Evangelicals* (Markham, ON: Faith Today, 1991). 'The days are over,' wrote one reporter about Stiller's influence, 'when the often-poor, marginalized evangelicals let the sin-filled world go to Hades while the righteous remnant waited for salvation in Christ's second coming' (Douglas Todd, 'The New Face of Evangelicalism,' *Vancouver Sun*, 4 May 1991, D13).

31 'Submission by the Evangelical Fellowship of Canada to the Special Joint Committee on a Renewed Canada,' as printed in *Shaping a Christian Vision for Canada*, Van Ginkel, 85–92.

32 Unlike the membership as a whole, Anglicans were the largest group comprising the executive of the PSCF, but its chairpersons were consecutively an Anglican, Presbyterian, Christian Reformed, Pentecostal, and Catholic. Interview with Nick Van Duyvendyk, Ottawa, 18 May 1999.

Part Six

Bearing Witness: The Voice of Religious
Outsiders in Public Life

15

'Justice and Only Justice Thou Shalt Pursue': Considerations on the Social Voice of Canada's Reform Rabbis[1]

Gerald Tulchinsky

Reform Judaism's message of social justice and other universalistic values received eloquent expression in the first half of the twentieth century in Canada, just as it did in Germany and the United States, where this movement was thriving. The command issued in Deuteronomy by Moses, ever mindful of his people's waywardness, to pursue *tsedek*, justice or righteousness, mandating the performance of good deeds such as charity, freedom for the oppressed, and decency towards all mankind, in short *menschlichkeit* (the Yiddish term meaning human decency), resonated through the careers of four notable Reform rabbis who served in Canadian congregations between 1900 and 1960. This Canadian Reform expression, like its German and American counterparts, was shaped as much by its local contexts as it was by those broad universalistic values. It is my purpose in this chapter to outline some of this Canadian flavour through the voices of Nathan Gordon and Harry Stern of Montreal's Temple Emanu-El and Maurice Eisendrath and Abraham Feinberg of Holy Blossom in Toronto, all of them important examples of the interplay between context and culture in Canada's Jewish experience in the first half of the twentieth century. This interface between Judaism and Canadian society demonstrates that key Reform leaders became deeply involved in many important contemporary issues central to Canada's social and political transformation in the first half of this century, and that the story of religion in Canadian public life has had an interesting, if not significant, Jewish component.

Reform Judaism, unlike Orthodoxy, has always been predicated on active Jewish engagement in the world beyond the fences erected against the outside Christian world. Canadian Orthodoxy's leaders, such as Montreal's Hasidic 'ilui' (genius), Rabbi Yudel Rosenberg, stressed that the path towards redemption required the 'innerness' of the *Halacha* (the 613 *mitzvot* of Orthodoxy), especially those mandating the sanctity of the Sabbath. Emphasizing the importance of that sanctuary in time, in a 1924 pamphlet he put Canada's Jews on notice that Sabbath observance was essential before the Messiah's arrival – a stiff requirement for a community which, though nominally traditional, included many professedly antireligious left-wing elements.[2] Neither Rosenberg's nor other similar appeals were widely heeded. A 1938 sociological study of the Montreal community revealed that Jews – especially the immigrants' children – were rapidly falling away from observances while accommodating to the exigencies of living in a free society and, despite appeals and warnings, later trends revealed that the genie could not be put back into the bottle.[3]

Observances that built a fence around Judaism to keep its adherents free of the temptations from the outside world, while the very stuff of Orthodoxy, were in those days (Reform has become much more traditional in recent decades) precisely what Reform thinkers, like Isaac Meyer Wise of Cincinnati, abhorred, except in those few cases where *mitzvot* were supportive of the universalism which its founders proclaimed in their famous Pittsburgh Platform of 1885.[4] 'We recognize in the modern era of universal culture of heart and intellect,' it proclaimed, 'the approaching of the realization of Israel's great Messianic hope for the establishment of the kingdom of truth, justice, and peace among all men.' To Reformers, then, Judaism was a 'progressive religion,' which 'extend[s] the hand of fellowship to all who operate with us in the establishment of the reign of truth and righteousness among men.'[5] Such beliefs proclaimed outwardness, engagement, and service, and its rabbis, trained at Hebrew Union College in Cincinnati, followed that mandate in the pulpits they occupied throughout North America, including the few Canadian Reform congregations (called temples like their counterparts in the United States).[6]

Reform had a late, weak, and slow start in Canada, historian Michael Brown points out, compared with its early efflorescence in the United States, where, by 1880, an estimated three-quarters of all synagogues had affiliated with this denomination.[7] Reform rabbis were already dominant among the Jewish clergy with figures like Wise and David Einhorn, who were defining an American Judaism that stressed the need for a symbiotic relationship between Judaism and American culture. To them, it was essential that the religion become modernized, streamlined, and universalized – some would say even 'Protestantized' – and that, as much as possible, it be injected into public discourse. But British North America constituted a polity and society significantly different from the United States, and the Reform movement did not take root easily. Nor did Reform escape criticism from Orthodox rabbis, like Meldola de Sola of Shearith Israel, Montreal's Spanish and Portuguese synagogue, who (like many Orthodox leaders in the United States) ridiculed and scorned this new expression of the old faith.

Still, there were enough Reformers in Montreal to establish Temple Emanu-El in the early 1880s, while Winnipeg, Hamilton, and Toronto formed Reform-oriented congregations in the early 1900s. Toronto's Holy Blossom experienced serious factionalism for years and these tensions affected their choice of rabbis, of which more later.[8] Notably, too, all in time employed graduates of Hebrew Union College, including the four chosen for a closer look. These rabbis were all American-born or arrived in the United States at a young age and, with one exception, Abraham Feinberg, young men when they came north seeking to establish themselves before moving on to more prestigious pulpits in the United States. But some of them stayed in Canada for many years, and their careers form the bedrock of my story of the adaptation of Reform to this country's distinctive context. They reached out to non-Jewish, as well as Jewish, audiences everywhere; they wrote for the daily press, spoke on radio – and later television – and they interacted with Christian clergy and lay men and women to advance their vision of social justice. In many ways, they became Canadian Jewry's most visible and important ambassadors to the non-Jewish world.

When New Orleans–born Nathan Gordon arrived in Montreal in 1906 to take up his post at Temple Emanu-El, he was twenty-four years old.[9] While fulfilling a multitude of new responsibilities in this small and struggling congregation – and negotiating the tricky matter of choosing a bride from among the eligible young women of the community (he married Gertrude Workman, the daughter of a local tycoon) – Gordon took little time getting involved in Montreal public affairs. First, he did the almost obligatory tour of duty in various Jewish communal organizations, mostly in the uptown ones like the Federation of Jewish Philanthropies, which dispensed charity to the needy immigrants in the city's crowded downtown core. Gordon also spearheaded the campaign to build the Mount Sinai Sanatorium to meet the mounting tuberculosis rates prevalent there. Temple Emanu-El, by this time, was rapidly overcoming its early problems and Gordon – backed up by his wealthy father-in-law – presided over the construction of an impressive new edifice on Sherbrooke Street in the heart of fashionable Westmount, as if proclaiming to the Montreal Anglo Protestant élite that the venerable Jewish community had arrived and was claiming public space in the heart of the city's locus of power.

Gordon was developing some far-reaching additional interests, mainly in challenging municipal political corruption, which, in early twentieth-century Montreal, was the worst in Canada. He supported civic leaders like Herbert Brown Ames, whose 1909 pamphlet, *City Below the Hill*, was an arresting exposé of horrific slum conditions in the inner city. As well, corruption was rampant in the Montreal police force, the red-light district was a scene of violence and public debauchery, and patronage reigned ungoverned as municipal debt soared. Gordon took an interest in efforts to combat this moral and political degradation by the Committee of Citizens, which was formed in 1909 to examine and recommend changes to Montreal's governance.[10] Meanwhile, he was also serving as one of the Jewish representatives on the city's Non-Catholic Juvenile Court Committee, which addressed the severe problem of youths engaging in petty crimes that brought them before the courts.[11] He also found time to lecture on Oriental languages at McGill University.

Not content with these activities, Gordon decided after only a few years to make a significant career change: he became a part-time law student at the Montreal branch of the Université Laval (now the Université de Montréal). In 1916, by then qualified for the Quebec bar, he resigned from the rabbinate, but not from the cause of municipal reform. After a short apprenticeship with Peter Bercovitch, member of the Quebec Legislative Assembly for the riding of St Louis, Gordon joined the City Prosecutor's office, where he served until 1921. He then entered private practice and, although no longer a pulpit rabbi, continued to labour in public affairs while becoming an increasingly prominent local lawyer.

While Gordon's tenure had lasted a full ten years, he was not able to bridge the divisions in the Montreal Jewish community caused by bitter disputes over education. After a 1903 Quebec court decision, Jews were defined as Protestants for purposes of schooling in the confessional systems confirmed at Confederation. On grounds of economy, though in reality reacting to alleged administrative difficulties and to what they believed were cultural problems in their schools located in Jewish districts, in 1924 the Protestant School Commission of Montreal moved radically to revise the terms of the Jewish presence.[12] The Jewish community's reaction was divided; broadly speaking, those living in the west end, or the 'uptowners' as they came to be known, who tended to be well-to-do and integrationist-minded, supported compromise with the Protestants. Many of the 'downtowners,' who were more influenced by cultural nationalist ideas emanating from religious and Zionist organizations, favoured a separate, publicly funded Jewish school system on the same basis as those of the Protestant and Catholic communities. Temple Emanu-El lay leaders, like those at the nearby upper-middle-class synagogue Shaar Hashomayim (Gates of Heaven), and their rabbis, like Rabbi Max Merritt, who had succeeded Gordon, sparked furious debate in the Jewish community by acting in ways downtown spokesmen depicted as craven. In this atmosphere, Temple Emanu-El did not have a positive image among the immigrants.

Harry Joshua Stern, who took up Merritt's pulpit in 1927, was an ideal rabbi for the Montreal scene. He not only possessed enormous energy, imagination, and courage, but he also had great empathy for the poor downtown Jews. The Lithuanian-born son of impoverished immigrants, Stern grew up in Steubenville, Ohio, in a deeply pious Orthodox household in which Torah was the moral guide and Yiddish the medium of discourse. He attended the University of Cincinnati before taking rabbinical training at Hebrew Union College, graduating in 1922.[13] During his fifty-seven years at Temple Emanu-El, while energizing his growing congregation with a variety of educational activities intended to deepen its members' knowledge of and commitment to Judaism, Stern also pursued an active program of outreach to local Christians, whom he tried to interest in a better understanding of Judaism and in ongoing dialogue. The Christian triumphalism which regarded Judaism as a displaced religion and Jews as potential candidates for conversion to the true faith Stern saw as his prime target.

Stern was also an outspoken and active Zionist, an unusual and unwelcome enthusiasm for a Reform rabbi in the interwar years when, though several prominent Reform rabbis were outspoken Zionists, most professors at Hebrew Union College strongly opposed this expression of Jewish nationalism. Leaders of the Union of American Hebrew Congregations – the organization governing Reform congregations in North America – were deeply concerned that Jewish nationalism conflicted with their own concepts of Jewish-American symbiosis and the theology of universalism so prominent in its Pittsburgh Platform of 1885.[14] Stern, however, was one of the few Reform rabbis who believed that Zionism was an important and legitimate vehicle of Jewish religious expression and that a Jewish commonwealth or national home in Palestine – few Zionists then spoke in terms of a Jewish state – was a political necessity in an uncertain world and an important vehicle for cultural and spiritual revival.[15] Though he recognized that 'Judaism is greater even than Palestine,'[16] Stern took up the Zionist cause with enormous enthusiasm and, despite some rumblings in his own congregation, maintained an active speaking campaign on its behalf during the tense days leading up to the establishment of Israel in 1948.[17] First styling himself provocatively as 'an agricultural Zionist' (a response he gave to an aggressive interrogation at Hebrew Union by one of his anti-Zionist professors) by which he asserted this belief in large-scale colonization, he later became an admirer of the Revisionists, who demanded both sides of the Jordan River – in fact all of both Palestine and the Kingdom of Jordan – and after 1939 the establishment of a Jewish army to fight Nazi Germany on the side of the Allies. Stern befriended Menachem Begin in later years and invited him and other so-called right-wing Zionists to speak at the Temple. Always a believer in Zionist action, besides propaganda and fundraising, Stern visited Israel often, the first time in 1929, when he led a group of young congregants from the Temple on a tour of the Holy Land, including the new agricultural settlements. He never wavered thereafter.

Stern's principal outreach was to the Montreal Christian communities, notably towards the Roman Catholic hierarchy. His purpose was to establish some dialogue and mutual understanding that might possibly lessen the widespread and virulent anti-Semitism that, at least in part, emanated from sources within the Quebec Roman Catholic Church. In 1928, only a year into his appointment, he organized a fellowship dinner to bring together clergy from all Christian denominations. He also laboured to establish collegial relationships with individual sympathetic clergymen through private meetings and numerous lectures at churches. While these efforts were slow in bearing fruit, especially the early overtures to the Roman Catholic hierarchy, by the 1940s Stern's correspondence reveals that he had begun dialogue with some of its more liberal-minded clergy, who, quite independently, were working towards improved relationships with the Montreal Jewish community.[18] By the 1950s he was a well-recognized and popular figure for his lectures in various interdenominational forums and from church pulpits, and thus a major contributor to the weakening of anti-Semitism in the new Quebec of the late 1950s and 1960s.

While building bridges of ecumenism, Stern also fought highly significant battles for social justice within the local Jewish community, notably during the bitter and bloody disputes in the clothing industry, the second-largest manufacturing sector in Montreal. Here the Depression had bitten deeply; strikes and lockouts – with ensuing picket line violence – affected thousands of workers, including many poor downtown Jews, whose jobs were threatened by the Jewish factory owners moving production to small Quebec towns where labour costs were cheaper. Along with other community leaders, Stern spoke out for the workers and publicly castigated employers – some of them prominent members of Temple Emanu-El – for trying to throw their employees onto the street. He was not successful in stopping these 'runaway shops,' but his sympathy for the ordinary working man and woman, along with his fluency in Yiddish (a rarity among Reform rabbis, who ministered exclusively to the more assimilated and well-to-do uptown Jews) helped to endear him to the downtowners. In these working-class districts his outspoken advocacy of Zionism helped him, as did his favourable attitude towards the collectivist achievements in the Soviet Union, which he visited several times in the 1930s.

Holding the Temple Emanu-El pulpit until his retirement in 1972 and acting influentially until his death in 1984, Stern pursued his causes of social justice, Zionism, and Jewish–Christian dialogue with zeal, although with slowly flagging energy. When Kenneth Cleator, Canon of Montreal's St George's Anglican church, wrote Stern's biography in 1981, he concluded with Stern's own reference to his responsibility to continue spiritual leadership, mindful, no doubt, of the Talmudic injunction: 'You are not obliged to finish the work, but neither are you free to desist from it.'

Meanwhile, in Toronto, Holy Blossom since the 1920s attracted even feistier rabbis, the reflection, perhaps, of that congregation's stormy break from Orthodoxy that very decade. As if to underscore the seriousness of that congregation's commitment to the spirit of Reform's radicalism vis-à-vis traditional Judaism, the Temple's lay power brokers sought out Barnett Brickner, Maurice Eisendrath, and Abraham Feinberg, some of the liveliest and most daring of all Reform rabbis ever to occupy Canadian pulpits. At Holy Blossom, Eisendrath preached with the eloquence and passion that his biographer likened to a 'raging fire,' while Feinberg progressed so far to the left that he became known as 'the red rabbi.'[19]

Maurice Eisendrath arrived in Toronto in 1929 to fill the post vacated by the outspoken Brickner, who had served as Holy Blossom's rabbi for a few years in the 1920s. Almost immediately, Eisendrath made his mark by publishing what many in the congregation viewed as an outrageous statement in the *Canadian Jewish Review*, a Toronto weekly. As he saw it, the Palestinian Arabs who a week before had murdered 130 Jews (including eight American rabbinical students) and severely maimed scores of others in Hebron were simply expressing understandable and, to him, obviously acceptable, national sentiment. He urged Zionists to reconcile differences with the Arabs and accept a binational (Arab–Jewish) state in Palestine, instead of the Jewish national home that Zionists had been promised by the British government in the Balfour Declaration and affirmed in the mandate of the League of Nations.[20] Eisendrath shared the views of other Reform rabbis, who in efforts to shear away all manifestations of Jewish particularism, while emphasizing Judaism's universalistic values, stressed that Jews had no more right to Palestine as a national home than to any other country.[21] While many Reform laypersons in the United States supported this viewpoint, Canadians were far less likely to agree. North of the forty-ninth parallel, Zionism had become a normative mode of identity for Jews, and Eisendrath's attack was tantamount to serious heresy, even at Holy Blossom, which by now was thoroughly Reform in liturgy and other observances.[22] The ensuing furore there led to another bitter split and the secession of many Temple members. Undaunted and unrepentant, Eisendrath was only getting warmed up. His lengthy and eloquent sermons, which he delivered without notes, now attracting huge crowds of Gentiles as well as Jews, were replete with scorn for these Jewish nationalists.

In a February 1934 sermon he asserted that, while he supported developing Palestine as a 'cultural centre and haven of refuge,' he strongly disapproved of Jewish statehood.[23] 'The whole of Jewish history,' he contended, 'gives the lie to the ... vapid ... contention that ... Jewish hearts must ... pound ecstatically at the sound of a certain Oriental song.' Such ethnocentrism distorted Jewish values because 'Israel's roots ... lie ... not in the soil, but in the soul.' He warned that the Zionists' 'exclusive national aspirations will bring Jewry to its doom in a tragic anticlimax.'[24] Strong words these, but not unusual ones from a man with the conviction and self-confidence that Eisendrath evinced during his years at Holy Blossom.

While he never explicitly recanted, Eisendrath started singing a slightly different tune two years later. Following his first visit to Palestine in 1935, he waxed rhapsodic about Jewish colonization there and the emergence of the tough, agricultural, self-reliant, and assertive men and women. Their collective settlements, he even suggested, could serve as 'models for Canada's exploited toilers [who] should likewise band together and begin themselves to build a better and more comradely life.'[25] But he never endorsed the Zionist agenda of statehood. Nor did he countenance the rejection of the Jewish diaspora in North America, where, he realized, Jews enjoyed unparalleled peace, freedom, and opportunity. So, while he happily endorsed Micah's prophecy that 'Out of Zion shall go forth the Law, and the word of the Lord from Jerusalem' (Micah 4:2), throughout his career Eisendrath celebrated the prospects of the Jewish future in North America and even rejoiced in Canada's imperial connection, which, in a sermon delivered to mark the royal visit in May 1939, he called an 'impregnable tower to which we may tenaciously cling.'[26]

Eisendrath's enthusiasms extended far beyond the Jewish community. This was unusual for a newly arrived young rabbi with a demanding congregational agenda which included spearheading the campaign for Holy Blossom's move from the old Bond Street location to a new and imposing edifice (dubbed by local wags as 'the church on the hill') on north Bathurst Street, like its Montreal counterpart an assertive statement of Jewish legitimacy in the Anglo Protestant city. He became the president of the Toronto chapter of the pacifist organization the Fellowship of Reconciliation and, as historian Thomas Socknat points out, had quickly become one of that organization's most popular and active speakers.[27] His wife, Rosa, shared his views and worked in the Women's International League for Peace and Freedom.[28] In November 1930 Eisendrath presided over the All Day Peace Conference, a gathering of activists to discuss international disarmament and hold graveside vigils honouring 'heroes of peace.' Films were shown, poetry read, and an address heard from J.S. Woodsworth, arguably Canada's leading peace advocate. The cause of social justice in a nation undergoing serious economic and social stresses during the Depression also attracted the heat of Eisendrath's raging fire. Like Stern, he spoke out for fair labour practices and decent living standards for workers, concepts which, in the context of the tumultuous clothing industry in which some of his well-to-do congregants were employers, might well have resulted in grumbling and dark looks.

Eisendrath's pacifism did not last, however. By the late 1930s he had quit the Fellowship of Reconciliation, no doubt despairing of the prospects for peace in his time.[29] On 20 November 1938, only ten days after Kristallnacht, his sermon 'World without Jews' reflected his growing pessimism. Cognizant that German Jews faced imminent disaster from the 'looming menace' of the Nazis, he excoriated 'these savage sadists and barbaric pagans who would stain the entire earth with their trail of blood.'[30]

By 1939, after ten years at Holy Blossom, Eisendrath felt played out as a pulpit rabbi and, ambitious for a new challenge in the Reform movement, he accepted an important administrative position in the Union of American Hebrew Congregations (UAHC), in Cincinnati. He thus passed from the Canadian scene, to return only occasionally, once in 1964 – he was by then a widower and president of the UAHC – to marry his second wife, a former congregant at Holy Blossom.

What Eisendrath left behind at Holy Blossom was a reputation for outstanding oratory, first at the venerable old temple on Bond Street (hard by O'Keefe's brewery, a powerful influence when a south wind blew in from Lake Ontario) and then at the Bathurst Street edifice, which was completed in 1936. Week after week he drew enormous crowds with his eloquence, commanding presence, and passion. But the moral courage of his sermons was not confined solely to advocating pacifism, opposing Zionism, and advancing social justice. He had the audacity and imagination to espouse Jesus as a fellow progressive and brother Jew. His 1939 publication of eighteen sermons and radio addresses included frequent references to the Jewishness of Jesus' ministry and the strong similarities between various Christian hymns and prayers and older Hebrew counterparts. Jews and Christians meet, he contended, 'in spirit and in truth ... because both these treasured institutions were one.'[31] Through Christianity, he argued later, 'Israel has shed its luster over all humanity,' and 'if it had not been for Christianity, Judaism and the Jew might well have remained as insignificant as have been the followers of Zoroaster.'[32] Such pronouncements seem to have brought Eisendrath perilously close to Christian triumphalist doctrines, and I doubt that these thoughts would have endeared Eisendrath to some of his more traditional congregants. They certainly would have attracted strongly adverse comment from Toronto's Orthodox Jews, if they heard about these remarkable sermons in which Judaism is depicted as having failed 'to keep the torch ablaze, but handed it on instead to Christianity to tend.'[33] If this were true, one might ask, what was the point in continuing to be a Jew?

While Eisendrath saw Judaism as 'a never failing stream,' a spiritual resource from which Christianity and all humanity should draw continuing inspiration, his successor, Abraham Feinberg, was far less interested in such theological speculation. Judging from his autobiography, he seems to have regarded himself as more of a champion of minorities, not just Jews but the entire spectrum of ethnic communities, and not just as a mere pulpit rabbi, or an activist for peace and reconciliation.[34] Feinberg was prepared to go on the air and out into the streets – a Jewish advocate of the 'social gospel,' if you will – to fight the good fight for human decency and equal civil rights for all.

Born in Ohio, educated at the University of Cincinnati and Hebrew Union College, where he was ordained in 1924, Feinberg had considerable congregational experience, in Niagara Falls, New York; Wheeling, West Virginia; New York City; and Denver, before taking up his post at Holy Blossom in 1943. His family was poor and he had worked summers in steel mills in his home town; he was used to working-class rough and tumble and he had developed a very tough hide before attending seminary.[35] His search for truth took him far afield. Only five years after ordination in 1929, Feinberg deserted the pulpit and its 'servile rabbinate' for a singing career on Broadway as Anthony Frome, Poet Prince.[36] His melodious baritone repertoire ranged from 'When Irish Eyes Are Smiling' to 'Eli, Eli,' with 'Love in Bloom' and other 1930s favourites in between. In May 1935, stung to the very marrow of his soul by a *New York Times* report of Hitler's promise 'to exterminate the Jewish vermin,' the troubadour abandoned his well-paying stage career and applied for a small mid-Manhattan congregation's poorly paid rabbinical post that was going begging.[37] Anthony Frome, the Poet Prince of Broadway, was reconstituted Rabbi Abraham Feinberg of Beth Shalom. He had decided to fight for the Jewish people, or, as he himself wrote: 'My work was cut out for me!'[38]

And it was. By the time Feinberg reached Toronto, in November 1943, four million Jews had been destroyed and some two million more were to be murdered by the German Nazis and their enthusiastic collaborators throughout Europe before the war would end. Canada was at war and its soldiers had been bloodied at Dieppe, while a division was fighting the Germans in Italy. At the same time, Canadian society was being profoundly altered by the wartime mobilization of labour and resources. But the decisions to relocate Japanese Canadians from the west coast deeply offended Feinberg. Outraged by the poisonous anti-Black racism in his native Ohio and determined to speak out about it wherever it existed, he thundered against this horrible injustice. He was later to rail against persecution of Blacks in Dresden, Ontario. Later, in a famous cause, he almost single-handedly – the Canadian Jewish Congress deserted him – battled against the institution of Christian religious instruction in Ontario's schools, as R. Gidney and W. Millar explain in their contribution to this volume.

Not long after his arrival, Feinberg joined the Labour Progressive Party of Canada, the name adopted by the Communist Party in 1940, and soon became a member of its advisory board and of the Canadian-Soviet Friendship League.[39] From that point forward, he was known to all, including the RCMP who kept a file on him, as one of Toronto's leading leftists. He was especially notable in the campaigns against nuclear arms; there was rarely a demonstration or march in which Feinberg was not featured as speaker. On these and other matters he was a lifelong maverick. In the 1960s, as part of the antiwar protest, he led a delegation to Vietnam, where Ho Chi Minh gave him – his eyesight was failing – a cane, which he treasured for the rest of his life.[40] Five years before his death in 1986, he published a book entitled *Sex and the Pulpit* in which he made the then startling observation that he 'found gays to be amongst the most decent, law-abiding and peaceful people in a community.'[41]

In conclusion, then, Moses' admonition, 'Justice, justice thou shalt pursue' and Amos' exhortation, 'establish justice in thy gate,'[42] were not enough to keep the Lord's chosen behaving like a light unto the nations and following in his prescribed paths. Nor have Jeremiah's reproaches sufficed to keep some Jews from falling away from Torah observances. It was, essentially, this prophetic tradition that Reform Judaism embraced as its inspiration to rescue Judaism from what it regarded as moribund rabbinic ritualism and infuse it with transcendent universalistic values. Beyond the 613 *mitzvot*, Reformers believed, Judaism rested on a moral code stressing decency, charity, and love. Each of our four rabbis exemplified, in varying degrees, the universalistic humanist values in Judaism in their respective settings: Gordon at Temple Emanu-El joining the battle against municipal corruption in early twentieth-century Montreal, Stern trying to stem that city's virulent anti-Semitism, Eisendrath at Toronto's Holy Blossom tackling contemporary issues of Jewish religious and national identity and, finally, Abraham Feinberg protesting against postwar racial prejudice and nuclear armament. These four were not, of course, the only such examples of rabbinic forthrightness and courage in the Canadian Jewish community – Reform, Orthodox, or Conservative. Most rabbis, how-

ever, laboured within the fences of their congregations, quietly studying, teaching, and doing good works. But the quartet examined here
performed those vital tasks while also stepping out into the world
beyond the confines of their congregations to fulfil a larger vision.
While none of them, as far as I know, employed the term 'social gospel,' they were all, it seems to me, spiritually at one with Salem Bland,
James Shaver Woodsworth, M.J. Coldwell, Stanley Knowles, and
Tommy Douglas, among others, who tried to fulfil Isaiah's demand to
his people to 'Loosen the chains of wickedness [and] undo the bonds
of oppression.'[43]

What is clear, also, is that these rabbis moved out beyond the narrow
confines of *mitzvot* to embrace as much of the world as they could. Traditional Judaism was strongly, though not exclusively, oriented towards
observances (*mitzvot*) (though one of the founders of the rabbinic tradition, Hillel, when pressed, stated that the heart of Jewish law was 'do
not do unto others that which is hateful to yourself. All the rest is commentary.'). And the Talmud enjoins the building of fences to prevent the
rupture of these laws. Such boundaries, it can be argued, were major factors that kept Judaism alive for twenty centuries. But Reform put aside
such injunctions, pushing this particularism away to leap across the barriers that kept Jews from participating as Jews, in a Jewish spirit, and
with a Jewish message, in the wider context of all humanity. This outreach, it is clear, did not go far enough. One might question, for example, whether at least one vital Jewish cause, pressure for Canadian and
United States acceptance of Jewish refugees immediately before and
during the Holocaust, was adequately stressed, although at one point
during the war, Stern did urge a Quebec City audience composed
largely of French Canadians (whose leaders vehemently opposed Jewish immigration) to urge the Canadian government to allow refugees
into Canada.[44] Internal issues, such as Jewish recruitment to Canada's
armed forces was also not adequately addressed. This and other criticisms can come only after thorough research in these rabbis' papers at
the National Archives of Canada and the American Jewish Archives in
Cincinnati. However, what can be said with some confidence is that Isaiah probably would have been proud of these men, each of whom could,
fairly, I think, 'be called repairer, restorer of dwellings [and] old foundations.'[45] They spoke with the zeal of the Prophets in these northern
climes, addressing the eternal issues of justice, kindness, and peace,
while conscious of the distinctive context in which, to paraphrase historian Arthur Lower, colony was struggling to become nation amid the

demons of eternal human frailties, war, and endemic racism. These rabbis left an important legacy for Reform Judaism and for a rich tradition of religious engagement in the public life in Canada. In important ways they helped to put Judaism's message of *tikun olam*, repairing the world, publicly and dramatically on the Canadian religious map, while at the same time defining the nation's Jewish community that was seeking its own identity amidst domestic anti-Semitism, an exterminationist war, and the battle for a Jewish state.

Notes

1 I acknowledge with warm thanks the comments and suggestions made by Michael Brown, Louis Greenspan, and Ira Robinson on an earlier draft of this chapter.

2 Gerald Tulchinsky, *Taking Root: The Origins of the Canadian Jewish Community* (Toronto: Lester, 1992), 279.

3 Gerald Tulchinsky, *Branching Out: The Transformation of the Canadian Jewish Community* (Toronto: Stoddart, 1998), 24.

4 Jacob Rader Marcus, ed., *The Jew in the American World: A Source Book* (Detroit: Wayne State University Press, 1996), 241–3.

5 Ibid., 242.

6 See Mark Cowett, 'Rabbi Morris Newfield and the Social Gospel: Theology and Social Reform in the South,' *American Jewish Archives* 34 (April 1982): 52–74; and Alon Gal, 'The Changing Concept of "Mission" in American Reform Judaism,' Annual Lecture at the American Jewish Archives, Jerusalem, 1990.

7 Michael Brown, 'The Beginnings of Reform Judaism in Canada,' *Jewish Social Studies* 34 (October 1972): 322–42.

8 Arthur A. Chiel, *The Jews in Manitoba: A Social History* (Toronto: University of Toronto Press, 1961, published for The Historical and Scientific Society of Manitoba), 82–3; Stephen A. Speisman, *The Jews of Toronto: A History to 1937* (Toronto: McClelland and Stewart, 1979), 214.

9 Arthur D. Hart, ed., *The Jews in Canada: A Complete Record of Canadian Jewry from the Days of the French Régime to the Present Time* (Montreal: Jewish Publications Limited, 1926), 125.

10 See *Canadian Jewish Times*, 20 December 1912; Michel Gauvin, 'The Reformer and the Machine: Montreal Civic Politics from Raymond Préfontaine to Médéric Martin,' *Journal of Canadian Studies* 13, no. 2 (Summer 1978): 16–26.

11 Hart, *The Jews in Canada*, 125.
12 Tulchinsky, *Branching Out*.
13 Eli Gottesman, compiler, *Who's Who in Canadian Jewry: Compiled and Prepared by the Canadian Jewish Literary Foundation for the Jewish Institute of Higher Research of the Central Rabbinical Seminary of Canada* (Montreal: Jewish Institute of Higher Research, 1965), 93.
14 See Michael A. Meyer, *Response to Modernity: A History of the Reform Movement in Judaism* (New York: Oxford University Press, 1988), 326 ff.
15 See Kenneth I. Cleator and Harry J. Stern, *A Rabbi's Journey* (New York: Bloch, 1981), passim.
16 Harry Joshua Stern, *The Jewish Spirit Triumphant: A Collection of Addresses* (New York: Bloch, 1943), 32.
17 Tulchinsky, *Branching Out*, 240. See Harry J. Stern, 'Palestine and World Peace,' and 'The New Israel,' in *Martyrdom and Miracle: A Collection of Addresses* (New York: Bloch, 1950), 190–202, 203–6.
18 Ibid., 270 ff.
19 See Avi M. Schulman, *Like a Raging Fire: A Biography of Maurice N. Eisendrath* (New York: UAHC Press, 1993); Abraham L. Feinberg, *Storm the Gates of Jericho* (Toronto: McClelland and Stewart, 1964).
20 See Speisman, *The Jews of Toronto*; Lewis Levendel, *A Century of the Canadian Jewish Press: 1880s–1980s* (Ottawa: Borealis, 1989), 84.
21 Naomi W. Cohen, *The Year after the Riots: The American Responses to the Palestine Crisis 1929–1930* (Detroit: Wayne State University Press, 1988), 94.
22 Speisman, *The Jews of Toronto*, 216–17.
23 Maurice N. Eisendrath, *The Never Failing Stream* (Toronto: Macmillan, 1939), 233.
24 Ibid., 235.
25 Ibid., 264.
26 Ibid., 39.
27 Thomas P. Socknat, *Witness against War: Pacifism in Canada, 1900–1945* (Toronto: University of Toronto Press, 1987), 125.
28 Ibid., 127.
29 Ibid., 178.
30 Eisendrath, *The Never Failing Stream*, 336.
31 Ibid., 10.
32 Ibid., 341.
33 Ibid., 353.
34 See Feinberg, *Storm the Gates*.
35 Gottesman, *Who's Who in Canadian Jewry*, 92.
36 Feinberg, *Storm the Gates*, 230 ff.

37 Ibid., 236.
38 Ibid., 237.
39 *Toronto Star*, 31 December 1995.
40 *Canadian Jewish Outlook*, December 1986, 7.
41 Abraham L. Feinberg, *Sex and the Pulpit* (Toronto: Methuen, 1981).
42 Deuteronomy 16:20; Amos 5:15.
43 Isaiah 57:14–58.
44 Stern, *The Jewish Spirit Triumphant*, 115.
45 Isaiah 57:14–58.

16

Canadian Mennonites and a Widening World

Harold Jantz

In 1943, the Reverend Jacob G. Thiessen, a minister of the Mennonite Brethren church from Vancouver, reported on his mission work to the city at a Brethren convention in Saskatchewan. Thiessen launched into a passionate appeal to church leaders, imploring them to keep as many young people on the farm and out of the city as possible.[1] Profoundly suspicious of urban life, he tried to the utmost of his Mennonite convictions to steer his church community away from what he saw as the urban dangers to their moral and spiritual welfare.

In the years since Jacob Thiessen gave his report, Mennonites have undergone a remarkable transition in Canada. Two generations later, his own grandson, Gordon Thiessen, became governor of the Bank of Canada. Whereas Mennonites once formed communities relatively isolated from their British, Ukrainian, or French neighbours, today they have entered into the culture that surrounds them. According to the 1971 Census, Mennonites were the most rural of twenty religious groups, though studies showed they were already moving into the cities in large numbers. In the years that followed, while their rural ties remained relatively strong, their involvement with a wider, urban society and their growing ethnic diversity became more pronounced. Today, more than ever, they have become a part of the larger world. And while some have tried to shed their Mennonite past, many have managed to enter into and engage with a wider world while retaining a distinct Mennonite identity.

The Mennonite church in Vancouver, for example, became something very different from anything the Reverend Thiessen might have imagined. A commitment to evangelism has pushed his denomination to reach far beyond its original borders. In fact, one of the largest Mennonite churches in Canada is found just outside of Vancouver: the Will-ingdon Mennonite Brethren church of Burnaby today has a Sunday attendance of around 3,000, and greater Vancouver has at least thirty congregations of the Mennonite Brethren, plus a dozen or more churches of the Conference of Mennonites (renamed the Mennonite Church Canada in 2000). Willingdon Church simultaneously translates its services into Korean, Mandarin, Cantonese, Japanese, and Russian, and also has separate Spanish and Indonesian congregations.[2] Van-couver and the lower Fraser Valley additionally have some fourteen Chinese Mennonite churches, as well as Lao, Hindi-Punjabi, Arabic, Korean, Deaf, Indo-Canadian, Russian, Persian, Hispanic, Indonesian, German, and, of course, English-language churches. In 1999 five of thirty-five Conference of Mennonites churches in British Columbia were among visible minorities, as are twenty-one of ninety-two Men-nonite Brethren.[3] Within Mennonite congregations are members of Parliament, university faculty, businesspeople, social workers, labour-ers, teachers, land developers, medical staff – people involved in every area of business and community life in Canada.

How did the Mennonite churches make the transition from rural, ethnically homogeneous, and relatively isolated institutions to be-coming increasingly urban, diverse, and relatively integrated partici-pants in Canadian religious and public life? In this chapter, I address this question by examining two impulses, the evangelical and the Anabaptist, within the various Mennonite groups and how they have influenced a growing interaction with a wider world among Canadian Mennonites. The distinction between these two impulses is at times blurred: all Mennonites, of course, trace their roots to the Anabaptists of the Protestant Reformation, but some have found an additional source of identity in eighteenth-century Pietism and in the evangelical revivalism of the early nineteenth century. Both impulses have moti-vated Mennonites to move into new directions in their interaction with a wider world, though in different ways. I describe some of the many Mennonite churches, organizations, and individuals who have contributed to this growing interaction, and examine how the evan-gelical and Anabaptist impulses play out in Mennonite links to the broader culture.

The evangelical impulse, with its emphasis on the gospel and shar-ing the good news, steers churches towards witness and evangelism, first among fellow Mennonites but also beyond. This in turn has moved Mennonites towards church planting, working through mis-sion boards at home and abroad, education, greater autonomy of local churches, and linking with the Evangelical Fellowship of Canada (EFC) and a variety of evangelical agencies. For Mennonites who follow the evangelical impulse, much of the movement into the wider culture is motivated by a desire to embrace those with shared beliefs and to invite others to become part of their church. More generally, the evangelical impulse has helped Mennonites to negotiate and overcome cultural barriers: the most overtly evangelical Mennonites have made the greatest effort to integrate with the culture and have moved furthest into an urban environment where they have more opportunities to engage a wider community.

The Anabaptist impulse moves churches towards communal action, towards a service orientation, a theology of promoting the kingdom of God, conservative lifestyles, peace and justice issues, working with the disadvantaged, and working through the Mennonite Central Committee (MCC) and other agencies of Mennonite persuasion that act as means to be present on a larger stage. Their antiwar sensibilities and communitarian ethos have put them at the forefront of many NGOs, peacekeeping movements, and a long list of humanitarian organizations. In general, the Anabaptist impulse leads Mennonites towards a tension with the culture.

These two impulses play themselves out within the larger, diverse Mennonite experience and are at times found within the same Mennonite group. At the 'evangelical' end of the Mennonite spectrum are especially the Mennonite Brethren (MB), the Evangelical Mennonite Conference (EMC), the Brethren in Christ (BIC), increasingly the Evangelical Mennonite Mission Conference (EMMC), and, to a lesser extent, the Conference of Mennonites in Canada (CMC) and Chortitzer Mennonites. At the 'Anabaptist' end of the spectrum are, in the first place, the CMC and Old Colony and Sommerfelder Mennonites and, to a lesser extent, the MB, the BIC, EMC, and EMMC groups.

Within this wide range of Mennonite groups there is much cultural diversity. Groups like the Old Order Amish and Old Order Mennonites continue to use horses and wagons, operate their own schools, and tend not to use electricity and most new technology. They involve themselves only to a very limited extent in any outside organizations, even those of the wider Mennonite community. The Chortitzer Mennonites, on the other hand, until recently quite conservatively Anabaptist, have developed a strong missions emphasis and hold an annual missions conference for all their churches. Revival and deeper spiritual life meetings are a regular part of their church life. Their commitment to missions and their desire to be part of the larger evangelical movement have given them the means to make significant shifts towards easier access to the larger Canadian community.[4]

The evangelical impulse has played a major role in redefining the EMC's relationship to the wider world. The EMC has a long conservative history, from its beginnings in 1814 Russia as the *Kleine Gemeinde* (Small Church). It began making significant changes in the 1930s and 1940s, embracing an increasingly explicit revivalist and evangelical stance. In 1947 tensions in the church led to a split that saw a hundred families move to Mexico while the majority stayed in Canada and renamed themselves the EMC.[5] The role of the bishop was diminished and local churches gained the right to conduct their own affairs. In addition, the EMC embraced education. One of their leaders, Archie Penner, helped them write a Confession of Faith, and another leader, Ben D. Reimer, promoted a strong vision for missions among them. Of all the groups emerging out of the conservative wing of the Mennonites, the EMC is probably the most successful. At the same time, however, it has retained important elements of its earlier communal character.[6]

A growing concern for missions and openness to renewal brought about profound changes in the EMC. In 1957 it had 32 missionaries serving in Africa, Latin America, and northern Canada.[7] By 1996 that number had risen to 135, nearly one missionary for every 48 members. In 1957 the entire EMC membership in Canada included fewer than 20 people whose surnames indicated an ethnic background other than the Russian Mennonite.[8] Four decades later, every congregation contained members from the wider Canadian community, many who held leadership positions within their local congregations.

Church statistics provide a picture of the changing relationships between Mennonites and cities since 1943, the year the Reverend Thiessen gave his report on the Vancouver city mission. For the Mennonite Brethren, the most overtly evangelical of Canadian Mennonites, urban membership grew from 14 to 68 per cent of total membership between 1943 and 1998, and the number of churches in urban settings rose from 6 (of a total of 66) to 111 (of a total of 199).[9] For the Conference of Mennonites, who represented the more traditional Anabaptist stream, urban membership grew from 9 to 47 per cent during the same period, and the number of churches in urban settings rose from 6 (of a total of 62) to 110 (of a total of 242).[10] For the Mennonite Church in Canada, with a smaller Canadian membership but a long North American history, urban membership was 12 per cent in 1943; by 1998 much of this group (once called the Old Mennonites) had united with the Conference of Mennonites in Canada.[11] Of those remaining (the small North West Mennonite Conference in Alberta and Saskatchewan), 44 per cent of the membership lived in large urban centres in 1998.[12]

An examination of the 1994 statistics for 18 other Mennonite groups, ranging from the EMC to the Old Colony and Sommerfelder Mennonite churches, suggests that approximately 30 to 35 of 315 congregations were found in large urban settings, representing 10 to 12 per cent of a membership of some 40,000.[13] Of these churches, the EMC and the Brethren in Christ, both at the evangelical end of the Mennonite spectrum, were by far the most strongly lodged in large urban settings.

Mennonites guided by the evangelical impulse utilized that identity as a means to open doors to a wider world. These Mennonites liked to recall that the early Anabaptists were the evangelists of the Reformation, travelling throughout Europe to spread their new understanding of the gospel. For example, the convention minutes of the Canadian Mennonite Brethren from the 1930s and 1940s reveal an impressive amount of time given to overseas and Canadian mission matters. The Brethren heard reports on missions to India, China, Africa, and Oklahoma, and on work in city missions in Minneapolis, Vancouver, Saskatoon, and Winnipeg.[14] For Mennonite Brethren, the evangelical impulse and orientation towards missionary work had roots in the revivalism of the mid-nineteenth century. The Brethren were nurtured into being by Pietist and evangelical influences; heard preachers from Baptist, Lutheran, and Darbyist settings; and sent their young men to schools of several theological streams. Their desire for a renewed spiritual life sent them to seek contacts with other evangelical movements, schools, and itinerating preachers.[15]

In Canada, a number of prominent early Mennonite Brethren went off to well-known evangelical schools – such as the Baptist Rochester Theological Seminary, the Moody Bible Institute, and the Bible Institute of Los Angeles – and came back to spread their influence. The author remembers his pastor, John G. Baerg, of Virgil, Ontario, coming home from a convention of the National Association of Evangelicals in Buffalo in the fifties, and reporting that a group of Canadians there, including himself, had determined they wanted to start a similar Canadian Evangelical Fellowship.

When the first major Canadian Congress on Evangelism was held in Ottawa in 1970 – an event organized by Anglican evangelist Marnie Patterson and strongly supported by Canada's mainline United

Church and Presbyterian denominations – Mennonites and Brethren in Christ represented well over 10 per cent of the participants. Of these, Mennonite Brethren made up over half of the group of 62.[16] Twenty years later, in 1990, when the Evangelical Fellowship of Canada sponsored a Vision 2000 Consultation in Ottawa, launching an evangelistic emphasis for the 1990s, Mennonite Brethren were once again the group most actively involved.[17] Others, like the EMC, CMC, and BIC, were also present, though in smaller numbers. Mennonite Brethren also participated in the leadership of the EFC; most notably, John H. Redekop, sometime moderator of the Canadian Mennonite Brethren conference and political science professor, who served a term as EFC president during the early 1990s and has served continuously in the EFC General Council since 1969.[18] When he was elected president in 1991, Redekop wrote that it was the first time in the EFC's twenty-six-year history that an 'Anabaptist Mennonite' had been elected as leader, and said he saw his role as 'constituting an opportunity to strengthen cooperation among Canadian evangelicals, to build bridges to additional groups and to strengthen the collective voice and actual influence of Christians in Canadian society.'[19]

Other prominent Mennonite leaders in the Evangelical Fellowship included Victor Adrian, who became president of Ontario Bible College and Theological Seminary after serving as president of the Mennonite Brethren Bible College (MBBC); Frank C. Peters, who at various times was a faculty member at MBBC, moderator of the Mennonite Brethren General Conference, pastor of the Kitchener MB Church, and president of Wilfrid Laurier University; and William Janzen, the head of the MCC Ottawa office and a member of the Ottawa Mennonite Church. Both Redekop and Janzen have been active on the Social Action Commission, while Redekop also served on the executive and general council.

As far back as 1969, the author of this chapter spoke to his conference about the need 'for a sturdy evangelical press' that might '[reach] across to all evangelical bodies.'[20] In 1987, after editing the *Mennonite Brethren Herald* for twenty years, Jantz launched a biweekly tabloid, *ChristianWeek*, which has since served a wide Canadian evangelical readership as a 'window on Christian faith and life in Canada.' *ChristianWeek* is the only ecumenical national evangelical newspaper in Canada and owes a good deal of its success to its ability to embrace both those who hold strong evangelical convictions and those who place a greater emphasis on issues of peace and justice.

The Mennonite presence in the evangelical community appears to be welcomed. At the Mennonite Brethren Biblical Seminary's fall 1997 celebration for its BC Centre, former EFC president Brian Stiller urged Mennonites to continue to bring their 'vision of holiness, stewardship and missions' to the rest of the church in Canada. The Mennonite history of suffering and dispossession, he said, could uniquely help Canadian evangelicals to maintain a 'heart for the poor and dispossessed.'[21]

For Mennonites with a strong evangelical bent, this identification creates bridges for wider involvement, both with other evangelical groups and with the wider society. In most cases, this involvement began with a strong commitment to overseas missions. As language ceased to be a barrier and the cultural distances in Canada lessened, Mennonite efforts to embrace other cultures became stronger, and their success in establishing churches within diverse communities and among minority ethnic groups increased. It would be difficult to imagine a host of evangelical agencies in Canada without the support of Mennonite church communities. Points of entry include Youth for Christ; Crisis Pregnancy Centres; faith missions such as the Society for International Ministries, the Gospel Missionary Union, Samaritan's Purse, and Wycliffe Bible Translators; local ministries such as Living Bible Explorers in Winnipeg; or groups like the Christian Business Men's Committee, the Gideons, and others. The Bible institute and college movement, and schools such as Trinity Western University depend a great deal on both Mennonite students and Mennonite support. When Statistics Canada reports the Canadian communities that show the highest average per capita giving to charitable causes in Canada based on tax filings, Mennonite communities invariably appear high on the list. Much of it goes to evangelical causes.

But if the evangelical impulse has given some Mennonites the means for engaging a wider world, so too has the Anabaptist impulse, though in quite different ways and on different terms. Probably no entity created by Mennonites has more facilitated this engagement with the world than the Mennonite Central Committee (MCC). Created in the United States in 1920 to respond to famine in southern Russia, where brothers and sisters of the Mennonite faith faced imminent starvation, the MCC ultimately became a vehicle for a far wider response. It gained support within the diverse Mennonite and Brethren in Christ constituency and created initiatives that opened doors to new involvements. Through the experiences of volunteers, the MCC fed back into Mennonite churches perspectives that profoundly influenced the entire church community. Within Canadian Mennonite circles probably no group has supported the MCC more strongly than the Conference of Mennonites in Canada.

In its first years, the MCC was the means by which Mennonites helped their own. They sent aid to the Ukraine in 1920 and a few years later rallied to the aid of Mennonite compatriots who had flocked to Moscow in late 1929 and 1930 in a desperate attempt to escape an increasingly oppressive Soviet environment. But with the outbreak of the Second World War, the MCC's burden to minister to people in need in the name of Christ began to broaden beyond the needs of their own to those of the disadvantaged generally. By the time the response to the tragedies created by the Second World War had reached its peak, MCC volunteers were serving in twelve countries.[22]

The war encouraged the Anabaptist impulse in a number of ways. For example, alternative service programs in Canada and the United States took young Mennonite men off the farms and placed them in projects that broadened their worlds forever. In the United States, many young men served in hospitals and mental institutions through the Civilian Public Service (CPS). These experiences aroused in some an interest in care for the mentally ill that led to the creation of Mennonite Mental Health Services and Mennonite-run care facilities for the mentally ill in several states and provinces. These in turn have engaged in pioneering work in the care of the mentally ill, gaining insights that have extended far beyond the Mennonite community. The end of the Second World War also helped launch postwar programs that became the foundation for the enormous growth in Mennonite voluntary service during the decades that followed.[23]

Mennonites pledged that if they were going to take advantage of alternative service projects during wartime as a way of avoiding the military duties to which they objected on pacifist grounds, integrity demanded that they should do something similar in peacetime. So were born the Mennonite Service Units in the United States and the Voluntary Service programs in Canada. These programs boosted the numbers of young people available for work in places of genuine need, and also opened many to a much wider world. Overwhelmingly, the MCC was the vehicle through which the opportunities were created.

In Canada, both before and after the Second World War, Mennonites created several other organizations, some to represent their concerns to government, some to foster the peace witness, some to aid the immigration effort, and still others to do relief work. By 1963 the proliferation of organizations led them to form a single MCC Canada. They committed themselves to work together in all 'inter-Mennonite programs ... including relief, service, peace, disaster service, immigration and mental health.'[24] They began modestly with a budget of about $150,000 in 1964. By 1980 they had a staff of forty across the country and a budget of over $10 million, of which $3.16 million came from their own congregations.[25] During this period, Mennonite interaction with the culture increased most dramatically, and the number and variety of concerns the MCC embraced grew enormously. For example, in 1979 and 1980 Mennonites in Canada brought 4,000 Southeast Asian refugees into Canada (7 per cent of the total of such refugees) after leading the way for all Canadian denominations by negotiating an agreement with the Canadian government whereby churches could sponsor refugees.[26] Also high on the MCC's agenda were a foodgrains bank, Native concerns, a handicapped awareness program, and a host of other peace and social concerns.

The Handicapped Awareness program, Victim Offender Ministries, the Canadian Foodgrains Bank, and Mennonite Disaster Service all demonstrate how ideas had the potential to grow within the MCC. The Handicapped Awareness program originated when a wheelchair-bound Steinbach native, Henry Enns (who had already been working with disability concerns), approached the MCC in 1980 to propose that he work with them to develop greater awareness of the needs of the handicapped. The MCC agreed. Over a period of several years Enns pushed for greater awareness of the concerns of the disabled both within Mennonite churches and in the community at large. Through his position with the MCC he was able to access resources to build an organization called Disabled Peoples International, which now encompasses 120 member countries and in 1998 brought 2,000 people together in Mexico City for its fifth quadrennial conference. Its office is based in Winnipeg.[27]

The food bank was the brainchild of one-time MCC volunteer Art DeFehr, who tapped into a deeply felt concern within the MCC's Canadian constituency that less and less opportunity existed for food-rich Canadians to share their bounty with the starving elsewhere. Many of the leaders within the MCC had embraced 'development' principles that looked askance at shipping food aid abroad. DeFehr and his friends disagreed. Why not employ the biblical 'Joseph principle' and store up food during the good years so that when drought and famine struck, the reserves would be available to address the need?

The MCC embraced the idea, though with hesitation. Eventually, the

organization opened itself to a wider community. With the encouragement of the Canadian International Development Agency and the
Canadian Wheat Board (CWB), the food bank became the Canadian
Foodgrains Bank (CFGB), and membership was enlarged to thirteen
member groups. Both evangelical and mainline groups signed on, from
the Pentecostals and the Christian and Missionary Alliance to Luther-
ans and the United Church of Canada. Most critical to the success of the
venture was the acceptance of the concept by the CWB, which set up a
mechanism that allows farmers to deposit grains at any elevator point
throughout the country. A CFGB member group can in turn draw on
these deposits when it wishes to ship food to a place of need.[28]

The concept for the Victim Offender Reconciliation Program (VORP)
emerged in 1974 as a joint project between MCC Ontario and Waterloo
Region probation authorities, after two young men caused over $2,000
worth of damage to twenty-two victims in a night of drunken vandalism. Both pleaded guilty to twenty-two charges. Normally the young
men would have paid their fine, and restitution might or might not
have occurred. However, there were some who believed that genuine
reconciliation might result if the offenders met their victims, looked
them in the eyes, and accepted responsibility for their actions. As a
result, with a judge's agreement, the young men together with a third-
party mediator met each of the victims. In six months they had completed restitution. The VORP concept was transferred to the Mennonite community of Elkhart, Indiana, by probation officers who learned
of the Ontario model in 1977–8. Roughly fifteen years after the program began, a study identified 120 such programs in the United States
and about two dozen in Canada, of which sixty could be traced back
directly to the VORP influence.[29]

Mennonite Disaster Service (MDS) was an organization inspired by
the CPS and closely linked to the MCC. Its beginnings can be traced to
a 1950 Sunday school picnic at a Mennonite church in Hesston, Kansas,
where some former CPS people asked themselves, 'How can we keep
serving our Lord and others as we return to our home community?'
The answer to this question led to the formation of MDS.[30] This unique
organization, which operates with just a handful of full-time staff, has
provided a vehicle for Mennonites and many others who have joined
them to respond to natural disasters quickly, in large numbers, and
with time frames that fit the availability of the volunteers.

Why has the MCC played such an important role in enlarging the
engagement with a wider world for the Mennonite church commu-

nity? Many of its members from Russian German Mennonite circles were initially inspired by the powerful memory of how American Mennonites helped 'their brothers in need' in the Ukraine in the early years of the Soviet Union. That memory became the source of a great deal of financial and material support. Over time, both an emphasis on service to a world in need 'in the name of Christ' and a theology of the kingdom have guided the MCC into more areas of need. The emphasis on service prodded Mennonites to serve around the world, at times in a total of as many as fifty countries. And as they expanded their geographic reach, their world-view expanded. The over 13,000 alumni of MCC service have had a huge influence upon their congregations.[31] A theology of the kingdom of God, once so prominent in Protestant mainline social gospel denominations, gave leaders in the MCC the encouragement to be prophetic and speak out against militarism, racism, nationalism, and 'to give leadership in exploring and initiating new areas of service.'[32]

Mennonites have been unusually proficient in institution building, particularly since the midpoint of the twentieth century. In many cases Mennonite institutions began as a service to the church community itself, and over time began to serve the wider community. Scores of organizations have originated within Mennonite communities, many inspired by the communal impulse of the churches, others by evangelistic motives. Credit unions are one example. Winnipeg and Waterloo both have Mennonite credit unions – the Crosstown Credit Union and the Mennonite Savings and Credit Union – that began as exclusively Mennonite organizations and have stayed so to this day. Steinbach Credit Union and the Niagara Credit Union grew out of Mennonite communities, but later opened their membership to anyone living within their communities. Steinbach's was established in 1946; today, with over three-quarters of a billion dollars in assets, it is the eleventh-largest credit union in the country. The Niagara Credit Union, which began in the early 1940s, in tiny Virgil, Ontario, among Mennonites who had moved there little more than a decade earlier, is today the sixth-largest in the country, with assets of just under a billion dollars.[33] The latter two credit unions are centred in church communities in which both the evangelical and the Anabaptist impulses are strong.

A similar extension of influence is taking place in the area of Mennonite higher education. Both the Mennonite Brethren and the Conference of Mennonites in Canada began what they called 'schools of higher learning' in Winnipeg in the 1940s. Over time the MB school redefined its program as 'Christian university education,' while the CMC retained a more classical Bible college definition. In 1998 these schools, along with Menno Simons College, a school affiliated with the University of Winnipeg, received a charter from the Manitoba government to form a Mennonite College Federation – simply put, a Mennonite university. In the fall of 2000 the three institutions moved onto a common campus.

Creating a common program has required a blending of the emphases of the three institutions and the histories that have supported their approaches. Thus both the Concord College faculty and board members spoke of functioning with 'a face toward the culture.' The Canadian Mennonite Bible College, with deep roots in the Conference of Mennonites in Canada, on the other hand, hardly referred to the culture at all in its literature. By self-definition it faced first and foremost 'toward the church.' In acknowledging these different positions, both schools stayed true to their histories. It remains to be seen how effectively they will meld their programs and the aspirations of their church constituencies, but the opportunity to contribute their strengths to a wider Canadian community within a university context has exciting possibilities.[34]

Mennonite Economic Development Associates (MEDA) is an organization that has also had a significant role in channelling the resources of the Mennonite business community to a wider world. MEDA began as two organizations brought together in the late 1970s, one directed towards using Mennonite financial resources to help start businesses in developing countries, and the other towards bringing Mennonite business and professional people together to talk about issues related to living their faith in the marketplace. By the late nineties, with finances supplied by its more than 3,000 members, MEDA's in-country staff was helping launch 10,000–15,000 small enterprises annually in Nicaragua, Haiti, Jamaica, Tanzania, and Bolivia.

MEDA produces a bimonthly publication on ethical issues called *The Marketplace*, virtually unique in North America. It reports on how people in business and the professions try to live their faith in Christ with integrity in a complex world. Local chapters of MEDA hold monthly or bimonthly luncheons on the same topic, and once a year a convention brings hundreds of MEDA members together for a stimulating exchange on faith/marketplace issues.[35]

Individual Mennonites have played large roles in initiating projects that have significantly extended the borders of Mennonite involvement. No one, to this writer's knowledge, has had as significant a role as Art DeFehr, president of the family-run Palliser Furniture enterprise of Winnipeg, now the largest furniture maker in Canada. An entrepreneur with exceedingly broad vision, DeFehr's actions reflect strongly his dual evangelical and Anabaptist heritage. The key mover behind the Canadian Foodgrains Bank, DeFehr also helped found the Soviet Union Network, which brought North American Christians in business together with Christians in the former Soviet Union who wanted to engage in business ethically. DeFehr also assisted in implementing the vision of another Manitoba Mennonite couple, Dave and Elfrieda Loewen, who launched a Christian camping ministry to the former Soviet Union (FSU) called Kingdom Ventures.[36] In 2000 the organization gave training, direction, and inspiration to leaders and staff of 300 Christian camps in Russia, the Ukraine, and other countries in the FSU.

From their experience in the former Soviet Union and their daughter's involvement in a summer ministry in Lithuania, DeFehr and his wife Leona became interested in the possibilities for English-language instruction in Lithuania. They launched summer language institutes that evolved into a Christian liberal arts college called Lithuania Christian College in Klaipeda, which graduated its fifth class in 1999.[37] The school is known throughout the country, and has as pupils the children of some of the country's leaders. Two churches have emerged through the work of its students. Virtually all of the teachers and tradespeople who worked at LCC until the late nineties were volunteers; and more than 600 students have enrolled since its inception in 1990.

During one of several stints abroad, beginning in the late 1960s, DeFehr helped guide Bangladeshi agriculture toward greater self-sufficiency by shifting focus away from rice towards crops that could be raised in the off-season. During the years of the Khmer Rouge, when hundreds of thousands of Cambodian refugees were parked at the Thai border, DeFehr helped create a mechanism that in 120 days brought a total of 800,000 sacks of rice, vegetable seeds, plow tips, tools for oxcarts, chain, fishing hooks, and nylon, all of which allowed the refugees to go back into western Cambodia and make a new start. The program was estimated to have saved 100,000 lives.[38]

Since the Reverend Jacob Thiessen made his impassioned speech in 1943, Mennonites have indeed moved into a wider, urban world, but not with the resulting moral and spiritual decay that Thiessen predicted. Guided by the two distinct yet complementary evangelical and Anabaptists impulses, Mennonites in Canada have entered into and engaged with a wider world, with many able to retain a distinct identity.

Notes

1 *Yearbook of the Northern District Conference of the Mennonite Brethren Church of North America* (1943), held that year in Herbert, Saskatchewan. A few years later the title changed to Canadian Conference.
2 From an interview with Willingdon Church secretary, Lillian Klassen, March 1999.
3 See the *1998/99 Planner Directory* (Winnipeg: Kindred Productions, 1998); and the *1999 Mennonite Directory* (Scottdale, PA: Herald Press, 1999).
4 Interview with John Wiebe, pastor of the Steinbach Chortitzer Mennonite Church, 14 April 1999.
5 *Mennonite Encyclopedia*, vol. 3 (Scottdale, PA: Mennonite Publishing House, 1957), 196–9.
6 Interview with Harvey Plett, 16 April 1999. The EMC has grown from about six churches in the 1940s to fifty today, a number of them in urban centres. All EMC churches have as members people from backgrounds other than Mennonite. See also Frank H. Epp, *Mennonites in Canada, 1920–1940: A People's Struggle for Survival* (Toronto: Macmillan, 1982), 422.
7 *Mennonite Encyclopedia*, vol. 3, 199.
8 *EMC Yearbook* (1957).
9 Canadian MB Conference *Yearbook* (1943). During these years, Canadian MBs had more than quadrupled in membership, from 7,051 to 31,847 (*Planner Directory*, 1998–9). Furthermore, in 1998 some sixty of the Mennonite Brethren congregations either were composed of an entirely non-Germanic ethnic group or were located in areas of Canada where very few Mennonites of traditional Russian-German background were found. These represented slightly more than 11 per cent of the entire Canadian Mennonite Brethren membership. Eleven of those congregations were Chinese.
10 *Conference of Mennonites in Canada Yearbook* (1943). The Conference of Mennonites in Canada had a membership of 1,189 in large urban settings in 1943. In 1998 that number had increased to 16,398.
11 *Mennonite Yearbook and Directory* (Scottdale, PA: Mennonite Publishing House, 1943). The Mennonite Church in Canada had three of its forty churches, with 743 members, in urban settings in 1943.
12 *Mennonite Yearbook* (1999), 73–90. In 1998, 41 of 242 Conference of Mennonites in Canada congregations were composed of people of non-German or non-Swiss background or located in areas of the country where few if any Mennonites of Russian German or Swiss background were to be found. These represented about 5 per cent of the total membership. The North

West Mennonite Conference, located in Alberta and Saskatchewan, had nine out of nineteen churches in large urban centres, and six of nineteen congregations in places or among ethnic groups outside the original Swiss Mennonite communities, representing 18 per cent of the membership.

13 *Mennonite Yearbook* (1997), 220. In 1998, twelve of the EMC's fifty-two congregations were in large urban settings. Urban congregants represented 1,362, or 19.5 per cent, of the 6,963 members (*EMC Yearbook*, 1998).

14 *Yearbook of the Northern District Conference* (1936).

15 See *Moving beyond Secession: Defining Russian Mennonite Brethren Mission and Identity, 1872–1922*, ed. Abe J. Dueck (Winnipeg: Kindred Productions, 1997), 151.

16 See the list of delegates attending the Canadian Congress on Evangelism, 24–8 August 1970, in the possession of the author.

17 Interview with James Nikkel, former executive secretary for the Board of Evangelism, Canadian Mennonite Brethren Conference, March 1999.

18 Interview with John H. Redekop, March 1999. It is probably safe to say that during the past thirty years no one has had greater influence in moving Mennonite Brethren to become engaged with issues and to participate broadly in evangelical projects and affairs and inter-Mennonite causes than John Redekop.

19 Notes to the author, 10 April 1991.

20 Canadian MB Conference *Yearbook* (1969), 116.

21 *Mennonite Brethren Herald*, 9 January 1998, 6.

22 See *Mennonite Encyclopedia*, vol. 3, 606.

23 See T.D. Regehr, *Mennonites in Canada, 1939–1970*, vol. 3, *A People Transformed*; Paul Toews, *Mennonites in American Society, 1930–1970: Modernity and the Persistence of Religious Community* (Scottdale, PA: Herald Press, 1996); and Albert N. Keim, *Harold S. Bender, 1897–1962* (Scottdale, PA: Herald Press, 1998).

24 Regehr, *Mennonites in Canada, 1939–1970*, 393.

25 See the reports in the MCC Canada *Annual Yearbook* (1980), 17th annual meeting, 23–4 January 1981.

26 Ibid.; see report of the executive secretary. Also see interview with William Janzen, 26 April 1999.

27 From an interview with Henry Enns, 16 April 1999. Enns received an honorary doctorate from Queen's University for his work in disability issues. He led the development of a Centre on Disability Studies, a research institute that works primarily with the University of Manitoba to develop a discipline in disability studies.

28 The CFGB has become the largest private relief food supply in the world. In

1997–8, twenty-four countries received food aid, by far the largest amount going to North Korea. Over 50,000 metric tonnes were distributed, enough to provide emergency food for around 1.4 million people for three months. While the MCC is only one of a dozen groups in the organization, the Mennonite constituency collects fully a third of the food in its reserves, far more than any other member group.

29 See 'Mediating the Victim–Offender Conflict,' available from the MCC online news service at http://www.mcc.org/misc/mediating-conflict/index.html. In Winnipeg, between 700 and 800 victim–offender cases are referred annually to the mediation service, which began as a brainchild of MCC Canada in 1979. Of this total, about a third are resolved through mediation that would otherwise have gone to the courts (Dorothy Barg Neufeld, executive director, Winnipeg Mediation Services). Additionally, it is called upon to mediate many other disputes in the community.

30 See 'MDS – A Vision Born at a Picnic?' available from the MCC online news service at http://www.mcc.org/pr/1998/07–10/10.html; and 'MDS – All Deed and No Word?' available at http://www.mcc.org/pr/1998/08–21/13.html. In March 1990 an estimated 10,000 volunteers were recorded one week after a tornado left a hundred-mile path of destruction near Hesston, Kansas. In Manitoba, 1,822 MDS volunteers gave 14,690 volunteer days to clean and repair the damage left by the 1997 Red River flood (Paul Friesen, 20 April 1999).

31 See 'Mennonite Central Committee: A Snapshot,' available from the MCC online news service at http://www.mcc.org/misc/Snapshot-at-75.html.

32 See executive director's report in the 1982 *Annual Yearbook* of MCC Canada, 19th annual meeting, 20–2 January 1983.

33 See information sheet, 'Largest 100 Credit Unions by Asset Size (Excluding Quebec),' produced by Credit Union Central of Canada. The information is current to the fourth quarter of 1998.

34 For further reading on the colleges joining to form the Mennonite College Federation, see J.A. Toews, *A History of the Mennonite Brethren Church* (Fresno, CA: Board of Christian Literature, 1975); Regehr, *Mennonites in Canada, 1939–1970*; and the 1998 catalogues of the three schools. While the program will be rooted in the evangelical and Anabaptist traditions of the Mennonite communities that support the federating colleges, it is hoped that it will appeal to students beyond these traditions.

35 See *The Marketplace* (302–280 Smith St., Winnipeg, MB, R3C 1K2). MEDA has also inspired a similar organization in the Christian Reformed Church community in Canada.

36 See Kingdom Ventures, *Christian Youth Camps in the CIS & the Baltics Russia*

Report (Kingdom Ventures, Inc., Box 18, Grp. 540, RR#5, Winnipeg, MB, R2C 2Z2).

37 See *The Amber Link*, the Lithuania Christian College newsletter (7117 Hesslea Cres., Mt. Lehman, BC, V4X 2C2).

38 Interview with Arthur DeFehr, 21 April 1999. DeFehr was also a key player in the development of the Mennonite College Federation, especially in negotiating with the government, locating a campus, and articulating the concepts for its development.

17

Sikhism and Secular Authority

Hugh Johnston

In 1953 the U.S. Supreme Court declared that it was no business of a court to define religious practices or activities.[1] The court was endorsing the strict separation of church and state which Americans and most of Anglo Canada had long adopted as a principle of government. In neither Canada nor the United States, however, has it been possible to segregate religious and secular issues. Mormons, Seventh Day Adventists, and Jehovah's Witnesses and many others have all proven the difficulty. In recent years, Sikhs have added a new set of cases.

When fighting for the right to wear their religious symbols, Sikhs have presented a united front; but they have also ended up in court arguing with each other on issues of faith. A recent fracas over tables and chairs in a Sikh temple in Surrey, BC, has had that result. The incident drew an inordinate amount of media attention to a small and misunderstood community while dramatizing its bitter divisions. The courts ruled decisively in favour of one side, but the facts of the dispute are not simple: they reflect the ambiguities of a faith that has many strands within its tradition. The documentation prepared by the lawyers for each side demanded an understanding of the history of the Sikhs as well as their practices. Canadian courts were not versed in these matters, but they have made decisions that both sides have respected. The discussion that follows looks at both recent and historic developments within Sikhism and offers a context for the controversy that has brought Sikhs before the courts.

The Legacy of Sikh Rule

Modern Sikhism has inherited conflicting latitudinarian and conformist traditions. The latter is the more political and public tradition and the one that has most obviously brought the practice of Sikhism into the arena of the state. In many respects the Sikh story of church–state relations runs counter to the Western experience. Sikhs have learned to look to the state to protect their identity only in the last 150 years. An ambivalent reliance on the state – in the homeland and now in Diaspora communities – has come to be a feature of an increasingly institutionalized faith. This appears striking when one considers that the roots of Sikhism lie in teachings that were direct and personal – from guru to disciple – rather than formalized in texts, written codes, religious hierarchies, and instruments of government.

The early Sikh gurus attracted their disciples under a Mughal Muslim regime that did not interfere with the faith of its overwhelming non-Muslim subjects. The later gurus did at times find themselves in dramatic confrontation with their rulers. Politics, not religion, however, appears to be the principal source of conflict, as the Sikh gurus, having acquired territorial power and influence, assumed the roles of local lords.[2] In medieval and early modern India, rulers survived by tolerating diversity of faith among their subjects. What was true of the Mughals was also true of the Sikh rulers who followed them in Punjab. An integration of church and state on the Western model was never a part of the Indian experience. One can contrast the King of England, Henry VIII, who was obliged to change the faith of a nation to obtain a divorce, with the Sikh ruler, Maharaja Ranjit Singh, who respected the Muslim, Hindu, and Sikh faiths of his forty-six wives.[3]

Sikhism began and continued for over two centuries as the personal following of a living guru. Religious authority passed from guru to successor until the death of the tenth in the lineage, Guru Gobind Singh in 1708. Since then Sikh tradition has ascribed authority to the book of teachings collected by the fifth guru (Arjan) and augmented by Gobind Singh. Sikhs call this book *Guru*, or *Guru Granth Sahib* to give the full title. The problem of divergent interpretations of *Guru Granth Sahib* has never been formally resolved, although one set of interpretations has emerged as dominant. In the eighteenth century, leadership among Sikhs rested with contending chiefs who warred with each other as well as with Mughal rulers and invading Afghans. An instrument of unity existed in assemblies of all the chiefs and their followers, particularly on the occasion of the spring and autumn festivals, Baisakhi and Diwali. Resolutions – or *gurmattas* – passed at these assemblies in the presence of the *Guru Granth Sahib* were understood to be binding on all Sikhs.[4]

The assembling of chiefs and the issuing of *gurmattas* ceased, however, when one chief emerged supreme. This was Maharaja Ranjit Singh, who became the ruler of a unified kingdom in which Sikhs were a dominant minority, but in which Hindus and Muslims were also members of the ruling class. As a good politician, Ranjit Singh tolerated all religions and imposed conformity on none. A natural antagonism to rival authority led him to discontinue Sikh assemblies and, as a consequence, to deny his faith any unifying institution other than the holy book. Under his rule, divergent practices flourished among Sikhs and among sects closely related to Sikhism. Traditions based on the teachings of the first Sikh guru and his successors differed: in their conceptions of the personal or impersonal nature of God; on the role of gurus – some traditions accepting and some rejecting the existence of contemporary gurus; on the primacy of *Guru Granth Sahib* over other spiritual texts; on the true line of transmission of the original message; and on the importance of external emblems such as the turban and the *kirpan*. Sikhs were also immersed in the Hindu culture and attracted to spiritual teachers and traditions among their Muslim neighbours.[5]

Among the major beneficiaries of Sikh rulers were the Udasis – an ascetic, clean-shaven sect who revered Guru Nanak, the first Sikh guru, but who had their own religious texts and their own guru lineage. During a century of Sikh rule, the number of Udasi centres in Punjab multiplied from about a dozen to nearly 250, with healthy contributions from the coffers of the state.[6] In the twentieth century, mainstream Sikhs have targeted the Udasis as heretical and anti-Sikh. Tolerance, support, and even a sense of affinity have given way to deep antagonism. Other sects that at one time, like the Udasis, enjoyed acceptance within the broad community of Sikhs have also been affected negatively by modern trends: their teachings have become anathema to most Sikhs.

Sikhism under British Rule and since Indian Independence

The pluralism of belief, practice, and leadership that characterized the Sikh community under Sikh rulers was under attack within a generation of the establishment of a British administration in Punjab in 1849. This development was a product of both modernizing influences and the style of British rule. The British saw religion as the instrumental dividing line in Punjabi society and as a matter of policy co-opted élites from each major religious community – Hindu, Sikh, and Muslim. Their approach inevitably stimulated competition among religious communities and had a profound impact on Hindu–Sikh relations. The minority status of the Sikhs was a factor in this situation, along with a fear that Sikhs would be absorbed into Hinduism now that they were no longer the rulers of Punjab.

As in the era of Ranjit Singh, an influential element of the Sikh élite saw Sikhism as simply a branch of Hinduism. This view, however, steadily gave way to an emphasis among leading Sikhs on the unique and separate character of their faith.[7] By reserving places in the civil service for Sikhs and by creating Sikh regiments in the Indian army, the British encouraged this emphasis. In doing so they unleashed a process that is continuing to work itself out in the present. The recognition that the British-run state gave to religious identity was of critical importance in sharpening the boundaries around Sikhism and promoting conformity within it.[8] Conformity has meant the increasing identification of Sikhism with the *Khalsa* emblems and *Khalsa* ideals given to Sikhs by Guru Gobind Singh three hundred years ago. The best known of the *Khalsa* emblems are the *kes* and the *kirpan* – the unshorn hair and sword worn by Sikhs who have gone through the initiation ceremony instituted by Gobind Singh in 1699. (The other emblems, the *kara*, *kangha*, and *kachcha* – bangle, comb, and the shorts worn as an undergarment – are equally required but less visible and less contentious.) The British put a premium particularly on maintaining the *kes* by filling the military and bureaucratic posts that they reserved for Sikhs only with *kesdhari* or bearded and turbaned Sikhs.

In 1906 the British administration responded to pressure from Sikhs by legalizing marriages performed according to distinctive Sikh rites. In 1919, as the British administration moved minimally towards representative government, they conceded separate electoral rolls and separate constituencies for the Sikhs. In 1925 they sought to contain a mass Sikh agitation over the administration of historic shrines in Punjab by placing these shrines under the management of an elected committee of Sikhs.[9] This committee, called the Shiromani Gurdwara Prabandhak Committee (SGPC), is now the controlling body for several hundred shrines in Punjab, including the Golden Temple complex in Amritsar. Until 1925 most of these shrines had been managed on a proprietary basis by clean-shaven priests of the Udasi sect who had catered to both Hindu and Sikh worshippers. Displacing these managers meant removal of the Hindu iconography they had installed. More significantly, it meant the creation – by state legislation – of a central committee of Sikhs with immense resources to influence and direct the whole Sikh community. The prestige and income provided through the management of the shrines that they control have given the SGPC and its appointees a powerful and central role in Sikhism.[10]

As an early project, the SGPC initiated the development of a Sikh Code of Conduct and Convictions, which it adopted in its final form in 1945. This code has been widely – but not universally – accepted by Sikhs in India and abroad and it represents an important step in the formalization and standardization of the Sikh faith. It is a modern document, created in the absence of any preexisting, generally accepted code, and the natural product of an evolving and increasingly exclusive Sikh consciousness.[11]

The SGPC has been able to promote a standardized Sikhism through its publications and missions. It has also played a major role in the secular policies of Punjab by providing a power base for a Sikh nationalist party, the Akalis.[12] In the second half of the twentieth century, Sikh nationalist politics have gained unprecedented vitality. While Sikhs have always had a strong territorial identification with Punjab, it was an identification that they shared with the more numerous Hindus and Muslims. The partition of Punjab in 1947, and the consequent flight of Sikhs to India from the newly created Pakistan, have produced a greater concentration of Sikhs in a smaller Punjab than ever before existed. This present Indian state of Punjab is only one-ninth of the area of the old British province, but it is a Sikh majority state.

The creation of an instrument of religious government – the SGPC – and a Sikh majority state have been major milestones in the evolution of Sikh national identity. The institutionalization of the Sikh faith, however, is still far from complete. The modern Code of Conduct prepared under the auspices of the SGPC is silent on many aspects of Sikh practice. It does spell out procedures for resolving disputes within the faith, but Sikhs do not all adhere to the code and its procedures. The *Guru Granth Sahib* remains the one authority respected by all Sikhs, and its answers are a matter of interpretation, particularly because it contains devotional poetry, not codes or rituals.

A Question of Local Autonomy

These are facts that civil courts have had to deal with when Sikhs differ with each other. Recently, an American court set a precedent in accepting Sikhism as a congregationally organized religion without any supra-congregational or hierarchical controls. The case involved Sikhs in Fairfax, Virginia, who had organized a Sikh *gurdwara* (temple) society in 1979.[13] By the early 1990s, the Fairfax Sikh community split on the issue of Sikh separatism in India. A minority of the membership advocated a full commitment of the resources of the *gurdwara* society to the cause of Khalistan, an independent Sikh state. This same group demanded an open (and expanded) membership in place of the Fairfax society's existing fee-based membership. They were opposed by a majority who wanted no secular politics in their place of worship and sought to retain control by restricting membership.

The controversy ended up in the Fairfax County Circuit Court in 1993 after the pro-Khalistan faction challenged the constitutionality of the bylaws of the temple society, set up their own parallel management committee, and occupied the temple premises. The court faced a clear question about its own jurisdiction because under Virginia law it had none if it was dealing with a hierarchical church such as the Roman Catholic Church.

An intervention by Manjit Singh, the *jathedar* (or so-called high priest) of the Akal Takht in Amristar, Punjab, brought this question into sharp focus. The *jathedar* is an appointee of the management committee for Sikh shrines in Punjab – the SGPC. The Akal Takht is the first of five Sikh shrines whose historic association with the gurus gives them special prestige among Sikhs. These shrines are identified in the Sikh Code of Conduct as thrones (*takhts*) or seats of authority. The *jathedar* of the Akal Takht, who is essentially a shrine manager and a political appointee of the SGPC, nonetheless occupies a position of great prestige. In March 1994 Manjit Singh brought the full weight of the Akal Takht to bear on the Fairfax controversy. He did so with a written response to the *granthi* (temple officiate) of the Fairfax temple who was looking for help in resolving the conflict in his community.[14] In his response, the *jathedar* chastised both sides in the conflict and called on them to take their case out of the secular Virginia court and to settle their differences according to Sikh customs. He also said that the Fairfax temple community's management committee should include *kesdhari* Sikhs only, those who do not trim their hair or shave (in contrast to *sahajdhari*, or clean-shaven Sikhs).

By intervening in this way the *jathedar* bolstered the position of the pro-Khalistan faction who were in possession of the temple and whose ad hoc committee was exclusively *kesdhari*. Furthermore, he asserted the authority of this office with two statements: first, that the temple communities should inform the Akal Takht when they were drafting constitutions and second, that the Akal Takht should approve the makeup of any management board for the Fairfax temple. The pro-Khalistan side endorsed these positions with the implication that the governing structure of Sikhism was hierarchical and that ultimate authority rested in the Akal Takht. Their opponents understandably persisted with their case in the Fairfax County court.

The court referred the case to a special commissioner, who held hearings in the summer of 1994 on the structure of Sikhism and the validity of the bylaws of the Fairfax temple society. Evidence included testimony by Professor Gerald Barrier, a historian from the University of Missouri, Columbia, and a specialist on Sikh history, as well as Darshan Singh Ragi, a former *jathedar* of the Akal Takht. The hearings generated a formidable mass of material in testimony depositions and documents and it took the commissioner, John J. Karcha, two years to assimilate the evidence and to report his findings. The case is now before the courts following Commissioner Karcha's conclusion that the Virginia courts have jurisdiction and that they can rule on the legitimacy of the Fairfax temple society's bylaws.[15]

The Khalistan Movement

Much of the controversy, debate, and division among Diaspora Sikhs is factional in nature and would exist without any ideological underpinnings. Tensions between old and new immigrants, alliances based on kinship and locality, and competition for positions of prominence and influence within the community all contribute to a robust and contentious political environment. Rivalry among Sikhs can be a sign of a healthy democratic sense within their community, and if the Sikhs quarrel they also have their specialists in negotiation and conciliation. In recent decades, however, factional differences have revolved around issues of religious nationalism as with the Fairfax, Virginia, society. The policies of the British *raj*, the partition of the Punjab in 1947, the creation of a Sikh majority state in post-independence India, and the centrist policies of the nationalist government of India, particularly under the leadership of Indira Gandhi, have progressively intensified religious nationalism among Sikhs.

The idea of Khalistan or an independent Sikh state has never been embraced by a majority of Sikhs. But the religious nationalism that produced Khalistani agitators became the nationalism of nearly all

Sikhs when Indira Gandhi's government blundered into an extraordinary confrontation with their community. In 1984 Gandhi committed the Indian army to an action against Khalistani terrorists entrenched in Amritsar's Golden Temple complex (which includes both the Golden Temple and the Akal Takht). The resulting loss of life within a spiritual sanctuary and heavy damage to the sanctuary itself had a profound psychological effect on Sikhs around the world, shaking their sense of Indian identity to the core. The sequel came in that fall. In the aftermath of Mrs Gandhi's assassination by two of her Sikh bodyguards, Hindu rioters looted, burned, and murdered their way through Sikh districts of Delhi in the worst outbreak of communal violence in India since independence.[16] Fifteen years later, we witness a remarkable recovery of the Sikh sense of place in India. In the interval, however, Sikhs in Punjab have gone through a decade of immense turmoil and distress – as political and criminal terrorists flourished and the police responded with a brutality that put ordinary citizens in danger from both sides.

The events of 1984 provoked a tremendous outpouring of religious nationalism in the Sikh Diaspora. The streets of Vancouver saw a dramatic increase in the number of bearded and turbaned Sikhs, a consequence of the spontaneous adoption of *Khalsa* emblems by formerly non-*Khalsa* Sikhs. The momentum towards Khalistan among Diaspora Sikhs rapidly carried the day in every temple society with an open membership where commitment, organization, and the marshalling of hundreds and thousands of supporters could prevail. The only societies able to deflect the Khalistani movement were those like the Fairfax society with closed or limited membership. And even they were open to challenge. Even in these societies the public position was never open opposition to Khalistan. Instead their management committees took the line that secular politics had no place in a temple or that overseas Sikhs should not involve themselves in the politics of India and Punjab.[17]

Since the mid-1990s support for Khalistan has dissipated. Factional differences among Sikhs remain and religious nationalism is still a powerful force, but Khalistan has become a weak rallying cry. The change has been evident in Canadian temple elections in the last few years. In a close election in the fall of 1996 – in which 17,000 votes were cast – a pro-Khalistan faction lost control of one of the largest Sikh temples in Canada – the Guru Nanak temple in Surrey, BC. This was a temple they had run for more than a decade. A year later an election for the management committee of the Vancouver *Khalsa Diwan* Society –

the oldest and largest temple society in the country – produced a similar result. Sikhs uncomfortable with the more extreme positions of religious nationalists were entering temple politics in force and throwing their backing to leaders who called for an end to active involvement in Punjab politics.

There are several explanations for this development. One is the subsiding of the feelings of outrage generated in 1984. A second is the increasingly Canadian outlook of an immigrant community and their Canadian-born children. A third is the collapse of Khalistani activity in Punjab, where comparative peace and quiet now prevail. This last point is a key one. Peace came to Punjab at a cost. It was achieved by a Punjab government willing to give the police licence to target suspected terrorists without much regard for legal niceties. A two-year police campaign under the direction of Punjab Chief Minister Beant Singh had the benefit of eliminating terrorism by the end of 1993.[18] The results of this campaign have been welcomed by the people of Punjab and have reduced tensions among their relatives abroad. India's national politicians are now seeking to repair the damage of the past. In January 1998 the Congress party which Indira Gandhi once led issued a formal statement of regret for her action in ordering troops into the Golden Temple.

The Authority of the *Jathedar*

In Canada the chill in Hindu–Sikh relations that the Khalistan issue produced seems to have lifted and it has become easier to acknowledge common cultural interests. Among the Sikhs, however, religious nationalism, which has more planks to its program than a call for Khalistan, remains a formidable force. While pursuing conformity within Sikhism, religious nationalists have been promoting a revolution of their faith.

Their agenda has given the office of *jathedar* of the Akal Takht a prominence and visibility that it did not have before. *Jathedar* Manjit Singh's intervention in the affairs of a local temple society in Fairfax, Virginia, was probably without precedent, but it was part of a developing pattern. This same *jathedar* also took action against two Sikh scholars, one in North America and one in India, because he and his advisers found their scholarship blasphemous. The first was Dr Pashaura Singh, a professional *granthi* who completed a Ph.D. at the University of Toronto under the guidance of a visiting New Zealand scholar, Hew McLeod, the foremost student of Sikhism outside the Sikh community.[19]

In his dissertation Pashaura Singh discussed early textual variations in the *Mul Mantra*, the credal statement of the Sikhs, a composition of Guru Nanak, the first guru, which appears in the opening lines of the Holy Book, the *Guru Granth Sahib*. The implication of what he wrote was that these lines had been changed at some point before they were canonized in the *Guru Granth Sahib*. In May 1993, eighteen months after he finished his Ph.D., Pashaura Singh received a summons from *Jathedar* Manjit Singh to appear at the Akal Takht. Even though Pashaura Singh was intellectually convinced of the validity of his scholarship, he found the summons from the Akal Takht unanswerable. He presented himself before the *jathedar* in June 1994, accepted a guilty verdict, and performed a seven-day penance – two days at the Golden Temple and the balance at a Detroit temple convenient to Ann Arbor, where he occupies a chair in Sikh studies at the University of Michigan.

The *jathedar's* other target was an elderly and established Sikh scholar named Piar Singh from Guru Nanak Dev University in Amritsar. Piar Singh and Pashaura Singh had been following parallel lines of research and had reached similar conclusions. As Piar Singh pointed out in his own defence, earlier scholars had published similar work without furore and even with the endorsement of the SGPC. His study of the Sikh scriptures, published in 1992 by Guru Nanak Dev University, did not have such an easy passage into anonymity.[20] In Piar Singh's own assessment, the storm that rose around his work and that of Pashaura Singh was a direct product of religious extremism associated with Khalistani terrorism.[21] Nonetheless, Piar Singh did obey the summons that he received from the *jathedar* and performed the forty-day penance he was given.

Tables and Chairs

As these cases illustrate, the office of *jathedar* of the Akal Takht has commanded respect throughout the international Sikh community. The authority of the office is disputed, however, and the character of the occupant has been an issue for many Sikhs. As quiet has returned to Punjab and as Khalistan has receded as a political goal, an underlying tension within the Sikh community has risen to the surface. This is the tension between religious nationalism and a variety of other impulses within Sikhism: secularism, pragmatism, scepticism, and a tolerant spirituality. Ideological tensions compounded by factional rivalry have tested the authority of the *jathedar* of the Akal Takht and driven Canadian Sikhs into the courts for answers.

From their early days in Canada, Canadian Sikhs have furnished their temple dining halls with tables and chairs, although such furnishings are unheard of in Sikh temples in India. Many Canadians have been puzzled by the importance that Sikhs have attached to what looks – from the outside – like a mere question of furnishings. The explanation lies in a potent mix of symbolism and politics. The temple kitchen and the service of food are central institutions of Sikhism and have been so from the time of the first Sikh guru. Eating together has special significance in Indian society, where caste exclusiveness – especially around the idea of sharing food – has been so strong.[22] For that reason the Sikh Code of Conduct requires equal seating for everyone taking temple food, with no privilege, priority, or distinction for anyone.[23] Some Sikhs now interpret that to mean no tables or chairs, while others say that the long-standing practice in British Columbia is fine as long as no one has special seating.

Much of the heat generated by this issue has more to do with factional division than the merits of the arguments. Unfortunately, the middle ground has been hard to find. The compromise offered by one side – allowing individual choice with floor mats, tables, and chairs all available – has been rejected by the others as a compromise of true tradition. The issue has provoked violence or the threat of violence when one side has taken the tables and chairs out of a temple and the other side has brought them back. Police have been required in force on several occasions in the Vancouver area, in either the Surrey temple, the main Vancouver temple, or the Abbotsford temple. Each of these temples has been shut for a period by police order. Television cameras caught the most graphic outburst, a *kirpan*-swinging riot in the Surrey temple on Saturday, 12 January 1997, and the bloody injuries that resulted were the lead item on newscasts from coast to coast that evening.[24]

The tables and chairs issue took on a new dimension with the involvement of the *jathedar* of the Akal Takht. In April 1998 *Jathedar* Ranjit Singh issued an edict *(hukamnana)* requiring all Sikh temples around the world to remove tables and chairs by 29 May.[25] This was a challenge to more than thirty Sikh temple societies in British Columbia and to a number of societies in Britain, Australia, and New Zealand.

Most of these societies refused to comply, and in response the *jathedar* issued an edict excommunicating six BC Sikhs – five of them members of temple executives in the Vancouver area and the sixth a prominent Sikh journalist, the publisher of the *Indo-Canadian Times*. Their crime was opposition to the April edict. All six were instructed to present themselves at the Akal Takht in thirty days.[26] A large, active, and organized section of the Sikh community applauded the *jathedar's* action. An even larger section dismissed it.

Police intervention brought the matter before the courts. In weighing the evidence, the courts contemplated two views of Sikhism. One supported the authority of the Akal Takht and the edicts issued by the *jathedar*. In this view the *jathedar* of the Akal Takht is like the Pope in Rome, a supreme authority whose directives are binding on all members of his faith. In the opposing view the authority of the Akal Takht is qualified; the Sikh Code of Conduct sets a standard for Sikhs but they follow it voluntarily; and no individual or institution within Sikhism has the power of excommunication.

These positions were stated starkly in conflicting affidavits taken from two *granthi*s associated with the Vancouver Sikh temple.[27] Jagdish Singh, head *granthi* at Vancouver from 1991, endorsed the authority of the Akal Takht in uncompromising terms. Harkirat Singh, former head *granthi* at a Calgary temple and then at Abbotsford and briefly a *granthi* at Vancouver, was one of the six BC Sikhs named in the excommunication edict. His well-articulated reasons for ignoring this edict help to explain the reactions of a large part of the BC Sikh population. His main point was that no person or assemblage within Sikhism could take away a person's beliefs. In support of this point he observed that neither the Sikh Code of Conduct nor the Punjab legislation governing the administration of temples contained any provision for excommunication. This reference to an item of Punjab legislation in an affidavit before a BC court – in a matter of religious authority and faith – epitomizes the secular–religious crosscurrents of the case.

Harkirat Singh and others also questioned the procedure by which the *jathedar* had issued his edicts. The *jathedar* was not an infallible head of a church, but a vehicle for announcing rulings that had been developed through careful study and extensive consultation by a committee or convention of Sikhs. Moreover, in Harkirat Singh's opinion, and that of his allies, the *jathedar*s of all five *takhts* of Sikhism had to be signatories to an edict for it to carry weight. *Jathedar* Ranjit Singh had not acted in concert with his fellow *jathedar*s. He had recognized the principle of five by meeting with five other Sikhs, including the head *granthi* of the Golden Temple, but his edicts had not been signed by the *jathedars* of the other four *takhts*.

The exclusion of the *jathedars* of Patna Sahib and Hazur Sahib might have been expected because those *takhts* are far from Amritsar and outside the control of the SGPC. More surprising was the exclusion of the *jathedars* of Kesgarh Sahib and Damdama Sahib, the two *takhts*, besides the Akal Takht, within Punjab and under SGPC jurisdiction. The *jathedar* of Kesgarh Sahib was Manjit Singh, the former *jathedar* of the Akal Takht and, like Ranjit Singh, a member of the Sikh religious party, the Akalis, that dominated SGPC elections. In a war of letters in the summer of 1998 the *jathedars* of the Akal Takht and Kesgarh Sahib exposed deep divisions among Akali politicians.[28] Ranjit Singh and his supporters had overplayed their hands, and the proof became obvious six or seven months later. In February 1999, by a vote of ten to five, the executive of the SGPC suspended Ranjit Singh as *jathedar* and within a few weeks they had replaced him. On 15 March 1999 the president of the SGPC, Gucharan Singh Tohra, one of Ranjit Singh's strong allies, resigned.[29] With these departures a centralizing drive within Sikhism suffered a reversal, although it is too early to judge the long-term consequences.

Canadian Justice and the Sikh Response

In the summer of 1998 Ranjit Singh was still *jathedar* and, apparently, entrenched in office. Even if he had already gone, the questions before the British Columbia courts would have been the same because they were not about the person of the *jathedar*, but the authority of his office. Could a temple executive defy the edicts of the Akal Takht and retain its legitimacy? Could temple executives include individuals who had been excommunicated? The answer from the courts was yes, as long as the Sikh temple societies concerned respected their own bylaws and the provisions of the BC Society Act.

The decisions of the courts in separate cases involving the Abbotsford, Vancouver, and New Westminster temples were all disappointments for the anti–tables-and-chairs faction. In Vancouver their opponents retained control for the duration of their mandate. In Abbotsford and New Westminster the solution was not as simple. In each case the court named a neutral third party to run an election under court-imposed guidelines.[30] As a means of control in the

Abbotsford election, the court restricted voting membership to Sikh residents of the Abbotsford area. This restriction injured a fundamental principle for many (not all) Sikhs: that service and participation in the management and care of a place of worship should be open to all believers, wherever they come from or wherever they live. In this respect, the court was not just interpreting the law for Sikhs, it was making it.

The Canadian legal process may have been vindicated in the Vancouver area temple elections of the late fall of 1998, but not very emphatically. In the regular, biannual election in Vancouver, and in the special court-run election in Abbotsford, Sikhs made winners out of candidates who had defied the *jathedar* and ignored his edicts. The campaigns were intense and the number of votes mobilized extraordinary. In Vancouver, where membership was open and people came great distances to support one side or the other, 57,000 registered and 36,000 actually voted – twice the number who had voted two years earlier. In Abbotsford, where the court had imposed geographical boundaries on membership, 9,300 registered and 8,600 voted.[31] The results were victories for the advocates of local autonomy and individual liberty of conscience; but the margins of victory were arrestingly small. A swing of 200 votes would have reversed the Abbotsford result; 800 votes would have done the same in Vancouver.

What do these results say about the way in which Canadian Sikhs relate their faith to secular authority? In the struggle over tables and chairs, both sides have resorted to the civil courts to resolve their differences. But one side has also appealed to what its people consider a higher court – the court of the Akal Takht. In the absence of a well-articulated body of Sikh canon law, a set of precedents in Canadian and American courts are beginning to define the practice of Sikhism in North America. This is happening because Sikhs are divided. Two facts are striking in this context. The first is that more than 21,000 Sikhs supported the notion of the *jathedar* as a religious leader comparable to the Roman Catholic Pope. In other words, they did not agree with the British Columbia courts. The second is that these people, by their compliant actions, ultimately respected the decisions of the British Columbia courts and the temple election results that followed. This, of course, is an essential requirement of civil society. The police and the courts have become involved in Sikh affairs as a direct consequence of confrontations among Sikh temple worshippers; and civil order – not religious conviction – has been the first concern of the Canadian state.

Notes

1 *Fowler vs. Rhode Island*, 1953, cited in *Canadian Human Rights Reporter*, vol. 2, Decision 103, D1463.
2 Traditional Sikh historiography emphasizes persecution of their faith under the Mughals. This emphasis, however, does not easily accommodate evidence of the support that the Gurus gave to Mughal emperors or to rebellious Mughal princes. For a traditional interpretation, see Khushwant Singh, *A History of the Sikhs*, vol. 1, *1469–1869* (Princeton: Princeton University Press, 1963), 56–98; for a more nuanced account, see J.S. Grewal, *The Sikhs of Punjab* (Cambridge: Cambridge University Press, 1990), 59–81.
3 See Khushwant Singh, *Ranjit Singh, Maharaja of Punjab, 1780–1830* (New Delhi: Orient Longman, 1985), 185 n.
4 Grewal, *The Sikhs of Punjab*, 93; W.H. McLeod, *Who Is a Sikh?* (Delhi: Oxford University Press, 1989), 63; Andrew J. Major, *Return to Empire: Punjab under the Sikhs and British in the Mid-Nineteenth Century* (New Delhi: Sterling, 1996), 14–39.
5 See Harjot Oberoi, *The Construction of Religious Boundaries: Culture Identity and Diversity in the Sikh Tradition* (Delhi: Oxford University Press, 1994), particularly chaps. 2 and 3. For a critical reaction to Oberoi's picture of diversity within nineteenth-century Sikhism, see Gurdurshan Singh Dhillon, 'Singh Sabha Movement, a Revival,' in *Advanced Studies in Sikhism*, ed. Jasbir Singh Mann and Harbans Singh Saraon (Patiala: Sikh Community of North America, 1989), 234–62.
6 Grewal, *The Sikhs of Punjab*, 116; *Vancouver Sun*, 18 November 1998.
7 See Joginder Singh, *The Sikh Resurgence* (New Delhi: National Book Association, 1997), 49–59; Oberoi, *The Construction of Religious Boundaries*, 318–47; and J.S. Grewal, '*Nabha's Ham Hindu Nahin*; A Declaration of Sikh Ethnicity,' in *Sikh Identity: Continuity and Change*, ed. Pashaura Singh and N. Gerald Barrier (New Delhi: Manohar, 1999), 231–51.
8 See Ian J. Kerr, 'Sikhs and State: Troublesome Relationship and a Fundamental Continuity with Particular Reference to the Period 1849–1919,' in *Sikh Identity*, Singh and Barrier, eds, 147–74; Joginder Singh, *The Sikh Resurgence*, particularly chap. 1 and conclusion; and Oberoi, *The Construction of Religious Boundaries*, particularly chap. 7.
9 See Attar Singh, 'The Management of Gurdwaras,' in *Punjab in Indian Politics: Issues and Trends*, ed. Amrik Singh (Delhi: Ajanta Books, 1985), 184–212.
10 In 1985 the annual budget of the central committee of the SGPC was reported to be 120 million rupees or 4.8 million Canadian dollars. See Rajiv A. Kapur, *The Politics of the Faith* (London: Allen and Unwin, 1986), 195.

11 W.H. McLeod, *Textual Sources for the Study of Sikhism* (Manchester: Manchester University Press, 1984), 8–9; W. Owen Cole and Piara Singh Sambhi, *The Sikhs: Their Religious Beliefs and Practices* (Sussex: Academic Press, 1995), 200–8; Shiromani Gurdwara Prabandhak Committee, *The Code of Sikh Conduct and Conventions: English Version of the Sikh Reht Maryada* (Amritsar: SGPC, 1994), 43.

12 See Kapur, *The Politics of the Faith*, 194–229; Gian Singh Sandhu, 'The Roots of the Problem,' in *Punjab in Indian Politics*, Singh, 61–70; Grewal, *The Sikhs of Punjab*, particularly 195–6.

13 N. Gerald Barrier, 'The Fairfax, Virginia Gurdwara Case and Sikh Identity,' in *Sikh Identity*, Singh and Barrier, 365–78.

14 Barrier, 'Fairfax,' 371–2.

15 Ibid., 374.

16 Robin Jeffrey, *What's Happening to India? Punjab, Ethnic Conflict and the Test for Federalism* (New York: Holmes and Meyer, 1994), 148.

17 See, for example, Hugh Johnston, 'The Development of the Punjabi Community in Vancouver since 1961,' *Canadian Ethnic Studies* 20, no. 2 (1988): 14–15.

18 K.P.S. Gill, who was Director General of Police in Punjab during the anti-terrorism campaign, says that the police had terrorism under control in 1993, although the government publicly announced success only in 1994 after six months had passed without a terrorist incident. See K.P.S. Gill, *Punjab: The Knights of Falsehood* (New Delhi: Har-Anand Publications, 1997), 12.

19 Pashaura Singh's 1992 University of Toronto Ph.D. dissertation is titled 'The Text and Meaning of the Adi Granth.' For a synopsis of the content of this thesis, see J.S. Grewal, *Contesting Interpretations of the Sikh Tradition* (New Delhi: Manohar, 1988), 229–31. For an example of the criticism that Pashaura Singh encountered from within the Sikh community, see Bachittar Singh Grewal, *Planned Attack on 'Aad Sri Guru Granth Sahib': Academics or Blasphemy* (Chandigarh: International Centre of Sikh Studies, 1994), 401.

20 Piar Singh, *Gatha Sri Adi Granth* (Amritsar: Guru Nanak Dev University, 1992).

21 Piar Singh, *'Gatha Sri Adi Granth' and the Controversy* (Michigan: Anant Education and Rural Development Foundation, 1996), 55–72.

22 W.H. McLeod, *Guru Nanak and the Sikh Religion* (Delhi: Oxford University Press, 1968), 210. Cole and Sambhi, *The Sikhs*, 21–2.

23 The wording of the English version of the Code of Conduct published by the SGPC in 1978 is: 'No invidious distinction is made between man and man, between a Sikh and a non-Sikh, between a caste man and a so-called

outcaste, when making seating arrangements or serving food in the Guru's kitchen.' The wording in the 1994 English version is: 'All human beings, high or low, of any caste or colour may sit at the Guru's kitchen-cum-eating house. No distinction on the grounds of country of origin, colour, caste or religion must be made while making people sit in rows for eating. However, only baptised Sikhs can eat off one plate.'

24 See *Vancouver Province*, 12 January 1997.

25 *Vancouver Sun*, 28 April and 25 May 1998; Supreme Court of British Columbia, Vancouver Registry, in the matter of Khalsa Diwan Society, no. A982044, translation of Akal Takht *Hukamnana* of 20 April 1998, exhibit 'A' of affidavit of Sarjit Singh Gill, 8 August 1998.

26 *Vancouver Sun*, 21 August 1998; Supreme Court of British Columbia, Vancouver Registry, no. A982044, in the matter of *Khalsa Diwan* Society, translation of Akal Takht *Hukamnana* of 25 June 1998, exhibit 'A' of affidavit of Sarjit Singh Gill, 8 August 1998.

27 Supreme Court of British Columbia, Vancouver Registry, in the matter of Khalsa Diwan Society, no. A982044, affidavit of Harkirat Singh, 1 September 1998, and no. A982260, affidavit of Jagdish Singh, 27 August 1998.

28 *Times of India*, 28 August 1998; *Tribune News Service*, available at http://www.tribuneindia.com, 19, 20, 25, 26, and 28 August 1998.

29 *Vancouver Sun*, 16 March 1999; *Times of India*, 16 April 1999.

30 Supreme Court of British Columbia, New Westminster Registry, Docket SO47061, Judgment of Madam Justice Stromberg-Stein, 19 June 1998, in *Rupinder Singh Pannu vs. Khalsa Diwan Society, Mohinder Singh Gill et al.*

31 *Vancouver Sun*, 24 November and 7 December 1998; Khalsa Diwan Society, Vancouver, Polling Station Reports for 5 December 1998 election

Index

Abbott, Edith and Grace, 212n43
Aberhart, William, 238, 242; and
Ernest Manning, 239; motivation
and religious beliefs, 237, 239;
political career, 237; radio evangelism, 237, 238–9; religious and secular pursuits, unity of, 237. *See also*
Calgary Prophetic Bible Institute;
fundamentalism
Addams, Jane, 214n65
Akalis (Sikh religious/nationalist
party), 350, 358
alcohol use: ties to tobacco use, 177–
8, 180–1; at Twelfth of July celebrations, 78. *See also* Salvation Army;
WCTU
Allen, Richard, 199; on United
Church and social gospel, 225
Ames, Herbert Brown: *City Below the
Hill*, 316
Anabaptist, 333, 334; influence in
contemporary Mennonite identity,
15, 330, 331, 332, 335, 336, 339,
341
Anderson, Benedict, 270n1; on imag-
ined communities, 74
Anfield, Earl, 122

Anglican Church. *See* Church of
England
Anglicans, 54, 124, 202–3, 230, 319,
333; evangelical, 33; missionaries,
137, 139, 140; and Native missions
and schools, 110, 115, 121, 122, 123,
124; political affiliation, 59; in
PSCF, 297, 310n32; and public education, 28, 31–4, 60, 63. *See also*
Church of England
Angus Reid World Survey (1997),
153, 169
Annand, Joseph, 133, 148n4
anti-tobacco movement: campaigns
and strategies, 177–8, 181, 183,
184–5, 189, 191; educational
efforts, 177, 179, 180, 185, 188–9;
evangelical input and/or influence, 177, 178–9, 183, 189–91; links
to temperance movement, 178,
184; literature, 185–9, 190–1; medical community involvement in,
177, 190–1, 192n5; phases, 179, 183,
189, 192n5; and role of the state,
178, 183; scientific community
involvement in, 189–91, 192n5; scientific hygiene, 184, 188–9. *See also*

Church of England, 7–8, 43, 51, 53, 59, 117; denominational representation, 8, 51; and disestablishment, 51, 65; and education, 8, 51, 54, 60–6; influence of, 51, 65–6, 179, 183, 191; interdenominational cooperation, 50, 52; and Mennonite identity, 330–1; and moral reform, 8, 11, 51, 52, 249, 295; and Mormons, 249; organizations, 50, 52; and politics, 8, 51, 59, 61–2, 65; and prohibition, 8, 56, 65; and public religion, 8; radical, 53–5, 59; societal goals, 50, 66; on state's role in defining moral behaviour, 178; strongholds, 51, 65; and teetotalism, 55–6; on tobacco use, 177, 178, 180, 182, 183, 189, 191. *See also under* individual denominations

Evans, James, 117

Falwell, Jerry, 307n6

Farías, Gómez, 160

Feinberg, Abraham (Anthony Frome), 313, 315, 319; causes supported, 323, 324; on Christian instruction in schools, 324; early religious career, 323; family upbringing, 323; political affiliation, 324; secular career, 323; social activism of, 323–4

Fellowship for a Christian Social Order (FCSO), 220, 231, 232; purpose of, 228

Fenety, George, 54

Fenian Invasion (1866): religious component in, 159

Fernandez, Aniceto, 262–3

Ferretti, Lucia, 101

Fisher, Charles, 58, 61

Fleming, Donald, 245

Fosdick, Harry Emerson: influence on Stanley Knowles, 222

Franciscans, 94

Fredericton: plebiscite on prohibition in, 65

Free Christian (free will) Baptists: educational agenda, 61. *See also* Baptists

Free Church Presbyterians. *See* Free Church of Scotland

Free Church of Scotland, 8, 51, 53, 133; and prohibition, 56, 65; statistics, 52

free will Baptists, 51, 52; on religious establishment, 53. *See also* Baptists

French Canadians (Québécois): adaptation of traditional culture, 101–2; and assimilation, 90, 100; national liberation of, 258; outside of Quebec, 89; redefinition of, 270n1; religiosity of, 94–6; as volunteers in papal army, 98

Front de libération du Québec (FLQ), 267

Frye, Northrop: on Charles Trick Currelly, 136–7

Fuller, Charles E.: *Old Fashioned Revival Hour*, 240

fundamentalism, 250n2; in Alberta, 237; and *Back to the Bible Hour*, 238; contrasting visions of, 239. *See also* Christian Right

Gallaway, J.C., 54

Gandhi, Indira, 352, 353, 354

Gavazzi, Alessandro, 159

Geddie, John, 133

gender roles, 202; in Canadian Girls in Training, 198; celebration and

Insurrections of 1837–8. *See* Rebellions of 1837–8
Irving, John: on Ernest C. Manning, 237
Iturbide, Agustin de (Emperor Agustin I): *Plan de Iguala*, provisions of, 159–60
Ivens, William, 205, 226

Janzen, William, 334
Jehovah's Witnesses, 240, 347
Jesuits (Society of Jesus), 110, 117, 120, 133; as conservatives, 260; and Native missions, 118, 122; *Relations*, 259
Jews, 198; Chinese, 138; Conservative, 324; defined as Protestants for education purposes, 316; education of, internal debates over, 316–17; as refugees, 200; and social reform, 15. *See also* Orthodox Judaism; Reform Judaism
Johnston, James, 58
Jones, Peter, 118, 119
Juárez, Benito: *Ley Juarez* (1855), 161; anticlericalism under, 162

Karcha, John J., 352
Kelley, Robert: on evangelicals within the British Empire, 66n3
Kellogg, J.H.: *Domestic Hygiene and Rational Medicine*, 190
Kerr, Walter, 243–4
Khalistan movement, 16, 351; changing attitudes towards, 353–4; roots of, 352–3; Sikh support for and against, 353–4
King, George Edwin, 51, 62–3, 64–5
King, Mackenzie, 200, 211n35

King's College (Fredericton): secularization of, 60, 61
King's College (Toronto): contrasted with Trinity College, 29; demise of, 23, 28; as establishment institution, 29; inclusive nature of, 29; secularization of, 24. *See also* Trinity College
Knowles, Lois, 221, 222
Knowles, Stanley, 12, 325; and CCF, 219, 229; on Christian tradition and purpose, 219, 220, 231; on church dealings with social and economic issues, 227; education, 220–2, 225–6; election experiences, 229, 231–2, 232n1; family background and upbringing, 220–1; and FCSO, 228; ministry, 221, 222–3, 226, 227, 229–30; pacifism, 231; political career, 219, 232; on purpose of theological education, 226; relationship with father, 221, 223–5, 229, 232; relationship with wife, 230, 235n39; religious and secular pursuits, unity of, 219, 220; theology of, 222–3, 225; theology and politics, unified purpose of, 220, 223, 232; Winnipeg influences, 225–6
Knowles, Stanley Ernest, 220, 223–5, 232; religious ambitions, 223–4

Labour Church (Winnipeg), 200, 205, 214n65, 226, 227
Labour Progressive Party of Canada (Communist Party), 324
language: as defining identity, analysis of, 88–9
Laurendeau, André, 87
Laurier, Wilfrid, 79, 159